I0114202

AGAINST TIME

Letters from Nazi Germany

1938–1939

Francis W. Hoeber

AGAINST TIME

Letters from Nazi Germany 1938–1939

AMERICAN PHILOSOPHICAL SOCIETY PRESS

TRANSACTIONS OF THE
AMERICAN PHILOSOPHICAL SOCIETY
HELD AT PHILADELPHIA
FOR PROMOTING USEFUL KNOWLEDGE
VOLUME 105, PART 1

ISBN 978-1-60618-051-8
US ISSN 0065-9746

Library of Congress Cataloging-in Publication Data

Hoeber, Johannes U., 1904–1977.
Against time : letters from Nazi Germany, 1938/1939 / Johannes U. Hoeber and Elfriede Fischer Hoeber ; translated and edited by Francis W. Hoeber.
pages cm. —(Transactions of the American Philosophical Society held at Philadelphia for promoting useful knowledge ; v. 105, pt. 1)
Includes bibliographical references and index.

ISBN 978-1-60618-051-8

1. Hoeber, Johannes U., 1904–1977—Correspondence. 2. German Americans—Pennsylvania—Philadelphia—Biography. 3. Hoeber, Elfriede Fischer, 1904–1999—Correspondence. 4. Immigrants—Pennsylvania—Philadelphia—Biography. 5. Philadelphia (Pa.)—Biography. 6. Political refugees—United States—Biography. 7. Germany—Emigration and immigration—History—20th century. 8. Frankfurter Zeitung und Handelsblatt (Frankfurt am Main, Germany : Daily—Employees—Biography. 9. Düsseldorf (Germany—Social conditions—20th century. 10. Düsseldorf (Germany)—Biography. I. Hoeber, Elfriede Fischer, 1904–1999. II. Hoeber, Francis W. III. Title. IV. Title: Against time, letters from Nazi Germany, 1938/1939. V. Title: Letters from Nazi Germany, 1938/1939.

F158.53.H63 2015
943'.5534—dc23

2015021664

Book design by Sharka Hyland.

Editing and composition by Adept Content Solutions, Urbana, IL.

The text is set in 10.5/14 Sabon, with additional typography in Berthold Akzidenz Grotesk.

CONTENTS

Individuals named in the letters

Name	**Identification**	**Nicknames**
Johannes U. Hoeber		Jo, Jonny, Peter, Peterchen
Johannes's Family		
Rudolf Höber	Johannes's father	Rudi, Papi, Pa, Daddy
Josephine Marx Höber	Johannes's mother Mutti, Mu	Seppi, Seppchen,
Gabriele Höber Blaschy	Johannes's sister	Gri
Manfred Blaschy	Gabriele's husband	
Juliana	Manfred & Gri's daughter	Janka
Monika	Manfred & Gri's daughter	Moni
Ursula Höber	Johannes's sister	Ulli
Elfriede Fischer Hoeber		Friedel, Fri, Peter, Peterchen
Elfriede's Family		
Clara Fischer	Elfriede's mother	Oma
Günter Fischer	Elfriede's brother	
Herbert Fischer	Elfriede's brother	
Elisabeth Fischer	Herbert's wife	
Peter	Herbert & Elisabeth's son	
Paul Fischer	Elfriede's brother	
Heidi Fischer	Paul's wife	
Düsseldorf Friends and Acquaintances		
Dr. Betz	Regional Circulation and Advertising Manager, *Frankfurter Zeitung*	
Prof. Hans von Baeyer	Physician, friend of both Johannes and Elfriede and Rudolf and Josephine	the Magician, the professor-friend
Erich and Annemarie von Baeyer	Son and daughter-in-law of the Magician, living in Cleveland	

Name	Identification	Nicknames
Karl and Hilde Lenzberg	Karl was arrested on Kristallnacht, and they decided to move to Venezuela.	
Till Jaffe	Hilde's 14 year old son by a prior marriage	
Gerhard and Marlies Trömel, Hendrik and Gerlinde Zech, Mac Hannasch	Friends	

American Friends and Acquaintances		
Walter and Mary Phillips	Walter was Research Director at the Charter Committee, and Johannes's "boss," as well as his best friend in America	
Frederick Gruenberg, Walter Millard, Roger Scattergood, Eleanor Davis	Directors and staff members at the Charter Committee	
Erich and Annemarie von Baeyer	Radiologist and portraitist, living in Cleveland	Brüdi
Erich and Friede Stötzner	Journalist friend from Frankfurt and his wife, living in New York since 1937	"Stös"
Wolfi Huber	Son of a friend of Josephine, living in New York	
Hans Schlossmann	Pharmacologist friend of Rudolf and Josephine, living in Cambridge, England after 1933	

INTRODUCTION

A Folder of Old Letters

My mother had to remain behind when my father fled Nazi Germany on November 12, 1938. His train took him from Düsseldorf to Zürich, Switzerland; from there he planned to travel to America. Their plan was that my mother, Elfriede, and my eight-year-old sister, Susanne, would join Johannes once he got to the United States. Had they known at the outset the odds against Elfriede and Susanne's getting out, Johannes might never have left without them—and they might never have gotten out of Germany at all.

Johannes Höber was my father; he died in Washington, DC in 1977 at the age of 72. A year later, my mother came to live with me and my wife, Ditta, in Philadelphia. Elfriede brought several file cabinets of papers with her. I did not know then that those papers included records of my parents' lives in Germany. My parents rarely spoke of Germany or of their experiences under the Nazis. Once they came to America, before I was born, they became Americans in every way and focused on the future of the nation they had made their own, not on the past.

As Elfriede grew older, she would occasionally ask me to handle some of her affairs—small things such as paying bills. One summer day in the 1980's, when Elfriede was away for a few weeks, I found myself at her desk working on her mail. Without giving it much thought, I began to explore the file cabinets in her study. I was amazed at what I found: hundreds of letters from Elfriede's mother and brothers in Germany spanning over forty years; dozens of folders with detailed records of the numerous international trips she and Johannes had taken; every income tax return they ever filed; everything that my sister, my brother, or I had ever written; and correspondence with friends, relatives, and political figures. All of it was carefully organized in dozens and dozens of the light-tan manila folders that were ubiquitous in American offices during the mid-twentieth century. Every folder was labeled in Johannes' meticulous spidery script or in Elfriede's distinctive, regular but nearly indecipherable hand.

Jammed at the back of an over-filled file drawer was something different: a black cardboard folder stuffed with yellowed pages. It was not an American manila folder like all the others, but something old and foreign. It looked like no one had opened it for many years. When I cautiously turned back the cover and began to read, I found a set of long letters written by Johannes and Elfriede. They were all in German; many were typed but some were written with a fountain pen in my mother's unique script. The earliest letters and postcards at the back of the folder were dated in November 1938, and the latest at the front were dated October 1939. I slowly came to realize that these were the letters the two of them exchanged during a most dramatic period in world history.

From November 1938 to November 1939, when Johannes and Elfriede were apart, they wrote each other as often as they could. During the first weeks, when Johannes was living in Zürich, they could exchange letters daily. Once Johannes escaped Europe and was in the United States, their correspondence was dictated by shipping schedules, because almost all mail traveled by sea. This usually meant that they were able to write only

A letter written by Elfriede

A carbon copy of a letter typed by Johannes

Phila, den 2.1.39.

Liebstes Peterchen,

es ist fürwahr ein Segen, dass nur einmal im Jahr Weihnachten
und Neujahr ist. Diesen Anlass benutzen nämlich sämtliche
grossen und schnellen Schiffe sämtlicher Linien um cruises
nach den Bermudas, nach Cuba oder sonstigen besseren Plätzen
der südlichen Hemisphäre zu unternehmen und dem Publikum dieser
cruises und den daran verdienenden Aktionären der steamship
companies ist es offenbar ganz egal, dass mittlerweile Ehegatten,
Eltern und Kinder von allen means of communication abgeschnit-
ten sind. Denn seit der Normandie am 26.12. ist effektiv überhaupt
kein Schiff mehr von New York eastbound gesailt, das "drüben"
vor der Europa ankäme, die nun diesen Brief morgen mitnehmen
soll. Fast schlimmer noch ist, dass seit der "Hamburg" die am
21.12. Hamburg verliess und die Du offenbar als letzte Gelegen-
heit des Jahres 1938 übersehen hast, kein decent boat mehr an-
kam, sodass das letzte , was ich mittlerweile von Dir hörte,
die beiden Briefe waren, (vom 16.12.), die ich schon am 24.
beantwortete. Umso netter war es, dass ein Teil der Weihnachts-
post vom customs house erst [illegible] - übrigens restlos zoll-
frei-ausgespuckt wurde und so im Laufe der Woche eintröpfelte.
Das von mir als weich und biegsam diagnosticierte Couvert enthielt den wunderschönen Schlips, der mir restlos gefällt und
meiner hier allgemein als elegant gepriesenen Farbensymphonie
in Blau nun die ganz vornehme Note verleiht. Das andere Couvert,
das ich hier schon vorfand aber erst am Heilig Abend öffnen
durfte, enthielt Günthers Photos. Danke ihm sehr dafür, er hat
sich wirklich Mühe damit gegeben. Dass nur das von Dir am
Schreibtisch so weit vor meinen Augen Gnade fand, dass es jetzt
die Wand meiner Bude über dem Bett schmückt, liegt nicht an ihm
sondern an der allzugrossen Nähe des Empfängers zu den aufge-
nommenen Objekten. Neben dem Bild von Dir hängt übrigens jetzt
das von Brüdi hier hinterlassene Photo seines Potraits von
Suna, das ich auch jetzt noch überzeugend finde. Das nächste
Düsseldorf-Paket, das unter dem Weihnachtsbaum ausgepackt
wurde, war die Bittner-Kiste. Das hast Du wirklich gut gemacht,
lieber Schatz, die Stollen sind schon restlos vertilgt, von
sämtlichen Pralinékästen befinden sich nur noch schäbige Reste
in meinem und Daddys Privatbesitz und das Säckchen Marzipan-
kartoffeln als ausschliesslich für mich bestimmt zu deklarieren
gelang mir nur unter nachdrücklicher Berufung auf Deine dies-
bezügliche schriftliche Aeusserung. (Ich identifizierte darin
doch richtig die für mich allein bestimmte Kleinigkeit, die
Du der Kiste einverleibtest?) Am dienstag - an Sonn- und Feier-
tagen wird hier keine Post ausgetragen - erschien Susas Päck-
chen mit Püppchen und Lesezeichen und Täschchen, das ich an
Hand ihrer Prosa- und Poesiekommentare mühelos verteilte. (A

once a week. The letters were long and detailed, with Elfriede describing her tedious daily life in the deteriorating conditions of Nazi Germany and Johannes reveling in the excitement and challenges he found in America.

When I first found the letters, my knowledge of German was sketchy. My parents rarely spoke German at home, so most of what I knew I had learned in high school. I could make out only a few parts of the typed letters; the handwritten letters eluded me entirely. My task was made more difficult because the letters were full of unintelligible terms that appeared in no dictionary—*Abo*, *Wobla*, *Staka*, *Affi*—and perplexing names—*Onkel Karl*, *Onkel Paul*, *Felix*, *Nepomuk*—that didn't belong to anyone I had ever heard my parents mention. In the beginning I felt that I would never figure the letters out and that I would be stymied by the handwriting, the foreign language, the mysterious terms, and the unidentifiable names. But their secrecy, their mystery, and the dark times in which they were written kept calling me back.

I enrolled in evening German classes for several years and kept struggling with the language. I eventually figured out that the odd words were a code that Johannes and Elfriede understood but others would not. I realized they wrote the letters under the assumption the Nazi authorities might open them. If that happened, Johannes and Elfriede wanted to ensure that their words would endanger neither themselves nor their friends and family. From context and research, however, and from repeated readings, I was eventually able to decode the letters.

I never discussed the letters with my mother and never told her I found them. The letters are extremely personal, written by a husband and wife for one another's eyes only. I knew I was intruding on their privacy by reading them. Both my parents—my mother especially—were reserved people who did not talk about their private business and did not share their emotional lives. My parents were particularly reluctant to speak of their experiences under the Nazis or about how they got out of Germany, leaving me with the sense that there were painful stories wrapped in their reticence. The letters showed me, however, that the story was not so dark as I had imagined. The letters are full of cleverness, good fortune, and a persistent optimism in the face of frightening difficulties. On the day my parents reached America, they turned their backs on Germany and on the past and became enthusiastic citizens of the New World. While my mother was alive, I never felt comfortable breaching the secure walls of the life that she and my father had made here in America.

I often found it draining to work on the letters. There is a tension, a sense of strain, that I feel each time I pick them up. Although my parents were, in the end, more fortunate than millions of others, their lives under the Nazis were lives of fear. I often felt their anxiety transmitted to me through their words. There were periods when I gave up work on the letters for a year or two at a time.

Although Johannes died in 1977 and Elfriede in 1999, I was able to meet and know them through these letters as two new people. As the father I knew, Johannes was high strung and unpredictable, with a volatile temper that might be set off by a child's minor transgression. To tell the truth, I was often afraid of him. But in the letters he is charming, caring, clever, ambitious, and loving, concerned for the welfare of Elfriede and my sister Susanne. As the mother I knew, Elfriede was reserved, even stolid, often painfully shy and determined to maintain an exterior of solid imperturbability. I believe she was depressed much of her life, and my experience of her rarely included warm displays of motherly affection. But in these letters I discovered an affectionate, witty, engaged, and loving wife and mother. She deeply loved my father and relied on him. Her whole strength was aimed at reuniting herself and Susanne with him, and that objective kept her going as the prospect of getting safely out of Germany became more and more daunting.

In these letters I also discovered two fine, passionate writers. They write very differently, however. My father's letters are carefully organized and precise, self-conscious and at the same time full of colorful detail and rich accounts of people, places, and events that convey his deep interest in the world he observed. My mother's letters are sometimes slightly chaotic, but they convey a full sense of her strong feelings about what she was experiencing. Her letters are often laced with a breezy wit, though the humor is often ironic and sometimes witheringly sarcastic. I never knew my mother was as funny as she is in these letters.

The letters in this book were Johannes and Elfriede's lifeline to one another during the tense year they were separated. Everything in their shared lives was included, and everything, from the smallest tedious detail of the newspaper distribution business that supported them, through the frightening delays in Elfriede's departure from Germany, to the highs and lows of their emotional relationship, had to be captured on the typed or handwritten page. After several months, Johannes asked Elfriede in a letter whether she ever found the letter writing burdensome. Elfriede wrote back:

> When I read your letter, for the first time in—how long is it? months?—I came within a hair's breadth of really crying. A sentence like "I wouldn't want writing to me to become an obligation or even a burden to you, etc." is something I never, never want to hear again and never, never want to read again. Of course one writes letters in different moods, sometimes with more, sometimes less, of a positive attitude—you do too. But these letters, both those that I write and those that I get, are now simply my daily bread and I have to write them, even when I am feeling completely miserable and even when I am dead tired.

Readers will note the extent to which the letters do *not* discuss the major world events that formed the daily context of Johannes and Elfriede's lives and that constantly threatened their future. They referred to world events obliquely as "the macrocosm," and wrote mostly about "the microcosm" of their daily lives. How real the threat of Gestapo surveillance of mail was is unclear, but a totalitarian state creates a fear of omniscience that may be greater than the reality. In any event, it is not surprising that the letters contain only fleeting mention of the great events of world politics, as any comment on those events could pose unknown dangers.

In the letters, Johannes and Elfriede often addressed each other as "Peter" or "Peterchen" [Little Peter], apparently as a term of endearment. Why they did so is a mystery. I never heard them address each other this way until I discovered these letters.

The German name "Höber" is spelled Hoeber in English. Few Americans, however, are able to pronounce the "ö" sound, and the name is always pronounced here as "HO-ber." When Johannes and Elfriede came to the United States they switched the spelling from Höber to Hoeber.

The mechanics of international mail in 1938–39 were not simple. There was no transatlantic telephone connection, and airmail was a costly rarity. Telegrams were outrageously expensive—it cost the equivalent of $50 in today's money to send a one-line message by cable. As a result, sea mail was the primary means of communication. Letters and packages went most often via passenger liners that made the fastest trips between European ports — Hamburg, Bremen, Cherbourg etc. — and New York. People who wrote frequently would buy a copy of the monthly European shipping schedule that listed the ships, the dates they were scheduled to leave a particular port, and the dates of their arrival in New York, as well as return trips to European ports. A person sending a letter would note on the envelope not just the address of the recipient but also the ship that should take it. The postal service would pick up the envelope from the mailbox and deliver the envelope to that ship, usually in one day. With a fast ship, a letter mailed from Düsseldorf could be delivered in

An envelope showing routing "Via airmail from Cologne to Cherbourg to the steamer 'Bremen,'" mailed November 8, 1938. The handwriting is Johannes'. The note on the lower right is Josephine's, indicating "arrived 18 November 1938, answered by Rudolf and me 19/20 November" ["angek. 18 XI 38, beantw. Rud u. ich 19/20 XI"].

Philadelphia in nine or ten days. In both Germany and the United States, mail was delivered twice daily, once in the morning and once in the afternoon, except on Sundays and holidays.

What follows is an introductory chapter that describes the context in which the letters were written and introduces Johannes and Elfriede and the people around them. The letters themselves, divided into chronological chapters, make up the bulk of the book. I have added notes to explain people, code words, and events referred to in the letters. I have erred on the side of explaining events or terms that may be familiar to some, but not all, readers. The Epilogue describes the subsequent lives of the Hoebers and their family and friends, as well as the world they made for themselves in America.

CHAPTER 1

Johannes and Elfriede

Johannes and Elfriede's flight from Germany in 1938–1939 was the culmination of years of resistance to Nazi ideology and their ever-increasing revulsion at what Germany had become. When they did finally decide to leave, the obstacles to getting out were daunting. The letters in this book tell the story of Johannes and Elfriede's passage out of the homeland that had become intolerable to them to their new life in a new world.

Johannes Höber (1904–1977) and Elfriede Fischer (1904–1999) made a strikingly good-looking young couple when they met at the age of nineteen. It was 1923 and they were first-year students at the University of Freiburg. Although of slight build, Johannes was dark and handsome—black hair, brown eyes, olive complexion and a strong, inquiring gaze. Elfriede was light and very pretty—light brown hair, blue eyes, pale skin. Her eyes were often downcast, but then she would surprise you by looking up at you with her direct, intelligent gaze. Johannes was outgoing and gregarious, often utterly charming, with an air of confidence unusual for his age, a confidence that could occasionally devolve into stubbornness and arrogance. Elfriede was quieter, with a manner that was at once shy and reserved and yet self-possessed. She had a slightly sad air that veiled a ferocious determination to achieve what she set out to do. In personality and temperament they were quite different, and in some ways they were mismatched. The glue that held their love together was their intelligence and their commitment to the world of ideas, the world of the mind, the world of sociology, economics, and political science. They both embraced an intense analytic intellectualism centered on the public sphere. They engaged the political and social issues of their time with deliberation and never ceased in their struggle to understand the world around them and to effect positive change in the society in which they lived. Johannes was a more political person and Elfriede more intellectual, but for both of them, lives focused on public affairs, social policy, and the resolution of social injustice were the natural course of existence.

In June 1924, less than a year after they met, Johannes and Elfriede became engaged. They were just 20. The next year Elfriede insisted that she and Johannes attend different universities. It was common at that time for students to move from one university to another within Germany, and Elfriede wanted to test the strength of Johannes' commitment. She transferred to the University of Berlin while Johannes attended the University of Kiel. In March 1925, Johannes joined Elfriede again at

Johannes Höber and Elfriede Fischer around the time of their marriage, December 22, 1928.

the University of Berlin, where he became a delegate to the student senate [*Allgemeine Studentenaußschuss* or *AStA*]. It was the first of many political activities for him.

In 1925, Johannes and Elfriede transferred to Heidelberg University, but a year later they were separated again, this time because Johannes was selected for a year of study at the London School of Economics. He was the first German foreign exchange student in England following World War I. That year in England was pivotal for Johannes. Most significantly, he became fluent in English. In addition, he became steeped in democratic socialism and the sense of being a member of an international liberal political community. In this period he also became a correspondent for the monthly journal of the International Metalworkers Union [*Internationaler Metallarbeiter-Gewerkschaft*], introducing him to both journalism and the trade union movement.

Returning to Germany in the fall of 1927, Johannes plunged into the tumultuous politics of Heidelberg University, which reflected the political upheavals then battering Germany. In the years following World War I, German democracy developed a full spectrum of vigorous political parties from Communists on the left; through Social Democrats, centrist, and religious parties; to aristocratic, militaristic, and fascist parties on the right. Embracing the socialism he encountered in England, Johannes became the president of the Social Democratic Student Group. He served as their representative in the Heidelberg Student Senate [*AStA*], where he regularly butted heads with the dueling fraternities, the militarists, and the rising National Socialists. His activism made him sufficiently notorious that he was attacked and badly beaten one night by a group of right-wing students in the Heidelberg tavern *Zum Ritter*. But he persisted in promoting the Social Democrats as a political force within the university.

Concurrent with his involvement in university politics, Johannes managed to keep up a respectable academic record. Elfriede, in the meantime, focused more intensely than Johannes on academic work. She completed her doctoral studies and dissertation in political science and economics under Alfred Weber in less than two years.[1] In 1928, the University of Heidelberg awarded many doctorates but only four of them with the *summa cum laude* distinction, all to women. One of the four *summas* went to Johannes and Elfriede's acquaintance Hannah Arendt and one went to Elfriede. Following her receipt of her doctorate, Elfriede was retained by Heidelberg University to run its pioneering international student exchange program, the *Internationaler Studentenaustauschdienst*. In 1930, Elfriede co-edited and published *Der Student im Ausland* [*Students Abroad*], a collection of essays by students who participated in the exchange program.

Also in 1928, although he had not yet completed his dissertation, Johannes got his first job, as press secretary to Hermann Heimerich, the Social Democratic *Oberbürgermeister* of the nearby Rhineland city of Mannheim. One of Mayor Heimerich's programs was to increase the general population's understanding of city government. He approached Emil Lederer, a professor of economics and sociology at Heidelberg, and asked for a recommendation from among his students. Professor Lederer recommended Johannes, and Heimerich took him on. Johannes finished his thesis, *Die Nachkriegsentwicklung der englischen Arbeiterbewegung* [The Postwar Development of the English Workers' Movement] under Lederer's supervision in 1930.

Johannes and Elfriede got married just before Christmas 1928 and moved into a modern apartment complex in Mannheim. Elfriede had strong interests in art, architecture, and modern design, and she and Johannes proudly indulged themselves in a set of five Breuer chairs, the then ultra-modern seating of bent tubular steel, for their dining room.

Johannes' job in Mannheim was at the outset everything he could have wanted. At the age of twenty-four he was seriously involved in the real work of running a city with a population of a quarter million. He worked hard and absorbed everything he could about public administration. He learned to polish his writing, developing a clear, declaratory style that even modestly educated readers could understand. He produced report after report filled with photographs and clear, engaging graphics, expounding on the city's importance as a commercial and industrial center

1 Elfriede Höber, *Grundlagen der Interpretation der Politik der deutschen Sozialdemokratie durch die sozialdemokratische Presse* [The Basis of the Interpretation of German Social Democratic Policies by the Social Democratic Press], Heidelberg, 1928.

and promoting the city's cultural resources in theater, music and the fine arts. The reports also explained the new roles of the city administration: city planning, parks and recreation and providing housing and health care for all citizens. Beginning in 1929, Johannes also compiled and edited a bimonthly magazine, *Die Lebendige Stadt* [*The Living City*], which reported on activities and developments in the city and its government. His work connected him with all the departments in the administration as well as with journalists in Mannheim and throughout southwest Germany. His position also brought him into regular contact with trade union leaders and members, with whom he developed an enduring sympathy.

Publicity magazine produced by Johannes as press chief to the Mayor of Mannheim, December 1929.

While he was working to achieve the official goals of the city by day, Johannes was continuing his political activities on behalf of the Social Democrats [*Sozialdemokratische Partei Deutschlands* or *SPD*] by night. Those political activities, like all politics in Germany at the time, were growing more confrontational and more dangerous. Germany's many political parties had been in ferocious conflict throughout the 1920s. Then the international financial crisis that followed the Wall Street crash of 1929 launched mass unemployment in Europe as well as in the United States. Political parties were quick to blame their opponents and their policies for the economic suffering, and political street violence became part of daily life. Parties established their own militias, paramilitary units whose nominal function was the protection of party officials but who regularly were involved in street fighting and intimidation of the adherents of opposing parties. Historically, the most remembered of the paramilitary organizations was the *Sturmabteilung* or SA, Hitler's jackbooted, brown-shirted Stormtroopers. But there were also the right-wing *Stahlhelm* [Steel Helmet], the very large *Rotfrontkämpfer* [Red Front Brigade] of the Communist Party, and the *Reichsbanner Schwarz-Rot-Gold* [National Banner Black-Red-Gold], originally a nonpartisan group defending the Weimar Republic but later the paramilitary arm of the *SPD*.[2]

Beginning in 1930, despite the fact that it created problems for his mentor, Mayor Heimerich, Johannes became increasingly involved in the militant activities of the Social Democratic Party. He became the chairman of the *SPD* organization for the part of the city he lived in (Mannheim-Lindenhof) and a member of the Baden state leadership committee of the *Reichsbanner* paramilitaries. At the height of these dangerous activities, Johannes acquired a pistol that he carried at night. He and a group of *SPD* cohorts would go out to Nazi meetings and take seats at the back of the meeting room. After the main speaker spoke for a time, Johannes would begin to shout questions and challenges. As the conflict escalated, the *SPD* men would begin throwing chairs. If the *SPD* men outnumbered the Nazis, they would chase them out of the meeting hall. On other occasions the Nazis would chase the *SPD* out of the hall and chase them down the street. Either way, the Nazis' meeting was disrupted. Johannes continued these risky activities until 1933, when the Nazis took power and made this kind of resistance suicidal.[3] While Elfriede certainly hated the Nazis just as much as Johannes, she found his participation in these activities alarming, fearing that one night he would go out to a political meeting and never return. Mayor Heimerich, though sympathetic with Johannes' objectives, also found his militant activities troublesome. To avoid exposing himself and his press chief further, Mayor Heimerich transferred Johannes to a less visible position in the welfare office in November 1932.

In the midst of all the political upheaval, Johannes and Elfriede continued the ordinary activities of daily life, enjoyed family and friends, and took joy in special events and special occasions. On April 3, 1930, their first child, Susanne, was born, delighting them and both sets of grandparents. Her arrival brought big changes, of course, as Elfriede gave up her job with the Student Exchange Program Office at Heidelberg to devote herself full time to the care of their daughter.

The young family's life was structured around the holidays of the Christian calendar. Advent, Christmas and New Year, *Karneval* (the Rhineland variant of Mardi Gras), Easter and the Pentecost weekend

2 On paramilitary organizations and political violence, see Richard J. Evans, *The Coming of the Third Reich* (New York: Penguin Books, 2003), 72–76, 220–23.

3 With regard to Johannes' student activities and Mannheim work, see Achim Bonte, *Werbung für Weimar? Öffentlichkeitsarbeit von Großstadtverwaltungen in der Weimarer Republik*, (Mannheim: Historisches Institut der Universität Mannheim, 1997), 196–98.

were occasions traveling and for celebrating with family and friends. Each holiday was anticipated and celebrated with pleasure, as were birthdays and vacations.

Johannes was the son of distinguished parents. Rudolf Höber (1873–1953)[4] and Josephine Marx Höber (1876–1941) were half-cousins,[5] and married in 1902. They became attracted to one another as teenagers, not least because of their shared interest in natural science. By the time they married, Rudolf was an instructor in physiology at the University of Zürich. Before he was thirty, and in the same year he and Josephine married, Rudolf published a groundbreaking work in cellular biochemistry, *The Physical Chemistry of Cells and Tissues*. Over the next 45 years, Rudolf authored seven further editions of this treatise.[6]

After they were married, Rudolf urged Josephine to continue her studies and obtain a medical degree as he had, an unusual ambition for a young woman in Europe at that time. Josephine's studies at the University of Zürich were interrupted by the birth of Johannes in 1904 and a daughter, Gabriele (called "Gri"), in 1906, but she persevered and received her medical degree and license to practice in 1909.

Also in 1909, Rudolf and Josephine returned to Germany when Rudolf was appointed associate professor at the University of Kiel, a center for physiological research. In 1912, a third child, Ursula, was born. In 1915, Rudolf was promoted to full professor [*ordentlicher Professor*] at Kiel as well as Director of the Physiological Institute there. In 1919, Rudolf published his second book, his *Textbook of Physiology*, which also went through eight editions and whose royalties substantially supplemented the family income for years.[7]

Rudolf's advancement to full professor came only at the sacrifice of Josephine's medical career. In the context of the prevailing social mores, the authorities of the Prussian Ministry of Culture and Education, who had to approve Rudolf's appointment, deemed it inappropriate for a professor's wife to engage in the private practice of medicine. Accordingly, they made it a condition of Rudolf's appointment that Josephine relinquish her medical practice. She was, however, allowed to participate as a volunteer physician in the Women's Clinic in Kiel, an activity she continued for many years. She also became active in liberal politics and in 1919 was elected a member [*Stadtverordnete*] of the city council. In the 1920s, Josephine collaborated with Rudolf in laboratory research and published the results jointly with him. Although Josephine did not achieve the international recognition Rudolf did, her contributions to the science of membrane physiology were significant.

4 See William R. Amberson, "Rudolf Höber: His Life and Scientific Work," *Science* 120 (1954):199-201; Albrecht Bethe, "Rudolf Höber," *Pflügers Archiv* 259 (1954): 1–3; H. Netter, "Rudolf Höbers Wissenschaftliches Werk," *Pflügers Archiv* 259 (1954): 4–13; Uta Cornelia Schmatzler und Matthias Wieben, "Professor Dr. Rudolf Höber (geb. 27. Dezember 1873)," *Vertriebene Wissenschaftler der Christian-Albrechts Universität zu Kiel (CAU) nach 1933* (Frankfurt a.M., 1991): 51–53; W. Wilbrandt, "In Memoriam: Rudolf Höber," *Experientia* 9 (1953):1–3; and W. Wilbrandt, "Rudolf Höber," *Ergebnisse der Physiologie, Biologischen Chemie und Experimentellen Pharmakologie* 49 (1957): 22–46.

5 Rudolf and Josephine had a grandfather in common named Eduard Höber who was married twice. Rudolf's father was Eduard's son by his first wife and Josephine's mother was Eduard's daughter by his second wife.

6 Rudolf Höber, *Physikalische Chemie der Zelle und der Gewebe*, First Edition (Leipzig: Verlag von Wilhelm Engelman, 1902), Eighth Edition [with David L. Hitchcock, David L. Goddard, J. B. Bateman, Wallace O. Fenn] (Bern: Verlag Stämpfli & Cie, 1947).

7 Rudolf Höber, *Lehrbuch der Physiologie des Menschen*, First Edition (Berlin: Verlag von Julius Springer, 1919), Eighth Edition (Bern: Stämpfli & Cie., 1939).

In 1930, Rudolf Höber was appointed *Rektor* [Chancellor] of the University of Kiel. In that capacity he presided over a confrontation with Nazi students who tried to interfere with a speech delivered by a retired liberal theologian, Professor Otto Baumgarten. Rudolf's passionate defense of free speech and his disciplining of the disruptive students in the Baumgarten Affair would be remembered by the Nazis and would be revived as an issue less than three years later when Hitler took over Germany. Professor Baumgarten was a member of the German delegation that signed the peace treaty that ended World War I and later was a leader of the Association Against Anti-Semitism. In his article "The Cross and the Swastika" (1926), Baumgarten established himself as an early opponent of the Nazis. When he was scheduled to speak at the University of Kiel in 1930, a group of Nazi students unsuccessfully tried to stop him. *Rektor* Höber issued the judgment of an appointed faculty hearing board, which expelled one student and prohibited a second from matriculating. Several weeks later, the national Nazi Student Association convened a mass rally in the city of Halle to protest the "Baumgarten Affair" and Rudolf's role in it, thereby making him notorious among right wingers throughout Germany.[8]

As far as the Höbers were concerned, they were not Jewish. Like many European intellectuals of the time, they were primarily secular, and most of their limited religious activity was connected with nonreligious celebrations of holidays in the Christian calendar. But while they were not Jewish, Rudolf and Josephine had Jewish ancestors. Rudolf was baptized and confirmed as a Protestant when he was a child in the 1870s. His father, Anselm Höber, however, had been born into a Jewish family; he formally converted to Protestantism when he married a non-Jewish woman in 1865. Josephine was born into a Jewish family but converted to Protestantism when she was in high school [*Gymnasium*]. This transformation of the family's identification from Jewish to Protestant/secular was a fairly common story among educated families over the course of the nineteenth century. The Höber children, Johannes, Gabriele (Gri) and Ursula, were baptized and confirmed in the local church, but otherwise the family's religious observance was limited. Elfriede came from a completely nonreligious family[9] (with Protestant ancestors), and when she and Johannes married, the wedding in her parents' home was conducted by an officiant from the Ethical Culture Society.

8 Hermann Mulert, *Baumgarten und die Nationalsozialisten* (Neumünster in Holstein: Wachholz Verlag, 1931).

9 In Germany, church taxes are collected by the state unless an individual registers formally as a nonbeliever [*ungläubig*]. Elfriede's parents, Franz and Clara Fischer, registered themselves as nonbelievers in the Düsseldorf civil registry office when they married in 1902.

While Elfriede's parents did not share Rudolf and Josephine's professional prominence, they too were intellectuals. Franz Fischer (1868–1937) was born the son of a prosperous farmer in the village of Küingdorf in the north German state of Westphalia but decided early that farm life was not for him. He moved to Düsseldorf, apprenticed in business, and joined a firm that dealt in bicycles and sewing machines. He made a respectable living and, in a period that did not make social mobility easy, succeeded in converting himself into a gentleman, dressing elegantly but conservatively, reading widely, and taking advantage of the cultural offerings of city life. He married Clara Schallenberg, from the small town of Rheine. She had a remarkably broad knowledge of German and classical literature. Franz and Clara led a good life in an ample apartment near the center of Düsseldorf.

As liberals and freethinkers [*Freidenkende*], Franz and Clara conveyed to their children a strong sense of moral rectitude and social responsibility grounded in a philosophically principled atheism. In addition to their daughter Elfriede, they had three sons. Günter (1906–1979) went into his father's business. He and Johannes became great friends and together would frequent the bars of the Düsseldorf *Altstadt*. Herbert (1907–1985) also went into business and after World War II took over the family farm in Westphalia. Paul (1909–1945?) became a lawyer and was helpful to Johannes and Elfriede in dealing with legal questions in the newspaper business. In his university years he was briefly a member of the Communist Party. Franz and Clara recognized early that they had a gifted daughter in Elfriede. When the time came, neither Franz nor Clara hesitated in sending Elfriede to the *Gymnasium*, the upper level public school that would prepare her for university studies. They were fully supportive of her attaining her doctoral degree.

The takeover of Germany by Adolf Hitler and the Nazis in 1933 changed everything. On January 30, 1933, President Paul von Hindenburg appointed Hitler Chancellor, with the understanding that elections for the Reichstag would occur in a number of weeks. Hitler immediately began issuing "emergency" decrees limiting the political activities of the Nazis' opponents and the rights of the press. In Berlin on February 27, the Reichstag building was burned. The next day, Hitler blamed the fire on Communists and banned the Communist Party. On March 5, the Nazis received a plurality of the votes cast in the Reichstag elections. On March 23, the Reichstag voted (with only SPD members dissenting) to pass the Enabling Act turning over to the Chancellor the authority to adopt any legislation whatsoever in the name of an "emergency." In a matter of a few weeks, the German people's surrender to Hitler was complete.

On April 7, 1933, the regime enacted the Civil Service Reform Act [*Gesetz zur Wiederherstellung des Berufsbeamtentums*], which prohibited the employment of "Jews"[10] in government positions. Thousands upon

10 The terms "Jew" and "Jewish" had multiple meanings in Germany and elsewhere, including the "racial" definition used by the Nazis from the time of their 1933 takeover of the government. This definition was codified in the Nuremberg Laws of 1935 (see footnote 16, below). I have adopted the practice of some historians of placing these terms in quotation marks except when referring to members of a Jewish religious congregation or people who self-identified as Jews. See, e.g., Sonja Niederarcher, "Eigentum und Geschlecht. Soziale und ökonomische Handlungsspielräume von Wiener 'Juden' und 'Jüdinnen' in der ersten Hälfte des 20. Jahrhunderts: Eine sozialhistorische Studie über Vermögensbildung, NS-Verfolgung und Restitution." (Vienna: Stiftung Kreisky Archiv June 2008), 56. Web. May 6, 2014.

thousands of civil servants who were practicing Jews, as well as Christians and nonbelievers of "Jewish" ancestry, were to be fired from their jobs or forcibly retired. Every civil servant in Germany was required to fill out a questionnaire listing his parents and grandparents and documenting their dates of birth, death, and marriage as well as their religion. A "Jew" was defined by the Nazis based on heredity and bloodlines, not religious practice; conversions were of no legal significance. Since all German universities were governmental institutions, every professor and instructor was a civil servant subject to the law. And since all doctors in Germany might potentially participate in the national health plan, every physician in Germany was subject to the law. Thus Rudolf, in his position as professor, and Josephine, in her position as a medical doctor, were subject to the provisions of the Civil Service Reform Act. This meant they were required to submit the detailed questionnaire and to obtain copies of birth, marriage, and death records for their parents and all four grandparents.

Johannes was the first in the Höber family to be affected by the Nazi takeover, and it had nothing to do with the Civil Service Reform Act or his grandfather's "Jewish" origins. Immediately after the March 5 national Reichstag elections, the Nazis' central organization moved to take control of the government of every state, city and town in the country, a process formalized in the coordination acts [*Gleichschaltungsgesetze*] of March and April, 1933. Even in advance of directives from Berlin, however, the local Nazi Party moved to take over the governance of Mannheim by force. On March 9, a large contingent of Stormtroopers led an assault on the Mannheim *Rathaus* and seized control of the city administration. They dragged Mayor Heimerich from his office onto the balcony overlooking the main square and forced him to watch as the black, red, and gold flag of the democratic Weimar republic was lowered and burned in the square and the Swastika banner was hoisted in its place. On March 12, Stormtroopers seized half a dozen Social Democratic officials in Heimerich's administration and imprisoned them in the city jail. Johannes was one of them. The stated rationale was that "the people" had become enraged by the supposed misdeeds of the Social Democrats and the officials needed to be placed in "protective custody" [*Schutzhaft*] to protect the public order.[11]

11 The events in Mannheim are described in Herbert Hoffmann, *In Gleichschritt in die Diktatur? Die nationalsozialistische "Machtergreifung" in Heidelberg und Mannheim, 1930 bis 1935* (Frankfurt: Verlag Peter Lang, 1985), 105–118; Friedrich Walter, *Schicksal einer deutschen Stadt: Geschichte Mannheims 1907–1945* (Frankfurt a.M.: Fritz Knapp Verlag, 1949), 180–185. See also Angelika Tarokic, *Hermann Heimerich: Ein Mannheimer Oberbürgermeister im Spiegel seines Nachlasses* (Mannheim: Verlagsbüro v. Brandt, 2006), 77–79.

Johannes' arrest and incarceration were terrifying for him and Elfriede and their families. At home, Elfriede's concern focused on the gun Johannes had acquired, which she decided she must get rid of. At night, she called a friend, Marianne Daniels, to help her. They cautiously removed the gun from the linen closet where it was hidden in a pile of bed sheets and put it into a brown paper bag. Fearing all the while that they might be stopped by police or Stormtroopers, Elfriede and Marianne walked onto the Rhine Bridge that linked Mannheim with Ludwigshafen on the

In Schutzhaft genommen

Der Polizeibericht meldet:

Im Laufe der letzten Tage wurden folgende Führer der SPD. in Schutzhaft genommen:

Ortsgruppenvorsitzender Landtagsabgeordneter Ernst Kraft,

der Gauleiter des Reichsbanners, Zahnarzt Dr. Helffenstein,

Dr. Höber, Mitglied der Gauleitung des Reichsbanners,

die Bezirksräte Werner und Meier und Nervenarzt Dr. Stern.

Ueber Oberbürgermeister Dr. Heimerich, der sich zurzeit im Theresienkrankenhaus befindet, wurde dort die Schutzhaft verhängt.

Folgende Personen, über die ebenfalls die Schutzhaft verhängt wurde, sind nicht auffindbar: Reichstagsabgeordneter Roth, Landtagsabgeordneter Reinbold, Schriftleiter Harpuder, Schriftleiter Dr. Schifrin, Rechtsanwalt Dr. Hirschler und Berichterstatter Diamant.

In Schutzhaft genommen—"Taken into Protective Custody." Clipping from the Neue Mannheimer Zeitung, *March 13, 1933. The list of those arrested includes "Dr. Höber, member of the regional leadership of the Reichsbanner [pro-democracy paramilitary group]." Courtesy Institut für Stadtgeschichte/Stadtarchiv Mannheim.*

opposite shore. In the middle of the bridge, they dropped the bag with the gun into the black waters of the Rhine.

There was no way to know how long the Nazis would hold Johannes in prison. After two weeks of incarceration, he and the other jailed SPD officials appealed for their release. Instead, the police led them to a balcony overlooking a courtyard within the *Rathaus*. They packed the courtyard with brown shirted Stormtroopers screaming for the death of the prisoners. The Nazi functionaries told the Social Democrats that this raging gang confirmed the need to keep them in "protective custody."

After nearly a month, Johannes' father, Rudolf, made the long trip from Kiel to Mannheim to attempt to secure Johannes' release. Rudolf was able to meet with the new Nazi commissar of police, who treated him with respect, deferentially addressing him as "Herr Professor." Rudolf offered the commissar a deal in exchange for Johannes' release: if allowed out of prison, Johannes would leave Mannheim and not return. The police agreed, and on April 13 Johannes was released. Shortly thereafter he, Elfriede, and Susanne moved to Düsseldorf. They would not return to Mannheim for more than 25 years.

After Rudolf secured Johannes' release from jail in Mannheim, he returned to his teaching duties at the University of Kiel. A week later, on April 24, 1933, he was in the midst of administering examinations to students in the medical school when a contingent of Stormtroopers and SS men stormed in and ordered him to break off the examinations. Rudolf indignantly refused. The Stormtroopers threatened to kill him if he returned to teaching classes or if he continued administering examinations. Again he refused. Faced with Rudolf's implacable stance, the Stormtroopers and SS men retreated. The next day Rudolf wrote an outraged letter to the Ministry of Culture and Education in Berlin protesting this mistreatment of a tenured professor and within a few days returned to his teaching and to his laboratory. But this victory was only temporary.

At the end of April, the Prussian Ministry of Culture began implementing the Civil Service Reform Law that required the removal from public positions of individuals classified as "Jews" under that law. As noted above, Rudolf was not Jewish, but his father, Anselm, was born into a Jewish family, and that made Rudolf a half-Jew [*Mischling*] in the eyes of the Nazis. Although the law allowed for exceptions to the termination order if an individual was uniquely qualified, and although the medical faculty and student body pleaded with the Ministry of Culture to grant Rudolf such an exception, once the Ministry learned that Rudolf had been a member of the liberal German People's Party and a supporter of the *Reichsbanner* prodemocracy organization, the Minister of Culture refused to grant him an exception. Rudolf's expulsion of Nazi students from the University during the Baumgarten Affair three years earlier also weighed against him. In October 1933, Rudolf was placed in forced retirement.[12]

12 An account of Rudolf's expulsion is contained in Uta Cornelia Schmatzler and Matthias Wieben, *Vertriebene Wissenschaftler der Christian-Albrechts-Universität zu Kiel (CAU) nach 1933: zur Geschichte der CAU im nationalsozialismus: eine Dokumentation* (Frankfurt a.M.: Peter Lang, 1991), 51–53. The documents concerning Rudolf's expulsion from the university faculty—indeed, his entire personnel file from the Ministry of Culture and Education—are preserved in the Prussian Secret State Archives in Berlin.

Crushed and bewildered, Rudolf and Josephine moved out of their apartment and placed their belongings in storage. They were among some 6,000 senior scholars and intellectuals expelled from German universities that year. All over the world, universities and scientific institutions scrambled to find places for these talented individuals. Rudolf was invited by Prof. A. V. Hill, a Nobel Prize–winning physiologist, to join him at the University of London as visiting professor. But his placement there did not last long. Dr. Alfred Stengel, Dean of the University of Pennsylvania Medical School in Philadelphia, was keenly aware of Rudolf's work and reputation, and upon learning that Rudolf was available invited him to Penn. In April 1934, Rudolf and Josephine, accompanied by their 22-year-old daughter Ursula, arrived in Philadelphia, where they would spend the rest of their lives.

In the meantime, Johannes and Elfriede settled into life in Düsseldorf, living at first with Elfriede's parents. Like many Germans, they did not expect the Nazi regime to last, but in the meantime Johannes needed a job. He first tried unsuccessfully to find a position as a reporter or correspondent. Finally, through reporter friends at the *Frankfurter Zeitung*, Germany's leading daily newspaper, Johannes found an opening as circulation manager for the paper in Düsseldorf. It was a comparatively low-status and low-income job, but it would support the young family adequately for the time being. He started work on August 1, 1933, and he and Elfriede and Susanne moved into an apartment on Pempelforterstrasse that could double as an office. Then, as today, the *Frankfurter Zeitung* had a role in Germany similar to that of the *New York Times* in the United States. In the 1920s it had a liberal editorial policy and was read daily by most educated and business people in the country. Although the Nazis forced the replacement of "Jewish" reporters and editors in 1933, they allowed the newspaper to continue publishing with a surprising degree of independence through the 1930s.[13]

Despite the upheaval in Germany and all of Europe, the lives of Johannes and Elfriede and their families remained relatively stable from 1933 to 1938. They frequently visited with Elfriede's mother and father and three adult brothers, who lived nearby, and developed a large circle of friends. They also remained close with Johannes' sister Gri and her husband Manfred Blaschy, who was a doctor at an exclusive sanatorium in Dresden. Although Johannes' parents, Rudolf and Josephine, were in Philadelphia, they exchanged long letters with Johannes and Elfriede in Düsseldorf several times a month.[14]

Although Rudolf had been expelled from his position at the University of Kiel, he and Josephine retained strong ties with family, friends, and colleagues in Germany. They returned to Europe for vacations in the summers of 1935 and 1936. In addition to visiting Johannes and Elfriede in Düsseldorf, they visited Gri and her husband in Dresden and then arranged joint family vacations for several weeks in the Alps. The European vacations were funded with Rudolf's modest pension from the University of Kiel that could be spent only in Germany and parts of Switzerland and Austria.

In Philadelphia, the University of Pennsylvania provided Rudolf with a small laboratory where he was able to continue his experimental research. Because the university did not provide him with adequate research support staff, however, Josephine became a full partner with Rudolf, working

13 See Modris Eksteins, *The Limits of Reason: The German Democratic Press and the Collapse of Weimar Democracy* (London: Oxford University Press, 1975).

14 Just as Johannes preserved the letters he and Elfriede exchanged in 1938–1939, Josephine preserved the letters Johannes and Elfriede sent her and Rudolf from Germany between 1934 and 1939. Much of the narrative in this chapter is drawn from those letters, which are in the Rudolf Höber Papers collection at the American Philosophical Society in Philadelphia.

in the lab four or five days each week without compensation. Together, Rudolf and she continued to make significant advances in biochemistry and cellular physiology, publishing the results of their research jointly.[15] Still, it was a far cry from the research facilities at Kiel, where Rudolf had access to cutting-edge electrical and electronic instruments and technical personnel to construct the new apparatus he designed.

In the summers, Rudolf and Josephine carried on their scientific work at the Woods Hole Marine Biological Laboratory on Cape Cod. Supported by research grants from the American Philosophical Society in Philadelphia, these annual stays in Woods Hole allowed Rudolf and Josephine to continue their research while escaping Philadelphia's oppressive summer heat.

When Johannes and Elfriede first moved to Düsseldorf in 1933, money was tight, and to help ends meet, Elfriede took a job as a salesperson for Electrolux vacuum cleaners. Such work was unsuited to her shy personality, however, and she gave it up after a few months. Later, as the newspaper business began to pick up and as Susanne got a little older, Johannes and Elfriede were able to afford a live-in housekeeper/babysitter. Helma was a solid, no-nonsense, unsentimental caretaker, but Susanne felt secure and comfortable under her watchful protection.

Johannes and Elfriede's newspaper business warrants some discussion here, as it occupies a considerable place in their letters. The couple did not receive a salary from the *Frankfurter Zeitung* but rather received a percentage of the subscription fees for the newspapers delivered and commissions on advertising they sold. Johannes was the head of the *Frankfurter Zeitung* agency for Düsseldorf, Duisburg, Krefeld, Gladbach, and the surrounding areas. The newspapers were printed in Frankfurt and delivered by train to Düsseldorf and the other towns, where carriers picked them up and delivered them by bicycle. The carriers also collected subscription fees from subscribers each month. The business was full of tedious annoyances that included unreliable carriers, complaining customers, and the need to keep complex accounts for the home office. A bright spot in this tedium was a valued part-time employee, Mrs. Natalie Freyberger. She could be relied on to take care of the business if Johannes and Elfriede wanted to go on vacation for some days or even weeks.

Johannes and Elfriede enjoyed a circle of close friends who shared their opposition to the Nazis and could be trusted not to reveal conversations when they turned to politics. A particularly close couple of friends were Karl and Hilde Lenzberg, who lived nearby. Hilde was Elfriede's best

15 See, e.g., Rudolf Höber and Josephine Höber, "The Influence of Detergents on Some Physiological Phenomena, Especially on the Properties of the Stellate Cells of the Frog Liver," *The Journal of General Physiology*, 1942, 705–15. A complete bibliography of Rudolf's publications, including over a hundred articles he published, is in W. Wilbrandt, "Rudolf Höber," *Ergebnisse der Physiologie* 49 (1957), 22–46.

friend and appears often in the letters as a continual source of sympathy and support, even when the Nazis wrecked her house, arrested her husband, and forced her family to emigrate. Another regular source of moral support was Hans Ritter von Baeyer, a retired professor of medicine whom the family called *der Zauberer,* the Magician. Prof. von Baeyer became a warm father figure, particularly after the death of Elfriede's father, Franz, in 1937.

Making the decision to leave Germany, to leave their friends, to leave Elfriede's family, to leave everything that was familiar to them, to leave hope behind, was a long process for Johannes and Elfriede. Despite Johannes' imprisonment and Rudolf's expulsion from the University of Kiel in 1933, Johannes in particular harbored the hope that the German people would drive the Nazis from power. But even if the Germans had wanted to do so, the state power apparatus made resistance increasingly dangerous, and the terrifying string of repressive measures against political dissenters, Jews, foreigners and other nonconformists intruded more and more into the daily lives of the entire populace.

On September 15, 1935, the regime adopted the Nuremberg laws, depriving "Jews" of German citizenship and forbidding marriage between "Aryans" and "Jews." These laws directly affected many of Johannes and Elfriede's close friends. According to the implementing regulations issued on November 15, 1935, anyone with three Jewish grandparents was a "Jew" and a noncitizen, and anyone with just one Jewish grandparent was a non-Jewish "Aryan" with citizenship rights. Those with two Jewish grandparents, so-called *Mischlinge,* were subject to some restrictions but were not subject to the same legal discrimination as "full Jews." Johannes' grandparents on the side of his mother, Josephine, were indisputably Jewish, but as far as Johannes was concerned, he was not Jewish. He had been raised in the Protestant Church and later lived an entirely secular life. Josephine's conversion to Protestantism as a teenager was irrelevant under the Nuremberg laws, which regarded "Jewishness" as a hereditary racial characteristic. Johannes' grandmother on his father's side was clearly not Jewish, but the status of his grandfather on his father's side was not so clear. Grandfather Anselm was born to Jewish parents but converted to Protestantism in 1865. Since Johannes had the records of this Anselm's wedding in a Protestant church, he concluded his father's father should not be calculated as Jewish. So Johannes simply continued living as the non-Jew he had always been.[16]

In 1937 Johannes and Elfriede visited the United States. In June that year, Johannes' younger sister Ursula graduated from the University of

16 In discussing the Nuremberg Laws, historian Richard Evans notes that they presented the question of "... who exactly was a Jew? ... To such questions there was no rational answer, because there was from the beginning no rational basis to the assumptions on which they rested. All solutions the Nazis arrived at in the question of mixed-race Germans and mixed marriages were thus in the end entirely arbitrary" *The Third Reich in Power* (New York: Penguin Books, 2005), 545. For Johannes, therefore, threading his way through these laws was a matter of creative ingenuity rather than rigorous legal analysis. See also David S. Wyman, *Paper Walls: America and the Refugee Crisis 1938–1941* (Boston: University of Massachusetts Press, 1968), vii: "... Confusion results when one tries to ascertain what the word Jew meant at that period. ... [Persons] with two Jewish grandparents ... [were] technically 'non-Aryans.' In theory, non-Aryans had fewer legal disabilities than full Jews. In practice, non-Aryans were hardly less oppressed. Many whom the Nazis classified as full Jews ... were members of Christian denominations. Others were nonreligious."

Hundreds of thousands of German Christians and nonbelievers found themselves confronted with similarly confusing—and dangerous—identity questions. The challenges facing non-Jewish Germans of Jewish descent are treated in Bryan Mark Rigg, *Hitler's Jewish Soldiers: The Untold Story of Nazi Racial Laws and Men of Jewish Descent in the German Military* (Lawrence: University Press of Kansas, 2002), 6–63. See also James F. Tent, *In the Shadow of the Holocaust: Nazi Persecution of Jewish-Christian Germans* (Lawrence: University Press of Kansas, 2003).

Johannes and Elfriede on the boat to the United States for a three-week visit including Ursula's medical school graduation, May 1937.

Pennsylvania Medical School. Rudolf and Josephine invited Johannes and Elfriede and Johannes' other sister, Gri, and her husband, Manfred, to the United States for the occasion. The trip was a huge success. Johannes and Elfriede got to see Philadelphia and the environment in which Rudolf and Josephine lived and worked and visited Washington, D.C., New York, and Cape Cod, where Rudolf and Josephine worked in the summer. Elfriede later wrote a long diary of the trip in which the heat and humidity of the northeastern United States in summer occupied much of her attention, but otherwise Johannes and Elfriede were charmed by all they saw. During the visit, Rudolf and Josephine spent a lot of time trying to persuade their children to leave Germany. At this point, however, neither Johannes and Elfriede nor Gri and Manfred were yet ready to give up on their country. In addition, Elfriede found the idea of leaving her mother and brothers very difficult, especially since her father died shortly before the American trip. At the end of their trip they all returned to Germany, but at least now they had an idea of where they would go if they eventually decided to leave.

Returned to Germany, Johannes and Elfriede had to deal with shipping Rudolf and Josephine's belongings, which had been in storage in Kiel since Rudolf's dismissal from the University four years earlier. Rudolf and Josephine now decided that nothing was going to change in Germany any time soon, and they would make America their permanent home. Elfriede and Gri went to Kiel to sort through the storage warehouse and arranged to ship half of the furniture, antiques, paintings, and fine china immediately. Somehow all the goods made it past the German export authorities and arrived safely in Philadelphia. Half of the belongings, however, remained in storage in Kiel.

In the fall of 1937, an event occurred that shook Johannes' confidence considerably. He and Elfriede's close friend, Erich von Baeyer, a doctor, who like Johannes identified himself as "half Jewish," had married a "half-Jewish" woman, and they had a child. Von Baeyer thought he had a secure position as staff physician in a Düsseldorf hospital. Abrubtly, however, the hospital's administration asked about his marriage, concluded it was illegal under the Nuremberg laws, and fired him with virtually no notice. Johannes wrote to his parents in Philadelphia and solicited their advice on finding von Baeyer a job in the United States, which they were able to provide. But the capricious manner in which the officials suddenly declared a person to be unemployable rattled Johannes' confidence in his own position, and caused him to think more seriously about emigrating. A couple of months later, another recently married pair of friends, Erich and Friedel Stötzner, were forced to leave Germany because some official determined that the wife fell within the law's definition of "Jewish" and that their marriage was not legally recognized.

Early in 1938, the government's policies hit Manfred and Gri in Dresden. Gri wrote her parents that

> On 31 January Commissar Mutschmann, governor of the *Weisser Hirsch* area, issued a decree that from now on German and foreign Jews may no longer be lodged in the sanatoriums in the *Weisser Hirsch* spas. Since the SaK [*Sanatorium am Königspark*, the place where Manfred was employed] belongs to the *Weisser Hirsch* spa area, we had about 15 patients depart in the last few days.

This loss of about 25 percent of the Sanatorium's clients all at once threatened the security of Manfred's employment there, not to speak of the message sent about the intensification of pressure on "Jews" generally. For Johannes and Elfriede, the notion of remaining in a country that had abandoned any pretense of law or humanity had become intolerable. Raising a child in such an environment was unthinkable. Elfriede said years later that a decisive point for her was the enactment of a law that would have required Susanne to enter the *Hitlerjugend*—the Hitler Youth—the Nazis' child indoctrination organization, when she turned ten. She saw it as essential to leave before that time arrived.

By early March 1938, in a letter to his parents, Johannes now referred to the subject of emigration as "the subject of all subjects, ... the subject—why shouldn't I admit it—[that] hasn't been out of our thoughts awake or asleep for weeks."

Then on March 12, 1938 came the *Anschluss,* Germany's bloodless annexation of Austria. With Hitler having forced the resignation of the

Austrian Chancellor and having replaced him with a puppet government, tens of thousands of German troops occupied Austria without serious opposition from other European nations or England. Once again, Johannes and Elfriede were forced to reckon with Hitler's actions in Europe (what they called the Macrocosm) as they affected their personal situation (the Microcosm).

At the end of March 1938, Manfred was in Düsseldorf for a conference and met with Johannes and Elfriede to discuss leaving Germany. The couples were agreed that their plans had to be coordinated, because they would both be dependent on Rudolf and Josephine's financial support in America. Because Manfred's job at Weidner's Sanatorium was now seriously threatened, it was decided that he and Gri would leave as soon as they could get American visas that would permit them to enter the country as permanent residents rather than tourists. Johannes and Elfriede would then follow. It seems surprising, from today's perspective, that none of them felt a greater sense of urgency, but of course they could not foresee what was to come from the Nazi regime. The biggest problem with their plan was that they underestimated the difficulty of obtaining American visas. In early April, writing to Rudolf and Josephine about the results of the family conference, Johannes wrote:

> The only right thing to do is to make the American move with finality right away. In concrete terms, that means that Gri and Manfred won't bother getting a VV [Visitor's Visa] again but rather will apply from the outset for the IV [Immigration Visa], not only because that will dispose of problems that will otherwise undoubtedly arise later, but also because, from everything we know, Gri and Manfred can count on getting the final visa without much difficulty. The granting of visas is, as you probably know, entirely in the discretion of the American consuls. We believe that our qualifications are so favorable to us—much more favorable than for many others who have gotten visas—that this presupposition is justified.

Johannes apparently believed that all of them were highly desirable immigrants, respectable, educated, connected to the great professor at the University of Pennsylvania, and that these factors would ensure quick approval of their visa applications. What was missing from Johannes' calculations was that hundreds of thousands of other Germans were also coming to the realization that it was time to get out of Germany.

As it turned out, everything took longer than anticipated. The application process was tedious and exacting, requiring multiple copies of notarized birth certificates, marriage certificates, police certificates of good conduct, photographs, detailed affidavits from relatives living in the United States, and comprehensive application forms for each individual providing precise details of the applicants' residences, education, and work history. Any flaw in the application could result in denial or delay of the visa. The initial processing did disclose a vital bit of information, however: Gri came under the Swiss quota, not the German quota. Under U.S. immigration law at the time, there was a numerical quota for citizens of a particular country each year. Germany's quota was around 27,000 and was vastly oversubscribed, with over 310,000 applicants for immigration visas between July 1, 1938 and June 30, 1939. The Swiss quota was, however, undersubscribed, as there were not a lot of Swiss citizens seeking to move to the United States. It turned out that a person's place of birth determined the quota he or she fell under. Even though they grew up in Germany, Johannes and Gri were both born in Switzerland when Rudolf was at the University of Zürich, so they both came under the Swiss quota.[17]

One of the problems with leaving Germany was having enough cash, as German foreign exchange laws sharply restricted the amount of money a person could take out of the country. There were, however, tourism treaties that authorized conversion of up to 50 marks each month in certain countries. Starting in May, therefore, Johannes visited the Foreign Exchange Office [*Divisenstelle*] each month to get a traveler's letter of credit [*Reisekreditbrief*] entered in his passport, each time permitting him to convert German marks to Swiss francs when he eventually left. This was the kind of forethought that was needed for successful emigration.

In July 1938, another alarming event occurred that lent even greater urgency to Johannes and Elfriede's departure. One of Johannes' current newspaper carriers, a man named Kehl, and a former carrier named Weinand were arrested by the Gestapo for activities on behalf of the banned Communist Party. When arrested, one of them was carrying a copy of *Oil*, a banned socialist novel by the American Upton Sinclair, with "Höber" written on the flyleaf. Gestapo agents came to Johannes and Elfriede's home on Pempelforterstrasse to get Johannes. Elfriede was at home alone, and the agents demanded to see her books. She told them they wouldn't like what they found, because they were economics books and included a lot of Marx. The agents were nonplussed, but Elfriede quietly told them she was an economist and needed these books for her professional work. The agents departed but ordered Elfriede to tell Johannes he must report to Gestapo headquarters for questioning. When he later reached the police station, Johannes was informed he was being charged with distributing banned literature. He managed to keep his composure throughout his interrogation, so that the statement he was required to sign reveals very little. His statement is preserved in Gestapo records in the state archives [*Hauptstaatsarchiv*] for the state of Nordrhein-Westfalen:

17 Regarding the U.S. laws that severely restricted refugees from Germany in the Nazi period, see Richard Breitman and Alan M. Kraut, *American Refugee Policy and European Jewry, 1933–1945* (Bloomington: Indiana University Press, 1987); Barbara McDonald Stewart, *United States Government Policy on Refugees from Nazism, 1933–1940* (New York: Garland Publishing, Inc., 1982); David S. Wyman, *Paper Walls: America and the Refugee Crisis, 1938–1941* (University of Massachusetts Press, 1968).

Appearing in response to a summons, Dr. Johann [*sic*] Höber states:

> I studied national economics and from 1928 to 1933 was employed by the city of Mannheim as director of the press office and later as an expert assistant in the welfare department. After the nat. revolution I was dismissed because of my pol. activities.
>
> I belonged to the SPD [*Sozialdemokratische Partei Deutschland*] from 1926 until its mandatory dissolution and I was last a local party official in Mannheim. Because of my activities as a party official I was placed in protective custody from 12 March to 13 April 1933. There was no judicial case brought.
>
> In 1928 I married and after I was released from protective custody in 1933 I moved in with my parents-in-law in Düsseldorf, where I lived for several months. I was then employed as a subscription agent for the *Frankfurter Zeitung* and took over the local agency on 1 Aug. 1933. Today my agency includes several more distant locations in the Lower Rhine region.
>
> I met the driver Heinrich Weinand through my brother-in-law, Günter Fischer. He worked for me as a carrier from 1934 to 1936 with a couple of short breaks. Weinand recommended the barber Heinrich Kehl to me, who was employed as a carrier from 1935 until he was arrested. I had no idea that both of them were active for the illegal Communist Party in Düsseldorf and the surrounding area. I spoke with both of them occasionally, mostly about business matters.
>
> Until 12/31/35 I kept my library in my business office, and it is possible that Heinrich Weinand borrowed a book once. I don't remember which books Weinand borrowed from me over time.

This statement ended up being quite innocuous, but Johannes' interrogation indicated he was on the Gestapo's radar. Any suspicious activity could endanger his chances of escape, if only because the American consulate required a police good conduct certificate from every visa applicant.

In July, Weidner's Sanatorium in Dresden demanded Manfred's resignation. Although the Director admired Manfred's skills and liked him personally, he said that Gri simply "looked too Jewish." This final rupture was a harsh blow, especially for Manfred, who took it personally that his former boss and mentor turned on him. He and Gri packed their belongings for shipment to America and then arranged to stay with Johannes and Elfriede in Düsseldorf while they waited for their American visas.

As the wait for Manfred and Gri's visas dragged on, Johannes and Elfriede realized they could no longer delay their own visa application. The American consulates were being flooded with applications, and the annual German visa quota was quickly being used up. It was then that Elfriede hit upon an insightful scheme. As noted above, when Gri had applied in May, she learned that because she was born in Zürich her visa would be counted against the Swiss quota, not the German quota. She also learned that if one spouse was settled in the United States, it would raise the other spouse's priority for a visa. Putting these facts together, Elfriede suggested that Johannes apply for a visa in Switzerland and travel to the U.S. and get settled there. That might make it possible for Elfriede and Susanne to get German quota visas with some kind of priority and follow him. The dangers in this scheme were substantial, but it seemed that it had to be risked. In light of Johannes' recent interrogation by the Gestapo, however, he was fearful of sending inquiries to the American consulate through the mail. Consequently, Johannes and Elfriede decided to go to Switzerland, where they could get answers directly. They turned that trip into a farewell vacation.

In the midst of all the anxiety pressing upon the family, taking a vacation in Switzerland might not seem like the most obvious thing to do. But there was money to pay for the vacation in Rudolf and Josephine's account in Kiel that could not be expended outside of Europe. In addition, the vacation travel would cover the trip's real purpose—to get information from the American consulate in Zürich. Manfred had learned enough about the newspaper business that he could take it over while Johannes and Elfriede were away.

On September 2, 1938, Johannes and Elfriede set out by car for the Italian Alps. Two weeks later, at the end of the trip, the American consulate in Zürich confirmed that Johannes could, indeed, get an immigration visa there comparatively easily under the Swiss quota.

On September 10, while Johannes and Elfriede were away, Manfred and Gri were finally notified that their visas would be granted. But then events in the "Macrocosm" intervened in the form of the Sudeten Crisis, and for a time all transatlantic travel was halted. For months, Hitler had been fomenting protests among the ethnic German minority living in the Sudetenland in northern Czechoslovakia. In a speech in Nuremberg on September 12, Hitler threatened war against Czechoslovakia if the Sudeten Germans were not granted self-determination. Since the British and French had previously guaranteed Czechoslovakia's territorial integrity, Hitler's threat amounted to a threat of a general war in Europe. The British and French, however, were desperate to avoid war. Over the next two weeks, negotiations continued between Germany, French Premier Daladier, and British Prime Minister Neville Chamberlain. Finally, at the Munich conference on September 29, Chamberlain capitulated to Hitler and turned the Sudetenland over to Germany, in exchange for what Chamberlain famously called "peace in our time."

For the time, war was averted, and Manfred and Gri were able to leave. On Friday, September 30, they cabled Rudolf and Josephine from Hamburg:

> INITIALLY DELAYED DEPARTURE HAMBURG CONFIRMED SATURDAY 1 OCTOBER. WAITED EVERYTHING OUT HAMBURG. WILL CABLE ARRIVAL FROM ON BOARD.

Manfred and Gri and their two little girls arrived safely in Philadelphia ten days later.

In anticipation of the arrival of their German family, Rudolf and Josephine had found a large house at a reasonable rent that could accommodate the entire family. The Germantown section of Philadelphia has been called "a suburb in the city" because it has mostly large homes surrounded by trees and generous yards. The house Rudolf and Josephine rented on Cresheim Road was not new, but it was in good condition and in a good neighborhood and had a large garden and eight bedrooms. Their idea was that the extended joint family of six adults and three children could live together in one house and share expenses until the new arrivals got settled and could live on their own. It was a wise arrangement, as the costs were modest, and it was uncertain when Johannes and Manfred would begin to draw any regular salary.

In the meantime, with this part of the family's emigration accomplished, Johannes and Elfriede started seriously to make their own arrangements, with Johannes initially planning to leave in the early days of November. Preparations included instructing Elfriede in how to run the business on her own so she could maintain an income after Johannes had left for America. Johannes took her to Duisburg, Krefeld, and Gladbach to meet the carriers she would have to supervise there and to orient her to the newspaper operations at these outlying locations. Johannes wrote his parents that he intended to leave on November 4, but making final arrangements caused him to postpone his departure a week, until November 11. That postponement was almost disastrous.

The rest of this story is told in the exchange of letters that follows. The first letters are from Johannes to his parents, Rudolf and Josephine, in Philadelphia.

CHAPTER 2

Getting Out, Part 1

On Saturday, September 3, Johannes and Elfriede drove from Düsseldorf to Füssen on the German-Austrian border. Gri and Manfred stayed in their Düsseldorf apartment, ran the newspaper distribution business, and took care of Susanne in their absence. On the second morning of their trip, Sunday, they drove four hours further to Solda (or Sulden) in the Italian Alps. There they spent the afternoon writing letters to Johannes' parents.

SUNDAY, SEPTEMBER 4, 1938

Letter from Johannes in Solda, Italy, to Rudolf and Josephine in Philadelphia. Despite the fact that this letter would be sent by Italian mail and not be subject to surveillance by German authorities, Johannes was circumspect in his wording. Much of the letter concerns the strategy Johannes and Elfriede were developing for getting out of Germany. Johannes' use of various code words and obscure abbreviations (explained here in the footnotes) illustrates the difficulties involved in deciphering these letters. In later letters the code words are not as dense as in this one.

The last part of this letter concerns Rudolf's obligation to file a report required of all those defined as "Jews" under the Nuremberg Laws. Johannes discusses the applicability of the reporting laws to Rudolf and Josephine in this letter

---

Solda [Italy], 4 September 1938

Ihr Lieben,

Where should I begin this letter and where should I end it? There is such an endless amount to write about. I had saved everything up so Gri and Manfred could convey all of it to you orally [when they reached America], but now those poor people are waiting and waiting and waiting, so I am using our first day in Solda to entrust to the Italian mails those things that cannot be delayed any longer.

Alea est iacta was how Daddy began that fateful letter in September 1933 with which your "great trip" began.[1] *Alea est iacta* now applies to us too. So: we're coming! And indeed just as fast as we possibly can.

1 *Alea est iacta* = "The die is cast." *Daddy* = Rudolf, Johannes' father. *Great trip* = emigration from Germany to the United States.

Now that this decision is firmly settled, the rest is only a matter of our convenience.

After careful consideration and research, we have concluded that there are two avenues open to us: by means of VV from D. or IVfrom Zürich.[2] Let me explain. IV from D., which would have been the only sound option just a half a year ago, has in the meantime become impossible. As a result of the most recent measures [taken by the Nazi regime], the onslaught on the respective Uncles[3] has become so immense that the one in Berlin as well as the one in Stuttgart have announced that they will not accept a single additional [visa] application for consideration before May–June 1939. Quite aside from the fact that we no longer want to wait that long, it seems to us to be vital that we precede the tens of thousands who are going to undertake the "great trip" in the next few months if I hope to have any luck at all over there [in America]. Since the logjam at the Uncles is neither the result of any ill will nor a result of the exhaustion of the German quota (and in light of Gri's surprising experience with her birthplace), we have come up with the idea of Zürich. So next week, when we are in Zürich, we plan to get definitive information as to whether it would be possible to get IV's via Zürich (we have a Swiss letter of credit[4] in addition to our Italian one). The Uncle there naturally does *not* have a logjam. Whether we will be able to use him, therefore, depends on how long we would have to be "resident" there in order to qualify, and whether it's possible under Swiss regulations that we could be temporarily "resident" in Switzerland long enough for this purpose. Since there is a travel treaty between Germany and Switzerland, we would be able to take more money with us than we would actually need to live there.

I hardly need to tell you how very much preferable an IV would be to a VV. It would not only spare us the trip to Cuba[5] but it would also be psychologically a very different kind of start for us. And we wouldn't have to book return passage *à fonds perdu* as we would for a VV. But as I said, whether this route is actually possible will be revealed only by our upcoming research in Zürich. Our desire to conclude that research is one of the reasons we ultimately decided we would still make this trip.

The other possible route looks as follows: Immediately following our return [to Düsseldorf], and assuming that the Zürich route turns out to be impracticable, I will obtain a VV from the Uncle in Cologne. I went there last week with Manfred to get the most current information and it turns out that I can indeed get one. I don't even need a new affidavit: I told them I had one from last year, and they told me that will suffice. But VV means I would have to travel alone and that Elfriede and Susie would

2 *VV* = Visitor's Visa, allowing a temporary stay in the U.S. *IV* = Immigration Visa, allowing permanent residence. *D.* = Düsseldorf.

3 "Uncle" or "Uncle Karl" is a code word for the United States, here used as a code for the U.S. Consulate, which had visa granting offices in Stuttgart, Berlin, and Zürich. In the fiscal year between July 1, 1938 and June 30, 1939, the American consular offices in Germany received some 310,000 requests for Immigration Visas but granted only about 27,000, the maximum allowed under the existing immigration statute.

4 A letter of credit [*Reisekreditbrief*] was required to permit a German to change Reichsmarks into the local currency and thus essential for travel outside of Germany.

5 For a fee, Cuba allowed refugees to live there temporarily while awaiting an American visa.

have to remain in D. at first. I don't need to tell you what that would mean for us, given the current state of affairs. But if the Zürich route doesn't work out there will be no alternative. First, it's very unlikely that all three of us could get VVs, because the Uncle would certainly suspect something if we all showed up *en famille*. But second, under the current circumstances, he would demand some documented proof that I have a steady job in Germany to which I could return. I could give such proof to both Frankfurt and the Uncle, without grossly deceiving them, only if Elfriede continues the business on a temporary basis. Finally, given how much more difficult the start would be under the restrictions of a VV, it will be much easier for you and for us if Elfriede and Susie remain here for a while under Oma's protective roof.[6]

And now I come to a problem that I would much rather have left to an oral discussion between Gri and Manfred and you, but unfortunately the deadlines no longer permit that. I'm referring to the extremely vexatious Assets Inventory required by the government Order of 4/26/38. There can be no doubt that Daddy is obligated to file this Inventory, because even the pure Aryan spouses of non-Aryan husbands and wives must report, and indeed their own assets, not just those of the spouse.[7] While the deadline was 6/30 for those who are obligated to file the Report who live inside Germany, it is 9/30 for those who live abroad. So it's high time, but I delayed telling you about this in writing in the belief that Gri and Manfred would be with you by the beginning of September. I've filled out the form [for you] in pencil to the best of my knowledge and belief so that all you have to do is review it and rewrite it in ink. There's only one question, and that's with respect to the blank IV(c). Here you need to insert a specific dollar amount converted into marks ($1 X 2.50 RM) that only you can determine. How much did you have in your wallets on 4/27?

It remains to clarify to whom your report is to be sent. Normally it is with the authorities where the reporting individual resides, but for all those living abroad it is with the Chief of Police in Berlin. I therefore recommend most strongly that you address it to Chief of Police, Berlin, and please send the form there directly to arrive before 30 September! Please don't send it again via D. But *sub titulo* "Form," please let me know what you did and any part of my draft that you might have changed.[8]

So, that's all, but it strikes me that there's an awful lot in this letter. Believe me, the decision as to our departure hasn't gotten any easier for us. Our dearest Daddy formulated it in his classic way in his last letter, which moved us just as your departure moved us five years ago. But now that we've made a decision, we are almost in better spirits than before. Now for the next two weeks we will fortify our strength,

6 *Oma* = grandmother. Oma Clara Fischer, Elfriede's mother, lived a few blocks away from Johannes and Elfriede's Düsseldorf apartment.

7 *Aryan* = non-Jewish. The Order of April 26, 1938 required all German Jews to file a report of all assets they owned if their total value exceeded 5,000 marks. Under Nazi "racial" laws, Johannes' father, Rudolf, was 50 percent "Jewish" because his mother was Protestant and his father was born to Jewish parents. Johannes' mother, Josephine (Seppi) was the daughter of two Jewish parents. Failure to file the Asset Report could result in imprisonment and confiscation of all assets. In fact the Asset Reports were later used to seize Jewish property generally.

8 In 2013, the author located a copy of the "Inventory of Jewish Property" [*Verzeichnis über das Vermögen von Juden*] that Rudolf filed in the Federal Office for Central Services and Unresolved Property Questions [*Bundesamt für zentrale Dienste und offene Vermögensfragen*] in Berlin. The form showed that he owned about RM 19,000 in negotiable securities.

hopefully with lots of sunshine, and then, "bristling with energy," we will face the future.

In alter immer neuer Liebe,
[With old-fashioned, ever new love,]

Euer Jo

PS. Don't be concerned about the peculiar return address. If for some reason this letter should want to make a return trip, it should make its return trip to that address.[9]

Following this letter, Elfriede and Johannes spent three leisurely weeks travelling to Verona, Padua, Venice and back to Lake Como, sending cheerful tourist postcards to Rudolf and Josephine along the way. Then, after three weeks, they reached Zürich, where Johannes sent the following letter.

WEDNESDAY, SEPTEMBER 22, 1938

Letter from Johannes in Zürich to his parents in Philadelphia.

Zürich, 22 September 38

Ihr Lieben,

The faint hope that we might already get an answer from you [here in Zürich] to our letter of 4 September did not, in fact, come to pass. Nevertheless, we are sending you this mail on this our last travel day, as there is news to report that is not unimportant and not unpleasant. Early today we went to the US Consulate General here, where the responsible official explained (1) that I can apply for an IV here if I come here, that the Swiss quota is not exhausted, and that for that reason "it would only depend on me" how long I would have to wait for the visa; (2) that, once I have the visa, Elfriede and Susie can follow me more easily and more quickly than we assumed up to now. Without knowing your opinion, at the moment we are inclined to favor this route. This afternoon we're visiting "old friends," this evening we are visiting the Laquers [unidentified] in Basel. At both places we will try to clarify the question whether under the new Swiss regulations I can stay here as long as I need to until I get the visa. We went directly from the Consulate to the Civil Registry Office and got three official copies of my birth certificate, and from there to the church office in Aussersihl, where I obtained two baptismal certificates. The name Uto[10] opens every door to me here and changes every bureaucrat's expression into that of a kindly uncle. Praises to those who gave it to me.

9 On the envelope, Johannes put a British return address, the residence of their friends the Schlossmanns. He wanted to avoid any possibility that, if the letter went astray, it might make its way back to Düsseldorf and the eyes of the Gestapo.

10 Johannes' middle name was Uto, taken from the Ütliberg outside Zürich, where he was born. Uto was a stereotypically Swiss name. Johannes needed the birth and baptismal certificates for his visa application.

You can see that we are expending all the energy we saved up in the last twenty days in the direction of the USA. May the coming weeks be equally fortunate for all ten of us.[11]

In Liebe,

Euer Jo

The six weeks following Johannes and Elfriede's return to Düsseldorf from Zürich were tumultuous. The Western world was transfixed by the Sudeten Crisis, which ended only with the Munich Pact on September 28. Before that crisis was resolved, Manfred and Gri received their American visas and scheduled their departure for October 1. Writing to his parents later, Johannes described being glued to the radio day and night listening to the news, deeply fearing war would break out and all of them would be trapped in Europe. With Chamberlain's appeasement of Hitler, the crisis was temporarily averted, and Manfred and Gri left on October 1, the same day German troops occupied the Sudetenland.

Consistent with the previous letter, Johannes began to plan his departure for Switzerland for the early days of November. He introduced Elfriede to his newspaper carriers and business contacts in outlying locations so she could run the business in his absence, and he informed his immediate superior at the *Frankfurter Zeitung*, Dr. Betz, of their plan. He asked his parents to write to various old friends in Zürich so he would have a support network there while waiting for his American visa. He also settled various tax bills and bank accounts for Rudolf and for himself so things would be in good order for Elfriede once he left.

On October 25, shortly before Johannes intended to leave for Switzerland, Elfriede's youngest brother, Paul Fischer, 25, was arrested by the Gestapo and interrogated about his activities as a former member of the Communist Party. This arrest was directly related to the Gestapo investigation the previous July in which Johannes had been implicated. Although the Gestapo interrogated Johannes at that time, they took no action against him immediately. Paul's October arrest (described in the letters that follow) lent even more urgency to Johannes' plans to leave Düsseldorf as soon as possible.

Before leaving Germany, Johannes had to purchase a steamship ticket for the United States. He did that at the Cologne office of the United States Lines. Although he booked passage for a specific ship leaving in December, the ticket could be changed for another ship if he didn't get his immigration visa in time. By a fortunate chance, Johannes bought the ticket at 6 P.M. on Wednesday, November 9, 1938. Just six hours later, the Nazis launched *Kristallnacht*, the massive assault on German Jews in

11 By "all ten of us" Johannes means Rudolf and Josephine; his sister Gri, her husband Manfred and their little girls Juliana and Monica; himself and Elfriede and their daughter Susanne; and his sister Ulli.

which Nazis destroyed hundreds of thousands of homes, placed thousands in concentration camps, and murdered hundreds of innocent citizens. It was the beginning of the worst repressive measures of the Nazi regime.[12] The next day Johannes would probably have been unable to purchase his ticket.

The next two writings include Johannes' descriptions of *Kristallnacht* as he and Elfriede experienced it.

UNDATED MANUSCRIPT

Unaddressed, written shortly after Kristallnacht, *November 9–10, 1938. Elfriede discovered this account, written in English in a tiny, painstaking script on small sheets of tablet paper, among Johannes' papers many years after his death. No one had ever read it and there is no indication for whom Johannes wrote it. The immediacy of the narrative and the clarity of the details make it likely that it was written shortly after the events, probably during the brief period Johannes was in Zürich. On the one hand, Johannes found it critical to record what he had witnessed and, on the other hand, he wanted to protect himself if the Nazis discovered it. That explains why he wrote it in English and included no names or the location of the events. The spelling and punctuation appear here exactly as in the original.*

Wednesday 9 November 1938.

The Nazis had been celebrating that day, as every year, the anniversary of Hitler's abortive 1923 putsch. That night an old friend of ours had come to see us. We had been associated in the early days of the Third Reich in some underground activities, trying to build out of the remainders of the Catholic, liberal, Socialist and Communist opposition a group of resistance against the rising tide of Fascist tyranny. He had been caught in 1934 circulating illegal leaflets and sentenced to 18 months hard labor. He had served his term and now lived in a small village far remote from his former center of activities. He rarely could risk to come to see us, because no Gestapo agent would have believed either him or us that we would talk anything but politics. Only a few weeks before he and we had again been subject to a Gestapo investigation and therefore had to be more on our guard than ever before.[13]

The conversation had centered around the recent political events, Chamberlain's Munich surrender and its repercussions on Germany's internal policy. Munich undoubtedly had bolstered the regime's declining morale and everybody viewed with alarm the reviving arrogance of the Nazis after a period of relative moderation.

13 The visitor fits the description of Hendrik Zech, an old friend who lived with his wife, Gerlinde, in Schalkenmehren in the Eifel Mountains.

Johannes Höber's handwritten eyewitness account of Kristallnacht in Düsseldorf. *Elfriede found this among Johannes' papers many years after his death.*

Wednesday November 9, 1938. The Nazis had been celebrating that day every year, the anniversary of Hitler's abortive 1923 putsch. That night an old friend of ours had come to see us. We had been associated in the early days of the Third Reich in some underground activities, trying to build out of the remainders of the Catholic, Liberal, Socialist and Communist opposition a group of resistance against the rising tide of Fascist tyranny. He had been caught in 1934 circulating illegal leaflets and sentenced to 18 months hard labor. He had moved his home and now lived in a small village far south from his former center of activities. He rarely would write or come to see us, because no Gestapo agent would have believed either him or us that we would talk anything but politics again. Only a few weeks before he and we had been subject to a Gestapo investigation and therefore had to be more on our guard than ever before.

The conversation had centered around the recent political events, Chamberlain's Munich surrender and its repercussions on Germany's internal policy. Munich undoubtedly had bolstered the regime's declining morale and everybody viewed with alarm the reviving arrogance of the Nazis after a period of relative moderation. Incidentally our friend told us that he had heard on his way to our house that Herr vom Rath, secretary of the Nazi German embassy, who had been shot by a young Polish Jew driven to despair by the treatment of his parents by the Nazis, had died that afternoon. We did not discuss the implications of this news item. Not because we did not fear them. But in the past six years of our life under the Nazi government we had developed a habit that might be called a technique of mental self defence: not to speculate on the possibilities of disaster implied in any

Incidentally our friend told us that he had heard on his way to our house that Herr vom Rath, secretary of the Paris German embassy, who had been shot by a young Polish jew, driven to despair by the treatment of his parents by the Nazis, had died that afternoon. We did not discuss the implications of this news item. Not because we did not fear them. But in the past six years of our life under the Nazi government we had developed a habit that might be called a technique of mental self defense: not to speculate on the possibilities of disaster implied in any news, before we were confronted with this disaster and could cope with the concrete emergency by concrete maneuvers. No one of our company that night was Jewish but we all had some very close Jewish friends. I myself have some Jewish ancestors, not enough to make me subject to the humiliating clauses of the infamous Nüremberg laws, yet enough to brand me as a second class citizen in the Germany of today, the Germany of the Bohemian born Hitler, the Egyptian born Hess and the Baltic born Rosenberg.

The possible consequences of vom Rath's death were upmost [*sic*] in my mind, when I drove to the station at about 11 P.M. to mail some letters. [Illegible] in the streets I noticed an unusually large number of brownshirts. First I thought they were on their way home from some of the day's celebrations. Then I noticed that they did not go in the direction of the residential quarters but hurried towards the center of the city. So, on my way home, I drove through some of the main thoroughfares of the downtown business section and found on two different places brownshirts gathering quietly in front of Jewish business establishments. I went home and without telling my wife what I had seen offered our friend who had to leave at midnight to drive him to the station and asked my brother in law to accompany us. After having dropped our friend at the station we hastily drove downtown. We had not to drive very far to find what we had anticipated. In front of a large shoe-store, owned by a Jewish woman whose husband had been killed in action in the world war and who therefore, despite of six years of Nazi boycott, had still one of the largest businesses in the field, a detachment of brown shirts had assembled. We just came in time to see two of them starting—on a given signal—to break the shop windows. This done they forced the entrance and the whole group rushed into the store. It was one of those modern outfits with plenty of glass, attractive wood panneling on the walls, every shelve [*sic*] full of shoe-boxes. Twenty minutes later it was so completely devastated that no bombshell could have done a more thorough job. No piece of glass, no piece of wood was unbroken. The carpets were cut up, the lamps torn from ceiling and walls, shelves, tables, chairs smashed to pieces. The problem to destroy thousands of shoes in a hurry otherwise than by fire had been solved in an ingenious way: they had been strewn all over the place and then oil paint had been poured over and into them. When they had finished their job the wrecking crew on the blow of a whistle assembled in front of the store, in line two deep, stood at attention in perfect military discipline, drilled into them by endless training, and marched off.

We got into our car and drove on. A few blocks away we encountered another group of Stormtroopers looting a fashionable lady's outfit store. This was on our city's "Fifth Avenue" and the wrecking crew corresponded to the distinction of the district. Our city is the seat of a higher district leader of the Nazi party. Every such district leader has a staff of his own and a body guard of his own whose members are easily recognized by red squares on the lapels of their brown uniform coats. The squad that wrecked this store was composed almost entirely out of members of the district leader's staff and body guard under the personal command of a well known Nazi-Lawyer and S.A. officer. A few yards away a police car with two higher police officers was parked at the curb. The two officers watched with apparent interest the work of destruction carried out under the leadership of the chief aide of their superior.

The next time we stopped in front of a tailor's workshop. Here a particular problem presented itself to the wrecking crew: how to destroy the stock of bales of cloth. It was solved no less efficiently than the shoe problem had been solved: one man unrolled the bale and another poured ink over it from one end to the other. Then they left it lying in the street.

After an hour of driving around Town we were convinced that not one single Jewish business in [Düsseldorf] would survive that night and that more than a hundred thousand people would have to pay for one man's act of despair with the destruction of their lives' work and their basis of existence.

What happened during the next hour, however, outgrew the wildest anticipations any one of us, trained by six years' lessons of terror and used to incredible brutalities, had ever entertained. At 1.30 A.M. we stopped in front of an apartment house, because we noticed two SA sentries guarding the house-door. On the opposite pavement stood a small group of civilians looking at a brightly lighted apartment on the fourth floor. We joined them and asked one of them what was going on. "They are revenging vom Rath" he said. "Which firm has its offices up there?" I asked. "That is no office, that is a private apartment occupied by a Jewish tenant." Before we could continue our conversation one of the S.A. sentry came across the street and ordered us to move on. A few seconds later the windows of the apartment came down in splinters and one after the other the lights went out in the apartment, the last one being a large crystal lamp that we saw wildly swinging up and down before we heard it crashing to the ground.

Then panic gripped us.

[*The manuscript breaks off here.*]

Johannes and Elfriede spent most of the day after *Kristallnacht* helping friends whose homes had been wrecked and trying to locate some of the men who had been arrested. That was Thursday. On Friday, Gestapo agents came to the apartment and took Johannes to police headquarters and interrogated him again about the Weinand affair of the previous July. Once again Johannes was fortunate in being released. As everything had been prepared in advance, he was able to leave for Switzerland early the next morning, Saturday, November 12, 1938, carrying only two suitcases. He wrote to his parents the following Wednesday.

WEDNESDAY, NOVEMBER 16, 1938

Letter from Johannes in Zürich to his parents in Philadelphia. He writes of having a "model passport," meaning that unlike most other refugees, his passport was not marked "J" for Jew, which was the signal for particular harassment from the German border guards. His passport also indicated he was born in Switzerland, providing a credible reason for him to travel there.

Two days after arriving in Zürich, Johannes contacted Lilly Reiff, his godmother. He had had little contact with before this. A concert pianist and student of Franz Liszt, Reiff conducted a salon in Zürich frequented by such cultural figures as Arturo Toscanini, Bruno Walter, Richard Strauss and Thomas Mann. She was an old friend of Rudolf and Josephine and was holding an affidavit of support for Johannes that Rudolf had sent from Philadelphia. In the affidavit, Rudolf guaranteed to support Johannes once he got to the United States. In Zürich Johannes also met with his godfather, Professor Eugen Bleuler, and his wife Hedwig. Professor Bleuler was the renowned psychiatrist who first coined the term "schizophrenia."

Zürich, the 16th of November 1938

Ihr Lieben,

When will all of you at last be able to live through an uninterrupted period of months—I don't dare speak of years—in reasonable peace?

Because if I know you, the days from Thursday [*Kristallnacht*] until early Sunday, when you got my telegram, must have been like those days preceding 1 October.[14] I can only hope that the American newspaper reports were as sketchy as the ones here and didn't report on the especially significant role that Düsseldorf played in last week's events.

But more of that later. Let me first tell you something about the fairytale world in which I find myself living here. First and most important: since early this morning my [visa application] papers have been on file with the local American consul general. They are perfectly complete and, thanks to your foresight in taking care of everything, I believe the granting of my visa depends only on how long it will take the Consul to dig down to my application in the mountain of papers that tower over his desk. The only thing missing is my good conduct certificate from the Düsseldorf police, which I will ask for once it is certain I will get the visa. The reason I didn't submit my papers until today is that I was unable to get the affidavits from Lilly Reiff, who was holding them for me, until Monday. Then yesterday [Tuesday] it took me the whole morning to fill out the application forms at the Consulate. Gri and Manfred will be able to describe to you what the offices of the Consulates look like these days, based on their experiences in Berlin. Here, in addition to Germans, there are Austrians, Czechs, and Italians. The second document that is still sitting in Germany is my fully paid passage as well as the receipt for 150 marks in shipboard money.[15] I didn't dare take the ship's ticket along in my baggage and endanger the whole plan if my luggage was searched by the Germans at the border. Elfriede will send it to me as soon as I need it. I won't even tell you the departure date for which the ticket was purchased, because it is completely hypothetical at this point. I chose the United States Lines because if everything goes right I'll travel directly from here to Le Havre. Incidentally, I got the ticket last Wednesday evening in Cologne—and that very night the fateful events broke out that probably would have made any such financial transaction impossible after that.

The trip here went unbelievably smoothly. Getting through passport control, customs, etc. at the Basel border crossing, about which I was so worried, was done in 30 seconds. My model passport turned something that was unattainable for other people into child's play for me. The other things I needed to carry out the Zürich plan are also done. It took me only four weeks after 26 September to get the travel letters of credit I needed, so I am the fortunate possessor of 700 Swiss francs, and they should last until I can leave here. On three separate occasions yesterday I heard the Consul's secretary say in my hearing: for the Swiss quota there is *no* waiting time. The completion of the work now depends solely on

14 October 1, 1938 was the day Gri and Manfred and their two little girls left Germany. The previous three weeks had seen the Sudeten crisis. By the time of this letter, Manfred and Gri were safely in Philadelphia.

15 *Shipboard money*: shipping companies required passengers to deposit cash to cover on-board expenses.

the quality of the papers I submitted—and on the pace of work at the Consulate. May my legendary good luck of the last five years continue to hold out!

The last days of these last five years in the Third Reich were, however, days of horror that were unequaled by anything I've ever experienced, and the images of the 24 hours from Wednesday at midnight until Thursday at midnight are things that I will never forget for the rest of my life. On Wednesday night we had a visitor from the Eifel, whom Günther and I took to the train at half past midnight. On the way back from the station we stumbled on the first stages of the operation. Groups of Stormtroopers in full uniform, under the direction of the highest levels of officers, and sometimes accompanied by the local leader of the Party organization—either a ward captain or a block warden—first headed for the *Königsallee* and went from store to store. They would line up in front of each store in two rows and, on a command from their leader, each detachment would turn to its work of destruction. Not a single civilian took part! The Party officials had lists with them, on which every Jewish store and Jewish home in their district was identified, without exception. Immediately behind every detachment of Stormtroopers was a police car that dropped off a policeman at every place where the Stormtroopers had finished their vandalism. I don't know whether the police were left there to guard the ruins or the crowd that immediately collected at each place.

Günter and I watched for about a half hour, when something began about which I have read nothing in any newspaper, and which apparently took place only in Düsseldorf:[16] After 1 A.M., the demolition teams began to invade every single Jewish residence, and to destroy everything, but absolutely everything, and this part of the action then went on uninterrupted for the next 14 hours. As long as it was night, this activity was played out in the interiors of the residences—but when it got light around 6 A.M. they started throwing the broken furniture through the windows and out into the street. Before that began, however, there was a pause of an hour, after which the formerly uniformed units reappeared in civilian clothes, because in the meantime it must have become clear to the leaders of the operation that not even an idiot would believe in the spontaneity of the "demonstration" if the gang of vandals continued their work in daylight in full uniform with the numbers of their units on the collars of their shirts.

For all practical purposes we didn't get to bed at all that night; we tried to help where we could, but it was almost impossible to do anything. I got to the Oppenheimers (the wife, née Luise Morgenstern, was a classmate of Elfriede's during her first semester at Freiburg) five minutes

16 Johannes was in error in believing the destruction of residences was unique to Düsseldorf. The Nazis launched attacks similar to those he describes in Düsseldorf in towns and cities throughout Germany.

too late, because the Stormtroopers were already in the apartment. When I came back there a half hour later they were gone, but everything, absolutely everything, was wrecked, the furniture smashed, china and glass pounded into splinters, every single knife and fork broken piece by piece. Mrs. Oppenheimer had been badly wounded in the head, evidently because she tried to protect her husband, and had to be taken to the hospital immediately. She was still there when I left Düsseldorf. The husband's brother had been punched in the mouth. Their three-year-old daughter then stayed overnight with us. The husband, who brought the little girl to us, insisted on returning to their apartment, where he was arrested the following morning.

At 2 A.M. an old acquaintance of Elfriede's mother's showed up at her house half crazed because she had been chased from her home when Stormtroopers forced their way in and took her husband into custody. At 3 A.M. I was finally able to get in touch with the husband from a pay phone and, thank God, nothing had happened to him. Their huge beautifully furnished house met the same fate as all the others.

I last spoke to the Lenzbergs[17] in person at 12:30 and again by phone at 2:30. We hoped until the last moment that they would be spared. During the night the Stormtroopers had been "working" very close by, but then they moved on in the other direction. But our hopes were dashed. On Thursday, in broad daylight in the middle of the day, Elfriede and I arrived just as their beds, carpets, furniture and everything else came flying out of their windows into the street. I drove by again in the evening, but was forced to drive on immediately because a huge contingent of police, Gestapo, and Stormtroopers were out searching for Karl. Around the corner I saw a whole busload of men who had been arrested. Elfriede was then able to connect with Till on Friday night at Frau Weddell's [unidentified]—fortunately nothing happened to her either. Karl found refuge in the home of some Aryan[18] friends, but what will become of him now is unclear.

As you see, I have seen so much of all this with my own eyes and up close that I think I can really objectively evaluate the judgment of the general public. Since 30 June 1934,[19] nothing has unleashed such outrage and revulsion as the events of 9–10 November, even deep into the Party circles. The mob that gathered wherever a new residence was demolished howled in support, as you would expect, but the reaction of every person there who didn't look like a hoodlum was one of outraged indignation. On Thursday morning there wasn't a single street in Düsseldorf that wasn't filled with heaps of household furnishings, and the fire department kept racing around the city nonstop because the Stormtroopers, evidently

17 Karl and Hilde Lenzberg were long-time close friends of Elfriede and Johannes. The nearly-new house that they had built for themselves was heavily damaged by the Stormtroopers. Till Jaffe was Hilde Lenzberg's 14-year-old son by a previous marriage.

18 Here, as elsewhere, Johannes uses the term "Aryan" to mean non-Jewish.

19 *June 30, 1934* = "Night of the Long Knives," when Hitler had many of the leaders of the SA murdered.

Karl and Hilde Lenzberg's house before it was vandalized by Stormtroopers on Kristallnacht, *November 9–10, 1939. Johannes witnessed the Lenzbergs' piano being thrown out through the second-floor French windows.*

lacking any orders as to what they should do, amused themselves by setting fire to these piles of debris in the streets. Herbert[20] saw one incident in which the crowd gathered around one of these funeral pyres harassed the Stormtrooper who was watching it so much that he called for reinforcements, who arrested 5–6 people. At the home of some acquaintances of ours, the first order of business for the police officer—in full uniform!—who was sent to watch over some of the debris was to prevail upon the maid to pack everything that was at all usable into two suitcases. When she told him she didn't know where she could store the suitcases, he said she could leave them in his own house. On my way here to Zürich, a man wearing Party insignia got on the train in Karlsruhe and sat down in my compartment. He maligned "those bandits" so furiously that I got so concerned that he might be a *provocateur* that I hardly said a word until he got off the train in Freiburg.

20 Herbert Fischer was Elfriede's middle brother.

While these last days were days of extreme concern for us, from which at least we didn't suffer any immediate damage, the weeks before that were weeks of the greatest possible anxiety. On October 25, [Elfriede's lawyer brother] Paul was suddenly arrested by the Gestapo in Leipzig. Paul's name had already come up in July in connection with the business about my newspaper carrier, whom Paul had previously known slightly, but we had hoped he was out of danger since three months had passed without anything further happening.

It was Heidi's [Paul's fiancée's] truly amazing adroitness that succeeded in finding out after only 24 hours what usually is impossible to find out in such circumstances, namely what he was accused of. For the most part the accusations related to acquaintances, meetings, and assemblies from way back in 1933. After Heidi figured that out, she got Paul's former boss and a lawyer friend of his to make such a fuss with the investigating officers that they released him from jail after just ten days. But you may imagine what those ten days were like for all of us who have had experience with the political methods of the last five years. With his release from jail, the greatest and most immediate danger was alleviated for him, but not completely because, as the warrant for his arrest came from the state prosecutor's office—and not from the police—a formal and final withdrawal of the action against him is still required. Paul still hadn't received the final papers when I left on Saturday, but if he does get it he fortunately will be spared the destruction of his legal career, which previously was a cause for great concern.

The origins and development of this whole affair are so tragic and inexplicable that it's hard to describe it in detail. How insecure a state must be when it has to make such a big deal and capital case out of political misdemeanors committed years earlier under completely different times and circumstances! (By the way, if you write to D[üsseldorf], please don't give any indication in your letters that you know anything at all about this matter!)

You may well imagine that after weeks like these this city of Zürich and its people, indeed life here generally, seems like a fairy tale to me. On Sunday, the first full day I was here, Lilly Reiff was away all day, so in the afternoon I went by myself up to the top of the Ütliberg.[21] Down in the valley it was foggy, but there were yellow signs on all the trams that announced: "Ütliberg clear." And so it was: the entire chain of mountains from the Berner Alps to the Santis Alps in bright sunshine, and below the valleys full of white clouds.

21 The Ütliberg, which overlooks Zürich, has an inn on its summit. The tram from the Zürich suburb of Albisrieden still takes visitors to the inn today as it did in 1938. Johannes was born in the inn thirty-four years earlier, when his father and pregnant mother went up in the tram for a Sunday afternoon excursion and Josephine went into early labor.

After five nights in the expensive and shabby City-Hotel, yesterday I rented the 22nd of the 26 furnished rooms I looked at that day. It costs 70 francs, it is light and clean, and it is one room in a three-room suite that I share with two French-speaking Swiss fellows.

At any rate, my address: 26 Alfred Escher Strasse, care of Mottier. Undoubtedly this street didn't exist at the time you lived here.[22] It's close to the train station, between Seestrasse and Mythen Quai, in other words quite close to Lilly Reiff's.

Since I was invited to lunch at Lilly Reiff's on Tuesday, the social life has flooded in on me around here. Lilly Reiff, with whom I was at first somewhat angry because I couldn't locate her for two days, has been really nice to me and immediately called me by my first name. I call her Aunt Lilly and since then I have been invited again to dinner, am invited again next Monday, and on Tuesday, after the other guests left, she took me along with her and her housemaid to Baden, where she had some business, for the sole purpose of being able to chat with me. We get along very well and she really couldn't be nicer to a lonely temporary bachelor like me.

On Tuesday at her place I met—in addition to Dr. Golo Mann, one of the sons of Thomas, who flattered me by allowing that he had some idea who I was since he studied at Heidelberg in 1930—Dr. Eugenie Schwarzwald from Vienna, who is now a refugee here. I was invited to her house for lunch the day before yesterday (her husband was formerly a department head in one of the Austrian ministries), and since she is a close friend of Hedwig Bleuler's I have now been invited to the Bleulers' for tea. And so on and so on.

If I keep on going, this letter will grow into a book and the *Normandie* will sail before I finish writing it. So at least let me turn now to the important things.

Elfriede will now continue running the business in Düsseldorf. We took our dear friend Dr. Betz,[23] who is the business manager for western Germany for the *Frankfurter Zeitung*, completely into our confidence. On his advice I didn't tell the home office in Frankfurt anything about my trip. As soon as it is certain that I won't have to return for anything, he will report that directly to Frankfurt. Either the agency will be taken over entirely by Elfriede or else he will take it over himself and install Elfriede as business manager.

Lieber Daddy, please send me $50 here by return post. Not that I want to use it. If everything goes smoothly here, my francs will be sufficient. But according to the Swiss foreign exchange regulations—yes, such things do

22 Rudolf and Josephine lived in Zürich from 1899 to 1909, when they moved to Kiel.

23 Anton Betz (1893–1984) had been the head of one of Germany's largest publishing companies but was removed by the Nazis. He thereafter earned his living in a much lower status position with the *Frankfurter Zeitung*. After the war he again became one of Germany's most prominent publishers. See Peter Henkel, *Anton Betz. Ein Verleger zwischen Weimar und Bonn* (Düsseldorf: Düsseldorf University Press, 2011).

exist—it is forbidden to purchase railroad tickets for travel outside Switzerland using money from a travel letter of credit. If things work out right and I want to travel from here directly to Le Havre, I want to be able to show the Swiss border officials the receipt from your postal money order as proof. I hope to be able to bring all those dollars back to you, but please take care of this right away!

Now I'll bring this letter to the train and go have lunch at an alcohol-free restaurant next to the station. As soon as things settle down here I'm going to see if I can take an English stenography or business correspondence course.

In the hope of being with you soon in good condition,

In Liebe,

Euer Jo

CHAPTER 3

Waiting

Germany was in an uproar. On the morning of Saturday, November 12, 1938, just two days after *Kristallnacht*, Johannes boarded a train in Düsseldorf for the eight-hour trip to Switzerland. The station there, the *Basel Badischer Bahnhof*, has a peculiar status. Although the station is several miles inside Switzerland, a 19th-century treaty provides that the tracks and arrival platforms are legally German territory. The train platforms are connected to the station by an underground pedestrian tunnel, and the German-Swiss border is in the tunnel.

Years later, Johannes described his arrival at the station and his fear as he approached the German exit checkpoint. Would he be stopped? Would the Gestapo be looking for him after his interrogation the previous day? Would the border authorities check whether he had paid the emigration tax? Might someone have informed the authorities about his past activities as a Social Democrat or about his Jewish grandparents? Would he be arrested as so many were on *Kristallnacht* two days earlier? With his anxiety built up, it almost seemed like a trick when he was allowed to pass through the German exit control without a single question. But the Swiss passport control was some 50 meters away at the opposite end of the tunnel—a kind of no man's land separated the checkpoints. Carrying his suitcase, with his head up but with his heart pounding, he walked straight ahead, trying to look confident. Johannes told his children years later that those 50 meters were the longest walk of his life. To his immense relief, he quickly swept through the second checkpoint, out of Nazi Germany and into the security of Switzerland. He got away from the *Badischer Bahnhof* as quickly as he could, and took a fifteen minute tram ride to the *Schweizer Bahnhof*, the station for Swiss trains. There he got the train to Zürich. He was free.

Shortly after 11 P.M., Johannes sent two telegrams, one to Elfriede in Düsseldorf and one to his parents in Philadelphia, letting them know he was alright.

SATURDAY, NOVEMBER 12, 1938, 11:38 P.M.

Telegram (in English) from Johannes in Zürich to his parents, Rudolf and Josephine, in Philadelphia, where it was received at 6:46 P.M. (there was a five-hour time difference).

WESTERN UNION
PJ170 VIA RCA=ZURICH 11 12 2338
LC HOEBER 6701 CRESHEIM ROAD PHILA

SO FAR EVERYTHING ALLRIGHT.

JO.

He sent a similar telegram to Elfriede.

SATURDAY, NOVEMBER 12, 1938

Reply telegram from Elfriede in Düsseldorf to Johannes in Zürich.

DDF, 12 NOVEMBER 1938 23H

JACTA EST ALEA[1] OR WHERE HE STOPS NOBODY KNOWS.
GOOD LUCK.

E.

SUNDAY, NOVEMBER 13, 1938

Letter from Elfriede in Düsseldorf to Johannes in Zürich. Elfriede was left to run the business alone that Johannes had primarily run in the past. Her daily letters to him include operating details of this tedious enterprise. There are references to the names of subscribers as well as several of the problematic paper carriers they employed. Delivery complaints were handled on the telephone, which rang incessantly in the office in the Pempelforterstrasse apartment in Düsseldorf.

In this letter, Elfriede uses a code word that appears in many of the following letters. "Uncle Karl" was Johannes and Elfriede's code word for the United States Consul who issued immigration visas.

Düsseldorf, 13 Nov. 1938

Lieber kleiner Jo,

The day is well begun said the man, when a brick fell on his head. This brick is apparently a disappearing carrier by the name of Gröbbels. He writes: "I respectfully request to see you on Monday, 14 November shortly after 12 o'clock for the purpose of an important discussion concerning myself." Doesn't sound good to me. But Herbert[2] will drive me there. The Dresden Bank in Gladbach made a stink again about not getting their paper. Frau Hucks [one of the carriers] got only 70 papers instead of 79.

1 *Jacta est alea* = "The die is cast."

2 *Herbert* = the middle of Elfriede's three brothers, then in his early thirties.

A man who wouldn't give his name made a stink about a missing paper. The written cancellation of his subscription will be here tomorrow. Mrs. Breidenbroich [a subscriber] doesn't want to pay. Should I cancel her? The invoice for Weissenberg came back from [carrier] Zinnmann—he said you asked for it. What should I do with it? Mr. Hannasch hasn't seen a paper in two weeks. [The home office in] Frankfurt writes that G. Lindemann paid RM 13.50 on 4 November. I don't understand, I thought he already paid in advance up to 31 December?? Explain to me, Count Oerindur, this contradiction in nature.[3]

Susanne is in bed. Right after we came back from the train she said she didn't feel well. Then she went to the mailbox and on the way met her professor friend,[4] who was just on his way over here. In the afternoon we put her to bed, in the evening 102.2, this morning after a restless night in your bed 100.7. Otherwise no diagnosis. I'll wait the thing out until tomorrow, because Susie is still relatively cheerful. Mother was here yesterday evening and helped me wait until the doorbell rang [with your telegram] around 10:45.[5] My equanimity was fading.

If Herr Gröbbels quits tomorrow, I'll curse you, but otherwise I hope Uncle Karl will greet you with his customary geniality.

Tonight Susie has 101.5, so it's going up.

Deine Fri

MONDAY, NOVEMBER 14, 1938

Letter from Elfriede in Düsseldorf to Johannes in Zürich. Part of the letter is about hiring and firing carriers. Most of the carriers worked two jobs, delivering the paper by bicycle early in the in the morning and then going on to another job. If a carrier was sick or quit, Elfriede would try to get one of the others to double up and handle two routes until a new carrier could be hired.

Düsseldorf, 14 Nov. 1938

Caro mio,

It's 10 o'clock at night and I just got back from Gladbach after leaving with Herbert at 11:45 this morning. What you left behind for me is an utter pigsty, and please don't attribute it to my incompetence if someday I resign from this position. Well: Mr. Gröbbels hasn't delivered any papers since Saturday!!! Reason: he has to start earlier at the department store. It's probably not true, but if I had been able to prove he was lying

3 An approximate quotation from *Guilt,* by Adolf Müllner, Act II, Scene 5.

4 *Professor friend* = Hans Ritter von Baeyer, a former professor of medicine at Heidelberg University. He was dismissed from his post by the Nazis in 1933 and now practiced orthopedics in Düsseldorf. (Dorothee Mußgnug, *Die Vertriebene Heidelberger Dozenten* (Heidelberg: Universitätsverlag Heidelberg, 1988), 24, 136.) Elsewhere in their letters Johannes and Elfriede refer to Prof. von Baeyer as the Magician. His son, Dr. Erich von Baeyer, also appears frequently in the letters.

5 Elfriede and her mother, Clara Fischer, who lived nearby, were waiting for word that Johannes had arrived safely in Zürich. The doorbell signaled the delivery of the telegram from Johannes with that news. Elfriede replied at 11:00 P.M. with the telegram at the beginning of this chapter.

I probably wouldn't have a carrier any more. So we went to the Employment Office, but with no success other than the addresses of a couple of cleaning ladies. Then to Mr. Overhage [another carrier], who couldn't take it over himself but who told me the name of a man who delivers the *Niederrhein* paper. That fellow couldn't do it either because he repairs heaters after he delivers papers. He referred me to the church office at St. Mary's. Closed. Then lunch at the train station. Pig slop—I left three-quarters of it behind. Then we delivered some of Mr. Gröbbels' many undelivered papers. A little after 3 to the church office again, still nobody there. By 5 we had delivered most of the papers.

Again to the church office; they gave us two addresses, nobody home at either one. Then to another address I got from the man Overhage recommended. Also not there. Once more to the church office addresses. One was at home, 70 years old, no bike, otherwise quite nice. A cup of coffee, then back to Mr. Jacobs, whose address I had found out in the meantime. Finally landed Mr. Jacobs. He'll drive tomorrow if God wills it and he doesn't change his mind in the meantime. He will also deliver the missing papers from the last few days that we weren't able to finish. It'll cost RM 2 extra. Then on the way home a flat tire at Gerol Place.

Day's activities of a wife alone. In the meantime the usual Monday morning complaints. Mr. Böcker on Grafenberg still hasn't seen a paper. Makes me want to throw up.

This is what you call a blooming business.

You might imagine that I didn't have a lot of time in the middle of all this to think about you. Susanne has no fever right now and even let me to go the train station to take the mail.

I hope to hear from you tomorrow.

This whole thing seems a lot like the old formula of throwing her in the water and seeing if she drowns. At least today I swam, even if with difficulty.

1000 Grüsse von deinem geplagten Weibe
[Love and kisses from your afflicted woman.]

TUESDAY, NOVEMBER 15, 1938

Letter from Elfriede in Düsseldorf to Johannes in Zürich. Here Elfriede responds to a not-preserved letter from Johannes similar to the one he sent his parents about his arrival in Zürich and his tram trip up the Ütliberg outside the city.

Düsseldorf, 15 Nov. 1938
Pempelforterstr. 11.

Mein Lieber,

All at once two letters [from you], but they still don't answer all my questions. As incredible as your account of the Ütli[berg] sounds to me, I can picture it somewhat when I think of the time in 1923 when we went hiking and [woke up in the morning and] found ourselves sleeping in the sun.[6] Susie feels better this morning, 99.3, but I decided not to let her go back to school this week so she can recover a little more. She looks thin and pale as soon as she gets up.

[*Additional business details omitted here.*]

There is no way this is something you could call a love letter. But I'm in a bit of a muddle over the business. When I tell you that yesterday after Gladbach, that is, after 10 P.M., I still wrote five letters and two cards, made up six postal deliveries and wrote out three complaints to carriers, got back from the train station at midnight and then did filing until 1. But how else can I do it? And I don't have anybody to whine to when things don't work right.

Tomorrow is a holiday, Penance Day,[7] but I don't think I need it. I think I've already done penance for my sins.

Afternoon

Mr. Jacobs, the new carrier, just called from Gladbach to say everything worked out. In the meantime another man came here, sent from the employment office, who wants the job for himself temporarily and then later for his wife. I kept his address for later use.

You poor thing, you get a heap of mixed-up questions from me, but every day the number of things I figure out gets bigger and the number of questions gets smaller. At least I hope so. What else do I hope? I hardly have to write you that. I'm already excited about tomorrow's letter from you.

1000 Grüße von uns beiden!

Deine Friedel

WEDNESDAY, NOVEMBER 16, 1938

Letter from Elfriede in Düsseldorf to Johannes in Zürich.

At this time, Rudolf and Josephine Höber in Philadelphia were awaiting two shipments of furniture from Germany. The moving firm of Pfütze

6 In 1923, when they were just 19, Johannes and Elfriede met for the first time at the University of Freiburg. A few weeks later they took a hiking trip into the Black Forrest. When they went to sleep after a day of hiking it was foggy, but in the morning it was clear and the clouds were below them.

7 *Buss und Bettag* [Penance and Prayer Day, a Protestant observance], was a legal holiday in Germany until 1994.

in Dresden was shipping the belongings of Manfred and Gri, who had left Dresden at the beginning of October, and the firm of Tischendorf in Kiel was shipping belongings of Rudolf and Josephine that had been in storage since they left Germany five years earlier. In the letters the names Pfütze and Tischendorf become abbreviations for these transactions. The shipments were packed in oversized shipping crates that could hold several rooms of furniture. Elfriede's letter also discusses a telegram Johannes' parents in Philadelphia sent her about the shipments. Telegrams at the time were costly and used only for matters of exceptional urgency. With Johannes in Switzerland, delivery of a telegram late at night frightened Elfriede with the possibility that something might have happened to him.

This letter discusses the need to get permission from the authorities to spend money that Johannes' parents had in German banks. Following his forced retirement from the University of Kiel in 1933, Rudolf received a pension that was paid into an account at the Kiel Savings and Loan. The account was blocked in the sense that pension funds could only be expended in Germany. Shortly before this letter was written, Johannes asked the bank to sell bonds to pay Tischendorf to transport Rudolf and Josephine's furniture to Philadelphia. Immediately after Kristallnacht, *however, the Nazis prohibited the sale of negotiable instruments by Jews, and the bank included Rudolf's bonds under that prohibition. Following* Kristallnacht, *the Nazis perversely fined Germany's "Jews" one billion marks ($400 million) to cover the damage caused by the Nazis that night. Withdrawals from "Jews'" bank accounts were blocked until that "fine" was paid.*

Düsseldorf, 16 Nov. 1938

Liebes Peterchen,[8]

It's Wednesday morning and I am all tired and depressed and nobody's here to comfort me. Susanne is still in bed. Yesterday afternoon she made the first attempt at getting up, but after half an hour she felt so bad she wanted to go back to bed. This morning 99.8 but her overall condition is much worse than the temperature. I think the whole thing is an after effect of the angina made worse by the effects of a shock.[9] If only I had a decent doctor. Engel may be good enough to distinguish angina from diphtheria, but not for this kind of nervous thing. As long as she stays in bed she's cheery and chipper, plays little games, reads and knits, but she's still not quite right.

On top of that, I didn't get any letter from you this morning and since this is a holiday there's no hope that one might still come. Our professor friend, who looks in on us every other day, has been very sweet. Yesterday evening Hendrik [Zech, a friend] came by, apparently just to be nice.

8 In most of the letters, Johannes and Elfriede addressed each other as Peter or Peterchen, a term of endearment whose origin was known only to them.. They never addressed each other this way later in their lives.

9 *Angina*: Elfriede's basis for using this term is not clear. Susanne remembers being told as a child that she had a "weak heart," but it never bothered her. The shock presumably refers both to *Kristallnacht*, the aftermath of which Susanne witnessed, and Johannes' abrupt departure.

Then at 12 I had just gone to bed very tired when the doorbell rang and a mail man brought me a telegram from Philadelphia asking, "When did Pfütze ship and with which ship?" Of course I don't know that and those people over there will be sure to notice when the crate arrives! I can't do anything about it today because of the holiday, but the telegram caused me to lose my night's rest and gave my nerves another jolt. Eventually it occurred to me that there were some sleeping pills in your night table, which I took and I finally fell asleep around 4:30, but now I'm thoroughly tired and down. I confess I could conceive of a telegram of greater urgency. While I can imagine that living over there without furniture can be inconvenient, this telegram really struck me as mean. Besides, why these intelligent jackasses—excuse me, but I am really angry—didn't cable directly to Pfütze is incomprehensible.

Then this morning a letter came from the Kiel Savings and Loan saying they can't carry out your order to sell bonds from the blocked account because, under the regulations issues by the Reich Finance Minister on 14 November, financial institutions are prohibited from selling negotiable securities from Jewish accounts. In what manner should I inform the Savings Bank that their belief that your father is a Jew is erroneous? What will happen with Tischendorf? Please bring this to your family's attention right away.

Those are my problems. What are yours????

With respect to our blooming correspondence, this is the 5th letter—from me naturally—that I have put into a new file folder. You must write me every day without fail.

Now I feel a little better and I'm going for a walk. Helma[10] is with Susie now.

Have a good time, good luck; be charming to all old aunts and uncles.

Deine Friedel

I wrote Saturday	briefly
Sunday	
Monday	Report about Gladbach
Tuesday	with a lot of business papers
Today	this letter

You'll hear from me every day from now on.

THURSDAY, NOVEMBER 17, 1938

Postcard from Elfriede in Düsseldorf to Johannes at the City Hotel in Zürich. This responds to a letter from Johannes that probably contained

10 *Helma* was employed full time by Elfriede and Johannes as both housekeeper and caretaker for Susanne.

information about his arrival in Zürich (see Johannes's letter to his parents in Chapter 2). In this postcard, Elfriede uses another code word that appears in the letters. "Uncle Paul" was Johannes and Elfriede's code word for Germany or the German authorities. Here the reference is to Elfriede's need to secure from the police in Düsseldorf ("Uncle Paul") a certification that Johannes did not have a criminal record. Johannes had to have the certification for his American visa application to "Uncle Karl," the American Consul.

Mein lieber, just quickly about Susie's condition. Yesterday her temperature went up to 103.4. This morning she had 99.9. Now 98.7. This second fever jump caused me to call Dr. Engel despite her normal temperature this morning, but after a thorough examination he found nothing and prescribed Prontosil tablets.[11] There was quite a bit of business today (invoices, carriers) but nothing problematic. I'm waiting for your answers to my last questions. Your advances with your business [in Zürich] impress me greatly as well as your "encounters." I wrote to Uncle Paul today about a recommendation to Uncle Karl. Thank God he wasn't too nasty. Don't flirt too much with the Pfau lady; that should be your first moral challenge.[12] Nothing more with her. Lots of love, from Susie too. *Deine Friedel*

FRIDAY, NOVEMBER 18, 1938

Letter from Elfriede in Düsseldorf to Johannes in Zürich, accompanied by a letter from Susanne.

Düsseldorf, 18 November 1938

Lieber kleiner Jo,

Or great or wonderful Jo. At which tea, lunch, dinner or mess, at which cabaret and with which pretty woman should I look to find you? Who did you just meet in the street? Which collar button went missing and to whom did you complain about it?

Many thanks for finding the time in the midst of such auspicious and time-consuming occupations to take care of the monthly reconciliation report. An answer typed in final form—that's more than I expected in my wildest dreams.

Today everything was pretty unexciting. Even the complaints remained within bearable bounds. Two ads,[13] one for RM 36 and one for RM 38. And two new subscribers.

11 *Prontosil* was an antibiotic sulfa drug manufactured from a dye base. A side effect of this medicine was a yellowing of the patient's skin.

12 *Alexander St. Pfau* was a famous Zürich biochemist, a friend of Johannes' parents. The "Pfau lady" was probably his wife or daughter.

13 In addition to distributing the newspapers, Johannes and Elfriede sold advertising.

Susanne is still free of fever. She got all yellow from the Prontosil she is taking. She's still in bed, but if she's like this tomorrow we'll try getting her up in the afternoon. I haven't seen many people. The Trömels call almost every day, but because their child is sick I haven't seen them since Sunday.

Tischendorf sent a furniture list that you're supposed to sign and have notarized by the police. It certainly is convenient that the mail between here and Zürich functions relatively quickly. Everything gets here in two days. Your first letter was routed through customs and for that reason took longer. So you know accurately: up to now I wrote every day, but yesterday only a card. On Sunday morning I will visit the Betz's.[14]

Paul's case[15] hasn't been decided yet, but that's not bad.

Keep having a good time; I'll muddle through somehow.

Deine Friedel

Accompanying letter from Susanne:

Dear Papi,

Thank you very much for the pretty card. Yesterday I wrote to the *Christkind*[16]. Today Lotte sent me an Advent calendar. Now I have two of them. [For Christmas] I am going to send Monika[17] a hand crocheted little case. Helma said I should do that because I really wanted to send it to Janka. Now I am going to send Janka a little rubber doll, Gri a handmade bookmark, Manfred a fake cigarette, you know like the one he had here because he said he would need a new one soon. We laughed a lot over your card. Do you know if you were pulled out of the fountain that is on the card or did you fly through the air the way you see it on the card? Everybody calls me skinny bones and piggy because Helma told Oma I eat so much. In my heaviest clothes I weigh 56 pounds. You can see how much I took off. When I was sick Fräuken visited me. She gave me a toy horse. When I was at her house with Mutti I liked the little straw animals so much I asked her for one. She said she remembered that. She brought a big apple too. For St. Nicholas Day I asked for a pair of leggings. On Sunday the 4th is the first Christmas pageant, Sleeping Beauty.

Lots of kisses, because 1000 don't fit on the letter. But here are some OOOOOOOO *Deine Susanne.*

---

14 *Dr. Betz* was a circulation manager for the *Frankfurter Zeitung* to whom Johannes and Elfriede reported.

15 The Gestapo's arrest of Elfriede's brother Paul is described in Johannes' letter to his parents dated November 16, 1938. See Chapter 2.

16 In Germany, Christmas presents are brought by the Christ Child [*Christkind*] rather than by Santa Claus.

17 *Monika Blaschy* was Susanne's little cousin who was in America. *Janka* was Monika's sister and Gri and Manfred her parents.

SUNDAY, NOVEMBER 20, 1938

Letter from Elfriede in Düsseldorf to Johannes in Zürich. He had written her that the American Consul in Zürich immediately accepted his application for an immigration visa and scheduled an appointment for an examination, in contrast to the consulates in Germany, which were not even accepting applications because of their backlog.

Düsseldorf, 20 November 38

Mein lieber Peter,

It was nice with the phone call today, and I am still sufficiently amazed at technological miracles that it seems like a fairy tale to me to speak from hundreds of kilometers away. It's really more than one could have hoped for that Uncle Karl would respond so quickly. I will speak to the police tomorrow to see if I can speed up [your good conduct certificate].

Susie is noticeably better. She's still worn out and we'll have to count on a little convalescence, but she's quite cheerful today. On Friday I went to the movies with my mother to see a tolerable French movie. This morning I went to the Betz's and the Daniels, but no one was home so our living room is decorated with two calla lilies that were intended for Mrs. Betz and the walk in the cold sun was good for me

Business: I seem to have carried off the Düsseldorf carrier recruitment pretty well. I'm beginning to feel generally more secure. And I am going to write to Pfütze [about when they will ship Gri and Manfred's furniture].

Where and in what neighborhood of the beautiful city is your current residence? The fact that you can be reached by phone is a comfort to me. You can never know what that might be good for.

Alles liebe, Deine Friedel

TUESDAY, NOVEMBER 22, 1938

Letter from Elfriede in Düsseldorf to Johannes in Zürich. She refers to "Seppchen" and "Seppi," nicknames for Josephine, Johannes' mother. "The Philadelphians" refer collectively to those living on Cresheim Road, namely, Rudolf, Josephine (Seppi), Manfred and Gri.

Düsseldorf, 22 November 38

Mein liebes Peterchen,

Yesterday went by without a letter to you, but I did get your nice one from Sunday night, which arrived here in a little over 13 hours. Up to now most of them have taken much longer. Today there was mail from Philadelphia and a letter from the Stös,[18] both of which I'm enclosing. The fact that the furniture issue has now become the central problem for the Philadelphians—now that some of their children have arrived—seems to be a significant misallocation of priorities. Pfütze hasn't answered yet, indeed they couldn't have, but I really don't see what basis Seppchen has for her belief that they still haven't shipped things. The whole thing leaves me pretty cold, and if nothing worse happens than that they have to sleep on Salvation Army mattresses for a couple of weeks, then I would be quite ready to trade their problems for mine.

I called the police yesterday, at first without success but then later got an appointment for Wednesday. I'll do everything I can for you.

Susanne is doing better. She was up for several hours today. I suspect that she has jaundice. She got Prontosil last Friday, and that changes the color a lot, but after she finished with that on Sunday she looked quite normal again. Then yesterday it struck me that the whites of her eyes were yellow and from her face and body you could almost doubt whether she is a member of the white race. All that without taking any Prontosil. Now we put some of her pee into a little bottle and brought it to Dr. Engel for testing. As the Magician[19] says, jaundice would explain her fatigue. At any rate we're on the right track.

1000 Grüsse Deine Friedel

I had just sealed up the envelope when the afternoon mail came with your letter of yesterday. I also got the answer from Pfütze that the crate went on the Hapag steamer *Köln*. I'll cable that information [to Philadelphia].

Your report on your interaction with Bleuler is heavenly; different places in the world are indeed very different. Your social advancement brings to my mind the question of whether there might be some overseas connections to be made out of them. Your account of your visit in Baden was also nice. If you see those people again give them my best regards. In fact give my regards to everyone to whom you think my regards might be opportune. So long as it doesn't obligate me personally it is all the same to me.

Alles Gute weiter!

F.

---

18 *Stös* = Erich and Elfriede (Friedel) Stötzner, longtime friends who emigrated to New York. He had been a journalist with the *Frankfurter Zeitung.*

19 *Magician* = Professor von Baeyer.

WEDNESDAY, NOVEMBER 23, 1938

Letter from Elfriede in Düsseldorf to Johannes in Zürich. In this letter, Elfriede mentions a Mrs. Breidenbroich, a Jewish subscriber who disappeared without paying her newspaper bill. Elfriede's comment about her residence being destroyed indicates that she was one of the many victims of the Kristallnacht *pogrom. Her disappearance raised the question of whether Johannes and Elfriede would have to pay Frankfurt for subscribers who fled Germany without paying or whether Frankfurt would absorb the loss. Elfriede also makes reference to a Mr. Schindler, a troublesome carrier who appears repeatedly in the letters. At the end of the letter Elfriede discusses a plan to meet Johannes in Switzerland before he leaves for America.*

Düsseldorf, 23 November 38

Lieber kleiner Jo,

Well, Susanne really has jaundice and indeed seriously. Of course that's not good, but somehow I'm happy that we now have a diagnosis. The jaundice has been present at least since Sunday, because that's when I first noticed the symptoms. Dr. Engel was here last night and gave instructions for the diet. She is allowed no fat and no meat, only carbohydrates, fruit, and vegetables. That's hard because she already has no appetite and without fat and meat everything tastes terribly bland. Salt is also forbidden. So there's the worry that she'll take off even more weight than she already has. I feed her large quantities of apple juice with dextrose added. She likes that and doesn't notice the extra dietary sugar.

Business: I want to come back to the case of Breidenbroich. I sent her subscription card back [to the home office] with the notation "moved/address unknown." The Breidenbroich residence has been destroyed and I can't go looking for Mrs. Breidenbroich all over Germany. We can't be liable for that.

Mr. Schindler's truss is broken, so he couldn't make his collections on time. At least he delivered the paper. Your carriers are a pain about turning in their collections. About RM 300 are still outstanding; my ultimatums go unheard, or at any rate without any reply.

I just came back from a successful visit to the police [to get your good conduct certificate]. They gave me the runaround for a while but eventually it was resolved with the payment of RM 3. I called Mother right away and three minutes later she called back to say that Paul's case has finally been closed. So that's one more obstacle out of the way. I was told to send you the warmest regards from Mother and Herbert and Elisabeth and Peter. Now Paul will get married the day after tomorrow, and since you presumably would at least want to write to him I'll give you his local address: 9 Gohliser Street, c/o Schreiber, Leipzig. I don't know yet what I'm going to do about a present. Every evening when I leave at 6 there's so much to do, part private, part business, that the time vanishes too quickly. I have to do an awful lot that otherwise you would do, delivering missed papers, collecting, etc. etc. In addition Susanne takes a lot of time, for me and Helma both. And finally I have to write you nearly every day, which is nice but time consuming.

So now I have to say something about your letter. You don't seem to be entirely happy with me. So, in order: Susanne's shock was no shock but rather a serious infection, whose character could not be more precisely determined and so was called grippe, hereafter, however, jaundice. I was afraid that the various upsetting things that happened recently, along with the effects of her angina, had the effect on our extremely sensitive child of causing her to recover more slowly. For you to call this angina a bit of a sore throat is a pretty insensitive thing for a father to say.

I'm giving a lot of thought to 3–4 December but so far without a conclusion.[20] If I don't want to travel at night it will take practically 3 days in the middle of the first Ultimo I have to do alone. I could take the train [to Basel] on Saturday morning. Then it looks like there's a car with reclining seats on the train coming back Sunday night, so I could take that and be back here early Monday morning. Maybe Basel would be more practical after all; it costs less and saves two hours each way, which we might put to better use. First however I will wait anxiously for news about what happens [at the American Consulate] on Friday.

Machs gut!

Deine Friedel

FRIDAY, NOVEMBER 25, 1938

American Immigration Visa entered in Johannes' passport with a large rubber stamp with blanks completed in ink.

20 Johannes had proposed that he and Elfriede meet in Zürich 10 days after this letter, on the weekend of December 3 and 4. Elfriede suggested Basel instead because it was two hours closer to Düsseldorf. The train trip to Basel would already take eight hours from Düsseldorf. The *Ultimo* mentioned in the following sentence is Johannes and Elfriede's term for the business procedures at the end of every month to distribute bills, collect subscription payments, and balance the books with the Frankfurt home office.

~~Nonquota~~ Immigration Visa

Quota No. *132 from Quota*

Dated NOV 25 1938

Issued to *Johannes Höber*
(Name)

(signed) *Carl W. Strom*
CARL W. STROM VICE CONSUL

American Consul at Zürich, Switzerland

Identification Card Issued
No. *1050723*

Service No. *3769*
3770

$ *10* for which were collected Frs. 45.--

A few of Johannes' letters to his parents are inserted into this exchange to complete the narrative of his journey to the United States.

FRIDAY, NOVEMBER 25, 1938

Cable from Johannes in Zürich to his parents, Rudolf and Josephine in Philadelphia. He sent Elfriede a similar telegram.

RCA RADIOGRAM
RCA COMMUNICATIONS

PH73 VIA RCA ZUERICH 24 25 1845
NLT HOEBER
6701 CRESHEIM ROAD GERMANTOWN PHILA=

GOT VISA ALREADY TODAY DEPART WITH PRESIDENT HARDING LE HAVRE 8 DECEMBER ARRIVE 17 DECEMBER.

HAPPILY JO

FRIDAY, NOVEMBER 25, 1938

Letter from Johannes in Zürich to his parents in Philadelphia. In this letter, Johannes mentions his father Rudolf's Textbook of Physiology, *which was widely used in medical schools in Europe for nearly 30 years. First published in 1919, the eighth edition was published by Stämpfli Publishing in Zürich in December 1939. The first seven editions were published in Berlin, but the Nazis regarded Rudolf as Jewish and prohibited reprinting the book in Germany.*

Zürich. 25 November 38
26 b Alfred Escher Street, c/o Mottier

Ihr lieben,

I just cabled you. Now quickly a few lines to send via the *Queen Mary*.

There is still such a thing as miracles in this world! On Wednesday the 16th I submitted my papers to the Consulate here; on Saturday the 19th I was summoned to appear today.[21] Today I got my visa.

Now I can disclose that on the 9th of November in Cologne I booked a firm ticket for the *President Harding*, which leaves from LeHavre on 12 December and which arrives in New York on 17 December. It was my firm intention to be with you for Christmas—and now I will be! On Saturday and Sunday, 3 and 4 December, I will meet a last time with Friedel in Basel and after that I probably will not return to Zürich. The fact that the visa process went exactly according to plan gives me boundless optimism for the coming months.

Here in Zürich I've been unbelievably spoiled for the last 14 days.
Lilly Reiff treats me as though I am a son in her house. I was invited there for dinner four times, always with new interesting people. On Sunday I drove with her to Lake Lucerne. Yesterday afternoon at her house I met the Hirzels [unidentified], to whose house I was then invited yesterday evening. I was at the Bleulers for tea, and the Manghoffs [unidentified] are like old friends. (Yesterday they invited me to the premiere of a Zuckmayer[22] play.) Almost the nicest, however, was this: when I was being examined by the doctor at the Consulate, a Dr. Kauffman, as soon as I told him my name he immediately started talking about Daddy, about the *Textbook*, and I hope that I sold him the first copy of the new Stämpfli Edition.

When all is said and done, Daddy and Seppchen, without you I wouldn't have been born in Zürich, wouldn't now be able to travel to the USA, would not be a fast friend with this city—where will this chain ever end? Are we all always conscious—we seven big and small children—of how much we owe you?

Very much looking forward to seeing you again.
In seliger Wiedersehensfreude,

Euer Jo

21 *Summoned:* The visa application process included written forms and supporting documents, and if these were satisfactory, the applicant was summoned for a personal interview and a medical examination.

22 Carl Zuckmayer's play *Bellman* was originally scheduled to open in Vienna the previous March, but after the Nazi takeover of Austria that month, Zuckmayer was forced to flee. He found temporary refuge in Switzerland, where Johannes saw the first performance of the play.

P.S. Yesterday Friedel wrote that the case against Paul was finally and formally dismissed. So we lived through that one successfully as well. Today he is marrying his Heidi in a private ceremony without either family.

FRIDAY, NOVEMBER 25, 1938

Letter from Elfriede in Düsseldorf to Johannes in Zürich. He had sent her a telegram saying he got his American immigration visa. In this letter, Elfriede refers to the fact that the previous spring Gri was told that, like Johannes, she came under the Swiss quota rather than the German quota because she was born in Zürich. That was when Elfriede came up with the idea that Johannes should get a visa in Switzerland and emigrate before her.

Düsseldorf, 25 November 1938

Mein lieber Kleiner,

Just the sight of the outside of your telegram did me good, because if you had bad news you would hardly have sent a telegram to tell me. It's all really too improbable. If somebody had told me in advance that this could happen I would have taken him for some kind of trickster. That such a thing exists and no one knows about it! When my brain gave birth to this idea in August, stimulated by Gri's case, I didn't dare to dream that this idea was as good as it has turned out. Since my intelligence is so often undervalued, I would like some credit for having suggested this very productive idea. I take the success in this first step as a good sign for the further ones. *Quod dii bene vertant!*[23]

And now? A whole new crop of problems comes up, above all with respect to the newspaper, though there is no need to be too hasty about that. If we are to meet [in Basel] on 3–4 December, then I'll talk to Betz before then. There are already a lot of subscription cancellations and many of the people who have left won't pay, even if they haven't expressly cancelled. Please write down for me again how the monthly requisition form is to be made out. In the matter of the invoices things are very bad. At the beginning of this month, the carriers were sent a notice to the effect that the invoices that turn out to be uncollectible will be charged to the carrier after the 10th of each month. How we will handle that in each individual case is something we can still decide. In any event it's no good if, as now, RM 250 remain uncollected. So shake up your brain and help me some more.

23 *Quod dii bene vertant* = May the gods grant good fortune.

I don't want to deprive you of the contents of a letter that came today from Frankfurt about marketing: "We know that you have been working to replace the normal cancellations by means of soliciting new ones. Nevertheless we must tell you that at this particular time we place the greatest importance in not experiencing any disappointment. We do not have to expend a lot of words: you understand us. We can imagine that you have already increased your sales efforts so as not merely to maintain your level of subscribers but actually to increase them. We are counting on your understanding and we ask that you let us know that we can count on you when it is essential to hold the rudder fast. With German regards." Dictated by Wolter, signed by Schreiber. Isn't that a wonderful concoction? It really leaves me cold. What on earth is going on at the paper?

That's all for today. You can see that even when large matters are foremost in one's mind, there are little ones left over that we have to think about too.

Yesterday, together with Günter, I bought a small woolen rug (about RM 40) for Paul and Heidi for their wedding that will be shipped [to their new home in Leipzig] along with their furniture.

1000 Grüße Deine Friedel

MONDAY, NOVEMBER 28, 1938

Letter from Elfriede in Düsseldorf to Johannes in Zürich. She mentions Dr. Betz, who wanted Elfriede to keep running the business. He recommended against Johannes sending a letter to the home office in Frankfurt announcing that he was emigrating. She also tells Johannes that there was a 10 percent reduction in subscriptions in the two weeks following Kristallnacht, *indicating how quickly the attacks on Jews that night disrupted the city's population and its economy.*

Düsseldorf, 28 November 1938

Lieber kleiner Jo,

I am going to try to write with the typewriter, even though it isn't working right. It has a transmission problem that causes the letters to stick over each other once in a while. I don't know the trick for fixing it, because this happened before. Yesterday I typed both the business letters and the carrier accounts at my mother's. So this letter won't look good but I think you'll be able to read it.
At any rate, I went to the Betz's yesterday afternoon and it was very nice. I was happy he shared my opinion that the letters you wrote shouldn't be

sent yet. He'll be in Frankfurt next week and will talk the matter over with Hecht and Schreiber. I think he would rather continue the operation in its current form [with me running the business]. I don't know what I would actually prefer, to continue as now or as an employee of a new business operation. So I've put the whole thing off and you don't have to do anything.

Since I started this letter our little typewriter seems to have overcome the disturbance in its digestive tract.

"Oma" Clara Fischer, Elfriede's mother, in her home office at Prinzgeorgstrasse, Düsseldorf, 1938.

Susanne is getting better and better every day. The yellow is going away, her gall bladder is working as it should again and her appetite is practically alarming. We're still being careful about returning her to a normal diet. She's supposed to get a little heavier before she goes back to school but she's already well enough to play some. The after-effects in the form of a substantial bill [from Dr. Engel] will undoubtedly follow.

Your Sunday letter just arrived. Many thanks for the answers to my questions. I've already made a lot of progress with the invoices and feel very diligent. The reduction on the first of the month will be about 10 percent. So far there have been about 30 cancellations, but those aren't all of them.

1000 Grüße, Deine Friedel

WEDNESDAY, NOVEMBER 30, 1938

Letter from Elfriede in Düsseldorf to Johannes in Zürich.

Düsseldorf, 11/30/38

Liebes Peterchen,

I am completely drowning in the Ultimo and there's only a slight possibility that I might ever surface again. I'm just as far along as we usually are by the 30th, but the next few days are going to be a real rush. I'm anxious to know whether you got my letter of yesterday on time.

I'm very aware that you used to do a lot of things during the last few days of the month [that I now have to do]. I know you were in charge and in the end were responsible for everything. But in the morning I lie in bed from 7–8 A.M. and think about everything there is to do that day and it seems to me to be much bigger than it actually turns out to be as the day goes on. This morning it began with the fact that there weren't any newspapers in Gladbach. I still don't know when they eventually came. Then United Silk complained that yesterday's morning papers were delivered today, but otherwise the phone was pleasantly quiet today. Because of that I was able to get all of the invoices ready for the carriers, two carrier-books are made up (I didn't get more done in spite of my efforts), all invoices are ready to send and all previously pending cancellations have been worked through, that is, index cards filled out and duplicated. I have the feeling that I've done all that pretty well, and the next time around it won't cost me as much thought.

At lunch I went to Bittner's Konditorei and picked out a big fat box of candy for Philadelphia for Christmas. After I had made my selection the way I planned to—and it didn't seem very small in view of the fact that it's for a lot of people—I nearly fell over when they told me the shipping cost. But I took it anyway and I'm looking forward to hearing what you eventually think of it. In the middle of the box is something very small that's just for you. You'll have to see if you can figure it out. Otherwise I'm not at all in a Christmas mood because of all the preoccupation and work. I'd like to ask you nevertheless to get some Christmas wishes to me as soon as you can manage it. It will be a lot easier to carry them out now than after next week.

Just ordered a train ticket. Happy about that.[24]

1000 Grüße,

Deine Friedel

---

24 Elfriede means that she purchased a train ticket to Basel, where she was to meet Johannes on the following weekend, i.e., three days later.

CHAPTER 4

Getting to Philadelphia

FRIDAY, DECEMBER 2, 1938

Postcard from Elfriede in Düsseldorf to Johannes in Zürich. They were scheduled to meet the next evening in Basel for a last visit before Johannes left Europe for the United States.

Düsseldorf 2 Dec

Lieber Peter,

Lull between Duisburg and Krefeld. Just got 2 ads combined value about RM 150. Got your toothache letter. Can't you have them pull the damn thing? In spite of everything I'm looking forward to seeing you tomorrow at the S.B.B.[1] I just picked up my ticket. Yesterday evening very nice at the Magicians'. Their daughter-in-law is leaving [for America] on the 7th or 8th of December from Rotterdam, may pass you, or probably will.

Deine F.

MONDAY, DECEMBER 5, 1938

Letter from Elfriede in Düsseldorf to Johannes in Zürich, accompanied by a letter from Susanne. Elfriede had returned that morning by sleeper car from Basel. Her farewell from Johannes the previous evening must have been agonizing because they knew they would not see each other for many months—if intervening world events did not prevent their ever being reunited.

Düsseldorf, 5 December 1938

Liebes Peterchen,

Now I'm home again and I don't feel as horrible as yesterday evening, though Susie isn't back and I haven't spoken to my mother yet. I spent the first hour [after I left you] feeling pretty bad but it got better in the sleeping car. The conductor managed to place the woman who was supposed to get on at Freiburg and share my compartment somewhere else so I slept alone all night, though restlessly and waking up a lot but

1 *SBB* = *Schweizerische Bundesbahnen*, the Swiss railway system, here meaning the Basel train station where Elfriede was to meet Johannes.

overall alright until a little before 7 this morning. Unfortunately the train got here already at 7:13. Then I sacrificed 10 *pfennigs* for the streetcar so I didn't have to walk home alone in the dark hours of the morning.

Our little rabbit[2] is really chipper; we just talked on the phone.

Later: I'll quickly write a little more. It's almost 6 o'clock and I have to go out because tomorrow is St. Nicholas Day and Susie has certain expectations from such saints that I dare not disappoint.

Good luck. I'm really very excited about the way your things have been moving along. I hope for a letter from you tomorrow. With all the things I've had to deal with today I simply haven't had the time to worry.

Alles liebe

Deine Friedel

Accompanying letter from Susanne, December 5, 1938.

Lieber Papi:

I just practiced my recorder lots of pretty things. I made poems made two bookmarks, I will write more in a minute need to ask Mutti something.

So now I can write more. In the Advent calendar from Lotte there was so far a star an acorn a little sailboat. Yesterday Herbert was here for Mutti to. [*sic*] I have to ask again!

Mutti asked him to drive to Krefeld and Glabach. So he went to Mutti in the office and then I took his cane hid in the entryway behind the black chairs pushed the cane through the hole in the chair and hung the hat on it. Then Helma came out of the bedroom. Ssst! Ssst! came from behind the chair and the hat came out on a long neck I scared Mutti and Herbert the same way.

Many 10000000000 kisses your Susanne.

TUESDAY, DECEMBER 6, 1938

Postcard from Johannes in Zürich to Rudolf and Josephine in Philadelphia. Johannes had previously booked passage on the President Harding, *which was scheduled to leave from Le Havre and put in at Southampton before crossing the Atlantic. Because he was unable to secure a French transit visa to travel from Zürich to Le Havre, Johannes proposed to take*

2 *Rabbit* = Susanne, who stayed with Elfriede's mother, Clara Fischer, while Elfriede was with Johannes for the weekend.

a plane from Zürich to London (bypassing France) and catch up with the President Harding *when it left Southampton.*

Zürich, 6 December 1938

Ihr lieben,

I want to use this last mail opportunity—which will travel faster than I will—to fill you in. After things went so well at the American Consulate, new problems began to mount up quickly. Despite all my efforts, I have so far been unable to get my French transit visa for the trip to Le Havre, and if I wait for it I might have to sit here for another two weeks. So I decided to sacrifice the extra 100 frs. it would cost and tomorrow I'll fly to London and leave from Southampton. But whether I will actually arrive in New York on the 17th as planned is now doubtful because the *Harding* now will leave 1–2 days late because of strikes in Le Havre. Poor old Europe!

In liebe,

Dein Jo

P.S. My meeting with Freidel in Basel on Sunday was as nice as it could possibly be.

TUESDAY, DECEMBER 6, 1938

Letter from Elfriede in Düsseldorf to Johannes in Zürich. The travel agent, Lindemann, had written her in Düsseldorf that Johannes' ship would be delayed, and she wasn't sure how to get the message to him in Zürich.

In Elfriede's letters she complains quite a lot, mostly about little things—the business, her health, the weather, the logistics of international mail service. Perhaps this was a substitute for the much bigger things that she was constrained not to complain about. The home of her closest friends, Karl and Hilde Lenzberg, had been destroyed on Kristallnacht, *and they were emigrating to Venezuela. Many other neighbors, friends, and customers were fleeing Düsseldorf as well. Still, Elfriede almost never mentions the oppressive atmosphere in Germany in her letters, except once or twice in the most veiled terms. She felt it was dangerous to write of the threatening atmosphere of daily life under the Nazis. Still, she did not want him to forget the anxiety of her situation, and her writing so much about the smaller problems may have been a substitute for more serious concerns.*

In the following letter, for example, Elfriede has to write Johannes in very guarded terms about difficulties she was having getting money from Rudolf's bank account at the Kiel Savings and Loan. The money was needed to ship Rudolf and Josephine's furniture to the United States. The Savings and Loan's "erroneous assumptions" refer to the bank's belief that Rudolf was "Jewish," subjecting him to the government restrictions on "Jewish" bank accounts after Kristallnacht. *Elfriede believed the bank should be asked to remove the restrictions. Dealing with such setbacks was maddening and alarming, but Elfriede could not voice her frustration about them in her letters.*

Düsseldorf, 6 December 1938

Mein lieber Peter,

I haven't waited more anxiously for mail from you at any time in the last three weeks than I have today. I had no idea where I could find you and no way of knowing whether you would get my special delivery letter with the card from the Lindemann travel agency, which aggravatingly I only found in the mailbox late last night. I didn't know whether you took off [for England] already this morning and I kept wondering if I should phone or send a telegram. But since it was in the paper here that your ship could not leave because of a strike, I thought you would have seen the same thing [in the paper there] and then checked with Lindemann's agent in Zürich. I'm going to check the air mail connections with England so I'll know how I can still write to you.

Things aren't going smoothly here either. This morning Schindler didn't go out on his route; he hadn't been right for a couple of days. Last week he had a bike accident and twice after that he got completely soaked. Another carrier drove the route for him today so all I had to do was soothe the complaining subscribers. Tomorrow the other carrier will take over half the route and Schindler will do the other half himself again. So this situation is salvaged once more.

Enclosed is the letter from the Savings and Loan, whose erroneous assumption [that Rudolf is "Jewish"] in connection with the recent pronouncements needs to be clarified.

You should have your tooth pulled. Our friend Marlies gave a vivid description of your condition, which she lived through a little while ago and which was quickly and thoroughly remedied when it was extracted.

If this weren't the Christmas month our [financial] status would have improved quite a bit. But the current [gift] list, which I just made, now includes 15 people, among them such weighty ones as Susanne and Helma, although all of Philadelphia is already crossed off.

There is a whole bunch of work still left for today, but nothing too, too urgent. So I'll take this letter out first so you'll have it at least with the 2nd mail tomorrow And then bon voyage!

Deine Friedel

Accompanying letter from Susanne.

Düsseldorf, 6 December 38

Lieber Papi.

On Sunday I went with Oma to Shirley Temple's *Heidi*. It was very nice. Remember, the grandfather went seventy miles to Frankfurt, but it was not nearly as nice as in the book. This morning when I woke up I did not know at first if I was at home because I dreamed I was in Küingdorf. After a little while I figured it out. Also St. Nicholas was going tingalingalingaling. Mutti rang and then I called her. I went in the kitchen with her. There was a plate with a little sign that said Helma. There were nuts scattered all around. Mutti called that I should search around and right on the dining room table was a plate of cookies and leggings for me.

Viele Grüße und OOOOOOOOOO
Deine Susanne

P.S. I learned from Mutti that you won't be here for Christmas. Hopefully you will enjoy it over there and say hello to all of them.

WEDNESDAY, DECEMBER 7, 1938

Postcard from Johannes in Zürich to his parents in Philadelphia concerning the delay in his departure.

Ihr lieben,

For months I had so carefully planned every detail of my trip! And now everything is getting messed up. Because of strikes in Le Havre my passage tomorrow on the *President Harding* has been cancelled and the passengers are being transferred to the *Manhattan*, which leaves a week later. That means that instead of the 17th I'll reach you on the 22nd. Mess! I heard about the whole thing just 5 hours before my plane was supposed to take off for London. So now I'll travel from here [via Paris to Southampton] because in the interim I got my French transit visa. I have what I need for living expenses because after some difficulty I got the cost of my plane ticket refunded.

Anyway, see you on 12/22.

Euer Jo

THURSDAY, DECEMBER 8, 1938

Letter from Elfriede in Düsseldorf to Johannes in Zürich. In this letter she mentions Natalie Freyberger, a part-time employee who managed the business for Johannes and Elfriede when they went on vacation or had other business to attend to. She had wanted to divorce her husband for some time. Because the husband was not Jewish, Mrs. Freyberger took advantage of a Nazi law that allowed non-Jews married to Jews to divorce without court costs or attorney's fees. In addition to working for Johannes and Elfriede, Mrs. Freyberger also worked as caretaker to an invalid in a wealthy family.

Düsseldorf, 8 December 1938

Mein armes Peterchen,

If I hadn't called you yesterday I might have saved you a lot of trouble, but I pictured you in Southampton without any resources and without any information and no steamer there to carry you off. It's really disgusting when the important things go smoothly and the little things turn into disasters. What's happening with your tooth? I worry about it.

Things here are nearly enough to make me crazy. The newspapers finally got here 10:08 A.M.! I wrote a letter to all the subscribers warning them in advance that this sort of delay may happen more frequently in the coming weeks. That way the subscriber phone calls won't be as crazy. Betz called and said that Schreiber and Hecht are the only ones in Frankfurt who know [that you have left and I will leave eventually]. The only request they made was for me to let them know 3–4 weeks before things are wrapped up. You can't ask for more than that. I think you should write Betz when you're a little less overwhelmed.

Freyberger was here yesterday. First of all, she successfully got divorced with a no-fault annulment on grounds of racial difference. I told her that was the first time she ever got something for nothing. Secondly, her professor has gone to his wife and it's uncertain how long that will last or whether he will take a route similar to the one you are taking. Third, she confirmed that it's possible to travel to Shanghai without a visa—but only there, now that Paraguay is closed—and now she's planning to go there in February or March. She'll be without money, but she says that would be true anywhere. In the meantime she's going to come here next week for two days so I can do a little Christmas shopping. Up to now it's been pretty skimpy on that front.

Natalie Freyberger, Johannes and Elfriede's part-time office assistant.

Somehow it's a great comfort to me that I can still reach you for a couple more days.

Alles gute!

Von deinem auch seltsam geplagten Eheweibe Elfriede
From your exceptionally afflicted wife Elfriede.

FRIDAY, DECEMBER 9, 1938

Letter from Elfriede in Düsseldorf to Johannes in Zürich.

Liebes kleines Peterchen,

You are absolutely right that all these little problems really stink. Technical difficulties can get on your nerves because you're at their mercy even more than the big problems. But these obstacles will also be overcome.

It's not pleasant here either. At noon someone called up and said Schindler was sick in bed and his newspapers were still at the station. So good old Mrs. Mugler is now on her way with the papers and I'm still afraid to answer the telephone. I have no idea what will happen tomorrow when the newspaper is going to have a 40-page rotogravure supplement.

I got a really very nice letter from Philadelphia in response to your long one that went on the *Queen Mary.*[3] The letter is dated 11/27 and Manfred and Gri's furniture had not yet arrived but was still afloat somewhere on the Atlantic. It's comforting to know I can still write you for a couple more days. It will be hard for me when I'm no longer able to bring my cares and worries to my husband's attention and get a quick reply. Other than you, nobody understands what kinds of problems there are with the carriers, how much attention and effort they require, what anxiety they cause and so on.

At some point I'll go to the police in the Tischendorf matter,[4] but I don't know when. I really should have a car and know a little more about this typewriter. As you can see the typewriter is behaving badly. [*The text at this point in the letter became very pale.*] Being alone makes me feel like different parts of my body have been amputated one after the other. Annemarie and her son have been at sea since yesterday.[5] Yesterday we toasted all passengers everywhere. Oh, I hope so much that you will soon be able to follow them, but for myself I hope so passionately for a couple more letters from you before then. If you find that things aren't very nice these days, maybe you can comfort yourself with the fact that your letters are a real comfort to me and a great fortification for my psyche.

Susie is very cheerful. She's supposed to go back to school next week. She seems to have regained most of the weight she lost and her appetite is remarkable. If I now tell you that yesterday I bought a bottle of cognac and a small bottle of liqueur, then you will understand that I intend to have a little company in. [*In the last several lines the typing is very irregular and eventually stops and switches to handwriting.*] Oh God, the machine is suffering from constipation again!

So long --------

Deine Friedel

[*Handwritten*:]

How did you handle Christmas with the carriers in the past?

3 The letter Elfriede refers to is one Johannes wrote his parents (Chapter 3) telling them he had obtained his American immigration visa and would leave soon for New York.

4 A police notary was required to certify the inventory of Rudolf and Josephine's furniture that the Tischendorf firm was to ship.

5 *At sea* = on the boat for America. Annemarie was the wife of Erich von Baeyer, who had emigrated to Cleveland the previous summer.

If money, how much?

Cigarettes? How many?

For the moment our carriers are mostly as reliable as you could want.

Accompanying letter from Susanne.

Düsseldorf 9 December 38.

Dear Papi.

Mutti told me that Manfred sometimes shovels the snow away in front of the house. You can help him. I hope there is a Saint Nicholas over there, he has a lot of places to go. Hopefully he won't forget that you moved, otherwise your things will end up here. There was a concert at Miss Fleischauer's on the 21st. I am learning some Christmas songs. So now I have to wait with this letter until I eat lunch and exercise.

So now I have exercised and it was very nice with a lot of running and playing mop, that means that Erika who also takes recorder with Miss Fleischauer sits on the floor me too and and then we go swish, swish, swish, swish, swish across the room and then we were in the other corner. We did that ourselves but when Miss Fleischauer came she said that was not good for the seats of our pants.

Now lots of Christmas OOOOOOOOOOO and wishes *Deine Susie*

SUNDAY, DECEMBER 11, 1938

Letter from Elfriede in Düsseldorf to Johannes in Zürich.

Düsseldorf, 11 Dec. 1938

Mein lieber kleiner Peter,

Because the typewriter is entirely constipated you will have to try to read my handwriting. After I didn't sleep well again, and after I persuaded another carrier at the train station to do Schindler's route, and after Schindler did his route himself after all, and after the telephone was kind to me this morning, and after the Frankfurt balance sheets, which came this morning, weren't much different from mine, I'm in a slightly better mood.

I'm following the progress of your travels with some trepidation. If things don't change you still might have to use the air [trip] as a backup. Karl [Lenzberg] will go [to Holland] in the next few days and then in several months he will go to his relatives in Venezuela. A position there looks as good as certain for him, though there is sometimes some confusion because the letters from that wilderness on the equator often go astray. Anyway, it looks like Karl and Hilde's strenuous efforts of the last few weeks will be successful.

Yesterday afternoon I went for a Christmas walk with Oma and Susie and today, the Sunday when the stores are open [for Christmas shopping], everyone was amazed at how many people poured into the city in the glorious weather. The Christmas activities that I otherwise love so much now seem pointless to me, but I still have to play them out. During Christmas week Paul and Heidi will probably stay in our bedroom. They liked the rug we gave them jointly with Günter very much.

This evening I am going to Maxhi's,[6] because otherwise I will sit here in the office with balance sheets and after all it is Sunday. Is it possible that it's just a week since we were together? It is a day like that here today, but much, much lonelier. But Susie, who is sitting next to me now, is a real comfort to me. Too bad we can't have a weekend like that every week.

Susie is sitting here reading Elisabeth Forman-Lewis' *Young-Fu of the Upper Yangtze*, and is completely fascinated and captivated, loves it and suffers along with it, is outraged and terribly interested in all the amazing things in China.

With great satisfaction I sent a special present, very small, to Philadelphia for you for Christmas, though I can't say *vivant sequentes*.[7]

1000 Grüße, Friedel

TUESDAY, DECEMBER 13, 1938

Farewell letter from Elfriede in Düsseldorf to Johannes in Paris, with an accompanying letter from Clara Fischer, Günter Fischer, Elisabeth Fischer, and little Peter Fischer. Johannes was in transit from Zürich to Le Havre where he would finally be able to board the S.S. Manhattan *for New York. The* Manhattan *was scheduled to stop in Southampton and Cobh before crossing the Atlantic.*

Düsseldorf, 13 December 1938

Mein liebes Peterchen,

I was rather torn up when I read your letter just now, so to be certain that you find a letter in Paris tomorrow I am writing you now in the light of the morning. The only reason it's light is that the floor lamp is on. We

6 *Maxhi* = Max and Hilla, friends.

7 *Vivant sequentes* = "Long live those that follow."

should be happy now that we have lived through the worst stages and the worst impediments of your leaving. Yet I'm really very sad that the regularity of our letter exchange of the last few weeks will now come to an end. The fact that your departure is now becoming a reality means some anxiety for me. I can imagine your ship leaving under full steam, thinking of nothing else other than how to get you to something better as quickly as possible. If only we knew a little more clearly what that something better is going to look like!

Karl was supposed to take off [for Holland] yesterday. He was lucky enough to get the papers he needs for the trip yesterday morning after a lot of formalities. The von Baeyers are very sad to see that the social environment they have come to love is being scattered to the four winds. It is indeed not pretty. [Their daughter-in-law] Annemarie and her son are probably nearly "over there." I'll be interested to see when you see her again. The business is running smoothly at the moment. I have a terrible cold, coughing and headache and a sore throat.

It's really funny that tomorrow you'll be in good old Felix.[8] How long it has been since we were there, how unbelievably long! It's ridiculous the way all the expectations we had then have vanished in the wind.

Please be good and don't go astray, otherwise I won't come along after you. Seriously, I don't want to be aggravated over such things any more. It was not really my intention to deliver a sermon to you at the last minute, but you have earned it only too well. Or should I suppose that during the last few weeks all of your bad characteristics have disappeared and that in the future you will be a model of virtue? If only that were true![9]

So long!

Enclosed in December 13, 1938 letter—handwritten notes attached on separate sheets:

From Clara Fischer, Elfriede's mother:

Lieber Jo!

At the commencement of your great voyage, may I wish you luck from the bottom of my heart. Hopefully you will have a good trip and be happily reunited with your parents and sisters. Greet them all from us here and please accept yourself my most heartfelt best wishes.

Mother

---

8 *Felix* = Paris. Johannes and Elfriede paid a memorable visit to Paris in June 1937, staying in the Hotel Félix, hence the code name.

9 Original: *Bitte sei brav und geh keine Abwege, ich komm Dir sonst nicht nach. Im Ernst, ich will mich nicht mehr über so was ärgern müssen. Es war zwar nicht meine Ansicht, Dir zum Schluss eine Predigt zu halten, aber Du hast das allzu sehr herausgefordert. Oder darf ich annehmen, dass in den letzten Wochen alle schlechten Eigenschaften von Dir abgefallen sind und Du jetzt und immerdar in strahlender Tugend stehst? Ach bitte doch!*

From Günter Fischer, Elfriede's brother:

Lieber Jo!

The old city seems barren and empty since you've been away. Every young lady I meet there asks me to send you her best wishes, that unfortunately I can deliver to you only in writing. I now see in what great esteem you are held here, particularly by the blonde, Star. Mr. Müller asked after you very cordially. He greatly regretted that the acquaintance was so brief and would gladly have extended it. I wish you all possible success for the future.

Merry Christmas, and best wishes to your parents and sisters.

Dein Günter

From Elisabeth Fischer, wife of Elfriede's brother Herbert:

Lieber Jo,

I send you my sincerest Christmas greetings and best wishes for a happy and fortunate New Year. The same also from Herbert. Best wishes also to your parents and sisters.

Deine Elisabeth

[*Elisabeth's note is followed by a small inky smudge, with an arrow pointing to it and a caption in Günter's handwriting: "This is Peter Cornelius' fingerprint." Peter was the one-year-old son of Herbert and Elisabeth.*]

WEDNESDAY, DECEMBER 14, 1938

Letter from Elfriede in Düsseldorf addressed to Johannes on board the S.S. Manhattan *before its departure from Southampton, England. The letter did not reach the ship on time but was forwarded to Philadelphia, where Johannes received it shortly after his arrival on December 22. When she wrote the letter, Johannes was still in Paris.*

Düsseldorf, 12/14/38

Mein lieber Peter,

This is the last letter that will reach you inside Europe. It's all too strange that after a sleepless night I should search for you in my mind in that beautiful city. It's quite proper that you allowed yourself a second class ticket—cabin class labels bring their own obligations. Did you meet anyone interesting? How relatively carefree we were in Paris last year—despite the concerns that traveled with us—as we walked through the beautiful streets. Will you get to the Musée Cluny, which Manfred recommended so emphatically, this time? I expect that tomorrow I'll still get a report from you and maybe one the day after tomorrow and then nothing until New Years. But at least I can catch up with you via the *Europa*, which leaves two days after the *Manhattan* but arrives there on the same day.

Now I have to convert the Christmas present from [your parents in] Philadelphia, which arrived today in the form of RM 700 deposited into your account (no explanation why it's 700.—, but anyway), into something appropriate for you.

Your *Manhattan* docks once more in Cobh. That is somewhere in Ireland. Maybe you will write once more from there. I'm acting on the assumption that you'll get this letter delivered to you on the *Manhattan*, but who knows if its mail arrangements are any better than on the *Europa*.

Yesterday evening I went to Mother's even though I wanted to go to bed early because of my cold. But the cold seems to be going away without having made itself too horribly noticeable. Then I went shopping. The *Manhattan* will bring you some of the results, but I won't tell you what it is. For Susie I ordered the book that is the companion to the book Betz gave her that she loves. I also bought *Bibi* by Karin Michaelis. Günter is giving her Mark Twain's *Tom Sawyer*. And then I got some blue silk for her for a dress with a lace collar and a new recorder. We won't have as big a Christmas tree this time as last year.

Mrs. Freyberger just arrived, will take care of the office and I can go shopping. In the meantime the Magician was here and said Karl is back again because of a missing visa. In fact there is no visa requirement but you have to have one anyway. I'll let you know as soon as I know more.

The very, very best of luck to you, a smooth sea, no rolling of the ship, nice people but no flirtation! Full steam ahead!

Deine Friedel

WEDNESDAY, DECEMBER 14, 1938

Christmas letter from Elfriede in Düsseldorf to Johannes' family in Philadelphia: his parents Rudolf and Josephine Höber, his sister Ursula Höber, and his sister Gri and her husband Manfred Blaschy.

Düsseldorf, 14 December 1938

Ihr lieben,

This is supposed to be a Christmas letter. But even though all signs outside show that it is Christmas, in my mind it really isn't yet. It's not just that Jo just started out [for America], separating us even further. I can cope with that by thinking of the goal that is the reason for this separation, but it still affects us.

Since you have all of your offspring assembled around you for the first time in five years,[10] those of us who are absent would at least like to be there in the form of a few meager words to wish you all happy and comfortable days. The Christmas box that Mr. Bittner sent off to all of you in ample time should take the place of the things I had wanted to make myself, but for which I didn't find the time since I am now not only the sole proprietor here but the sole slave. I hope I have properly selected products that this country makes better than yours does.

Today is the first quiet day in the business in nearly four weeks. All my feminine virtues have been extinguished, the cooking spoon and the sewing needle lie quietly in the closet waiting for better times. Instead of them, newspapers, typewriters, and the telephone reign. Last week the newspapers didn't get here until noon, and one of the carriers was sick three times (thank God he's better) before they had to deliver me to the insane asylum. Maybe it's because I had to soothe customers 100 times over but I am hoarse and can only whisper piteously. Or is it possible that getting up at 5:30 in the morning and making my way to the train station in the cold isn't good for me? Anyway, there is an old saying that a man who has troubles also has liquor, [11] so some friends gave me a big bottle of whiskey from the Münster country, even though they could have used it themselves in the battle against their own troubles.

The weekly edition of the *Frankfurter Zeitung* addressed to Manfred, which will arrive at Creshiem Road starting next week, is intended for Jo. The rest of you are welcome to read it to the extent he deigns to permit you to do so.[12]

In the garden shop next door they have Christmas trees. What does it look like at your place in Germantown? Yesterday I informed myself about the historical background of Germantown by reading the book that Johannes is getting [for Christmas].[13] But the circumstances in Germantown today are of greater importance to me. Have a good time, and be happy together!

10 *For the first time in five years*: Rudolf and Josephine had not been together with their children for Christmas since they left Germany in late 1933.

11 "*Es ist ein Brauch von alters her,/ Wer Sorgen hat, hat auch Likör.*" Wilhelm Busch, *Die Fromme Helene.*

12 Johannes' subscription to the *Frankfurter Zeitung* was taken in Manfed's name to conceal from the *Frankfurter Zeitung* home office—for a while anyway—that Johannes had left Germany.

13 Elfriede sent Johannes a copy of *America under the Rainbow*, by Alfons Paquet, a recently published book about travels in America.

Euer Friedel

FRIDAY, DECEMBER 16, 1938

Christmas letter from Elfriede in Düsseldorf to Johannes at his parents' house in Philadelphia. It's not clear what it was in his Paris postcard that made Elfriede so angry in her first paragraph.

Düsseldorf, 16 December 1938

Mein liebes Peterchen,

The *Europa* is about to leave Bremen and I have to hurry if I want this letter to catch up with it when it makes a stop in Cherbourg. Your postcard from Paris arrived first thing this morning, and I was very angry that you simply will not do what I want you to. I don't think that the man [unexplained] is an adequate excuse for that because you couldn't have foreseen meeting him. Your intention was bad, and if the reality didn't turn out to be as bad as you intended it's still not anything to your credit.

Your letter and your meeting with Abbott improved my mood a little.[14] Your meeting him is more fantastic than any fairy tale somebody could dream up. I now think that Abbot could have some positive results for you and I will be interested in seeing how that plays out. I thoroughly disapprove of the fact that you have become disloyal to Felix [i.e., the city of Paris]; one shouldn't treat such good old friends so badly.

In the meantime I am still plagued with business problems. Schindler didn't show up again yesterday. He hasn't really recovered from his grippe, so he always has relapses. But by noon the subscribers got their papers anyway. Then I had a blowup with Mr. Milchsack, who didn't get his paper and who ranted horribly because I didn't drop everything here to go and take it to him. With time I'm developing a thicker skin. On Wednesday, Freyberger was here to give me a breather for a day. Yesterday we baked Christmas cookies and Susanne was very helpful.

Also, yesterday I bought a Christmas tree next door, about 8 feet tall. That's smaller than usual in accordance with our reduced family complement. But I didn't reduce the presents—they're the least I can do. I hope the two packages actually get to you in Philadelphia, so you can celebrate a nice Christmas with your family and so I can get a detailed report of your trip and of how things are over there.

14 William "Bill" Abbott was an American Johannes and Elfriede had met on a visit to Washington D.C. in June 1937. In his letter the previous day, Johannes described fortuitously running into him on the street in Paris.

Good luck
have a good time
think of us

Deine Friedel

FRIDAY, DECEMBER 16, 1938

Letter from Elfriede in Düsseldorf to Johannes' parents in Philadelphia. This was an emergency letter written hurriedly to reach the mail ship leaving the next day. It concerned Helene Höber, called Tante Lene or Talene, who was the sister of Johannes' father, Rudolf Höber. She was to some degree mentally disabled from birth and could not live on her own. She was living in a private institution for disabled persons in Kiel, a six-hour trip from Düsseldorf, where Rudolf had supported her for years.

After Kristallnacht, *the Nazis issued regulations requiring the removal of "Jews" from various public institutions. The director of the institution where Tante Lene was housed apparently decided on her own that Tante Lene was "Jewish" and should be expelled. Under the Nuremberg laws of 1936, "Jews" were declared not to be citizens of Germany. Hence the term "citizen" (in German,* Reichsbürger*) became an alternate term for someone legally defined as not "Jewish." Because Tante Lene's and Rudolf's father, Anselm, was born into a Jewish family, she was legally half Jewish (mixed race or* Mischling *in Nazi terminology). The fact that Anselm converted to the Protestant religion as a young man before Rudolf and Tante Lene were born was not of legal significance under the Nuremberg laws. More details on this problem follow in Elfriede's longer letter to Johannes of December 19 and 20, 1938.*

Düsseldorf, 16 December 38

Ihr lieben,

Unfortunately I must send you a letter with bad news. Helene has been given notice to leave the Institution by 31 Dec. and wants to come here [to Düsseldorf] because we are her only relatives in Germany. I will write to the Director [of the institution] immediately to get a postponement at least. Please think the matter over quickly and thoroughly and give a quick answer. Also a letter from you to the Director—it's no longer the old one but a new one appointed recently.

Friedel

MONDAY AND TUESDAY, DECEMBER 19 AND 20, 1938

Letter from Elfriede in Düsseldorf to Johannes in Philadelphia. Before discussing the issue of Tante Lene's expulsion from the institution where she lived, Elfriede tells Johannes about a visit she made with Susanne to their friends Hendrik and Gerlinde Zech who lived in Schalkenmehren in the Eifel mountains, about two hours' drive from Düsseldorf. Hendrik was a political associate of Johannes' who had had to leave Düsseldorf because the Gestapo was watching him.

Düsseldorf, 19 December 1938

Mein lieber Peter,

I hardly know where I should begin, there is so much running around in my poor little head again. 1st, it is rotten cold, 11 degrees F on our balcony today; 2nd, it is now 9:45 A.M. and the newspapers aren't here yet; 3rd, I just got a call from Betz with some news worth relating; 4th, we were in Schalkenmehren yesterday; 5th, last but not least, your letter that left the ship in Cobh arrived, making it clear that the letter I wrote to you to the *Manhattan* didn't reach you. Much more important for me was that your letter arrived today from Cobh, that mysterious city that is not to be found in my atlas. But this city must exist, otherwise your letter could not have come today to warm my freezing heart, because both the exterior and interior temperatures here are at a barbaric level. I find it hard to imagine that in the near future I'll be moving to a country where barbaric temperatures like these are more common, but since I have to imagine it I've decided to invest the little money I have in a pair of high boots.

It is now 11 o'clock and the newspapers just got here, but no complaints yet, probably because it's Monday and because I made everyone aware of that possibility in a recent letter to all subscribers.

I find the problem of Tante Lene very pressing. I wrote to the Director [of the institution] that she should keep her there "until Miss Höber's relatives are able to take some steps in the matter." I also asked for a statement of the reasons [for expelling her] because Lene didn't write anything about them and I was making assumptions based on her questions about Jewish welfare organizations. I wrote to the Director right away that racial grounds are not a an issue, since Lene is of mixed race and a citizen. I sent that letter, as well as one to Lene, on Friday evening. I told Lene she should stay there for now. The situation for her would be far less favorable here because she gets welfare payments in Kiel and can't just move. If that support is terminated, I'll initiate a letter war with the welfare office. I intend to delay everything as much as I can, making reference to the actually responsible relatives being in America. In any event, I explained to the Director that I'm prepared to jump in financially on a temporary basis if that's necessary. Right now I have no idea how things actually stand with Helene, what the terms of the contract are with the institution, whether there's any money for her somewhere or anything at all, or how much is paid to the institution and by whom.

It's a big mistake that Lene is legally responsible for herself and it seems absolutely essential to me to have a conservator appointed for her. I have no idea whether that can be done without a court proceeding, but it is imperative that someone be appointed in Kiel immediately who can take of her affairs professionally.

> §1910 Civil Code: An adult who is not under an order of guardianship may obtain a conservator for himself and his property if he is unable to manage his affairs as a result of physical disability, particularly if he is deaf, blind or dumb. If an adult who is not under an order of guardianship is unable to manage some of his affairs, or a particular category of his affairs, especially his financial affairs, as a result of physical or mental disability, then he may obtain a conservator for these affairs. The conservatorship may be directed only with the consent of the disabled individual unless such a consent is not possible.

This lays out an option that must be initiated immediately, if it hasn't already been done. If Lene has to move out on 12/31 without a new residence having been obtained, then things will become dreadfully complicated, and indeed not just for now but also for the long term because of the welfare department jurisdiction. If we were going to be available here for a longer time it would be worth thinking about whether we could house her here. But the way things stand now that makes no sense and just creates needless costs and difficulties. The most important thing seems to me to be the appointment of a conservator. As you know I can't arrange to have that done, and I request urgently that that be done with all possible haste. What facilities for such a thing exist is something that Seppchen will know better than I as a result of her previous occupation.[15] I know almost nothing at all about that. Ridiculously, no fast ship is departing now or for the foreseeable future. I will put this letter on the *Hansa*, which leaves from Cherbourg on the 22nd.

12/20/38

There was once a German mail system and that was a praiseworthy institution. You used to be able to give them letters and newspapers and they used to send them on the next train to the place where they were

15 As a former member of the Kiel City Council and as a public health physician, Josephine was familiar with the work of various welfare organizations and social service agencies in Kiel.

supposed to go, and when they got there, there was a man called a letter carrier who took the things to the people who were supposed to get them. Unfortunately it was that way once but it's not that way anymore. It is now 6:30 p.m. and the newspapers are not here yet. Nice! True, at 12:30, 59 copies arrived and a part of the business section. But I have found that it's better for no subscribers to get the paper than for 59 to get it and 400 not to.

As a result of the hours-long [train] delays resulting from the cold weather, both the mail and the trains are totally disorganized. Nobody can tell anybody anything, nobody knows anything, you can't find out anything specific. Because of all that I'm going to send you this letter today, even though it shouldn't have to be mailed until tomorrow. Maybe then it will get to Hamburg today and to Cherbourg the day after tomorrow. I'm anxious to hear whether the ocean is frozen solid too. If "over there" it's like it is here, then the crossing must have been a pleasure of a peculiar kind. I'm very happy with the high boots I bought yesterday. I wear heavy socks in them and that way I keep reasonably warm feet even here on my iceberg. My first cold of the season has got me in its grip too. I know I can't move your cold heart with coughing, sniffling, back, throat, and joint pain, but I still have to write you that it's got me. I'm proud of the fact that I didn't get my first cold until December.

Yesterday [our friends] the Trömels and [my brother] Günter were here. At least they had the requisite sympathy for me. Then we boozed it up. The wine was completely cold after 15 minutes outdoors, and the club soda bottle that spent the night outside is now in pieces, both the soda and the bottle. The bottle of cognac I just bought is already half empty.

By the time this letter leaves with the *Hamburg*, it will be our tenth wedding anniversary. Where will our second decade take us? I hope we don't have to wait for our next anniversary to be together again. Your letter did my heart good; how would it be if we could spend my birthday[16] together somewhere in the wide world? I am very anxious to see how things turn out.

Quod dii bene vertant![17]

Deine Friedel

WEDNESDAY, DECEMBER 21, 1938

Radiogram from Johannes aboard the SS Manhattan *underway in the North Atlantic to Rudolf and Josephine in Philadelphia.*

MACKAY RADIO
EXTRA NO PHONE RADIO VIA MRT=

16 Elfriede's birthday was May 12, about five months from when she was writing this letter.

17 *Quod dii bene vertant* = May the gods grant good fortune!

SS MANHATTAN AMAGANSETT NY 111P 21

HOEBER=6701 CRESHEIMROAD PHILAPA

ARRIVE THURSDAY AFTERNOON=
JO

THURSDAY, DECEMBER 22, 1938

Letter from Elfriede in Düsseldorf to Johannes in Philadelphia. This is their 10th wedding anniversary.

Düsseldorf, 22 December 1938.

Mein liebes Peterchen,

Today your good ship should arrive in New York and I am hoping for a cable once you get there. What does the weather look like on that side of the ocean? Are you stuck in fog or in icebergs or in anything else inconvenient? Since yesterday Düsseldorf has lain under deep snow, which doesn't make anyone happy except the children, and the newspapers are more delayed than ever.

[*Business details omitted*]

Your roses [for our tenth anniversary] just got here. That is really a great joy. And Mother came and brought me a pot of flowers. In the midst of troubles there are still comforts to be found. I hope your comfort today is that you land in N.Y. in one piece. May everything go well for you and may our second decade together begin well. You really have much occasion for good wishes. If only reality lives up to those wishes!

The day after tomorrow we will celebrate a somewhat problematic Christmas here, but we'll make it as nice as we can.

Mrs. Freyberger just got here and I will take this opportunity to go to the police station to have the furniture lists notarized [for Tischendorf]. I haven't heard anything from Philadelphia since 27 November. Are they all snowed in? Did Manfred and Gri's furniture finally get there? Please give your father all my best wishes for his birthday [on December 22]. I am really not going to be able to get to writing him a letter.

Best wishes to all of you. But to you most especially good luck and all my love.

Deine Friedel

SATURDAY, DECEMBER 24, 1938 (CHRISTMAS EVE)

Letter from Johannes, two days after his arrival in Philadelphia, to Elfriede in Düsseldorf. This is Johannes' first letter from the United States. Once he reached the United States, he typed most of his letters to Elfriede and kept the carbon copies that are transcribed here.

Readers who have grown up with computers and copy machines may be unfamiliar with carbon copies, the universal method for making duplicates until the 1960s. Carbon paper was a lightweight sheet with a pressure-sensitive ink on one side. The carbon paper was placed behind the original, a second sheet of paper behind the carbon paper, and the three sheets were inserted into the typewriter as a package. The impact of the typewriter keys produced the original image on the first sheet and a duplicate copy by transferring the ink from the carbon paper onto the second sheet. When Johannes typed his letters, he sent Elfriede the original and kept the carbon copy.

In this letter Johannes describes his arrival at the house at 6701 Cresheim Road in Philadelphia, which was big enough for the entire Höber family. Germantown was a pleasant middle-class area of large old single-family houses. The rent was low enough for Rudolf to afford on his modest stipend from the University and would accommodate the new arrivals until they got jobs and their own homes.

There are references to problems with Manfred in this letter and a couple of later ones. What Johannes writes is not completely clear, but there is no further explanation of the incidents available. It should be remembered, however, that Manfred had been fired from a prestigious and well-paid physician's position in Dresden because his wife, Gri, "looked too Jewish." He found it very difficult to start from ground zero in the United States, a country that had no way to recognize his accomplishments.

Philadelphia, 12/24/38

Liebster Peter,

Since the letters I sent from on board at Southampton and Cobh should have been in your hands on the 17th and 18th, and since in the interim nothing has appeared in any newspaper reporting that the *Manhattan* sank with all hands, you know that I indeed I reached my destination on 12/22 [our tenth wedding anniversary]. Instead of bemoaning the fact that on this day of all days we were further away from each other than ever before, I will take the date as a good omen, and will continue to believe that I'll be able to maintain the pace at which I've moved ahead since 11/12.[18] Hopefully the flower man in Zürich functioned in

18 11/12 was the date Johannes left Germany for Switzerland.

accordance with the orders I gave him so that you at least were able to see how very much I thought of you on our anniversary.

Some things about the days from Cobh to New York were already in the letter I wrote on board to Susanne but, like this one, that will probably only travel back on the *Normandie* on Monday.[19] The crossing once again confirmed my opinion about sea voyages: there isn't much pleasure in them and as a means of crossing the ocean they are most deficient. Saturday, Sunday, and Monday, the three days after Cobh, were extremely unpleasant and only by summoning all my energy was I able to prevent myself from becoming seasick, as three quarters of the other passengers did. I had just enough energy left to study the menu, to leaf through a couple of magazines and for the daily movie. After Tuesday, the ocean got calm, but in exchange my tooth, which had not yet been pulled, suddenly began rumbling again. Since among the 320 passengers in Cabin Class there was not a single person—man or woman—who might exercise some charm on me, I did not allow my new handicap to affect me very much—I read and ate and read and ate. (Reading: *Northwest Passage*, very much to be recommended, to the extent it is not too much like *Arundel*.)[20]

I was amazed at how little difference in comfort there turned out to be between Cabin Class on the *Manhattan* and Tourist Class on the *Europa*.[21] Aside from caviar, oysters, and lobster, which you are not exactly crazy about, the service was actually better on the *Europa*. And the passengers!—let's not mention them. Barely a quarter of them were American and among them were at most two who might have been worthwhile if there had been an occasion for a conversation. As a result of the late rebooking my cabin was an inner cabin, which I had to share with an unpleasant man from Berlin, but as the ventilation was better and the vibration less than on the *Europa* it was quite bearable.

After Zürich, everything that had to do with passport and customs went extraordinarily smoothly. The Swiss don't check anything anymore when you exit at the French border and it was hardly different with the French. It took me only 30 seconds with the Immigration Officer who came on board between the Ambrose Light and the Statue of Liberty. I didn't even have to be pulled aside like so many others; whether that was because of Daddy's influential position or because I still had almost all of my on-board money left I don't know. Thus I was able to enjoy my arrival in cold but very clear weather without any excitement in the negative sense but also, to my amazement, without the positive sensation of the first time we arrived here. Perhaps that's because I just can't be as happy all by myself. Perhaps also because, to my surprise, I just couldn't summon up the right sense of disjunction. I think that will only come when I pick you and Susie up in my own car to drive you to our own home.

19 The letter to Susanne was not preserved.

20 *Northwest Passage* and *Arundel* are historical novels by Kenneth Roberts set in the period of the American Revolution.

21 Johannes and Elfriede had taken a vacation trip to the U.S. the previous year (1937) on the *Europa*.

The house at 6701 Cresheim Road, Philadelphia, where Rudolf and Josephine lived with Gri and Manfred Blaschy and their two little girls, along with Johannes and later Elfriede and Susanne. Photograph by the author, 2012.

In spite of the icy cold, Daddy and Seppchen were waiting for me on the pier. That's almost exactly how I would have wished it. At 4 o'clock we docked, at 6 we got on the train for Philadelphia with my suitcases. Manfred and Ulli were at the station with Blue Boy,[22] and a half hour later I made my entrance into the Höber house.

This Höber house in Germantown belongs in the same category of "fairytales" as Uncle Karl in Zürich[23] and Mr. Abbott in Paris. A New England house like in the picture books, with a big porch of white wood, a red brick building with white windows behind a small front yard, with eight rooms and three stories, central heating, hot water, a large kitchen, a cellar, and lots of extra space. The whole thing for $55 [a month], though not counting heating etc. Inside was the furniture from Kiel and Dresden looking as though it had been acquired for this house. As soon as there is less to tell than today you'll get a really thorough description. As you already know, this mansion is one of a hundred other mansions in a spacious suburb surrounded by greenery.

Not as happy as the situation of the house is that of its residents. The tragedy that you and I feared concerning Manfred played out in their first days here. I don't know all the details yet, as I have not yet spoken to Gri by herself and the subject is understandably taboo in the family circle. I only know that during the first week he disappeared without a trace, taking with him his suitcase and leaving behind a slip of paper with three lines of writing, and only reappeared a day and a half later after Gri and Daddy had driven to New York to look for him. Gri was in fact able to whisper to me quickly yesterday, "We are over the hump," but the whole thing has still

22 Consistent with the Höbers' mania for naming cars, Blue Boy was Rudolf and Josephine's big eight-cylinder Model B Ford Sedan.

23 The "fairy tale" involving "Uncle Karl" was the fact that Johannes obtained his U.S. immigration visa in Zürich in less than a month.

cast a shadow over everyone. He is himself now, far more even-tempered than in the last days in Düsseldorf, is interested in his work in his training position with a roentgenologist and is full of hope for a position as an assistant in Saratoga Springs, for which he really has a well-grounded prospect. For this assistant's position he would need neither an internship nor the State Board, both of which he still strongly resists.

Daddy, fortunately, is far and away in the best shape. He seems to have been somewhat paralyzed by concern during the last few weeks over the reality of my arrival. By contrast, Seppchen looks disordered and haggard, so intense and unchanged is her level of activity. But it is important to everyone that I am here now and that you will be coming soon, because it's time for us to take on the role here that we had to take on for years as heads of the European branch of the family.

The first day I was here, however, related to anything but this role. Between Thursday night and Friday morning my cheek swelled up almost as big as it was in Zürich and so Seppchen dragged me from treatment to treatment from 12:30 until 6:30. With such a foul tooth you don't just go to one dentist who does everything that needs to be done. Instead, the lady dentist first stabbed the thing that was about to explode with a sharp pick, then I had to go an x-ray man who took an x-ray, then back to the dentist and on Tuesday I have to go to a third man who will finally remove the troublemaker. The dentist will then handle the aftercare. Since we didn't have the car and since Germantown is three-quarters of an hour from the city, and as the dentist lives at the Fairfax and the x-ray man at City Hall, it took us hours and hours to get around on preposterous transports.[24] But at least now it doesn't hurt anymore and an end to the suffering is in sight.

And now to you. Yesterday your postcard of 12 December arrived forwarded from Zürich, but I had already received your letter to Paris, which you sent later. This morning your Christmas letter to all of us arrived as well as your letter with the bad news about Tante Lene. This afternoon your Christmas letter to me arrived as well as a package that I wasn't allowed to open yet but which upon external examination of its overall condition showed itself to be soft and bendable. Furthermore a package of printed matter came from Günter for me. In addition, the Bittner package has been here for a long time. So I think all that is missing is a second letter you wrote to Paris and the second package you told me about. Is that right? Or did you write just once to Paris?

That you should now get the Tante Lene problem added to your load is really too much. We have therefore already done everything today that is possible for the moment. Daddy wrote to the Director demanding the grounds for the eviction—apparently resulting from mistaken

24 *"Preposterous transports"* = The Philadelphia public transit system at that time consisted mostly of antiquated, overcrowded, slow-moving trolley cars.

information—and asked for a postponement of the termination date on grounds of her misinterpretation of the law.[25] Moreover, Gri wrote on behalf of the family to Ilse Lask's [unidentified] parents—just about the only connection we still have in Kiel—to ask whether they might take her in as a boarder or can find out another place where she can live. Hopefully the Director will at least grant enough delay for us to be able to come up with a tolerable solution.

It seems really weird and implausible to me that today is supposed to be Christmas Eve. Right now I feel like the holidays are just an impediment to my urge to get going [on finding a job]. On the 27th I'll send off letters requesting appointments to everyone to whom I have an introduction or whom I want to search out, so that right after New Year's I can start off on the first exploratory trip (of who knows how many). I can probably get the car for that and head first to New York and Boston. In any event, I'm itching to get to work as soon as possible.

Johannes' photograph of the house at 6701 Cresheim Road, Philadelphia, decorated for Christmas, two days after his arrival in the United States.

Hopefully, *mein lieber Peter*, after all the upset and exertion of the last few weeks, you and Susie will be able to celebrate a nice holiday with the help of Mother and the boys. You certainly have earned it.

Sehr in Liebe,

Jo

MONDAY AND TUESDAY, DECEMBER 26 AND 27, 1938

Letter from Elfriede in Düsseldorf to Johannes in Philadelphia, accompanied by a letter from Susanne.

25 Johannes believed the director of the home thought Tante Lene was Jewish, and Rudolf was seeking to persuade her otherwise.

Düsseldorf 26 December 1938

Mein liebes Peterchen,

Christmas isn't a day when you have much spare time, particularly when the house is full of guests and you still have to operate a business that requires a lot more thought than it's worth. The business this past week was awful and nearly unequalled in our almost 6 years' experience. Even Frankfurt's attempt to bring order out of chaos by shipping the papers much earlier turned out to be less than successful. Nevertheless we were able yesterday [Sunday, Christmas day] to deliver 360 regular subscriptions and 50 weekly editions. And since by now our clients have heard about the chaos in the mail system and since most of them (not Mrs. Ilse Meyer-Rissman!) respect the peace of Christmas, it has now been quiet since Saturday afternoon. But I was really at the end of my rope. A horrible cough won't leave me alone despite all kinds of treatments, and having the telephone start ringing every morning at 6 o'clock for the last week was not exactly good for my health. Now here I wanted to write a Christmas account and it has turned into a newspapers account instead. If it keeps going like this I will become a complete monomaniac.

In any event, on Saturday afternoon it got quiet and then the mailman brought the card from the travel agency saying the *Manhattan* arrived safely on the 22nd. That was so nice—it seems strange that when one has a transport debacle like I've had this week that a mode of transport is so punctual over such a great distance—but I heard from a woman who traveled here from over there that the crossing was very stormy. Hopefully you found a way to enjoy your crossing a little bit anyway.

Shortly after lunch [my brother] Paul and [his new wife] Heidi arrived here to take a nap so that before the festivities they could recover from the long overnight train trip [from Leipzig]. In the meantime I made up a Christmas room in our old style. The tree is not as tall as usual, though still quite stately. It is a splendid Christmas room.

Shortly before everything was done the von Baeyers came by to inspect, actually to bring me a plant. I am regarded as worthy of pity and therefore I am treated nicely. This time Susanne could sing and play pretty recorder songs. She also memorized a pretty poem. I was in a rather off mood but maintained my composure very well, which in comparison with the young married couple [Paul and Heidi] wasn't too difficult. They really are too funny. Since they had slept here they wanted to take part in our sharing of presents. Then the Philadelphia letter to

Susanne was read (I was not honored with one) and little packages from Trömels, Lenzbergs, and Mrs. Freyberger were unwrapped. Hilde gave me a lovely sweater (undoubtedly she thinks I need things to keep warm) and a bottle of French perfume (for whom should I smell good?). For Susie a card game: "With North German Lloyd Around the World." Susanne was very proud of the sum of 2$ [from your parents] in the form of RM 4.90 and shows it to everyone. Helma's [housekeeper/babysitter] table, covered with pink and pale blue underwear, was a pleasure for the men's eyes and Paul, as an old married man (he has not yet fully developed his role) kept staring. Helma lined up a fabulous camellia for me (I mean the flower of that name) so that now my desk, from left to right, is bedecked with: roses from your father from our anniversary on the 22nd, pink flowers from Mother from the 22nd, a Christmas hyacinth from Trömels, an azalea from von Baeyers, and finally the camellia. On the round table red and yellow patterned tulips from Karl and Hilda. Karl is making his second attempt today to find himself better circumstances.[26]

Then we went to Mother's, where it was just the way it always is and very pretty. We plundered great treasures, I a beautiful red handbag that had seduced me with its voluptuousness, and a pair of very elegant woolen gloves (I had looked for some like them without success last year) with leather palms. In the face of the barbarous climate a very gratifying capture. In addition our kitchen forks were supplemented by 3 more. Our library added Pat Mullen, *Man of Aran*, some kind of Irish thing. For Mother I had a bed jacket (for her rheumatism) and the Silanpäa,[27] for Günter a lens for his Retina [camera] and a set of ceramic liquor glasses, for Herbert a superb paint box (since he was the one who got me the gloves I was glad I had picked out such a good one), for Paul a bottle of egg cognac[28] and a jar of marmalade, all on a wooden tray for Heidi. Elisabeth got French perfume. I can't remember now how everyone else was enriched; perhaps when it is written down it doesn't seem as nice as it was. Around 11 I went home with our child and lodgers.

On Christmas morning the telephone rang with the news that half the newspapers were here. In the afternoon the goose at Mother's was as good as ever. Little Peter sat with us in a new highchair. Afternoon coffee was at Herbert and Elisabeth's, from which Susanne and I went home so we could both take a nap.

Mrs. Freyberger cancelled because she has the grippe. Everyone here either has a cold or is sick. It's now 9 o'clock and I have to get to bed, dreading tomorrow and the nightly calls. But the Christmas room will stay as it is. I don't even have the heart to put on the bracelet you sent me

26 Karl Lenzberg had previously attempted to leave Germany for Holland but lacked the necessary papers.

27 Frans Eemil Silanpäa of Finland (1888–1964) of Finland won the Nobel Prize in Literature in 1939.

28 *Egg cognac* is a kind of eggnog.

because it looks so nice in the middle of my table and underneath is the postcard of the *Manhattan*. Everything else is only decoration around it.

Now I am anxiously awaiting your next letter with the account of the crossing. But from the shipping schedule I gather that no letter can be here before 2 January and no Christmas report until 6 January. The shipping is very meager at the moment.

27 December, 38

Once again a work day, but not as bad as I expected, though the papers are late again. The reviews about Heidi are pretty bad. She gets on all of our nerves. For a 24-year-old she is amazingly immature. Whether the intelligence that has not been developed up to now might still appear remains to be seen. They really are a funny pair. Whether Paul can be happy with this arrangement seems questionable to all of us.

Here is Erich von Baeyer's new address: City Hospital, Scranton Road S.W., Cleveland, Ohio. I'm sure you'll search him out and visit him soon. If you fulfill only half the expectations that all possible and impossible people have for you then things can't go wrong for us. Everybody says they aren't worried about you. If good wishes can do anything, then we certainly will be together again soon.

In that spirit, best wishes for the New Year.

Deine Friedel

Accompanying letter from Susanne:

---

27 December 38

Lieber Papi,

Since I have stationery I want to write you a letter. I got a fountain pen from Mrs. Freyberger that I am writing with now. The recorder I got from Mutti is very nice. The recorder from Miss Fleischauer is also swell. I got a book from Trömels: *Peik*. The books I mean are : *Bibi* and *Ho-Ming. A Little Chinese Girl Studies*. They should be very nice. We can be very happy with the snow too because it snowed a lot. But it's already melting and Mutti says: such cold and such snow I have not experienced yet. From Oma I got a "genuine gold" watch.

Viele Grüße und 10000000 O O O

Susie

CHAPTER 5

Philadelphia

MONDAY, JANUARY 2, 1939

Letter from Johannes in Philadelphia to Elfriede in Düsseldorf. Within six days of his arrival in the U.S. he had sent out seven job inquiries and organized a trip to New York with twelve appointments. Some of these were based on introductions he got from an American acquaintance, Bill Abbott, and others were connections from Germany. One of the latter, code named "Doktorpapa," was Emil Lederer, a professor of economics expelled from Heidelberg University in 1933. Lederer was Johannes' doctoral thesis advisor and co-founded the New School for Social Research in New York. "Taxi Dancer" is another code name, unidentified.

Johannes also writes in coded terms about the next steps in procuring immigration visas for Elfriede and Susanne. They had been told in Germany that if one spouse was "settled" in the United States, the other would get preference for a visa on the German quota. This "settled" status of the spouse in America was to be documented on a government Form 575, and that number became the code for the whole scheme. Johannes learned when he arrived in Philadelphia that he could claim "settled" status even before he got a job. There was a setback, however, when an employee of the Immigration and Naturalization Service was ignorant of the preference to be obtained with a Form 575. It must be remembered that in 1938 over 310,000 Germans applied for American immigration visas against a quota of 27,000 granted.

Johannes also addressed another unresolved issue, whether Elfriede would apply for visas for herself and Susanne at the American consulate in Stuttgart or the one in Zürich (code named "Lilly Reiff" after the friend who had hosted Johannes there).

Philadelphia, 1/2/39.

Liebstes Peterchen,

It's really a blessing that Christmas and New Year come only once a year, because these occasions are used by every single large and fast ship of every single line to take off on cruises to Bermuda, to Cuba, or to other such places, and it is apparently inconsequential to the customers of these cruises and to the stockholders of these steamship companies that in the meantime husbands, parents, and children are cut off from all

Elfriede at work at her desk in Düsseldorf. Photograph by Günter Fischer, December 1938.

means of communication with one another. Since the *Normandie* on 26 December, for all practical purposes no ship has sailed eastbound from New York before the arrival of the *Europa*, which is supposed to take this letter over there tomorrow.

Almost worse is the fact that since the *Hamburg*, which left Hamburg on 12/21 and which you apparently overlooked as the last opportunity [to write to me] in 1938, no decent boat has arrived, so that the last thing I heard from you was the two letters (of 12/16) that I already answered on the 24th. That actually made it better that the Christmas mail was only released *peu à peu* from the customs house, and so arrived bit by bit during the course of the week.

The envelope that I had diagnosed as soft and flexible contained the beautiful tie that I really love and that lends a very distinguished note to my symphony in blue, which is generally judged here to be most elegant. The other envelope, which I found here when I arrived but which I was only allowed to open on Christmas Eve, contained Günter's photos. Thank him very much for me; he really went to a lot of trouble with them. The one of you at your desk now decorates my bedside and next to it is the photo of Erich's portrait of Susie.[1]

The next Düsseldorf package unwrapped under the Christmas tree was the Bittner package. You really did that well, *mein Schatz*. The stollen has already been completely consumed and only a few crumbs of all the boxes of candies remain in my and Daddy's private cache. I only succeeded in my claim that the little bag of marzipan potatoes was intended exclusively for me by citing your prior written declaration

1 Erich von Baeyer, a physician, was also a portraitist. He painted Susanne in Düsseldorf and took photographs of the painting to show prospective clients. Passing through Philadelphia on his way to Cleveland, he left one of these photographs with Johannes. Nearly twenty years later he made a gift of the painting to Johannes and Elfriede, and Susanne inherited it when Elfriede died in 1999.

Susanne Höber, age 8. Oil on panel. Erich von Baeyer, spring 1938. Courtesy of Susanne Hoeber Rudolph.

relative to this matter. (I was correct in identifying this as the little thing intended just for me that you put into the package, wasn't I?)[2]

On Tuesday—no mail is delivered here on Sundays and holidays—Susie's package with the dolls and the bookmarks and the little purses appeared, and I distributed them without difficulty in accordance with her instructions in poetry and prose. (À propos, poetry, did she really do the poems all by herself? We find them all really astonishingly good.) And Mother's Baedeker [guide to the United States] came with the same mail. She really pleased me with that. I had no idea that such a thing exists and I think it's really nice that she unearthed it. (Just between the two of us, please check with Kemming whether a newer edition has come out since 1909. It's not important, because even this old edition is very useful. But if a newer one came out you might want to exchange it. In the meantime I will be careful with it so we can still exchange it.) On Friday the Paquet book

2 In her letter of November 30, Elfriede wrote, "Then at lunch I went to Bittner's and picked out a big fat box of goodies for Phila. . . . And in the middle of it is something very small that is only for you. You will have to see if you can figure it out."

arrived as the last Christmas package; after leafing through it, it looks very worthwhile. At the same time the first edition of the *F.Z.* arrived.[3] Many thanks to everyone who had a part in sending all these things.

The nicest thing on Christmas Eve was the kids. Monika [18 months old] was terribly excited about the lighted Christmas tree and beamed even more than usual, and [four-year-old] Janka sang two Christmas carols along with Gri. It was a really nice holiday, even in the near total absence of gifts because of our need for frugality.[4] I'm sure you and Susie won't hold it against me when I say that what I missed most was going with you from the Christmas tree in our house to the second Christmas tree at Mother's with the boys.

While we are on the subject of Christmas, all of us are looking forward to your report on what kind of Christmas present you decided to buy yourself with Kiel's help.[5]

Since Sunday it has been one social event after the other. Gri and Manfred are still chronically tired, especially in the evenings. Gri has more justification than Manfred because she really has a lot to do with the children and the housework, although she has been temporarily getting a lot of help from Seppchen, who isn't going back to work in the lab until tomorrow. A whole house with 7–8 people and only four hours of Suzy[6] really makes for an awful lot of work. So I take very seriously what everybody always says about America and make my bed every morning and dry the dishes. The day before yesterday I swept the entire staircase with a dustpan and brush and a couple of times I braided Janka's pigtails accompanied by much yelling on her part.

For my own purposes as far as contacting people is concerned, my arrival time in the middle of the holidays was, as expected, inopportune. Last Thursday [December 29], I sent seven letters to New York requesting appointments, five to addresses I got from Abbott and one each to Doktorpapa [Emil Lederer] and one to the valiant Taxi Dancer. On Thursday morning I will drive there myself and probably stay until the middle of the day Saturday. In addition, the agenda includes Wolfi Huber, Paul junior, Michels [unidentified], Stös[7] (if they're still there), Opps [unidentified] and maybe a previous *F.Z.* fellow manager (Mr. G.) who is also there now. I have also fired up a couple of things here [in Philadelphia] that are not uninteresting.

While these negotiations are pending, I've divided my time between the dentist, the immigration office, and preparing for the driving test. For the latter I have to learn the traffic regulations—the rest is a breeze and may even get taken care of this week. The dentist—a third one following the

3 Elfriede sent Alfons Paquet's *America Under the Rainbow* and arranged to have the weekly edition of the *Frankfurter Zeitung* mailed to Johannes in Philadelphia.

4 *Frugality*: at this time, Rudolf and Josephine were supporting themselves plus the four Blaschys and Johannes on an income of less than $400 per month, and their rent alone was $55 per month.

5 *Kiel's help*: as Christmas presents to Elfriede and Susanne, Rudolf and Josephine had sent a sizable check drawn on their Kiel savings account.

6 Suzy was a part-time maid on Cresheim Road. Like most middle-class Germans of the time, Rudolf and Josephine and Johannes and Elfriede had had full-time help in Europe and were not accustomed to doing most kinds of housework.

7 Wolfi Huber was a friend of the family and son of Josephine's best friend. Paul junior was the son of Rudolf's distant cousin, Paul Hoeber, the publisher. The Stös were Erich and Elfriede (Friedel) Stötzner, longtime friends who emigrated to New York. He had been a journalist with the *Frankfurter Zeitung*.

diagnosis woman and the X-ray man—rendered me totally insensible with some dreadful gas and then pulled the tooth, whose granuloma impressed even Manfred, who is familiar with granulomas. Fortunately the tooth doesn't have to be replaced.

More amazing was my first encounter with a real American bureaucrat [at the Immigration and Naturalization Service office]. I thought of all the stories about the "spoils system" when it became apparent that the guy I was dealing with didn't know the first thing about the law he was administering. He insisted steadfastly that Form 575 gives no preference, and it wasn't until I brought him the regulations to look at that he confirmed to his own surprise that I was right.

I need you to let me know as soon as possible about your wishes as to two points:

1.) Are you going to choose Lilly Reiff or would you rather go to Uncle Karl in Stuttgart? The good experience I had there speaks in favor of Aunt Lilly. But you know better than I whether Uncle Karl's good sides outweigh his bad ones. But since no one can say precisely how much 575 will shorten the process, there might be an advantage to the uncle who is closer to you.

2.) We originally thought that 575 would function only after I had a job here. But that's not correct. The preference works whether I'm employed or not. Since, as I said, no one can estimate how long the whole process will take, then perhaps it would be best to get the whole thing started now, in the belief that by the time this is over my lucky star will long since have flung a meteor of gold and silver into our backyard. But first I would like to hear your opinion with respect to this speculation.

If you decide against Lilly Reiff and in favor of acting right now, then you have to get an application form as soon as possible. Everything else will then be done from here. If you decide in favor of Lilly Reiff, then you just need to let us know that and indicate whether or not you first want to wait and see how things turn out for me.

Note: To understand the next paragraph, note that Manfred, like all immigrant doctors, was faced with the difficult task of obtaining an American license to practice, as foreign medical credentials were not recognized. Obtaining a license required mastering English, taking written and oral exams and, in some states, serving an internship. In Germany, Manfred was chief physician at a prominent sanatorium (Marlene Dietrich was a patient), and his indignation over being required to be reexamined in America did not make his transition easier.

In order to understand the situation here, you will be interested in Manfred's situation and why he hasn't begun an internship yet. Since I arrived I have learned something about this. First, all internships here begin in July and Manfred didn't get here until October. Second, it turns out that in the state of New York you can take the State Board without doing an internship. Third, he would like to avoid the year's internship if at all possible. Fourth, his language skills have turned out to be insufficient to begin a job immediately. And finally—and this is what tipped the scales in the analysis—Daddy has already prepared something so well—namely a summer job in Saratoga Springs—that he will almost certainly get the position that will open up there on 5/1. Since Saratoga is in the state of New York, he can do the exam from there, and maybe even more or less right after it. The fact that it's another five months until that starts is no problem. Every day now he works as a volunteer for four hours in the morning for the local University radiologist and works on the literature in the field in the afternoon so he makes progress at least as quickly as he would as an intern.

Your two letters of the 16th are indeed the last ones I got from you. Last week the New York office of the US Lines sent me the letter you had addressed to me "On Board the *SS Manhattan*, Le Havre" with the notation that it didn't reach the ship in Le Havre in time.

As to social events here: the nicest was a dinner at our house with Bazetts and McCouch's[8] and their son. They all asked warmly after you. In fact, you arouse almost more interest here by being absent than you would if you were here.

But I certainly cannot say that for myself.

In diesem Sinne,

Dein Jo

MONDAY AND WEDNESDAY, JANUARY 2 AND 4, 1939

Letter from Elfriede in Düsseldorf to Johannes in Philadelphia. Part of the letter concerns problems getting the newspaper carriers to complete their collections of fees from subscribers. The carrier named Schindler had become unreliable and by the end of December had still not turned in his collections from November.

Düsseldorf, 2 Jan. 1939

Mein lieber Peter,

8 Profs. H. C. Bazett and Grayson P. McCouch were on the medical faculty at the University of Pennsylvania. Johannes and Elfriede had first met them on their visit to the United States in the summer of 1937.

It feels like I haven't written you for a long time, but I didn't pass up any reasonable ship in the intervening period. Now this morning I finally got your letter and the connection is in place again.

Business: After Christmas things got better because Frankfurt started shipping the papers earlier and earlier so now we get the papers at the usual time—albeit a little out of date—and the phone doesn't perpetually irritate me [with complaint calls]. Then preparation for the Ultimo[9] demanded a lot of attention between the holidays, which is not a good time to get much work done. But on Saturday, the 31st of December at 6:30 I was able to leave to prepare for Paul's wedding celebration, having completed the invoices, balanced the accounts, and straightened up. I find the Ultimo to be a lot of work but I *can* do it. I still have a couple of small problems. Schindler works two days and then is sick for two days and in addition he is hasn't turned in RM 165 from last month. I have decided to end his situation one way or another once I have the money in my hands. Either he's going to deliver regularly or I'll hire a woman who was referred to me. I feel personally so worn out that I have to work up the nerve to make that kind of decision.

Last Wednesday we went over to my mother's, where the Trömels were visiting. Then all of a sudden some mulled wine appeared and for health reasons I couldn't turn that down and it ended up with Herbert and Günter getting into a ridiculous condition. Even days later I was laughing about it so much that it hurt. It was wonderful. And on Saturday the festivities for Paul began and that kept on going until today when the last guests left Düsseldorf. Paul had invited two people from Hamburg, six from Hannover, two couples, one married man (whose wife was taking care of sick children), and one single guy. It was a really nice crowd that felt completely at home with us after a short time. I had packed Paul and Heidi and Susanne on the couch and made Susanne's room available to the single guy. Mother's was very nice, and nicest was a great bar set up in Paul's former room, whose capacity for holding people we had previously greatly underestimated. Herbert was a terrific bartender. All the walls and doors were decorated with wonderful drawings. And just imagine that your inconstant bride had a great time carrying on until 4:30 in the morning and was among the last to leave. Very, very tired and in high spirits we found ourselves around the breakfast table around noon and made incredible quantities of toast. In the afternoon I was alone with Susie, because everyone else went back over to Mother's. But yesterday afternoon about 10–20 people gathered here, and in the evening all of us went to the Golden Kettle and later to Fatty's.[10] This whole group is usually quite orderly—Paul swears it—but on this occasion! I can't quite describe it, but it was one of these

9 *Ultimo* = end-of-the-month business procedures. See Chapter 3, footnote 20.

10 Both the *Goldene Kessel* and *Fatty's Irish Pub* are bars that still exist in Düsseldorf today.

fantastic, completely unlikely situations like the old days that once in a while becomes possible again. I regret that I lack the poetic capacity to do the situation justice. In the end it wasn't 11 o'clock, as we originally planned, but 2 A.M. when we got home.

The phone started ringing again at 6 this morning with complaints, but also two new classified ads. When you get down to it, everything here begins and ends with the newspaper.

Since your letter got here, I can already picture the whole Germantown setup a lot better. Does a house like that also have a furnished kitchen? And if so, with what is it furnished? And where will our house be? For my underdeveloped ambitions as a housewife it would be better not to have eight rooms.

Your tooth really aroused my sympathy, and I hope it's gone now. Your description of the dental expedition together with Seppchen was really nice. *Peterchen* led by Mommy's hand through the big world, or mother and son as playmates.

I can readily imagine that the last few weeks haven't been easy. Gri and Manfred lived on a Magic Mountain [in the Dresden sanatorium] up to now and only had to deal with Magic Mountain problems.[11] To have that [professional] situation not yet fixed up and then to have to deal with new things in a new country plus two small children—they had a lot happening. And different people vary in their ability to deal with problems.

In the business with Tante Lene you reacted the same way I did. Since I haven't heard anything more, I assume that my explanation of the "racial" circumstances put the matter off at least for a while, though it's not completely cleared up yet. Marianne suggested I might refer Helene to the Protestant church office. That's also the best place to secure a conservator for her. Or should we ask the Director to see to that, if she is willing to? I am very dubious about setting up anything with the Lasks because that might interfere with more permanent possibilities.[12]

Next the Finance Bureau was curious about Daddy. I was able to satisfy their curiosity. It seems to be rare for a citizen to file an inventory because of a non-Aryan wife.[13]

1/4/39

A dissipated life style and a full-time job are really too much for a woman like me. So I've now given up on the gay life and returned to the job. Yesterday I (1) hired a new carrier, a Mrs. Vossen, who will do Schindler's route and (2) was unable to connect with Schindler. He didn't

11 *Magic Mountain.* Elfriede alludes to Thomas Mann's novel of the same name set in a sanatorium in the swiss Alps. She is analogizing Dresden's *Sanatorium am Königspark*, where Manfred was a physician and had lived with his family, to the luxurious and introspective isolation of Mann's *Berghof.*

12 The Lask family were among the few remaining acquaintances the Höbers had in Kiel, and the family asked their help in arranging care for Tante Helene. This strategy was discussed in Johannes' letter to Elfriede of December 24.

13 *Non-Aryan* in this case means Jewish. For a discussion of the Nazi definition of *citizen*, see Chapter 1. For some purposes, Rudolf successfully maintained that he was not Jewish, but Josephine fell within the Nazi definition of "Jewish" because her parents were. As described in Johannes' letter to his parents from Solda (September 4, 1938, Chapter 2), Rudolf was required to file an inventory of all their property in Germany based on the fact that Josephine's parents were Jewish.

respond to my registered letter and I didn't have a lot of time yesterday to track him down at home, but he usually isn't there anyway. At any rate the deliveries to the subscribers are taken care of and tomorrow I'll go on the hunt for [Schindler's] money. If I didn't have to worry about the RM 165 from Schindler, things wouldn't be too bad at all. Since my clothing supply has recently been increased by the addition of woolen slacks I don't have to freeze as much as before.

Your letter to Susie arrived a day after the one to me and we both liked it a lot. Today the Magician was here again. Joy and sunshine reign in Cleveland because the family has been reunited.[14]

Alles Gute, alles Liebe. Deine Friedel

WEDNESDAY, JANUARY 4, 1939

Letter from Johannes in Philadelphia to Elfriede in Düsseldorf, thirteen days after his arrival in the United States.

Phila, 1/4/39, early morning.

Liebster Peter,

On Monday morning I mailed my impatient letter about your long silence, and yesterday both of yours from the 20th and 22nd arrived. Lord, mysterious are the ways of the European postal systems. I would like you to make a note of the date you get this letter. I will mail it later today from the main post office so it still reaches the *Manhattan* in New York, which leaves shortly after midnight. Let's see if it works. (*A propos* mail connections, don't forget to send American Express 5 marks so that you continue to get the mail schedules.[15])

All six of us really enjoyed both of your letters. After reading them over twice I decided they were appropriate for the whole family and we all admired the fact that in the horrible pre-Christmas days you retained your gallows humor undamaged. I only hope the nightly sojourn in the icy cold at the train station and the post office didn't make your cold worse and mess up the holidays. At a distance of 3000 miles your cold makes more of an impression on me than when I'm standing next to you. For our part, on New Year's Day we stood for hours in normal coats on the street with Janka and watched the famous Philadelphia Mummers Parade, a *Karneval*[16] type of procession *à l'Americaine*. The parade was much less entertaining than the neighborhood we accidentally landed in, a section of the eastern part of the city that is heavily populated with Negroes, who as spectators put on a much more interesting performance than the big show itself.

14 *The Magician* = Prof. Dr. Hans von Baeyer. His daughter-in-law Annemarie arrived safely in Cleveland, where his son, Erich von Beyer had moved some weeks earlier.

15 American Express published a monthly schedule of ships crossing the Atlantic, which Johannes and Elfriede relied on to time their letters.

16 *Karneval* is the week-long celebration before Lent that includes parties and costumed parades, most famously in Cologne. It is mentioned frequently in the letters in the coming weeks.

What you write about Tante Lene is of course the only correct way to regard the situation and since, as far as we know, the acute question of her placement since the 1st has been taken care of, we will take the necessary steps to get a conservator named for her. Everyone here agreed with what you wrote to the Director. Once we realized that Daddy's letter to the Director wouldn't be in her hands before the 31st, we sent Tante Lene a telegram. Now we are waiting anxiously for the reaction to all these efforts.

Yesterday I spent almost the whole day in the fantastic Public Library on the Parkway and informed myself as to what kinds of periodicals they have here. And tomorrow morning I'm going to New York. Doktorpapa responded very cordially, Stös very excited. I'll stay with Wolfi Huber, who has his own apartment. So far only one of Bill Abbott's addresses has responded, and that one very regretful to be away this week but invited me to dinner the next time I am there. The others could hardly have replied because of the holidays. Even so, there are twelve appointments on the list for 2½ days. You will get a report soon.

Jo

SUNDAY AND MONDAY, JANUARY 8 AND 9, 1939

Letter from Elfriede in Düsseldorf to Johannes in Philadelphia. Among other things, she describes her dealings with the German Finance Bureau. Elfriede planned to sell securities from Rudolf's Kiel bank account to pay the Tischendorf moving company to transport Rudolf and Josephine's remaining furniture to the United States. The Nazis, however, had restricted sales of negotiable securities by "Jews." The family conceded that Josephine was Jewish under the Nuremberg laws but asserted that Rudolf was not because his mother was "Aryan." The "Jewish levy" refers to the billion-mark fine the Nazis levied on Germany's Jews for "causing" Kristallnacht.

Düsseldorf, 8 January 1939

Mein lieber Peter,

My life is once again more or less normal. The woman carrier I hired to replace Schindler seems to be behaving herself. There haven't been any complaints for the last three days. The worst of the Ultimo—it was really bad—is behind me. After I threatened Schindler with prosecution in a registered letter he finally came here trembling and promised to pay this week. He told some confused story about "stolen or lost," which I didn't believe and told him so. I still have some small hope for getting the money back.

Today the enclosed letter arrived from the Lasks about [a possible residence for] Tante Lene, which I will answer gratefully tomorrow. But you clever people have probably long since had an answer from the Director and have already done something about it.

Yesterday Hilde and I got together. Karl writes very contentedly. He's in Utrecht at the university and can prepare himself there for tropical medicine. His letters sound as cheerful as yours from the Ütli [Zürich] when you were there. Things look really good for his future; he has a job, at least starting in the fall, and it's adequately paid. Hilde still has some things to take care of, but now she has at least one less worry. Karl's address is Heerenstraat 5, Utrecht.

1/9/39

I advised the Finance Bureau here—by telephone—that Prof. Höber is a citizen and reported his holdings to them only because his wife is of Jewish origin, and that Prof. Höber's property is therefore not subject to the Jewish levy.[17] If the Finance Bureau wants that in writing I will give it to them. I believe that is correct and I complained about their mistake because a simple person like me can't understand the thicket of regulations. At any rate I don't want to get caught up in all the twists and turns.

Everyone always asks after you so nicely and everyone sends you their very best wishes.

More soon.

Deine immer noch husten- und halswehgeplagte Ehefrau Elfriede
Your still-coughing and still-sore-throat-plagued wife Elfriede.

TUESDAY, JANUARY 10, 1939

Letter from Johannes in Philadelphia to Elfriede in Düsseldorf (two weeks after his arrival in America).

Phila, 1/10/39.

Liebstes Peterchen,

The week began as beautifully as possible yesterday at 7:30 in the morning when Janka brought me your letter about the New Year holiday

17 This is a follow-up to Elfriede's letter of January 2 and the explanation in footnote 12, above. In this context, Elfriede uses the word "citizen" as a code for "non-Jew," as the Nuremberg Laws revoked the citizenship of "Jews." Despite Elfriede's explanation, the Finance Bureau eventually assessed a levy of 3,600 marks, approximately 20 percent of Rudolf's holdings in negotiable securities. On February 19, 1939, Rudolf filed an appeal of this ruling with the Finance Bureau, which agreed, reversed the levy and marked Rudolf's file *Arier*—Aryan—meaning he was not subject to the levy on "Jews." The author located the original records of these transactions in 2013 in Berlin in the *Bundesamt für zentrale Dienste und offene Vermögensfragen* [Federal Office for Central Services and Unresolved Property Questions].

while I was still in bed. Peter, what wonderful letters you write, letters that make me feel close to you even over 5000 miles—or is it kilometers?—letters that don't lose their immediacy even when they are 14 days old, letters you write as soon as the business and your many obligations leave you a little time and quiet. Even when I tell myself it's just five weeks since we saw each other, and that at best this will be the smaller portion of the total time we will be separated, my longing for you and for Susie gets greater every day. As nice as everyone is to me here they can't possibly replace the two of you. Although it would be great if I had a job before you get here, I really miss you most during these first weeks of orientation and adaptation. If you add to that the family holidays I've missed, then it is not surprising that my heart travels over to all of you and can't be called back on command.

I was very glad that in spite of the cold weather and your cold, in spite of business worries and the general bitter-sweetness, you were able to have a nice Christmas. With the help of your letter, its warmth radiated all the way over here, and when I read it aloud to the whole family last night, I had the feeling that it was really soothing for Pa-Mu, who still feel wounded by Manfred's behavior and whom I try to comfort day and night by acting the part of "sunny boy," which I don't always feel like at all. In the interim I uncovered that when Gri went to New York with Daddy to look for Manfred, in her anxiety she told him about the experiences last year [not further explained], because Manfred had told her, when he informed her about his decision nearly daily during the preceding week, that he would leave Pa-Mu an explanatory letter. So you can imagine the work I've had trying to rebuild things here on top of everything else. Sometimes I think that in the two weeks I've been here things have gotten noticeably better, but Seppchen's emotional instability is shockingly greater than ever. When you think seriously about what it means for Pa-Mu that they had to experience this shock [with Manfred] just when they should have fulfilled what they had been hoping for for five years, namely reuniting the family here, it's no wonder that they haven't regained their equilibrium yet.

What pleased me most in your Christmas letter was the way all our old friends took care of you. I plan to write all of them a round-robin letter, but I will send it to you first so you can send it to make the rounds. You forgot to mention what you gave Susie and what she got from Mother and the boys, but that will surely be in her own letter, which hopefully is on the way. The Paquet book that you gave me is exceptionally charming. I am reading pieces of it in the evening here in the family circle and we're all enjoying it greatly. Did you see there's a whole chapter about Germantown and that Philadelphia is described extensively? One can't recommend this book too highly to people who want to learn something new about things here.

And now to me. I'm terribly busy. Seppchen just tested me on the 68 questions from the Pennsylvania Vehicle Code that I sweated over memorizing this morning. My learner's permit came yesterday and tomorrow I want to take the driver's test, because the day after tomorrow I'm going to Washington for two days, possibly three. I was invited to stay with Maurice and Sandy [unidentified], who were here for an hour on Saturday afternoon and greeted me like an old friend—Maurice even embraced me. In addition, I have been announced at his father-in-law's and at Papa Abbott's, and Maurice promised me at least one important interview. Before that I have an important appointment here tomorrow afternoon after the driver's test and on Monday I will go for the entire next week to New York.

The 2½ days [in New York] last week were completely fruitless, though I made some connections. Since then, three of the five New York addresses that I got from Abbott replied cordially and from them I hope for connections that may be less fruitless. The most disappointing were Doktorpappa and Taxi Dancer. The former was charming as always but completely unproductive and the latter terribly overworked though honestly interested. He will look around for something, but there isn't much to be expected from that bunch. Even shaking a lot of old hands was a lot less satisfying than I had imagined it would be. Café Krall in Heidelberg ten years ago was warm and exciting; discovering it again in New York feels like a rendezvous with a mummy.

Just as enjoyable as my meeting with Paul [Hoeber] junior was a lunch that followed with [his mother] Catherine and [sister] Jenny just before my trip back.[18] Jenny had to leave after ten minutes to shop for furniture; in two weeks she's marrying the assistant editor of a technical journal and said goodbye to me saying, "Now we two Hoebers have met at last and the next time we see each other my name won't be Hoeber any more." So I lunched alone with Catherine and was completely taken by this lively perfect lady, who last year stood somewhat in her husband's shadow.

When I got back here Maurice and Sandy were here, and for dinner Bettina Meyerhof[19] came from Swarthmore with a very nice American classmate. On Sunday, in radiant sunshine, all eight of us—Ulli had off—took a wonderful excursion to Valley Forge, a famous battlefield in the Independence War, which we missed last year and which has been transformed with great care into a National Park. It was so warm that we lunched outdoors on the tables and benches of the picnic area, and Daddy, Manfred, Janka and I stormed the slopes of the well-preserved ramparts of the fortification once defended by Washington.

18 Paul Hoeber Sr. was Rudolf's second cousin and a large medical book publisher. Johannes and Elfriede met him and his two sons and daughter the previous year, but he died shortly thereafter. Catherine was Paul Sr.'s widow and Jenny was their daughter.

19 Bettina Meyerhof was the daughter of Otto Meyerhof, who years before had been Rudolf's assistant at the Physiological Institute in Kiel and who won the Nobel Prize in physiology in 1922. He joined Rudolf at the University of Pennsylvania in 1940.

Enough! This evening Gri, Manfred, Ulli and I are going to a movie downtown for the first time, probably *The Citadel*. I went to my first one here in Germantown with Pa-Mu.

The next letter you get will probably be from Washington.

Dein Jo

WEDNESDAY AND THURSDAY, JANUARY 11 AND 12, 1939

Letter from Elfriede in Düsseldorf to Johannes in Philadelphia.

1/11/39

Mein liebstes Peterchen,

Damn the shipping schedules! Based on them, I concluded that the *Europa* would arrive in Cherbourg on the 9th, so yesterday I chased every mailman to see if your letter was here, but it didn't get here until this morning. Since the mail today from Frankfurt and similar places is uninteresting and doesn't require any work, I have time to write you so this letter can be taken by the *Aquitania* on the 14th.

The two weeks around Christmas still strike me as thoroughly dreadful even now that I have a halfway normal life back. With respect to the Christmas things I still need to note: Of course the marzipan potatoes were meant for you alone. A newer Bädeker than the one from 1909 indeed does not exist, and there was a long discussion here as to whether one could give something so old as a present, but in view of its many charts and maps we advised Mother, who discovered it all on her own, to go ahead with it. The Paquet should have been there for Christmas, since I dispatched it in time to reach the *Europa*'s Christmas sailing. I had even taken the delays that were common at that time into account. I am happy that the *F.Z.* [subscription] is already functioning. I still need to think over a Christmas present for myself. I think it's going to be a handbag, medium size, to replace the black one I use all the time. Then I'll be equipped for the next two years.

I find amazing your statement that Gri and Manfred are chronically tired, especially in the evening. Prize question: how long will this go on? At the same time I can readily believe that Gri really has a lot to do. The fact that in your current environment you are developing into bed-making, dish-drying, stairway-cleaning model husband fills me with great hopes for the future.

And that I now finally hear how things are going with Manfred! The way you describe it, things seem more plausible than we thought. But why didn't these jackasses ever write anything intelligible about this?

Oh and then that you went to the Immigration Office in the first week!!! I'm totally pleased and flabbergasted. Now I have to make a hard decision. With the help of a preference and your Swiss [quota] number, I think I too will be counted in [the Swiss quota]. If that's the case, then the whole thing can't take very long, since we heard here that other "Swiss" people were completed in two months. I'm therefore leaning in the direction of [the consulate in] Stuttgart. Overall it's much easier. It doesn't take so much time and money. A visit to Lilly Reiff appeals to me, but the timing would be so uncertain, since the Foreign Exchange Bureau runs a lot more slowly these days.[20] I never thought, by the way, that 575 wouldn't function until you had a job. It's possible that your father will have to provide an affidavit of support for Susie and me since you aren't employed yet.

I want to write you about something that is very much on my mind and that is bothering me a lot. That is Mrs. Freyberger. Please look around to see if there isn't some possible way to bring her into your vicinity quickly. The whole thing is too awful. She has already decided to sail to Shanghai with the next decent ship because you don't need a visa there, but it's pretty much the most hopeless place in the world. Her job is awful, and she has looked really pitiful for weeks. Last week, when she was here and told me about it, I told her she should just pack her suitcases and come here. I haven't heard from her since then, so I'll write her again today. If you can, ask around whether there isn't some way at all to help her out. Ultimately she can do everything and is ready and willing to do any kind of work. It can't be done with an affidavit of support alone, however, because that takes too long. Wouldn't it work as a "member of our household"?

I find the picture of 6701 Cresheim Road great. Dear Peter, please don't rent me such a big house—I would have to work too hard and I'm so lazy. Regrettably I have no opportunity these days to exercise this, my most pronounced and lovable characteristic. Never forget that an angry God punished Eve for the apple with work, and that by work he undoubtedly meant housework (not that I find other kinds any better). I'm more in favor of the apple and less of punishment. Who on earth cleans all the windows in the house? Don't forget that I have little or no need to show off, at any rate no more than is consistent with a reasonably comfortable lifestyle. That way we also get to keep all the money, to the extent we have any. By the way, since when are you Ph.D.? It looks very nice, but a

20 *Foreign Exchange Bureau*: If Elfriede was to go to Zürich to apply for an American immigration visa, she would need Swiss currency, which could only be obtained with the approval of the German Foreign Exchange Bureau. This would be difficult because by the end of 1938 the German government tightened up currency regulations, in part to prevent tens of thousands of "Jewish" émigrés from taking German currency with them.

little like titular pretentiousness. On the other hand, since you got your doctorate in the philosophical faculty it does have the appearance of justification. And that an American typesetter even has those cute little periods relieves me greatly.[21]

Do you know where I was last night? Not at the movies or any similar debauchery, but at an air defense course, evenings from 8–10 at the Scharnhorst school. For TEN evenings I will be introduced to the mysteries of cellars and skies.[22] And here I had the good intention of taking classes two evenings a week at Berlitz! Now that's out the window. Everything's out the window.

The 2nd mail just brought the letter from Seppchen and Daddy, which had to go through Customs because of its lumpy shape. The letter gives the overall impression that you have been given the role of the life of the party. You see? But I was right about your laundry. You could easily have had it laundered in Zürich, but it seems to be an eternal and unwritten law that sons must pour their unwashed laundry out upon their mothers. Paul did the same thing, but I am afraid that sons overrate the pleasure that they thereby provide to their mothers. So that you will not be dependent on members of your family who are prepared to darn things, I am sending you herewith another pair of socks that were here, as well as a single glove, whose twin will undoubtedly show up soon. If you have other wishes let me know, to the extent they lie in the area of wardrobe. Packages cost a lot, as I found out unexpectedly with the Bittner box.

[*Later.*] Mrs. Freyberger was here. Her regular employers are behaving so badly to her as to be beyond all imagining. They are now going to stay where they are until 1 March. After getting advice from a knowledgeable source, she has now given up on Shanghai and will try to get a position in a household in England. Those people should just help her find a position. I will write to the Schlossmans about this shortly and then Mrs. F. can do the rest herself. Jo, this is all very complicated for a lot of people, and for some a lot more complicated than for us.

In the long run I don't like a solitary life very much. It always seems so incomplete to me. That must be because it is.

1/12/39

I now have a written payment agreement with Schindler [for the RM 141 he stole]: 50 marks on 2/1, 50 marks on 3/1 and 41 marks on 4/1. He's boarding at his son-in-law's, and that way he can save up this amount. I'm only afraid he'll die first.

21 One of the first things Johannes did when he got to Philadelphia was to get personalized stationery printed. He did have a doctoral degree from Heidelberg, as did Elfriede, but the use of "Ph.D." on his personal stationery was an American—not German—practice. Throughout his professional life in the United States, Johannes insisted on being addressed as "Dr. Hoeber," while Elfriede was content with "Mrs. Hoeber."

22 Apparently the government at that time mandated that business people attend classes on air defense.

Now I'm going to wrap this up so I can get everything ready for the *Aquitania*.

Alles liebe, Deine Friedel.

FRIDAY AND MONDAY, JANUARY 13 AND 16, 1939

Letter from Elfriede in Düsseldorf to Johannes in Philadelphia.

Düsseldorf, 1/13/1939

Mein lieber Peter,

Now the letter stream is flowing and hopefully won't come to a halt again. Having to wait nine days for a letter is too much for your loving wife. Your *Manhattan* letter arrived promptly this morning and completely unexpectedly—because I thought that someone as elegant as you would disdain such a simple ship. Now when the *Manhattan* goes back it is supposed to take this letter along. By that time you'll have the pile of mail I sent on the *Aquatania*: two "printed matter" packages with the Mannheim brochures,[23] and a pair of socks and one glove. In the meantime I found the second glove here, which I will also send.

Yesterday at midday, prompted by your second inquiry, I went in town with Mother to get myself a Philadelphia Christmas present in the form of a dark blue handbag, squarish and very pretty. This was the result of a fairly long back-and-forth between a bag or a suitcase. I am very contented with this purchase. I will invest the leftover money exclusively in woolen underwear. I really don't know why I froze for 34 years of my life when there's something so nice and practical and not at all ugly, though that is not of such great importance. Being ensconced for a long-term stay in the ice cellar (read: office) leads to revolutionary decisions. If I had made this revolutionary decision a little sooner maybe my cold wouldn't have been so severe and long lasting. Now I'm only a little hoarse every couple of days with a frog in my throat, not a tonsil frog but rather red dots on the mucous membranes at the back of my mouth. At any rate I'm convinced it won't get worse this time.

The day before yesterday we translated Susie's $2 into a book she picked out herself: *Monika Travels to Madagascar*. Thus after *Ho-Ming*, which takes place in China, another piece of international education.

Enclosed I'm sending you a pile of stuff from the Kiel Savings and Loan. Enjoy it. I'm not ambitious enough to understand any of it. Last night I air defended again.

23 *Mannheim brochures* refers to publications Johannes wrote as city press officer in 1928–1933. Johannes used these as samples of his work while job hunting.

1/16/39

After two days devoted to household things, I decided on a real office day and will begin that by writing you. The fact that today, Monday morning, the mail consists solely and exclusively of a letter from you is really very nice. This letter of yours is the first from New York and I follow you very excitedly on your travels between the Battery and Harlem.[24]

You mustn't think that I expect concrete results from each of your reports. Take your time and do it properly and well. My current life here has dark patches, but the dark patches are more patches of mood than concrete ones, so it doesn't matter if they last a little longer or shorter. It has become clear to me in recent weeks that I'm not cut out for a single life over the long haul. The only thing with serious time constraints, however, is my passport, which expires soon, but I am going to have to renew that in any event before this year's summer trip. I can't tell you how much luck you had in this respect, but it was huge.[25]

On the question of the commencement of conversations with Uncle Karl, I would like to know if I should remind him right away about how he did it with you the last time (number, etc.). Maybe you should send me your file number. When I know that then I'll get in touch with him right away.[26]

I passed two quiet evenings at home, but yesterday afternoon Hilde was here briefly. The gatherings of straw widows are curious. We try to make the best of it, but there's not much good to be made. Early yesterday I was on the phone again at night because the newspapers got lost at the train station again. In the end they did finally show up on time, but my enthusiasm for night-time phone calls is quite limited. Susie always asks longingly after you. "When Papi is back again" or: "When there is an exhibition of hand work [at school] you'll come this time!" I: "You know I have very little time." She: "But by then Papi will be back." I had better not allow myself to start getting involved with longing!

Alles liebe Deine Friedel.

MONDAY, JANUARY 16, 1939

Letter from Johannes in Philadelphia to Elfriede in Düsseldorf.

Philadelphia, 1/16/39.

Liebster Peter,

Between trips a letter from you for me, between trips a letter from me for you.

24 Johannes' letter to Elfriede from New York was not preserved.

25 Elfriede's passport had expired, and she would need a new one for the trip to the United States. Johannes had been fortunate to have a current passport when he left. If he had needed a new one, he would have faced questions about his mother's Jewish ancestry. Elfriede, being what the Nazis called "pure Aryan," faced no such questions.

26 *Uncle Karl* = American Consulate where Elfriede would apply for a visa to immigrate. Here she is asking whether to mention Johannes' prior application and Swiss quota number.

I got back from Washington in Blue Boy on Saturday at 10 in the evening. Going there took barely four hours without ever exceeding the 50 mile speed limit by more than 10 miles, but coming back on icy roads without snow chains and in deep darkness took me six hours and I got here more dead than alive. Blue Boy, which handles badly on the road to begin with, began to slide around on the ice any time I went over 30 miles an hour. In addition, it was ice cold and the road (US Highway number 1!) was only cleared of snow or spread with sand in a few places.

The 2½ days in Washington were the most impressive and worthwhile I've experienced so far. I stayed with Maurice and Sandy, who not only cared for me like parents but the one recommendation that Maurice gave me turned out to be so topnotch that I have some hope for it. This concerns a very big big shot in the Department of Labor. The night I arrived I had dinner with him, Maurice, and Sandy in a very elegant hotel, but I was so tired from the long, fast trip in the car that I felt that I was in distinctly poor form—which immediately affects my English. When, after a relatively short time, our conversation about me came to an end with his invitation to visit him the next morning in his office, I had the feeling, well, the man will talk with you in a nice, non-committal way and then he'll be done with you. Nevertheless, I was pleased that after dinner he invited us to come with him to the Brookings Institute where an Arab leader was speaking to an invited group about the current situation [in the Middle East]. It was a remarkably interesting evening. After the lecture our old friend Mr. Sanders [unidentified] popped up, who had [previously] let me know he was so tied up with family business that he couldn't see me, and we all went to his house for whisky and similar good things.

Friday morning, awestruck, I made my way into the elegant building on Constitution Avenue—only to learn from the secretary that my big shot was so busy he couldn't see me, but I should come back Saturday morning, when he would have more time. You can imagine my ill temper, but what I took for an excuse turned out to be completely true. On Saturday I sat with this barely forty-year-old, very clever man for a full hour and a half, and the conversation became more and more intense and finally he came out with the fact that he might have a national economic research assignment for me. He had a phone conversation in my presence that included the following sentences: He speaks English fluently, and he is the man who should be able to do the job. Now tomorrow, at his instigation, I have an interview in New York with the man who is supposed to finance me. It turns out it's a matter of a one-time, narrowly limited research assignment, if anything at all comes of it. And yet I could hardly wish for a better and cleaner start.

Papa Abbott, whom I also visited, and who was very nice, turned out to be a total washout [on the job front], but to my surprise Bill is returning to Washington already at the end of this month, which naturally pleases me a lot. In addition to these two I stirred up a whole series of further interviews that in part were very pleasant and resulted in a load of additional connections. The old snowball system is still functioning well, and to my surprise my background in municipal administration and the London School of Economics turn out to be my strongest selling points.

Tomorrow I'm going to New York for the rest of the week where, in addition to the new Washington leads, I'll work more on those I began the week before, and then maybe already the next week to Washington again. Chicago is also crystallizing more and more as a third field of action, and I may have to go there soon too. Let me add that on Wednesday afternoon before my departure for Washington I passed both the oral and practical driver's test and yesterday afternoon we were invited to a large authentic American tea. So you now have an exhaustive account of my life since my last letter. The fact that my social life outside the family circle is and will remain nil will probably gratify you more than it does me.

And now to your letter of the 2nd/4th, which is the last one I have so far. Poor Peter, you never get out of the carrier problems! I am very disappointed at Schindler. Please, if you have to get aggressive with him—or with any of the others some other time—take Herbert or Günter or some similar masculine security along. These aren't encounters for a woman alone! And whether festivities like the one for Paul are appropriate for my wife alone is something I am not quite prepared to decide after reading your letter. You usually have liked things like that so little that your report this time seems almost too upbeat. Or am I doing wrong by you? Me jealous of you? Well, at any rate you can't complain about this alteration in circumstances.

In diesem Sinne,

Dein Jo

TUESDAY AND WEDNESDAY, JANUARY 17 AND 18, 1939

Letter from Elfriede in Düsseldorf to Johannes in Philadelphia.

Düsseldorf, 1/17/39

Mein liebes Peterchen,

I have a very productive day behind me, namely (1) the Frankfurt reconciliation report and (2) the quarterly sales tax return. Don't be shocked. I had gotten an extension to file the sales tax return and this morning I got the accounting from Frankfurt for December. You may be interested that ad sales for 1938 were about RM 3500 as compared to RM 2130 for 1937. Still, the absence of your guiding spirit is apparent, as the cancellations over the last two months won't be balanced by new subscriptions.

1/18/39

Office cleaned up, desk worked clean, or rather almost, because the left hand desk pile will never be totally free of a few bits and dregs. But I feel a little better again because the mountain in front of me has shrunk a little. On the other hand the next Ultimo is coming up and menacing me.

Right now it's ridiculously warm, up to 15° (Celsius, of course, if you remember what that is) during the day. But of course it's raining too; the sun seems to have given up on ever shining on Europe again. In the newspaper you begin to read about the first signs of *Karneval*, and if this year has any plus side, it's that for the first time I don't have to worry about you and *Karneval*. My standards are really becoming quite modest. The von Baeyer parents were just here. Erich has a job painting the portraits of the six children of a surgeon in Cleveland. But all the money they had went for evening clothes. How many gowns should I have made? Because I am sure that you won't let Erich outspend you in social climbing.

Alles liebe von Deiner Friedel.

JANUARY 20, 1939

Letter from Johannes in Philadelphia to Elfriede in Düsseldorf with an account of his third trip to New York since his arrival a month earlier.

Phila., 1/20/39

Liebster Peter,

I've been back [from New York] for three hours and am sitting with Pa-Mu here in the lab, where we just had a worrisome conference concerning Tante Lene and composed the telegram to you. More details on that subject shortly.

New York was quite strenuous again, as I met again with countless people. The most promising are the talks about the research assignment.

At least I made enough progress—in the short time from Saturday to Tuesday I got promising signals from Washington—that I was actually asked what my compensation requirements would be. I estimated the required time to be three months and asked for $200 per month.[27] Unfortunately I have no idea whether I thereby offered myself at too high or too low a price. The conversation ended with them saying they would review my proposal carefully and give me an answer in writing. In the meantime I'm not getting my hopes up, but if it did come through it would be very nice, despite the limited time of the assignment.

Manfred has made substantial progress. He formed a good impression of the boss in Saratoga with whom he lunched yesterday—also in New York—and the boss formed a good impression of Manfred. Starting on 1 May and for the next 6 months—that's how long the season lasts—he'll be working as this man's assistant at 200 a month. This man doesn't have a sanatorium but conducts his practice as a purely private practice and, as is usual here, places his patients in a sanatorium where they remain his patients. Despite the current limitation to six months, there's a possibility that Manfred can be extended. The disadvantage of this arrangement is that Manfred won't be able to take his State Board when it's given in September because in the high season there won't be time for him to cram and he'll have to wait until January 1940. We are all nevertheless strongly in favor of this bird in the hand.

My remaining New York talks were at least partially quite interesting. This time they included two of the addresses Bill Abbott gave me. One was an unrewarding young man who at least passed me on to a woman who in turn wrote me two introductions. Writing introductions seems to be one of the main occupations of the Americans. If it continues like this for a couple more weeks I'll know half of the 120 million people in this country. The other address was a very dignified older big business man who invited me to an informal supper at his wonderful estate on the coast halfway to New Haven. I was alone with him and there was a delicious, tender (!) duck for dinner accompanied in my honor by a bottle of quite good Deidesheimer. We talked nonstop for 2½ hours about the absurdity of economics as a science and a topic of study, but no suggestion of the word job emerged from his side, and I had been advised not to be the first one to mention that in our first meeting—it is not permitted with such big shots. So I took it simply as a good opportunity—even though naturally he complained for hours about Roosevelt's tax and social policies—and it ended with my having to promise him to have lunch with him the next time I'm in New York—and then I'll talk about a job a lot.

27 $200 in 1939 would equal about $3000 in 2015.

It was delightful again with [cousin] Paul junior, who introduced me to a man in his firm, and [a] very pleasant evening with the Stös, who for the time being are limiting themselves to a social atmosphere that deftly encompasses all their old connections. And really the best thing of all these days in New York, when I was feeling deeply discouraged after the 16th or 17th inconclusive interview, was to go to the film *The Good Earth*, which is such a great work of art that I was completely captivated by it for hours afterwards, above all by the lead actress, Luise Rainer, who, from all I had heard, I expected to be anything but a great artist.

The situation with Tante Lene is unfortunately not as good as we thought. Yesterday a letter came from the "spokesman" for the administration of the institution, that is to say the representative of the society, a lawyer, saying that the eviction can't be reversed. The two critical sentences say, "We do not care to express in detail anything about the grounds. The grounds do not lie merely in the area suggested by your daughter-in-law," and, "Naturally we are prepared to make accommodations respecting the moving-out date. We must, however, insist on having the room at our disposal on 1 March."

Your letter with the letter from Mrs. Lask [saying she found someone to take care of Tante Lene] arrived at the same time as the letter from the Institution. We are giving careful thought to Mrs. Lask's letter and are grateful that this heavily-burdened woman is so ready to help. We certainly don't want to miss out on this [potential alternative caretaker], but the address is not included in [Mrs. Lask's] letter, which is why we just cabled you. We didn't know any other way to be certain this woman gets an offer as soon as possible. That's why we asked that you cable us the address, so the woman can hear as soon as possible from Daddy as the legally responsible party, and also so that Daddy can write quickly to both the institution and to Lene. Lene's condition makes the move and the concurrent acquisition of new clothing, as well as the instruction of the new person who will provide her housing, a problem that is difficult to manage from a distance.

Financially, it appears Lene still has a savings account book (held by the Director) into which about RM 100 [of] interest accrue annually. In addition, Social Security pays RM 50 per month for her, while the Institution gets only RM 45 of that. Certain, although probably very limited, reserves are possibly also available. Daddy can take on the ongoing costs without difficulty, as least for a while yet. It's very painful to us all, *lieber Peter*, to have to hand some of these problems to you on top of all your other problems. We very much hope that by combining your letter writing abilities with ours we'll be able to avoid ultimately having to ask you to go to Kiel for a couple of days. I understand, of course, that it would be extremely difficult for you to do that, but we can't guarantee that things won't come to that point. It's not always an unalloyed advantage to be a smart woman and not just a little lady.

Fortunately it's now 6 o'clock. Since breakfast in Penn Station in New York I've only gotten a half dozen crackers, a hardboiled egg and a cup of tea in my stomach, and without a car it will take us about three-quarters of an hour to get to Germantown.

So, so long, and next time less about business.

Dein Jo

FRIDAY, JANUARY 20 THROUGH THURSDAY, JANUARY 26, 1939 (SEVERAL DATES, ONE LETTER).

Letter from Elfriede in Düsseldorf to Johannes in Philadelphia, accompanied by a letter from Susanne dated January 21. Exchanging mail continued to be a problem because ships sailed less often in the winter months and there was no airmail alternative across the Atlantic.

The letter captures a number of the disruptions in daily life following Kristallnacht, *two months previously, from nosy neighbors, to the mechanics of pursuing a visa, to the mournful departure of old friends for safe havens in foreign countries. Elfriede describes visiting Hilde Lenzberg, whose newly built house was heavily damaged by Stormtroopers on* Kristallnacht. *She also describes neighbors' curiosity as to Johannes' whereabouts. Johannes and Elfriede had not told their neighbors or business contacts—except the local manager, Dr. Betz—that Johannes had emigrated. This was in part to protect the stability of the business. Neighbors, however, were also watching, and one never knew which of them were reporting to the Gestapo or to the foreign exchange authorities, who levied taxes on emigrants. Peter Ameln, Mrs. Finger, Wulft, Lix, and Alwine the Pastor's daughter were apparently all neighbors.*

Düsseldorf, 1/20/39

Mein lieber, guter Peter,

Everyone always sends you their warmest greetings one way or another. That's why I'm starting another letter, even though there isn't the slightest possibility that a usable ship will leave before the *Bremen* on the 28th. It's terrible. Everybody around here who, like me, is waiting for mail from America is, like me, waiting in vain simply because no ships are moving. It really leaves a lot to be desired—even between here and South America you can communicate twice a week by airmail. Today I got a letter from Schlossman answering my letter in the Freyberger matter. He writes in addition to everything else that it's not good for a person to be alone. I could have figured that out on my own without his telling me, but right now a lot of people are thinking this.

1/21/39

Your letter of the 10th brought warmth to my freezing heart. I'm always fretting dreadfully for mail. That is not a complaint directed at you, because you write really sweetly and diligently. It's the fault of sparse transport conditions when a 4-day delay works out to be 7 days here.

Your telegram about Tante Lene soothed me less. But *nolens volens*[28] I will write today to Mrs. Lask about the matter. As noted above, it's now the 21st and your letter includes your response to my Christmas letter. And then in between your plans for Washington and your description of your first visit to New York—all of a sudden it's all mixed up in my head—but that is in the nature of things these days—I mean this uproar or, as I say, my head is spinning—my head has often been spinning recently. Only occasionally does that make me dizzy, but Mother is very helpful in restoring my balance. Actually my life would be impossible without her and my brothers. I really feel sorry for Hilde, who on top of everything else has to put up with family meanness and never has a penny's worth of help with anything. Till will be confirmed on Wednesday, and I will see today if a Spanish illustrated dictionary exists. If so I will give it to him. This Wednesday is also Hilde's birthday.

How different everything looks at Hilde's! Empty window frames, no carpets, no real lamps, a lot rebuilt—but for weeks it has looked like they're moving out. Only upstairs in the guest room Hilde set up a charming room for herself. Sometimes we set a couple of chairs for ourselves in front of the fireplace and don't look at what's behind us. It certainly is an amazing way to live.

Of course I found the chapter on Philadelphia and Germantown in the Paquet book. I even read it before Christmas.

The episode with Manfred is really sad.[29] He always did seem more like an opera hero than a real hero—but what he did wasn't even worthy of an opera hero. I can begin to understand that in the process your family lost their way somewhat respecting the rules for future transactions. That I became the victim in the process is something I can take with composure so long as the rules for me remain reasonable, and I'm not worried about that. But it always annoys me a bit when suddenly you

28 *Nolens volens* = here, willingly or not.

29 Johannes had written about Manfred running off to New York, but details of what he did are absent.

and I become the ideal married couple and it's the supposedly exemplary Gri and Manfred who end up acting out the tragicomedy.

Funny things happen sometimes. A few days ago Peter Ameln came down. He asked Helma to ask Dr. Höber if he could lend him a timetable. Helma got rid of him without asking Dr. Höber. Mrs. Finger, on the other hand, asked her whether the doctor was traveling. Yes, he was. For some time? Yes, for some time. Helma knows how to hold her tongue. It's so quiet in our place now, noted Mrs. Finger (presumably because we don't call to each other across the apartment either angrily or in a friendly way). Probably most of them think that Dr. Höber left his wife. Wulft asked once in December when they would see Dr. Höber again—I told him that was uncertain. Since then discreet silence from that corner as well. But when Lix was here recently, a sealed letter addressed to Philadelphia was on the desk, and I don't know whether he saw it. At any rate he didn't say anything. But do you know who was here and said she wanted to buy your business in the event you left permanently? Alwine, the pastor's daughter! Such arrogance and nerve took my breath away, but I smiled pleasantly, said certainly if it came to that it would be something to think over and similar noncommittal things. In any event that's one soup I'll gladly spit in. She really was something!

It was a great reassurance to me to see that your sister [Gri] hasn't completely forgotten how to write. I do understand that her available time is tight, but lack of time never counted in your family as an excuse for not writing. I agree that nothing should change that.

1/22/39

This is becoming a letter in stages. Yesterday Mrs. Freyberger came. Then I spent last evening at the Magicians' [Prof von Baeyer's]. They are watching the disintegration of their circle of friends with sorrow but are very kind about everyone's plans and are full of sympathy and helpful. He always has new ideas for you. And when one talks about things like that, then you start to fantasize about all sorts of things and allow your wishful dreams to expand. Washington would not be a bad place to live.

1/23/39

Betz was here today. I think this was the first time he was here since you left, but we often talk on the phone. He's going to Frankfurt and wanted to know how things are here, delivery time questions, etc. As far as the people there are concerned, you're still at the Ütli; your current stopping place is too far away.[30] But out of caution he wants to advise them that your return is in doubt. Did I have a suggestion for a successor [for

30 *The people there* refers to the *Frankfurter Zeitung* central office circulation managers. Dr Betz, the local manager, had told Frankfurt that Johannes was temporarily in Switzerland (code word = Ütli).

when I leave]? For the moment I don't. What did I think about Schell? It's difficult nowadays to get someone acceptable. The idea of a commission agency has become problematic because of the general uncertainty and because he sees that the business here would best be run by 2 people, preferably a married couple. Well, it doesn't make any difference at all to me. In any event, he was personally very nice though in general quite pessimistic.

Overall, I'm inclined to write immediately to Uncle Karl.[31] Since he's usually quite slow, I think he won't get the thing done until the end of March at the earliest. And then I'll have four more months [that the visa will be valid]. Please write me right away if you agree with that. If I could do it that way, it would relieve me of the necessity of applying to Uncle Paul[32] [for a passport], and I would rather not take on old Mr. Disgusting unless I have to. And then I would also have a little more space to maneuver. If it turns out the four months aren't enough, then I would still have to apply to Uncle Paul and thereafter to Uncle Karl. That would be dumb, but I still think I should risk it until then. If Manfred and his family take off for Saratoga (site of a famous battle of the Independence War) on 5/1, then maybe I could visit your parents in July.[33] You will get this letter on the 2nd or 3rd of February, and on the 4th the *Aquitania* leaves from New York. Maybe you can get an answer on that ship saying what I ought to do. After a lot of thinking it over backwards and forwards, this procedure seems to me to be the most practical. I would very much like to know your opinion. Once we decide on a plan we shouldn't delay it too much, but sending a cable isn't necessary. Something else: send me one of your birth certificates. I need it for my Ancestry Pass.[34] Similarly our marriage certificate, if you have it.

This time Susie is writing you a letter directly. She's always very busy and sweet and funny. She looks a little wintry-colored, but she's alright. I just got the doctor's bill from November. There were eight visits, but they were not as expensive as before (RM 43—total).

1/25/39

This morning I paid Hilde a birthday visit. Tonight there is a little celebration for Till's confirmation. Since there is no such thing as an illustrated Spanish dictionary, I will give him an ultraviolet filter for his Retina [camera], but I still have to get that.

1/26/39

This time I'm going to write this letter to the end, and I don't think I'm going to do one of these letters in stages again, because in the end it results in a longer letter but not a nicer one. Last night the gathering for

31 *Uncle Karl* = American consul in Stuttgart.

32 *Uncle Paul* = Germany or the German authorities. Elfriede's passport had expired, and if she went to the consul in Zürich rather than to Stuttgart for a visa she would need to apply to the German authorities for a new passport immediately

33 *Visit your parents* = arrive in the United States.

34 An *Ancestry Pass* [*Ahnenpass*] was a certificate the Nazis required of all citizens documenting their parentage back three generations. Extracts of civil and church registers of births, deaths, and marriages had to be presented to the local civil registry, which would then stamp the appropriate block of the *Ahnenpass* to certify that that ancestor was or was not "Jewish" as defined by the Nazis.

Till's confirmation was not a pleasant affair, about 16 people, including two old men. More than that, it was one of those dreadful gatherings of professional mourners, which are now really getting on my nerves. Only one pretty woman was there, whom you seem to have missed during your Düsseldorf days. Right away I was thinking that this would have been something for you, and Hilde then said the same thing, which amused us greatly. That was the only pleasant intermezzo, and otherwise it was very sad. It's raining and raining and never ends, and that's the way it always is.

Tomorrow the *Aquitania* arrives in Cherbourg. I wonder if she'll bring me something. Since you are a sweet letter writer, something will surely come to soothe my longing eyes.

Alles liebe, Deine Friedel

Accompanying letter from Susanne.

1/21/39

Lieber Papi.

Your letter this time was very nice. I really did write the poems myself. I got a very nice dress made out of the silk for Christmas. On Sunday I was at Oma's. Peter was there too and when she tried to explain to him that the person sitting across from him was Mama, he called her Papa, because he knew how to say Papa. Yesterday I was invited to Emil Waller's for his birthday. I brought him a third pocket knife because he already had two. We got ice cream in the shape of Max and Moritz. When we played strike-the-pot I won a bunch of flowers and a game of Black Peter. Tell the others that with the money they gave me I bought myself a book called *Monika Goes to Madagascar*.

Hello to the others and a thousand kisses O O O O O O O and wishes your Susiepuss.

TUESDAY, JANUARY 24, 1939

Letter from Johannes in Philadelphia to Elfriede in Düsseldorf. This letter includes coded phrases about the procedure for procuring immigration visas for Elfriede and Susanne. "Decision in favor of Stuttgart" refers to Elfriede's decision to apply for an American visa at the consulate in Stuttgart rather than in Zürich (identified by the code word "Aunt Lilly"). Form 575 is the form in which Johannes certifies to the Immigration Bu-

Susanne Höber, age 8. Photograph by Günter Fischer, December 1938.

reau that he is "settled" in the United States. The phrase, "It is not at all possible to determine clearly whether you will get a number analogous to mine or a number that you would ordinarily get on your own ..." concerns whether Elfriede would be counted against the Swiss quota or the German quota.

Philadelphia, 1/24/39

Liebstes Peterchen,

I'm all alone at home in our palace, so I have the time and quiet I need to write this letter, which *faute de mieux* the *American Trader* will take along tomorrow. The shipping connections are truly desperate at the moment; there isn't any decent ship all this week. I promised you on Friday that I would talk less about business in the next letter, but the Tante Lene problem has to be mentioned again today. In addition, your letter came yesterday with your decision in favor of Stuttgart, which I regard as both desirable and convincing, so first there has to be some business talk again.

Your letter was here for less than five hours before I sent the completed Form 575 as a registered letter to Washington. From there Stuttgart wi be provided with the official details about me that are supposed to hel you—hopefully without undue delay. But it is unfortunately impossib to determine exactly how much or how little these details will speed u the process, even by asking people who are experts in these matters. Th discretion of the authorized officials in this regard seems to be set with a very, very wide range, and it isn't possible to determine clearly wheth you will get a number analogous to mine or a number that you would ordinarily get on your own. In these circumstances it seems to me that your decision in favor of Stuttgart is the only right one, because at the moment the time factor remains completely unknown. If one day—G forbid—a situation develops like the one at the time of Gri and Manfred's departure,[35] you can still go straight to Aunt Lilly's and change the locality involved just by sending a letter. This morning Dad took the affidavit forms with him in town, and will ensure that they ha contents and accompanying letters that will be as effective for you as they previously were for me. As soon as they are done, they will go directly to you, that is, in two days at the latest. The only thing you hav to do right now is to get two application forms and send them back completed as soon as possible. The most important thing, whatever happens next, is to keep us informed as to what is going on. I can see th day coming when I may have to use some connections to get some pressure behind our various forms if they don't work out automaticall

Accompanying this letter you will get a whole file folder of material related to the Tante Lene problem. By reading it and Seppchen's letter you'll see how complicated it is. The maintenance of the former financ controls seems to be so important to all of us, because the Kiel resourc may one day become completely unavailable.[36] I have no idea whether the temporary solution we are currently considering is something we c rely on, but despite endless consideration we haven't been able to come up with anything cleverer. At any rate I hope the assignment of getting new underwear for her won't cause you a problem.

The fact that the people in Cologne have accused Mrs. Freyberger of insensitivity really makes me very sad. But it could have been foreseen for long time that she was going to become caught up in the disintegration o that household. Your question as to whether I could give her any suggestion for here is something to which the answer unfortunately is

35 *If one day ... a situation develops like the one at the time of Gri and Manfred's departure ...* Manfred and Gri left Germany in the midst of the Sudeten Crisis, when war seemed imminent. Johannes' circumlocution here means that if war broke out, Elfriede and Susanne could go to Switzerland and wait for their visas there.

36 Tante Helene's board at the Institution was paid out of Rudolf's Kiel bank account, which was replenished with his pension payments from his career at the University of Kiel. She was also partially supported by government disability payments. With the Nazis' ever-increasing restrictions on the finances of émigrés, Jews, and the disabled, the American Höbers were anticipating those funds being cut off entirely.

simply no. There are all the jobs she could want here, that is, in a household. Just yesterday I was told about one that is available immediately. She could even do everything in Germany that is necessary to get a work permit for such a position. But there is no way—or almost no way—to get her here any more quickly than by the normal route [of applying for an American visa]. A construct like "member of the household" or anything like that just doesn't exist, and everything that I've been able to determine here confirms that the pamphlet out of which we got our information about such questions is the best source, better informed even than many of the offices that deal directly with these things. So I find the plan for England to be the only correct one at the moment, and as far as I know it is also doable. I would just tell her what I tell everyone who asks me: regardless of anything else, file an application to come here. I hardly need to mention that you should give her my very best wishes.

And now to something more directly related to your letter. The fact that you wait anxiously for letters from me probably makes me feel as good as it makes you feel bad. I already anticipate that during the process that has now begun with 575 the two of us will have to pull ourselves together frequently to remain the model couple in the family. Part of that role, unfortunately, requires that I do not show the least sign of uncertainty, which I naturally suffer from from time to time, more so during a week like this one of relative inactivity than when the days are filled with non-stop interviews. But after all, as of Sunday I will have been here for just a month and at least 10 of those days were holidays when no one gave any thought to business. At any rate, given the current status of things I don't think you need to worry about my renting a place that's too big. On the contrary, maybe I should look for a place to live that requires as little work as possible so you can get a job outside the house. But any such thoughts are most premature. Did I write to you that the Stös live in a tiny hotel room for $50—and that Nuni [unidentified], who has now become a young woman and not nearly as whiny as two years ago, lives with friends all the time? But of course they are not really settled in yet.

It's funny, Peter, you write about all the people with whom you are together, and in addition to them you have Susie and the work, and I'm with countless people here—just yesterday we had 10 people here for a buffet dinner in addition to us six grownups—and I have the whole family, and despite all that we both complain about loneliness. Then how does it happen that when we are together we quarrel all the time? It doesn't make any sense at all.

I am very annoyed by the way the Schindler matter has ended up. What did the guy do with such a huge sum of money? And shouldn't you perhaps put more pressure on him than just with an indefinite restitution agreement, such as through Betz or maybe even by means of a criminal complaint? As near as I remember Schindler is in a position where he has some resources you could get hold of. Look at the case again a little more closely.

Note: For the next section the reader is reminded that the occupants of the Cresheim Road house included four doctors: Rudolf (Daddy), Josephine (Seppchen), Manfred, and Ursula (Ulli).

And now to the satirical play. On Friday I brought a pretty dreadful cold along with me from Washington, and on Saturday, when I could no longer defend myself against the combined pressure of the residents of the house, I took my temperature and it was 100.7. What happened to me then should happen to you sometime—you would never get a cold again. Ulli prescribed an inhaler stick which you drill into your nose, Manfred two Pyramidon, Seppchen two aspirin, then Ulli began again with hot tea, Gri supplemented it with a slice of lemon, Seppchen predicted a catastrophe because I smoked a cigarette, and Daddy was quietly sympathetic. The worst, however, came after supper. Manfred, whom I selected from among all the competitors as my personal court physician, wrapped me first in a wet towel, then from head to foot in a bath sheet, then in a wool jacket, then, since I still showed signs of life, threw two more woolen blankets over my bedcover and told me to lie there for two hours without moving. The next morning my temperature was still 99.3 and life still didn't look good to me, but I got up anyway because we had guests in the evening. In the evening I went to the party until 12, smoked, drank beer, etc. and when I took my temperature it was 98.2. But you should come here and just try to hang on to a sniffle for more than two days!

Which reminds me that you haven't written about the condition of Susie's health for a long time. She should also write again herself sometime. The letter with the report about Christmas was much too short for me, and she never answered mine from the *Manhattan*.

Tjüs, Gruß, Kuss.

Dein Jo

FRIDAY, JANUARY 27, 1939

Two letters from Elfriede in Düsseldorf to Johannes in Philadelphia.

Düsseldorf, 1/27/1939

Mein lieber Peter,

Yesterday evening I put the voluminous envelope with my 6-day letter and the Pfütze correspondence in the mailbox so I wouldn't have to go to the train station today (Elisabeth's birthday). Now I am writing again anyway, and Elisabeth will have to wait for me until nearly 10:30 after I have once more (the 6th time) increased my knowledge of air defense. This morning your card from Washington arrived completely unexpectedly because, according to my calculations, the *Aquitana* doesn't get into Cherbourg until today and I thought the letter would come tomorrow. So the card is a comforting advance notice, and since it was written on 1/15 the *Aquitania* on the 20th will certainly have a letter.

Item 1. Washington in snow is almost impossible for me to imagine. Based on our summer visit in 1937, it is for me the epitome of tropical heat and a southern environment, so I never thought there could be such a thing as a serious winter there. I am very much looking forward to your further report from this city that I love so much.

Item 2. Today I got an answer from Mrs. Lask that doesn't make sense. She was writing from Kiel but gives a Berlin address. The name of the woman [who can take care of Tante Lene] is: Mrs. Helene Lischke, 7311Waitzstrasse, Kiel. "Mrs. Lischke went to the institution yesterday and spoke with the Director as well as with Miss Höber. Next week she will pick up Miss Höber and show her her home as well as the room that Miss H. will occupy. Mrs. Lischke is happy to take over the care and I think that Miss H. will be in good hands there. She now awaits your instructions." I will now write to Mrs. Lischke today if I still can, otherwise tomorrow. But I think you should write her immediately also, on account of the financial arrangements, about which I know practically nothing. Who will pay? How will it be paid? What's up with Social Security? I will also write a thank-you to Mrs. Lask, 8511L Wiesbadenerstrasse, Berlin-Friedenau. I think it is really terrific that she did all that.

All my love from the midst of heavy production of invoices!

Deine Friedel

1/27/39

Liebster, bester Peter,

How and why your letter of the 16th arrives today is something I can't figure out, but here it is (though with the afternoon mail) and I'm very pleased with this delicious Washington account. It really makes me feel good in the midst of my solitary life, because that's what it is in spite of all the people around me.

I find it outrageous that you don't own any snow chains in such an arctic country. Chains are still no guarantee, but I would sleep better if I knew that you weren't sliding around on icy roads in the middle of the night in Blue Boy with its horrible handling. In my opinion your father should acquire some for the sake of his and your lives. I am also in favor of windshield wipers under all circumstances!! I noted during our icy return drive from the Eifel mountains in December that they can save your life. So please! But of course by the time this letter arrives you'll be enjoying spring breezes and think I am speaking in the *plusquam perfectum*!

Love and kisses to the Department of Labor man from me, that is, if it leads to something. No, even if it doesn't. I like the fact that he likes you and for that reason I like him. But first of all, the next time you drive to Washington D.C., please leave an hour earlier so you don't have to drive so fast and won't be so tired afterwards. I would find it much nicer and much better anyway if I were sitting next to you doing such things and chatted at you a little and if we then had a good time together and went somewhere chic. Apropos chic, what do you think of an evening gown for me? And what about your tux? Do we need it or not? And if you need some underwear or something like that, write me and I'll send it. Don't you need woolen stockings at the North Pole? Or a fur hat? Don't laugh at all this junk I'm writing, but I'm really happy about your letter.

Thank Gri for her answers to my cooking and household questions. She should routinely write down and put together all the things that come up in daily life [in America]. It makes a big difference whether you take a 3-week vacation trip [to America, as we did in 1937] or if you really do the thing right and live in the middle of it. Your reaction to my description of Paul's party was very funny, but unfortunately I can't give you any further occasion for jealousy, since all of the relatively more or less worthwhile objects of my social activity have decamped to remote places that are at present inaccessible to me. In that regard Düsseldorf is as barren as ever.

The Magician is still awfully sick. It's really not pretty. He has had the grippe for over five days now, with temperatures over 102. You really don't want any part of that.

Dein getreues Eheweib!
Your faithful wife!
F.

TUESDAY, JANUARY 31, 1939

Letter from Johannes in Philadelphia to Elfriede in Düsseldorf.

Philadelphia, 1/31/39.

Liebster Peter,

The ship traffic right now is really sickening. Last Wednesday I even had to use a cripple like the *American Trader*, and the *Deutschland*, with which mail can finally go off to you again, is not exactly a fast ship. In the next few days both the *Bremen* and the *Normandie* will land here, both hopefully bringing me mail from you, but both are scheduled to go off on southern routes instead of turning around to take mail from me back to Europe. Well, with spring approaching it will hopefully get better. To talk about spring at all is rather out of place today. Two days ago all automobile drivers rejoiced that the heavy thaw finally melted the frozen remains of the last snowfall, on which they had to balance precariously for a whole week both with and without snow chains, and last night as I took Ulli back to the hospital in Blue Boy at 12 it poured rain. But this morning the world appeared in the brilliant white of a heavy snowfall, and I had to take an hour clearing the sidewalk, which is twice as long for us since we occupy a corner house. The joys of a tenant of a private house with which I was not previously acquainted!

We just had lunch, Gri, Manfred, and I. We are the most usual combination at lunch when I'm at home. Otherwise I do it for 25–30 cents at Horn and Hardart or some similar large enterprise, where I'm getting used to the noise, impersonal quality and matter-of-factness. Our lunch is mostly cold—a big meal with soup, main course, and dessert only gets made at night. But you should not conclude from this that our lunch is a meager meal. Today there was first a huge half grapefruit for each, price for the whole fruit—larger than life size, sweet and juicy—5 cents. Then for each of us an egg; Manfred ate his fried, Gri and I, wallowing in childhood nostalgia, ate ours as a sugar egg.[37] A dozen, premium with a date stamp, cost 28 cents right now. And we recently profited greatly from a sale at the American Store that was sensational, even for the local circumstances: a special on a lightly smoked ham. We bought a huge chunk that weighed seven pounds for $1.08 that we ate cooked as a roast. So much for the subject of meals and prices, about which Gri will tell you more sometime.

And now to more important things. Since Thursday I have a full-time occupation. Actually it's purely voluntary—I won't get paid a cent—but

37 *Sugar egg*: an egg is beaten with a little sugar and eaten raw.

for all that it's more interesting and valuable as an experience than anything else that is a theoretical possibility at the moment. Specifically, I'm a consultant on the research staff of the City Charter Committee for Philadelphia. Now I have to explain that a bit.

You may or may not know that city administration remains the weakest spot in the government of this country, which is not exactly lacking in weak spots. This continues to be true for many cities, where the phrase "to the victor belong the spoils"—which has been partially overcome in many states and almost completely in the federal government—continues to be the governing principle. The city halls are mostly the fortresses of politicians and corruption, which is still amazingly widespread here, although probably not quite as widespread as the newspapers would lead one to believe, since of course scandals make such nice front-page stories. But in municipalities, corruption really plays as strong a role as ever. On the other hand, there has been a steadily growing reform movement for decades now which, as is typical in this country, is built on countless research organizations, citizens' committees, etc., which, in the battle against both parties, are not political organizations but fighting groups united against the reigning spoils cliques, and which give a lot of thought to government reform and have earned substantial recognition.

Such a battle has been under way for a long time in Philadelphia, which is of particular importance because of the size of the city and because Philadelphia, according to the *consensus omnium*, is particularly badly governed. Most people believe the city's antiquated foundational ordinance—called the City Charter—is or may be the cause, so the battle for a long time has been concentrated on giving Philadelphia a new Charter, for which an act of the Pennsylvania Legislature is necessary. The proposal for this new Charter, worked out by an official commission appointed by the Governor last year, is now in front of the Pennsylvania legislature as a bill, and the private City Charter Committee, a huge but completely private organization that has been leading the whole movement and is solely responsible for getting things as far along as they are, is now fighting for the second step, the adoption of the new Charter by the State Legislature. The third step then would be ratification of this State act by means of a plebiscite in the city of Philadelphia. These, then, are the purposes of the City Charter Committee. Its research staff now has the job of commenting on the Charter proposal for the second and third steps of the campaign and assembling the materials for the campaign to be carried out by the Committee proper. Its immediate assignment is the preparation of a speakers' manual, which will be given to the hundreds of speakers and campaigners who are supposed to popularize the reform movement in all possible organizations by all possible means.

Every staff member has a particular topic to develop, and when someone discovered that I knew a bit about municipal administration, and as German municipal administration is very well thought of here, I was assigned one of the principal topics. My paper is called, "The City Manager." If I wanted to explain in detail what that means I would have to write a whole paper to do it. In brief, it concerns the idea that while, up to now, the mayor directly elected by the voters was the political, ceremonial, and administrative head of the city, in the future the administrative functions would be transferred to a city manager appointed by the city council, whose position would approximate that of our *Berufsbürgermeister*. Only the ceremonial functions would remain with the Mayor, who in the future would be elected by the city council from among its own members as *primus inter pares*. The decisive question of the division of powers, which would necessarily arise in these circumstances, would be answered thus: the council is the policy determining body, the manager the chief executive. You can of course picture the kind of political, constitutional, and administrative problems that would be part of this arrangement. So now I've been sitting for a couple of days in the library of the Bureau for Municipal Research, buried in books, government reports, journals, laws, and bills, happy as I can be to be spinning at the old threads again and, well cared for and well sheltered by Pa and Mu, not having to ask too much what I personally might get out of it, but for the moment striving above all to do my bit as well as I can. I don't doubt for a moment that you will approve of this activity of mine.

I doubt it so little that I would like to ask you to help me with it a little as soon as possible. I need urgently: (1) the three volumes of *The Living City*; (2) the Mannheim report of the national cost reduction commission; (3) the Mannheim governance report 1933–1938; (4) my copy of the municipal ordinances for the state of Baden.[38] I know that I'm giving you a lot of work packing these to send, but I'm sure you can figure out how you can magically get these six books to me as quickly as possible for the lowest possible cost.

Whereby I now arrive happily at the pleasant subject of the bounteous mail that you have poured out upon me in such rich masses over the last few days. From my last letter you will already have seen just how much good you have done for me with the blue knee socks. Even more pleasant

38 These documents concerned municipal administration in Mannheim. *The Living City* [*Die Lebendige Stadt*] was a bimonthly magazine Johannes edited as press chief to Mannheim's mayor.

was the reunion with the sorely need mouse-grey gloves, which were joyfully reunited with one another and then with my hands. Many, many thanks. Also the Mannheim brochures, the two university transcripts, the diplomas and the appointment calendar arrived here safely. At the moment, therefore, outside of the the brochures, I only need the letter of recommendation from [*Oberbürgermeister*] Hermann Heimerich, which is to be found in my personnel file.

As modest reciprocation from us, this letter will bring you those three important papers that should continue what I have already begun with the 575. May they prove to be just as weighty and impressive for you as they were for me on my occasion.[39]

What you wrote about your attitude toward my efforts here made me feel very good. There are certainly not many men who in the same situation receive such sensible and comforting sentences from their wives as I. Actually Peter: what sweet and soothing letters you write, letters that even after 10 or 14 days make the recipient just as happy as if they were written yesterday. By the way, even without your suggestion I would have stuck with the principle that any non-business letters that I write would go to you. There may be occasional exceptions, but as far as friends are concerned I probably won't be able to get to more than a collective letter to Gunter, Herbert, Paul, Heidi, Elisabeth, Hilde, Gerhard and Marlies, Max and Hilla, Fräuken and Else, and finally the Magicians. And even that will go to you first. I will only make an exception for your mother, and as I recently asked, please read her anything out of these letters that you think might interest her.

Back once more to the subject of Uncle Karl. You don't have to write him about how he did it with me, because he will learn that officially through the 575. The one thing you might do is mention in a note accompanying your affidavit that this form is on its way.

Susie will get a separate letter from me again soon. Her observations about her absent father are sweet. But shouldn't you perhaps gradually start to tell her about the adventure that lies ahead of her? And above all you should begin to work on some English with her, or have someone do that.

Enough, this letter still has to be registered. Therefore let me just add quickly that I entirely approve of your business letter of the 17th/18th and highly appreciate it, and that now with the help of the Charter Committee hopefully you can brag about me as much as the Magicians about Erich's portrait commissions and Annemarie's evening gowns.

39 The enclosures referred to here were Rudolf's affidavit of support and related documents to be submitted by Elfriede with her application for a U.S. immigration visa.

How many evening gowns should you have made for yourself? Just one—you will achieve your triumphs in other arenas than Annemarie with her evening gowns.

Meint Dein sehr liebender
[So thinks your very loving]
Jo

CHAPTER 6

Getting "In"

WEDNESDAY AND THURSDAY, FEBRUARY 1 AND 2, 1939

Letter from Elfriede in Düsseldorf to Johannes in Philadelphia, accompanied by a letter from Susanne. Responding to Johannes' letter of January 20, Elfriede discusses the arrangements for housing Rudolf's mentally disabled sister, Tante Lene. The situation was complicated by the fact that Rudolf's bank, the Kiel Savings and Loan, refused to cash bonds for Tante Lene's care because of restrictions on the accounts of "noncitizens," i.e., those defined as "Jews" under the Nuremberg laws. Elfriede suggested to Johannes in December that they inform the Savings and Loan that Rudolf wasn't Jewish. It appears that Frau Lischke—the woman who agreed to house Tante Lene—was to receive RM *125 per month, more than double what Rudolf was paying the Institution where she lived previously. It was unclear whether the Social Security bureau would continue its monthly payment toward Tante Lene's support.*

Düsseldorf, 1 February 1939

Liebster Peter,

This is now the 3rd Ultimo I'm doing on my own, though the first one was done very much in your shadow. Oh, I'm learning the business and if it goes smoothly, as it has so far, then I'll know I'm up to it, even though it's still a mountain of work every time. Tomorrow I'm going to Krefeld and Gladbach, Friday to Duisburg. On Sunday Mrs. Freyberger was here and will come again one day next week so I can go to the hairdresser for a new permanent. People have to worry about things like that too. Yesterday at 7 I went to an air raid evening. Otherwise nothing uplifting is going on, and life is not greatly amusing.

I'll be very excited to see whether the research thing will work out for you. It would be very nice, but if not, then not. It's a lot that anything at all has appeared on the horizon this soon. I can imagine that this business of chasing down a thousand people isn't a lot of fun, but you can't really do it any other way. After all, you're just starting and our roof is still solid. In fact it—the roof—was beautifully restored by the roofers over the last few weeks. At the moment they're doing the gutters over our balcony so it won't pour on our heads in the summer.

Once more to the Tante Lene business. Your explanation of the finances is unfortunately somewhat skimpy. Tante Lene got the RM 5 left over from the Social Security payment as pocket money, so none of that will be available [to pay Mrs. Lischke]. The RM 100 annual interest [that you wrote about] won't even cover the cost of housing for a month. And will the Social Security payments continue? Of course I'm in favor of selling bonds and getting a permit to allow RM 125 to be paid out of the restricted account to Mrs. Lischke every month (I assumed that in the interim you've made it clear to the Savings and Loan [that Rudolf is not Jewish]!). Exceptional expenses can then still be paid out of the special account. But Mrs. Lischke has to see some money before 3/1. It would be good to arrange everything in advance so that as soon as we have Mrs. Lischke's agreement everything can be started up immediately. The move will also cost something. What will become of Tante Lene's things? As far as I know she had some furniture?? You really could be a little more explicit.

All of these questions back and forth take so terribly long, and it isn't going to be any better with the ships in February. No *Bremen*, no *Europa*, no *Columbus*, no *Normandie*. The *Queen Mary* is the only bright spot on the ocean. She will also take this letter along, as well as an old tie of yours that I had cleaned and that you will be sure to greet fondly and an old shirt so that your poor family members won't have to turn your cuffs for you too.

2/2/39

Last night I went to the movies with Mother for the third time since you left. *Napoleon Is Responsible for Everything*, a really witty comedy by Karl Goetz, who played one of the main parts along with Henkels. The story line was as silly as usual, but a lot of nice gags and charming acting made the evening worth it.

Thus may the modest events of my existence be described and I bid you farewell for the next few days.

Alles liebe, Deine Friedel

Accompanying letter from Susanne.

Lieber Papi.

I think it's high time for you to come home. If possible, you have to be back by *Karneval* or else ... ? Helma just said that you would take an airplane right away and come back. Here is something really sad, Klaus moved away. Saturday was the last time he was in school. In the afternoon he had a going away party and a birthday party ahead of time. I am sure he is now in Berlin.

Now best wishes to you and the others and think about what is at the beginning of this letter and a big fat O.

Von Susanne

P.S. Please send me a letter soon.

FRIDAY, FEBRUARY 3, 1939

Letter from Johannes in Philadelphia to Elfriede in Düsseldorf.

Philadelphia, 2/3/39

Geliebter Peter,

What riches of letters we've been showering each other with! Today both your letters of 27 January arrived. On the other hand, the six-day letter you mailed previously with the Pfütze correspondence hasn't arrived yet, so I can look forward to that. Funny, thick letters regularly take more time than thin ones. What could account for that? As a result we know only the second half of your answer to our call for help on behalf of Tante Lene, but that's already cheering enough. A letter came from Tante Lene at the same time as your letter, slightly confused but cheerful and not much upset. Mrs. Lischke was already at her place and dealt with the Director. We'll write to Mrs. Lischke right away, so fortunately it looks like this complex of worries will be resolved quickly and simply. Mrs. Lask [who made the arrangements] got a thank you letter with input from Seppchen, Gri, and me. We are all grateful for your quick intervention.

When I read your response to my Washington account, which I just got today, I noted again what a terribly long time always separates our original correspondence and the response. I really have to devote some care to reconstructing the time relationships, since so much has happened in the meantime. Right after New York I wrote a very nice letter to my big shot in Washington, but so far haven't heard back from him or from the New York man connected to the project. I comfort myself with the thought that it could be a good sign as much as a bad sign. For the moment, however, that project is overshadowed by the [Charter Committee] work I'm doing now, which has a lot of promise if I do it well. Yesterday I was summoned by one of the top bosses, who asked me to do a report for him about the problem of the separation of powers and parliamentary responsibility in the classic Anglo-Saxon literature of political philosophy. It feels to me like I've been transported back to my times in Heidelberg and London, and I realized with a shock that the intervening years wiped out everything I knew and I have to get accustomed all over again to doing long hours of concentrated intellectual work. If only you were here! I can hardly think of anything the two of us could work on better together than this. It's amazing how intensely this kind of debate is pursued here—it's all about the authority of the voters, the mayor, the city council, and the city manager of Philadelphia.

I never pass up an opportunity to orient myself to this world or to get around. Sunday I went with Pa-Mu to a tea in a private home at which one of the American delegates spoke about the Lima Conference,[1] and the week before that I attended a student gathering at the Wharton School—that is the business school here—where a Harvard professor spoke about the situation in Central Europe.

Getting back to your letter: you can now sleep securely: we have snow chains. True, not the kind that go all the way around but rather two separate ones, one for each wheel, but they are perfectly adequate and easier to mount and cheaper. A clear windshield? Do you realize that at five degrees below zero you have to drive with an open window here because how else could you give the mystical signals with your left arm?[2] Truly, truly the Americans are a nation of automobile drivers.

What is left? Oh yes, Tuesday I wandered around downtown by myself for the first time. Ended up in The Little Rathskeller—there is such a thing—and with a glass of beer and a whisky amused myself hugely with a floor show that was amazingly daring for the Quaker City, with dancing couples and with perfectly decent young men and women who were necking unabashedly *in coram publicum*, and confirmed once again that a single man can't possibly run into danger here simply because no girl ever shows up alone. Nevertheless, I'm the butt of my family's jokes because I didn't come home until 12:30. At any rate, that was Philadelphia from a new angle.

Enough! I need to take this letter out so the *Aquitania* takes it tomorrow.

Dein Jo

MONDAY, FEBRUARY 6, 1939

Letter from Elfriede in Düsseldorf to Johannes in Philadelphia, including a discussion of the high sum Mrs. Lishke was demanding to house Tante Lene.

1 At an international conference in Lima, Peru in December 1938, the twenty-one republics of the Western Hemisphere agreed on a declaration of solidarity for peace and in mutual defense against foreign aggression.

2 *Mystical signals*: in 1939, cars were not equipped with turn signals. Americans were required to use hand signals when turning or stopping.

Düsseldorf 6 February 1939

Ach mein liebes Peterchen,

I'm in a little better frame of mind now, because after a nine-day wait a I finally got a letter from you. It took a full 13 days to get here from Philadelphia. You're really a sweet writer, and this letter of 1/24 was written only four days after the previous one. Still, it's always too long for my pining heart. From time to time I'm in a state of mind where everything just seems like a lot of garbage and I don't feel like doing anything, it all seems so pointless and I really have to exert myself just to deal with the daily routine. I really can do all that technically and in terms of the work, but a lot of the time it's very bleak. Today the newspaper didn't get here until 7:30 for a change, and all hell broke loose again. Nevertheless I'm always at my post as a diligent woman should be. I must admit it's satisfying now that I finally have the whole operation in order. When I don't have it in order it's even worse, so most of the time I keep it very much in order. I just noticed a typographical error in an ad I sent that Frankfurt made worse with a transcription error. And now I have to see how to straighten that out. It doesn't take a lot of brains.

Now to the Tante Lene problem. Mrs. Lischke writes in response to my letter:

> I acknowledge receipt of your letter with thanks and note that you are in agreement with my putting Miss Höber up and with the boarding price. I can finalize the details as to how I will receive [the payments] with your respected father-in-law. I will arrange everything for the relocation with the Director [of the institution]. Hopefully Miss Höber will feel at ease with me, and I will make it comfortable for her. Today I picked up Miss Höber and showed her her future residence. She liked it very much and I believe we will get along nicely.

I am not inclined to see the whole affair in a rosy light, but I am afraid that Tante Lene is a lucrative object for exploitation. If you figure that of the 125 marks, 30 is for the room and 35 is for board, then there is a net profit of 60 marks, exactly 50 percent; that certainly looks like a profitable deal. On the other hand we came up with this resolution simply because it is so profitable. Thanks for writing the letters directly to the Social Security office; I would have had a hard time with those. Now I'll write to Mrs. Lischke about what to do about [Tante Lene's] things. I think I probably won't have to go to Kiel. For better or for worse we have to count on Mrs. Lischke doing things, and I don't think Tante Lene's possessions warrant the cost in either time or money that would be involved in my making a trip to Kiel. In addition, such a trip would only be of use at the end of the month, when it's impossible for me to get away from here anyway. On the other hand, I can somehow manage the shopping for underwear [for Tante Lene]. For the corset it will be easiest if a used sample is sent to me. Otherwise I can imagine approximately what kind of lingerie it should be. Something like that should be available in the Old City.

On Saturday I got a new dress from the seamstress (already another one?! You just got …) but it's not really any fun if I can't try it on for you, anxious about your judgment as to my new look. That's the thing, nothing at all is fun for me anymore.

On Saturday I was invited to Herbert and Elisabeth's for *Karneval*, but I didn't go. Herbert suggested I bring a man, but there wasn't one so I stayed away and invited the Trömels to come here and impressed them greatly with your last letter. It was really very nice. I'm terribly in need of amusement, only I don't know how and where to realize that need. And now for days there has been unbelievable sunshine in Düsseldorf, at night it's freezing but in daytime it's quite warm and wonderfully pleasant. Perfect weather for winter sports. Please ask your oh-so-dear-to-me father whether he wouldn't like to meet me in April in Sicily—it calls to me so. If you or someone else wants to come along that would be alright with me, but I prefer to travel as a pair. I would like to travel with you best of all, but I would also find a couple of weeks with your father in Sicily quite passable. You see, the nice weather and loneliness lead to all sorts of crazy thoughts. Yes, and do you know what I did on Saturday? Maxhi came at 11 o'clock in the morning on his way to Cologne and persuaded me to go along. I couldn't resist the nice weather and the BMW and simply left the office unattended and went with him. But that's the first and only time I abandoned my post.

I have to say something too with regard to your grippe. It doesn't seem to me to be such a momentous outcome for one's temperature to drop from 100.7 at night to 99.3 in the morning, and I would really like to know what sense all of medical science makes when they still use the methods of the wizard and the medicine man of the primitive jungles. It sounds more like exorcism than healing. I think the money for Manfred, Mu, and Ulli's medical training was totally wasted. The famous/infamous wet cloths were used on us by my mother while we were still children and couldn't put up any resistance, but later we refused to submit ourselves to such barbaric practices. I pity you from the bottom of my heart that you have fallen in with such a horde of sadistic barbarians. In this regard I omit your father, the better self of the family, but if you think I will voluntarily betake myself to such a society then you err gravely. Everyone has his own medicine and I have mine for me. I will come there only on condition that everyone will guarantee voluntarily and in writing not to murder me or my child under the guise of performing such purported medical procedures. If it's really necessary I can have myself murdered here. Save your skin is all I can say to you, in the most literal sense of that expression. And Manfred's medical reputation, which up to now has been relatively undamaged, is now permanently wiped out. If that is method, it is also madness. I would have expected better of him.

Susanne is very well. She got her former weight back and is eating well. Wednesday she is invited to Claudia's birthday, Thursday to Sonja's. In between she is often out on the ice, comes home mostly with red cheeks and lots of black and blue marks. Gymnastics and recorder are continuing, now on the deeper alto recorder, which sounds very pretty.

My cold is doing pretty well. I got a little thinner in the process, which is not a bad thing. I should add, however, that my becoming thinner was not empirically established by means of a scale but rather is asserted on the basis of the anecdotal evidence of my appearance.

Susanne was very annoyed when I told her you found her Christmas letter too short and that she should write more. She was really outraged: you had written her only a single letter and now you wanted to say something about *her* writing. The things I read to her from your letters to me are to totally inadequate in her eyes, and she's not totally wrong. She is very much an autonomous personality. I have to tell you a nice story. She read in a calendar "Hero's Death of Hermann Löns," and wanted to know in what way it was a hero's death. I explained to her that people spoke of a hero's death any time they spoke of someone who died in the war. Whereupon she asked how many had fallen in the war. Me: on the German side, 2 million. To which she expressed a certain skepticism that all 2 million were really heroes. Surely there were some who had fallen in the war who were not really heroic. Schlageter, he was a hero, and we could talk about hero's death about him, because he paid for his personal deed with his life. I found it very nice the way she resists overused expressions and really connects a concept with the word. A hero is actually only someone who, like Siegfried, is personally courageous and does something very special and independent. Her newest wish in books is for books about heroes. I will have to give her some for her birthday.

Recently Mrs. Freyberger made an incautious remark at lunch about our eventual plans, and your bright kid jumped in right away and said she didn't want us even to think about going to America. No, that was something she totally and completely did not want. And it's high time for you to come back. Then later: she always thought that maybe sometime when she was grown up she could travel to America, and now there was the possibility that she might go there now as a child and visit her grandparents. She could really show off about that at school. She very much likes the idea that we might visit the grandparents in the summertime. School right now is only sporadic. One teacher is sick so Susanne's teacher is now in charge of two classes.

Now Susanne dictates:

Lieber Papi,

I think it is not nice at all that you said that I write too little, because you only wrote me once and I already wrote you lots of letters. Now it's your turn to write back to me. I have been invited out two times in a row, once to Claudia's, once to Sonja's. Today the exercise class was very nice. I actually just came back from there. I borrowed three books. I like *Ho-Ming* and *Monika Travels to Madascar* the most. You see Ho Ming is a very brave girl. Monika too. And in Monika there are brown people in the book. I would like to live that way among brown people. But that would be in the forest, not like in America in the city. And now I have to practice my recorder.

Viele Grüße und Küße Deine Susanne.

Susie really wanted to draw the kiss for you because she thought that would be more effective. For myself I would actually be even more in favor of having the real thing, but some several thousands of kilometers are a bit of a hindrance.

The tax forms just arrived, and I'm forwarding the ones for your father. For our own return I'll get the papers together, enter everything in pencil and then send it all to you. I think I could to do it myself, but I still prefer to have you do it. Being responsible for something is really quite problematic. If you don't have the responsibility you want it, but if you have it then you'd be happy to be rid of it. It's the same with the "clever woman" thing. Oh, how much I would now enjoy being a helpless little lady! All these ornamental epithets carry so many obligations with them.

So, that will have to be enough for today. I still have to go and buy some *Karneval* cloth for a Mexican girl's costume for Susie that Mother will make for her.

Grüße! Küße! Deine Friedel

WEDNESDAY, FEBRUARY 8, 1939

Letter from Elfriede in Düsseldorf to Johannes in Philadelphia.

Düsseldorf, 8 February 1939

Mein lieber Peter!

The day after tomorrow the *Hansa* leaves Cherbourg and I have to betake myself to my typewriter, because when there are so few ships it would be a sin to miss out on one, even if I just wrote the day before. And I dreamed of you so sweetly and comfortingly. I am writing you, however, that I made a mess with an ad, i.e., I made a typographical error in transmitting it. And in the dream you appeared to me and advised me just to tell Frankfurt what had happened. Properly comforted and strengthened, I woke up yesterday morning and did just that. It's nice to have dreams like that. Then I took care of all the other chores—a letter to Mrs. Lischke about Tante Lene's furniture, a letter to Schindler. He has turned out to be a malicious swine. This afternoon at 2:00 he called and said he had mailed 50 marks, but they never got here. So I wrote him that the complaint to the district attorney is going out today, and it will, too.

This morning a letter came from Tante Lene. Getting underwear for her is no problem; she sent me a list of what she wants, which is very modest.

All the people here who are waiting for mail from America got mail on the same day I did. The von Baeyers are still very pleased with the letters from Erich and Annemarie. They have a car already, not from his doctor's salary but from painting. Now he has to paint the surgeons in the hospital for the lobby or something like that. I think you should write him. Who knows whether some of his good connections couldn't also be turned to good use for you?

I think often about your whole trial phase over there in America and about your plans. I wouldn't want you to do something too fast, *ut aliquid fieri videatur*[3] (hopefully my Latin isn't too far off). I find it so important that you find the right start. It doesn't have to be a big start, but the right one. Take your time and look around, and if I sometimes seem impatient, because I am not always in such a wonderful mood, then just remember that I'm an old grump and that and when I send you a rainy weather letter, by the time you get it the sun is already shining again. Of course I don't mean by that that you should make light of my cares, like my cold. I can't stand your not taking me and my needs seriously.

3 *Ut aliquid fieri videatur* = so something will appear to be done.

It's still sunny here and the air has been amazingly dry. That's good for the body and the spirit. Last night I completed the last air defense evening. Now I know everything. It's not really the last evening yet; that's not until Friday with a closing "fellowship evening" in the basement of the Rochus church, where the certificates of completion will be handed out. Unfortunately it will be impossible for me to go there for business reasons and Miss Kirchner will have to pick up the paper for me, but for that I have to write an excuse letter to the police station.[4] So once again another letter. And now I will take this letter out of the typewriter for now so that others can be done first. Your letter can still wait until tomorrow evening for the Paris train.

Deine Friedel

THURSDAY, FEBRUARY 9, 1939

Letter from Johannes in Philadelphia to Elfriede in Düsseldorf. The letter includes references to Prof. Stephen B. Sweeney, founding director of the Fels Institute for Local and State Government at the University of Pennsylvania in 1937. Johannes' attendance at Prof. Sweeney's weekly seminars was an important part of his education about American municipal government. He later worked for Sweeney writing materials on municipal government issues for the Bureau of Municipal Research, a branch of the Institute.

Philadelphia, 2/9/39

Liebster Peter,

I really shouldn't be writing this letter now. I stayed home specifically to write my report on the city manager with more concentration than in the library, because I promised to have it finished by Monday. The first 5 of about 25 typewritten pages have already been typed and fragments of the remaining 20 pages of the manuscript are also finished. Over the last ten days I've worked my way through an alarming wilderness of literature in the library, and now feel at least somewhat informed. In the course of my extensive reading, moreover, I accidentally made a pleasant discovery: an article by one of the leading men in the leading professional journal on municipal government about "The Information Bureaus in German Cities," excited about the institution, full of praise for their directors, e.g., "It is refreshingly true that the prestige of the office has attracted to the position a group of exceptionally well qualified men." I made myself a couple of transcriptions and will regularly make use of them.[5]

4 Elfriede was undoubtedly fabricating "business reasons" to get out of the "fellowship evening" convened by the authorities. It later turned out that the authorities made her attend a make-up session.

5 Johannes had been head of the Mannheim Information Bureau from 1928 to 1933 and planned to use the article to explain that experience to prospective American employers.

I recently visited Prof. Sweeney, the Director of the newly established Institute of Local and State Government and the university. He asked for my resumé and invited me to take part in his weekly seminar. All of that is very gratifying.

When my Manager study is completed, then I'm supposed to write a short outline of the history of city charters. On the other hand, I've never heard anything more from New York or Washington. At the moment, though, the work on the Charter is occupying me completely because I want to do it particularly well, so there's not much time or thought left over for anything else.

On Thursday evening I went with Ulli to a concert. This very famous Philadelphia Symphony Orchestra is really wonderful beyond words. Here the expression "bigger and better" really is appropriate. The Berlin Philharmonic is the only one I know of that is of comparable size. Unfortunately the only things on the program that evening were Wagner, and *Parsifal* and *Tristan* aren't any more palatable now than ever before. On the other hand they played the overture to *Tannhäuser* unbelievably beautifully and the "Festwiese" from the *Meistersinger*, and the "Holder Abendstern" sung by a great singer was something I found very moving again—alright, alright, just laugh! And then we had very charming guests on Sunday, namely Tönnies, eldest son of the great father. He is only a chemist but nonetheless smart and nice.[6]

Now to your six day letter, which also landed here on Tuesday, that is, it came on the *Aquatania*. Poor Peter, you really do have a lot on your back and in your head and I can readily imagine that it makes you dizzy once in a while. Once your thoughts get running, there's a chain of associations that finally gets so long and complicated you can't believe there will ever be an end to it.

Hopefully you are in agreement with everything we've done and sent so far in the matter of Uncle Karl. Fortunately what you suggested coincides exactly with what we did. We have also considered already whether and when we can do something to speed things up if it doesn't go quickly in the normal course. In any event you shouldn't feel for a second that you're all alone in this.

Note: The following two paragraphs deal with important financial issues, some of which Elfriede mentioned in her multi-day letter of January 21–26, 1939. The Höbers were facing several major expenses—payments to Tischendorf for transporting Rudolf and Josephine's remaining furniture to the United States, continuing payments for Tante Lene's residential care, and eventually the cost of Elfriede and Susanne's passage to the

6 The "great father" was the sociologist Ferdinand Tönnies (1855–1936), who taught at the University of Kiel and was expelled by the Nazis at the same time as Rudolf Höber in 1933. In writing that the younger Tönnies is "only a chemist," Johannes reflects his and Elfriede's bias in favor of the social sciences and against the physical sciences.

United States. Rudolf and Josephine had enough money in bank accounts in Kiel to cover these expenses, but there was a question as to whether they would be permitted to withdraw it. Following Kristallnacht, the government had restricted the use of funds held by "Jews." The Kiel Savings and Loan had treated Rudolf as "Jewish" and subject to these restrictions and therefore declined to cash securities in these accounts.

Johannes was concerned that if Elfriede (who held a power of attorney for those accounts) tried to argue over the asset sale, she might draw the authorities' attention to her and interfere with her planned emigration. In her letter of February 1, Elfriede reiterated her proposal to sell securities to provide a monthly payment of rm 125 to Mrs. Lischke for Tante Lene's room and board. She proposed something similar to pay some tax bills. Johannes was concerned that raising any questions with the Savings and Loan might also result in their questioning the regular monthly payments that Rudolf was making to Elfriede out of that account. Because the situation was so volatile in Germany, Johannes wrote in coded and circumspect language.

To stay for the moment with the paragraph of your letter that concerns all these things: the Kiel [bank] complex has gone through my mind again and again over the last few weeks, without my coming up with a plausible solution. There are two irreconcilable wishes that clash here: my one wish is to let sleeping dogs lie [and not try to withdraw money from the bank] as long as [you do not have a visa and] your plans are not fully developed, and my other wish is to liquidate the frozen assets for your use and for Tischendorf. For now, I have decided not to discuss correcting the Savings and Loan's letter of last November [in which they declined to liquidate Rudolf's securities because they considered him "Jewish"]. Instead, I asked them today under what circumstances a sale [of securities] would be possible and at the same time I asked Tischendorf, from whom we haven't heard anything, where things stand. In any event, from now on I'll take it over from here and the one thing I need for that is the folder of our letter exchanges with Tischendorf. Please send it to me.

I have some doubts about your suggestion as to [using money in the bank to pay] the taxes and the residential care for Tante Lene, because under the circumstances it would raise the question of the necessity for this kind of resolution and indirectly raise questions about the monthly payments to you, which I would like to avoid at all costs.

So dear Peter, once again this is not a sweet or inspiring letter, but the business things have to be addressed. And now I'm going to write to Karl [Lenzberg] right away. I always do right away whatever you tell me to.

Alles liebe,

Jo

SUNDAY AND MONDAY, FEBRUARY 12 AND 13, 1939

Letter from Elfriede in Düsseldorf to Johannes in Philadelphia. Johannes' registered letter of January 31, enclosing Rudolf's affidavit of support for Elfriede, had not arrived. In it, Johannes wrote about his unpaid work with the Charter Committee, reported on his work on Elfriede's visa, and requested her to send copies of brochures he had published when working in Mannheim. The loss or delay of so important a letter was one of many impediments Elfriede and Johannes had to endure during their separation.

In this letter, Elfriede writes about Rose Monday, the Monday before Ash Wednesday, when there are huge costumed Karneval *parades in Düsseldorf and Cologne. In 1939, Rose Monday fell on February 20.*

Düsseldorf, 12 February 1939

Mein liebes Peterchen,

After a week of waiting, the *Aquitania* today brought me your letter that I was waiting for so anxiously. But my joy at getting it has a dark streak, namely that apparently some other mail from you got lost. Today's letter is from 3 February, which replied to mine of 1/27. The last one I have before that is from 1/24, and I can't believe you would have written nothing between 1/24 and 2/3 without saying something about it. What you wrote to me about your work on the division of powers in government also seems to me to expand on things that must have been in another letter. This is really a pain—just like with my six-day letter that didn't reach you—because after two or three weeks you can't remember what you wrote any more. This way I also don't know which of my packages reached you and which ones didn't. The English letters of recommendation, the diploma, the blue socks, the glove, the books? You couldn't yet have acknowledged the later things (socks, shirt and tie). No, it isn't nice that it takes so long for letters to go back and forth. Still, it's really something that it took only16 days for me to get a response today to my letter of 27 January.

I don't know where this last week disappeared to. I just sent off the monthly reconciliation, but without a balance report. My problem with the classified ad, which I handled in accordance with the instructions you gave me in a dream, was subsequently straightened out simply by running the ad again without charging the client. I filed a criminal complaint against Schindler that was transferred from the District Attorney to the petty crimes prosecutor. I'm anxious to see whether any of the money shows up again. In any case the collection process is a serious concern to me. Some of the carriers are really good but others much less so.

2/13/39

My hope that some additional mail might come [with the second delivery] today has been disappointed, so I will never get to review the background of the division of powers. Just what I needed! The letters are always so slow and now they're getting lost too!

Everyone here has the grippe; Susanne is already coughing and we munch quinine tablets as fast as we can.

Karneval is in a week but that doesn't excite me much. The only question is how I can help Susanne have fun on Rose Monday. She has a Mexican girl costume which now is missing only the unavoidable cap pistol. At any rate she very much likes the way she looks in a brown skirt with fringes, a red and white checked blouse, a brown bolero, red neckerchief and belt and a huge hat (all from Oma) and she looks amazingly grownup in it. Maybe we can take a picture of her.

In the matter of Tischendorf, from whom I've still heard nothing, I wanted to write that everything has gotten much harder [regarding shipping belongings out of Germany]. According to what I've heard, for example, each book must be listed individually [on an inventory] and notarized, which makes things much more difficult.

I sent Tante Lene RM 20—but haven't heard anything since then. I hope everything works out without my being there.

This letter doesn't have a lot in it, but my life hasn't had much in it in the last few days. More soon. This letter should be taken by the *Île-de-France*. The *Queen Mary* goes 3 days later. It's still possible that I'll have heard from you by then.

Deine Friedel

TUESDAY, FEBRUARY 14, 1939

Letter from Johannes in Philadelphia to Elfriede in Düsseldorf. He tells her about the report he wrote on the use of city managers in municipal governments in the United States. The draft, left among his personal papers, was twenty-three typed pages long and analyzed how city managers functioned in Cleveland, Cincinnati, Rochester, Dallas, and Kansas City.

Note that he completed this after having been in the United States for just six weeks.

Johannes also refers to receiving a German government response to a "form that we sent from Sulden." While Johannes and Elfriede were vacationing in Sulden, Italy, they sent Rudolf a partially completed government form registering all his property in Germany, including bank accounts. See Johannes' letter to Rudolf of September 4, 1938, Chapter 2. This registration was required of those identified by the Nazis as Jews as well as of the non-Jewish husbands of Jewish wives. Rudolf arguably fell under the latter requirement because both of Josephine's parents were Jewish. The Nazi authorities were now demanding payment of a percentage of the inventory, presumably based on the levy imposed on Germany's "Jews" following Kristallnacht. *It appears that Rudolf was appealing the finding that he was obligated to pay, since he was not "Jewish" himself. If the appeal were granted, then he could get the bank (Kiel Savings and Loan) to lift the freeze on his negotiable securities.*

Philadelphia, 14 February 1939

Liebster Peter,

Yesterday I delivered my report on the City Manager to the Charter Committee right on time, after I spent almost all of Saturday and Sunday at the typewriter, and today I am squeezing in a mail day in order to give the *President Harding* something for you.

I will be excited to see what becomes of my first American manuscript. Yesterday I worked it over for two hours with the Research Director to correct minor grammatical and substantive errors before it goes on to the actual Committee. It got to be 23 typewritten pages long and Mr. Phillips—that's the name of the Director of the Research staff—thinks that for the Speaker's Bulletin (that is what the Speaker's Manual has become) an extract should be made and that it should become a magazine or newspaper article, either in its entirety or in edited form.

The way this Committee works and what the research staff is supposed to be for is pretty amusing. I already wrote you that last week Mr. Millard—he is the actual executive head of the Committee—asked to have a special report done for him about the division of powers and parliamentary responsibility in American political theory. The request, as I learned later, was occasioned by the fact that a significant labor group opposes an appointed City Manager and instead favors maintaining the elected mayor. It is now supposed to be made clear to them that people should vote for the legislative branch and that the executive should be appointed by the legislative branch. Then this morning Mr. Phillips called me to say that an important man from the Chamber of Commerce has taken the position that the difference between the new Charter and the old one is too great and that the changes have to be introduced gradually. Mr. Millard, whose job it is to sway such influential people, now wants classical citations and historical examples that a general reform is better than piecemeal. Sort of a funny assignment, I think, but if this forces me to study Anglo-Saxon political theory it won't do me any harm.

It's also a good thing my mind is kept occupied this way. For the moment I'm a little bit at a dead end in my [job-hunting] efforts. Lots of correspondence is still trickling in, but really nothing from which I can hope for any immediate success. I don't want to go to Washington again unless I know it's not a wild goose chase. I'm inclining more and more to a trip to Harvard to see [Professor Carl] Friedrich. But first on Thursday I'm going to Dr. Sweeney's seminar for the first time.

Things are quiet right now in the Höber House. Daddy came home Saturday afternoon with 101.1 and was immediately consigned to bed. He scared us on Sunday morning with over 102.2, but since yesterday the fever has gone down and today he's sitting at his desk again and in the face of united family opposition will only be permitted to go to the lab the day after tomorrow.

I just discussed various business [matters] with him and have to report the current status to you so you know it all. Tante Lene: I already wrote you that we wrote to Mrs. Lischke as soon as you sent us her address. We told her we were in agreement with RM 125 and that we will send her the first payment as soon as her agreement is here. No answer has come yet from the Social Security office. The furniture question seems to have been easily worked out because Tante Lene wrote that Mrs. Lischke told her she could bring all her things along. What is in Tante Lene's savings account should be sufficient to cover the move and other immediate expenses; any day now we expect a letter in response to ours in which those things were raised as well. So for now you don't have to worry about all this. But since all good things must come to an end, on Saturday Daddy received a demand for payment in full in response to the form we sent from Sulden in September. We are filing a formal appeal; if it is granted, as we hope it will be, then we can also start something up with the Savings and Loan.

I find Alwine's proposal to you [to buy the business] less grotesque than untimely, though Frankfurt won't think so. How would it be if you were to look around for a more suitable candidate? Shouldn't it be possible to dig up someone like that?

I would like to go out to dinner with you on the Kurfürstendamm too!

In liebe,

Jo

THURSDAY, FEBRUARY 16, 1939

Letter from Elfriede in Düsseldorf to Johannes in Philadelphia. In it she responds to Johannes' letter sending her Rudolf's affidavit of support.

Düsseldorf, 16 February 1939.

Mein liebstes Peterchen,

Joy reigns in the Halls of Troy,[7] since it has pleased God's and the German mail's inscrutable judgment to spit out your registered letter of 31 January after all. How come, where from, why now? One shouldn't ask such questions of the inscrutable judgment, but rather be pleased, and so that's what I am. I hope that the day after tomorrow the *Queen Mary* will follow the *Île-de-France* with this letter quickly so you won't have to go on worrying about the fate of your 31st of January letter, which is truly rich in content. This letter is a terrific combination: for you it's the end of your efforts and for me it's the arrival of the papers. Thus armed I will now charge into the uncertain War of the Documents [with Uncle Karl].

I think the thing with the City Charter Committee is really very, very nice, very appropriate and very decent. After I read your letter twice and then yesterday evening gave it my best at Mother's house, I even understood the whole thing. One really has to rethink what one knows about German municipal government, but please tell me more. To help you out, yesterday I packed up the five books you asked for. I haven't found the municipal ordinances for the state of Baden yet, but the Mannheim Reports from 1933–38 and the first volume of *The Living City* are already on their way. The two other volumes [of *The Living City*] and the Report of the Finance Commissioner will follow today. If I don't find the municipal ordinances [here at home] I will try to dig them up somewhere else. As far as I know they are no longer in effect. Good luck with what you're doing.

Enclosed is the recommendation from H.H.[8] It looks like it was drafted primarily from the perspective of your work in public relations, and

7 This phrase from Friedrich Schiller's *Kassandra* [*Freude war in Trojas Hallen* ...] became a cliché in the Höber family.

8 *H.H.* = Hermann Heimerich, *Oberbürgermeister* of Mannheim when Johannes worked there, 1928–33.

there's nothing there about the fact that your work gave you the opportunity to become familiar with the overall work of the municipal administration. I'm sure H.H. would add that if asked, if you need that or can use that.

Dear Peter, it's not necessary for you to write to our friends here either a collective letter or individually. I tell them everything and share your letters with everyone who would like to hear more. It's funny how they all see you as such a success, like a kind of foreign comrade. I really like it.

Everything here is starting to show signs of the *Karneval*, but not for me. Tomorrow Hendrik is coming to go to the little Movie Ball with Günther, and they are going to Cologne on Monday, but without me. As much as I would like to celebrate again at home and around here, it strikes me as absurd to drive to Cologne or something like that. I'm not sure how to help Susanne out so she can enjoy the Rose Monday parade, because that's really important to her. How can you help your child enjoy the essential pleasures of life when there's no *Papi* on hand?

I've been thinking about English lessons for Susie. Up to now I haven't thought of anyone suitable, but I hope to find someone. Maybe then we'll drop the gymnastics class so it doesn't get to be too much. In any case, we want to keep the recorder lessons going, which now take up a full hour once a week.

And then I have the income tax form ahead of me. I try not to think about it, but have to deal with it eventually. An abandoned wife has many worries.

1000 Grüße,

Deine Friedel

Oops, I almost forgot the further recent developments in the Tante Lene and Mrs. Lischke problem. Mrs. L. wrote:

> I received your letter of the 7th of this month with thanks. No information has yet arrived from your father–in–law, but I hope to hear from him in the next few days. If it is important to Miss Höber to move her own furniture into my place, I am willing to do that, but the furniture is in part in very poor condition and in need of repair. To what extent her underwear is in usable condition is outside of my knowledge and various new pieces may need to be procured. I have been in communication with your father-in-law and hope to receive notice from him by 28 February at the latest as to the extent to which he will assume responsibility. If, however, I should not be in possession

of your father-in-law's agreement, I cannot take responsibility for admitting Miss Höber.

In response, I wrote: Really bad furniture should not be moved. On the other hand, we would like to have things that are still good kept. Clothing will be supplemented. Dress is on the way. Money sent for underwear. Please let me know if anything else turns out to be necessary. The father-in-law has certainly written already, and the letter will definitely arrive in the next few days. Well, hopefully anyway.

FRIDAY, FEBRUARY 17, 1939

Letter from Elfriede in Düsseldorf to Johannes in Philadelphia.

Düsseldorf, 17th February 1939.

Lieber Peter,

Three letters and a card in a single week is really nice. As a result I'm feeling good. I sent a letter with its rich contents to Uncle Karl. Mrs. Freyberger got me the necessary records and that sped up the process by about two weeks. I have now decided as you suggest in your letter not to get impatient and to wait quietly for whatever fate wishes to impose on me. I do not feel like I'm on my own, especially when three letters come in one week. I called Mother to tell her of my good fortune, and she told me not to get despondent all over again if a week goes by without any mail.

Düsseldorf is sometimes remarkable. Last night I was at a farewell party at Luise's [unidentified], who on Sunday, the day after tomorrow, is going to England via Holland. Our dear lady doctor, whom everyone misses so much whenever there is any situation resembling illness, was there too. She's going to England too for the time being, where she has relatives who were able to get her the permit, but from there she too wants to go to the U.S. afterwards and hopes to meet us again sometime in Philadelphia.

All the printed matter [items you asked for] have now been sent off, but the municipal regulations are not to be found. Tomorrow, Saturday afternoon, I'll search all the bookstores one more time. If I didn't still have the tax return ahead of me I'd feel better. Just think, I've taken off nine pounds and I'm as slim as I was in May and I didn't have to go hungry to do that. I did it slowly so I didn't have to pay for a youthful figure with the facial wrinkles that make you look that much older. I still weigh 119 pounds, so you won't bruise yourself on my bones. It's just the right weight for a hot American summer.

After many nasty days of rain it's wonderfully fair again and everyone hopes it will stay that way until Monday. Rose Monday has the one advantage that it's almost like a holiday. Maybe then I will turn to the taxes. That's such a load on my shoulders, but since I took care of the things for Uncle Karl I really feel good.

Next door Susie is practicing the "The Moon has Risen" and that's very pretty too.

Alles liebe Deine Elfriede

FRIDAY, FEBRUARY 17, 1939

Letter from Johannes in Philadelphia to Elfriede in Düsseldorf.

Philadelphia, 2/17/39

Geliebter Schatz,

Your letter of the 6th, which the *New York* brought, starts out so sad and then continues so cheerfully that it struck me that our mood swings on this side and on that side of the Atlantic still run approximately in parallel. What a thin-skinned generation we have become! At the moment Gri, Manfred, and I are all depressed, I on account of jobs, Manfred because of the oral exams, and Gri because Manfred is and because they are getting along so well right now that they are more dependent on each other than when things weren't as good between them.

I delude myself that I succeed, at least outwardly, in appearing to be the most stable and most cheerful person here, but our clear-sighted and most sensitive Daddy still notices most of the things that are going on with his children. A few days ago, when I was really in poor spirits behind a smiling façade, he talked to me one evening as though he were taking a little boy on his lap. On occasions like that, if at all possible, you're not supposed to show that you're moved in some way. At the moment I'm keeping things pretty well bottled up, and I very much regret having no one around with whom I don't have to maintain some kind of assumed role. But Pa-Mu are themselves so unstable and besides, I always think that after the last five years they have earned some cheering up and as a result I feel doubly obligated to become a great success. I believe that the trouble with you and me and all of us is that we are all just sick of everything. I think everything would be much better if there were just some occurrence in the Macrocosm[9] that we could be really happy about. The fact that there's no sign of anything like that anywhere is what I find to be the worst thing of all.

That's not to say that there isn't a great deal that I really enjoy in my current life. Today I spent all day in the very lovely Public Library behind a wall of books consisting, for example, of *The American Commonwealth* by James Bryce, John Stuart Mill's *On Liberty*, Charles Beard's *American Government and Politics* and similar enjoyable things. The fact that I found much more material against rather than for the proposition that the Charter Committee wants to prove was less pleasant.

When I came home today, a children's party was under way for Janka's birthday. The best thing for the spectators was the pidgin English with which the children—partly German and partly American—were able to understand each other.

I drove home from town today in Blue Boy. Those of the family who are going into town drive together between 8:15 and 8:30 in the morning, after which the car is generously available for either Manfred or me for the rest of the day. The pleasure of driving an 85 HP, 8-cylinder car isn't diminished by repeated use. In addition, this daily trip from Germantown to Philadelphia and back, which is a quick 25-minute drive, is unbelievably lovely. The drive into town goes along the Wissahickon and then through the Schuylkill valley. Even now it's charming as a [winter] landscape and in the summer it will be a drive through green woods. The house in general and my little room in particular are also as nice as one could want. And you, first of all you have Susie, you have your mother and brothers, you have Gerhard and Marlies, Hilde, the Prof. and Mrs. Magician and Maxhi, who show up a lot in your letters, you have the nice apartment, you are your own boss. How tired and raw the last several years have made us, when all these good things aren't enough to keep us happy.

I think it's a good idea to draw up this kind of balance sheet for yourself once in a while. This is not intended as a sermon for the two of us. I think that we, and you in particular, *Schatz*, are behaving ourselves pretty well. But I think that putting together this kind of compilation of good things almost necessarily makes the balance seem more favorable. One thing, though, really surprises me. For several months now I've had that highly vaunted and often sought after "freedom," and I don't know what to do with it. I'm the kind of stay-at-home Jonny you could only wish for in your wildest dreams and I don't find being a stay-at-home at all hard.

9 *Macrocosm* = in the world at large. In this context, he means that everyone would feel better if anything went even a bit better in Germany.

You are responsible for that. Only you.

Jo

MONDAY, FEBRUARY 20, 1939

Letter from Elfriede in Düsseldorf to Johannes in Philadelphia. Among other things, the letter concerns individual income taxes for Johannes and Elfriede, as well as a separate return for the newspaper business.

Rose Monday [February 20, 1939]

Mein lieber Peter,

This is going to be a tax letter. Even taxes have to be done once in a while, and I think Rose Monday is particularly well suited for that. I already started working on it on Saturday and put together a pile of numbers and think it would be necessary for you to prepare the actual return. I'm enclosing the forms and a listing of receipts and expenditures. The revenue side of the thing is completely unproblematic because it was already assembled for the estimated tax return, first by you and then by me.

Note: An extensive discussion of income and business expenses for the business and personal income tax returns is omitted here.

Karneval time is progressing in its lively way without bothering me very much. On Friday Hendrik and Ellen came. Hendrik went to the Film Ball with Günter, but it wasn't fun because it was too crowded. On Saturday Günter went to The Barn while I had a ladies night here. Hilde hadn't been seen for three weeks, but she's had lots to do taking care of the liquidation of their house and other complicated things. Besides her, another relative was there, who is moving out of her house on 1 March and going to England with all the children. Then Mother came over during the evening and the gathering of war brides, as Hilde called us, was quite cheerful. First we emptied the half bottle of Mosel wine, then cognac and soda and when the soda was gone the cognac by itself, until the bottle was empty and we were very jovial. Last night I went with Mother to the Trömels, where I drank champagne with Gerhard, also until the bottle was empty and I was very cheerful. Mild alcoholic stimulation does me a lot of good. For this Saturday we all have bad intentions for a return engagement. In our cellar there are still a few bottles of punch wine that we want to use for a Cold Duck.[10] Hopefully something will come of that. It's nearly time to supplement our wine cellar, which aside from the aforesaid punch wine now consists of only three bottles. But when you left it was already pretty sparse.

10 *Cold Duck* [*Kalte Ente*] is a wine punch whose ingredients usually include wine, champagne, lemon juice, and sugar.

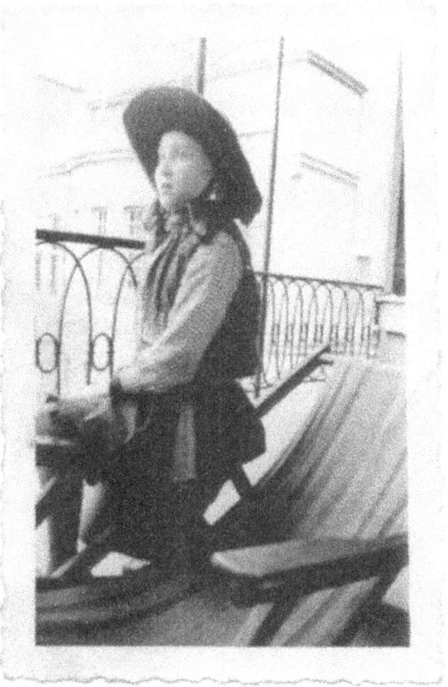

Susanne in her "Mexican girl" costume for Karneval. *On the left is her own drawing of herself, and on the right is the photograph taken by Günter Fischer.*

Now Susanne has taken off to watch the parade outside the train station with Marlies and Christof. I am staying here on the pretext of having to finish up the taxes, but I'm really happy that something nice could be worked out for Susanne. On Saturday afternoon, when I went shopping with her for the missing items—a cap pistol and brown makeup—she became thoughtful about her missing *Papi*. It wasn't nice that you were away: 1st it was sad, 2nd was tiresome, 3rd it wasn't nice. Then yesterday at dinner: it now looks almost like we're going to America—because I had said something about English lessons. She is strenuously opposed to the idea. Arguments: friends, Oma, and "all the Fischers." She has grasped the whole thing quite thoroughly.

Deine Friedel

FRIDAY, FEBRUARY 24, 1939

Letter from Elfriede in Düsseldorf to Johannes in Philadelphia.

Düsseldorf, 2/24/39.

Lieber, guter Peter,

Last week, when there were so many letters from you, I had to promise my Mother not to get down in the dumps when the next interruption inevitably arrived—but that's easier said than done. I just find life pointless when there aren't any letters from you. I notice more and more how very married I am and that even a grouchy, nasty Jo is better than none at all. Life may be calmer without you here, but it feels quite empty. The household and the business take a lot of time and are tiresome, but it all seems so unimportant when I know I won't hear the sound of car door slamming, won't hear the repeated ringing of the doorbell, and won't hear Jo running up the stairs. What used to seem to be too much time spent running the business now seems too little. As a result I'm terribly affected by mood swings. Yesterday, when the sun was shining and I amused myself with Peter Fleming's "With Only Me," I was content and in good spirits, but today everything, both sky and mood, are again gray and bleak. Tomorrow it will probably be different again.

Betz was here a couple of days ago, and it was especially nice because it wasn't about anything in particular. The conversation, which raised my spirits, showed me again that our mode of proceeding was the right one.[11] I have to tell you that just now because other times I complain about the details. I was all ready to start on the [subscriber] invoices today, but those miserable people [in Frankfurt] haven't sent them yet,[12] so now everything will be squeezed together needlessly. I have no idea how I'll deal with the collections next week. On Monday Günter is leaving with the car for two weeks, so it won't be available. Herbert suggested I rent a car, and I will in fact do that if it is not too expensive. Herbert can drive me and I must say I would prefer that to doing all three places by train. It's particularly tedious to do Gladbach that way.

Since I can't do anything for you here, I sent off two packages to you today, one with a shirt and one with two pairs of socks. Undershorts will follow next week.

Deine Friedel

FRIDAY, FEBRUARY 24, 1939

Letter from Johannes in Philadelphia to Elfriede in Düsseldorf.

Philadelphia 2/24/39.

Liebster Peter,

Following my mother's example, I passed an almost completely sleepless night. That was because when your letter of the 12th/13th arrived with the complaint about my long silence, I quickly checked my file of your letters and confirmed that of all things it was precisely the registered letter of 1/31 that hadn't reached you. I tried to console myself with the

11 Johannes and Elfriede had taken Dr. Betz into their confidence as to their plans for leaving Germany, and he supported them, particularly in their relations with the *Frankfurter Zeitung* management.

12 Subscriber invoices were prepared each month by Frankfurt. Elfriede then sorted the invoices and distributed them to carriers to collect. If Frankfurt sent the invoices late, the monthly collections would be delayed.

thought that maybe the post office routed it to the *Deutschland*, which sailed on the 2nd instead of the *President Harding*, which sailed on 2/1 and so it wouldn't have arrived in Hamburg until the 12th. But now everything is alright again because this morning the *Queen Mary* spat out your two letters of the 16th and 17th and they bring me the response I was hoping for from the doubly noteworthy contents of that wandering letter.

Note: The following paragraph illustrates Johannes and Elfriede's use of circumlocutions to conceal sensitive facts from possible government surveillance. "Uncle Erich" refers to Erich Marx, Josephine's brother, a pioneering physicist in the study of radiation. The Nazis expelled him as professor of physics at the University of Leipzig in 1933 because of his Jewish parentage, after which he ran his own research and testing laboratory. The oblique references to Uncle Erich's "grandmother" and "denomination" suggest that Rudolf and Josephine needlessly disclosed Erich's Jewish ancestry. The references to the "satisfactory address" and the "unsatisfactory address" may refer to places where Erich was seeking employment. He and his family eventually escaped Germany, and he became a professor of physics at Rensselaer Polytechnic Institute.

My bad night was also partly due to the fact that we sat up late with Daddy's colleague Amberson, who arrived at 10:30 at night from New York where he had been working on behalf of Uncle Erich. He is doing everything he can to resolve this case, which is getting more and more urgent, but unfortunately had completely unnecessary difficulties because my otherwise truly good and sweet Pa-Mu, who even after five years here are amazingly unfamiliar with certain things, didn't keep quiet about the grandmother on the one hand and the denomination on the other, so that Amberson had already negotiated something with the unsatisfactory address when the true state of things became known. Fortunately the satisfactory place jumped into the breach and so now he has $100 monthly altogether and the only thing that is missing is the formal invitation from the university.

My dear, all my nightmares have been driven away by the good news in today's mail. And the nicely laundered blue and white striped shirt appeared here as ordered, and when the tie—really a good old friend—appeared I put it on right away.

Now I have to interrupt [this letter] for a while and drive into town. At 1:00 there's a big lunch for the Charter Committee staff "for the purpose of coordinating their activities," and I want to go since I was personally invited. Apparently there was some disturbance in the ever-expanding machinery [of the Committee], whose gentlest waves broke on the shores of the quietly serious research staff and even washed over my ankles. When I got assigned my Manager paper, it was supposed to be for a speaker's manual, but by the time I delivered the chapter a week ago Monday the speakers' manual had turned into a series of speakers' bulletins and my good Mr. Phillips, a bright young lawyer but somewhat awkward and inexperienced, read the 23 pages and then murmured much verbiage in response about thanks and praise along the lines of "it's so excellent it ought to be published in a magazine or periodical," but also "couldn't I have just a short abstract of about two pages for the speakers' manual?" I'm not irked about that in the least. I won't believe the publishing thing until I see it in front of me in black and white, but I delivered the short abstract yesterday.

If my big paper isn't circulated more widely I would be sorry, but I wouldn't complain, because I learned an endless amount by being under pressure to write it. It seems, however, that some of the American staff who had experiences similar to mine were less peacefully minded and I'm sure that's the reason for the peacemaking luncheon today. There, too, I will hold strictly to my line that I'm a technical expert who is happy to make his subject matter expertise available but that I don't want to get mixed up in the discussion of what kind of Charter Philadelphia should get or how it ought to be publicized. Don't be surprised at so much modesty on my part, because it's really hard for me. Sometimes my fingers—and my tongue—itch to do more, but it would be very wrong if I were to succumb to that temptation.

Afternoon. In the interim the luncheon has taken place. It was interesting, as is every glimpse into the internal workings of the local machinery, and I have the feeling that the people with whom I have come into contact over the last few weeks think I'm alright.

Now to your letters. I'm most anxious to hear about Susie's reaction to the disclosure of our plans, referred to in your letter of the 6th and confirmed by her in writing today. I think it's terrible that she had to learn about what's ahead because Mrs. F. ran her mouth off, but it won't help matters for me to scold that good woman, whose strong points just don't seem to include discretion. Still, I hope the appealing aspects of this upsetting situation will quickly cause Susie to forget about the sad aspects. It's perfectly amazing how well all halfway normal children get along here. I'm pondering my letter in which I will lay this all out for Susie, but that can't be written on command when there's a ship leaving in 18 hours.

I hope your promise to take a picture of her as a Mexican girl came off, assuming Günter wasn't drunk the whole time, otherwise it could be done again after Ash Wednesday. That such a thing as *Karneval* exists at all feels like a fairy tale from a long ago time. I almost completely forgot about the holiday until someone said to me the day before yesterday that today is Ash Wednesday. If you had been here you would have had less trouble with me this year than any other time. On the other hand, Gri, Manfred, and I went on Tuesday to one of those burlesque shows, which were forbidden when we were in New York but which are amazingly enough permitted here. Well, it doesn't do any harm but what are you going to do? Our attempt to go bar hopping afterwards came to naught because it was Washington's Birthday and all the bars were closed, where otherwise you can watch a floor show while sipping a 25 cent drink with a one dollar minimum. Right now that's beyond our means.

In reading through my last letter to you I discovered that I didn't tell you anything at all about my first seminar with Dr. Sweeny. It wasn't very stimulating and it struck me as very odd to be sitting at a school desk again. But it's welcome to me that my daily activities, my reading, and everything else I do and work on at the moment is uniformly concerned with municipal administration. Your very justified observation that you had to read my Charter letter twice to understand it demonstrated to me again that the whole system of state and governance law here has been developed in a completely different way and that it has to be learned from the ground up. On Monday I experienced my first radio discussion. It, too, was about the Charter and was broadcast from Philadelphia, and a large audience was not only permitted but encouraged to call in.

I think that gets me through with your letters—up to your and my closing topic, Tante Lene. A letter came today from Mrs. Lischke, written before she had ours from the 6th and urging confirmation. We cabled right away: letter received, March rent already transmitted to my sister, letter follows.

Gosh, I just noticed that this whole letter doesn't include any response o everything you told me about the business. Very typical. But it's remarkable how my usual tendency to think I know everything better and want to do it myself has grown into the conviction that you know everything better and must do it yourself. Which is not to say that I won't be glad to look at the tax form and do my best with it. For that, please type up the tax rates up to 30,000 marks, because I also have to do Daddy's return. The problems with the carriers are always the most enduring and most difficult of all the problems. In the matter of Schindler, in my opinion, it is of utmost importance to make it clear to the prosecuting attorney that this is not the big rich publisher [i.e., the *Frankfurter Zeitung*] but a small poor agency that has been injured in this case. That will weigh heavily in the evaluation of the circumstances. If it's not too indiscreet for me to ask, I would like to have the subscription figures for February for all four locations. But it's not essential.

So now I really do have to bring this to a close. I've arranged for the second time to get together with a very nice young doctor, Dr. Samter, with whom I went walking (!) and then to the movies last Saturday, an English production of *Pygmalion*, much nicer of course in terms of language but otherwise weaker than the German version. But if Charles Laughton in *The Beachcomber* should come to your neighborhood go see it.

Schluss, schluss, schluss, Kuss!

Dein Jo

SUNDAY, FEBRUARY 26, 1939

Letter from Elfriede in Düsseldorf to Johannes in Philadelphia.

Düsseldorf, 2/26/39.

Mein lieber Schatz,

It is nice to begin Sunday morning with a letter from you when the previous one is only two days old. It's aggravating that your letters always get here just after I sent one off to you. But now on 3/1 the *Île-de-France* or is it the *Paris* is going and can take this letter along.

We had a very cheerful evening here yesterday, Trömels, Ellen, Herbert and I. Günter could only come for a short time because he had to leave at 10:30 for the nighttime showing of a guaranteed genuine Swedish film that was only being shown this one time at night. At any rate by 1 A.M. we had demolished six bottles and were very cheerful. Then on top of that we went to the restaurant at the main train station, [which is open all night] for chicken soup. We had actually planned only to go for chicken soup, but since you can't do that without having first had something else to drink, we made a virtue out of necessity and made a Cold Duck out of our left over punch wine, supplemented with some [sweet] Feist champagne *au goût americain*. All that arduous labor earned us the right to said chicken soup, which was then as nice and rich as ever.

This afternoon Günter and Mother were here for dinner. In view of our shrunken households, we decided it would be good to eat Sunday dinner here one week and at Mother's the next. It's really only fun to make a full dinner with all the good things (beef broth with marrow dumplings, roast tenderloin, French fries, remoulade sauce, celery root salad, wine pudding) when you do it for other people as well.

Something very sad happened to me. On Friday, on my way to the train station, where I was taking several packages, I lost my beloved wrist watch. I put an ad in the paper today, but of course I have little hope. I can take the unavoidable blows of fate with greater equanimity than something like this that might have been avoided with a little more care. But in the big picture I can still stand it. Everything in the realm of "things" has evaporated in my scale of values. But the watch was not only a thing but something of sentimental value.

I don't like it one bit that in Philadelphia you're such a homebody, if that's what you really are and this description isn't just put there to reassure me. I'm very much in favor of your thoroughly cultivating your desires for going out, unreliability, drinking, girls, and independence as long as I'm not there. If I'm not there it can't hurt me, at least as long as you keep writing me nicely—but if you save up all these cravings until we're together again then it will be a lot less nice. I'm also very opposed to your playing the model husband in front of your parents. That means that afterwards no one will ever believe how mean you can be and every disagreement we have will be laid to my account. But maybe it would be justified to lay everything to my account, since your cravings for unreliability are only aroused when I'm around. Is it my fault that you feel the need to stray when I'm around but not when I am far away??? I'm beginning to become skeptical of my own ability as a wife and of my ability to make you happy. On my side it's much simpler. There's no special art to avoiding temptation when there are no temptations around. Virtue arising from a lack of opportunity was never something meritorious, and I was never very talented at either seeking out or finding opportunities.

You're quite right that it's good and advisable in times of depression to calculate the balance of assets and liabilities. Once in a while it even works, but it's much harder to resist the frequent mood swings. On a long-term basis the usual moral prescriptions, like hard work and so on, turn out not to be very effective. But even the strongest emotions fade over time.

I have taken some steps with respect to the question of a successor [to me in the business]. I mentioned the question to Maxhi and through friends of his got to a Mr. Müller, who is interested. I set Betz on his trail and he will inspect the man. I accidentally ran into Alwine again when Herbert and I were eating at Mulfiner's after the last collection trip to Gladbach. She began all over again and got me very angry again. A little arrogance can be quite nice, but some people carry it too far!

Our conversation yesterday evening added a humorous note to the latest tax increases. It's mainly Günter who is affected and it will be an exercise in reckoning whether, in view of the taxes on bachelors, a marriage might not be worth it. Unfortunately, however, the designated candidate is missing. For us the elimination of the deduction for household help will have a substantial impact on us, but not until the next [return]. By the time you get this letter you will hopefully have sent off the tax papers I prepared so beautifully. If not, do it right away. It's very important to me to have these things done completely correctly. It already won't be as correct as I would like because I didn't manage to get my own [personal return] done before *Karneval*.

E.

Accompanying note from Susanne, with an enclosed drawing.

Lieber Papi,

How are you in America? Mutti said that if I am coming to America I have to learn English first. The people over there [in America] have forgotten it [German]. Playing the alto recorder is real hard. In addition it is very low. I don't want to move to America at all. Here I have friends and so many other things. Now lots of OOOOOO

From . . . . . . ? who will be a Mexican girl for Rose Monday.
Susie!
Susie!

TUESDAY, FEBRUARY 28, 1939

Letter from Johannes in Philadelphia to Elfriede in Düsseldorf.

Philadelphia, 2/28/39

Liebster Schatz,

With the author's compliments, with his kindest regards, with his cordial greetings, with all his love, enclosed for you herewith is my first American opus. It's not yet a printed one but nevertheless mimeographed in an "edition" of 250 copies sent today to all of those who are interested in the Charter Campaign. Maybe I will make my fortune with this; maybe I already have. In any event I'm proud of it. I'm swimming in deeper and deeper water, and my whole family is having a good laugh about how much I am already "in" in Philadelphia. In any event I'm being swamped with additional assignments: two days on the division of powers, two days on finance statistics, two days of departmental division of responsibility. When you realize that for every topic I first have to translate the basic commonly used terms into American, you can imagine how arduous it is to live up to my reputation. I sit either at the Charter Committee or in the Bureau of Municipal Research, where I now have a room of my own, from 9 in the morning to 5 in the afternoon with only a 20 minute break. The nicest part for me is that my boss's prestige makes it possible for me to talk through every problem that comes up with the most knowledgeable subject matter experts. It's too bad that you aren't here! Women who can do things are regarded here in the same way as men who can do things, and in this sense the organization of this steadily growing Committee still really has a place for people with initiative.

I actually didn't mean to write this much today, because the letter I will send Friday on the *Normandie* will probably arrive at the same time as this one. And you'll probably have to chew on my Manager piece longer than on an equally long and problematic letter.

Cheerio!

Jo

CHAPTER 7

Jo Has a Job

WEDNESDAY AND THURSDAY, MARCH 1 AND 2, 1939

Letter from Elfriede in Düsseldorf to Johannes in Philadelphia. The Depression was winding down, and employment opportunities were expanding in Germany, in part because Hitler was spending hugely on military expansion. The improving economy enabled Paul to get a well-paying job but also made it more difficult for Johannes and Elfriede to hire and keep good carriers, who could now get better-paying jobs elsewhere.

Düsseldorf, 1 March 1939

Mein lieber Schatz,

Joy reigns in the halls of Troy because I got my wristwatch back (actually, why *did* joy reign in the halls of Troy? Surely not just to provide us with an apposite expression to use today!). I just picked it up at the office of the Rhine railway. Cost: RM 1, in addition to which I left RM 10 for the conductor. I'm really happy I got it back—it's very dear to me.

Before that I was at the Criminal Police about Schindler. He claimed that he lost the money, that he didn't think he was guilty, and that he would pay it back as soon as he could. It now turns out he concealed from me the fact that he owes RM 180 on a loan from a consumer loan company which he won't have paid off until May!! Then he wants to pay us off at the rate RM 30 monthly. [The police] recommended that I enter into another payment agreement with him, the details of which I should share with the Criminal Police. That would be on file along with whether he complies with the agreement or not. The problem is that in the absence of a guilty plea the misappropriation isn't substantiated, so I'll dispatch yet another letter to Schindler to get him to come here. Interestingly, the Criminal Police told me he agreed to garnishing his pension to pay off the loan from the Consumer Credit company. What's possible for the Consumer Credit company has to be possible for us too, so I'll tell him he has to bring the agreement with the Consumer Credit company. That way I can see how you do that and I'll also finally have papers showing just how indebted he is. As before, I don't consider him a big racketeer, but a lot of money can be lost to a big thirst. He used the RM 180 from the Consumer Credit company for clothes and underwear. It's scandalous that they would give him a loan for that.

Thirst was also Linnmann's undoing—he's on the hook for RM 88. I wouldn't have let him collect on the invoices already in February if his wife hadn't said she would do the collections for him. But she got a job as a helper in a department store, gave him the invoices to collect, and now part of the money is missing. She wants to pay the money back with her son's help, and since Linnmann is still working for us something is still coming in by means of his wages. For this month I transferred Linnmann's collections to another carrier. And just so my troubles shouldn't be over, Wulff, the pillar of my business, is leaving next. I'm really upset about that. The instability of the carrier crew is so high because the good workers we once had and could always get are now doing more profitable things than delivering newspapers.

On Friday Paul is going skiing in the Alps with Heidi, then to Lake Garda and then following our tracks to Venice and Verona, Padua and Vicenza. Things are also happening for him career-wise. The Executive Director of the national Leather Business Association in Berlin asked him if he would be interested in taking over the Association's legal department. They're talking about a salary of RM 700–800. It's not certain yet whether anything will come of it, since he doesn't have the qualifications that several other candidates who weren't able to go [to Berlin] had. It's becoming apparent that the time has come when capable people will be able to get themselves well placed. It's significant that lawyers, who were a surplus just two years ago, are becoming scarce too.

The *Queen Mary* arrives in Cherbourg today. If I'm lucky I'll get a letter from you tomorrow. The ships are beginning to go a little more often. With two letters in one week my emotional stability is much improved.

3/2/39

Life isn't pretty in the Ultimo. Everybody has the grippe. Not me yet. But the waves of the business are breaking a little bit over my head. In a minute I'm off for Krefeld and Gladbach.

Alles liebe, Deine Friedel

THURSDAY MARCH 2, 1939

Letter from Johannes in Philadelphia to Elfriede in Düsseldorf.

Philadelphia, 3/2/39

Liebster Peter,

If it weren't for the fact that the *Normandie* is leaving tomorrow, and if it weren't a mortal sin to miss out on such a nice fast ship, you wouldn't get a letter from me today. After seven hours in the office and two hours in the seminar my poor head is just a little tired. After three days of preparation, I spit out ten typewritten pages about the division of departmental responsibilities in Philadelphia under the old and new Charters, and the sheer mechanical process of dictating that kind of manuscript is hard. My enthusiasm makes it possible for me to overcome these issues quite readily these days, and the kindness of the Research Director to whom I am assigned, Mr. Walter Phillips—remember his name, he warrants it—will keep that enthusiasm alive for a good while. Phillips is a young lawyer who just graduated from Harvard. After working together for five weeks we get along extraordinarily well, and I hope to visit him at home soon with his wife, who just had a baby two months ago.

I'm actually beginning to pick up a few people of my own. On Saturday night I was invited to dinner at the home of a lovely young woman and her husband, who seems to be a pediatrician but otherwise totally superfluous, though apparently married to her. This invitation was thanks to my assiduously sweet–talking the elderly mother of the young woman at a Charter luncheon. Yesterday I went by myself to dinner at the home of a young couple—he a businessman, she a nearly graduated doctor whom Pa-Mu have known for years—who I talked to until one in the morning about topics that were completely different from anything Pa-Mu would ever discuss with them. On Sunday the university's zoologist was at our place for tea, a remarkable man whom even I liked. I hope to incorporate him into my private stable soon, so I'll have something to show you when you get here. As I write this I realize that right now I'm imagining I might be able to stay in Philadelphia *á la longue*.

[Later]
In the interim we had dinner and there are guests downstairs, but they understand my absenting myself. I'm happy to be up here alone with the typewriter, because I find myself a bit worn out after the last few nights. I'm also not used to the fact that the lunch break passes nearly unnoticed, and a couple of times at lunch, in addition to the cup of coffee that I get routinely, I ordered a second one or got it from the spigot at Horn and Hardart for 5 cents. You eventually get used to the dreariness of these lunches in one of the overcrowded city restaurants.

Charter headquarters are on the 7th floor of a skyscraper on Broad Street, two minutes from City Hall, that is, as much in the center of things as possible. But in addition to Saturday and yesterday I was also out on Monday evening, and that was for the "Town Meeting of the Air," a round table discussion broadcast every Monday from the auditorium of the Benjamin Franklin Museum. I'm very proud of the fact that I've never opened my mouth in any of the many meetings and gatherings I have now attended—including the seminar—though the temptation is often very great.[1]

Speaking of the Benjamin Franklin Museum, it occurs to me I haven't told you about our recent Sunday morning visit to the Art Museum, which you and I missed when we were here two years ago. To my more than pleasant surprise, it turns out that this Museum, while not sensational, nevertheless includes an abundance of very decent representative pieces of all genres, schools, periods, and countries, German, Dutch, Italian, Japanese, Chinese, and above all a lot of wonderful modern French pieces. There was so much that we barely got an overview and want to go there again soon. On Sunday Pa, Mu, and Gri were at the Rodin Museum, which is also on the Parkway, for the first time and they returned very impressed.

I believe that in all my letters up to now I've hardly mentioned Ulli. I don't know why that is, now that I think of it, because the big brother and the little sister, who as adults have hardly ever lived this long in the same city, are getting along particularly well. Ulli is really deeply involved in her work. She has decided to specialize as an obstetrician and is looking for an appropriate residency for next year. It's a somewhat problematic specialty, but it's her particular interest and she's comfortable with it.

The mailbox will be emptied shortly so no time for an additional sheet.

Alles Liebe,

Jo

SUNDAY AND MONDAY, MARCH 5 AND 6, 1939

Letter from Elfriede in Düsseldorf to Johannes in Philadelphia.

Düsseldorf, 5 March 1939

Mein liebes Peterchen,

For two days it was sunny and we had warm spring weather here. Yesterday afternoon Susanne and I sat out in lounge chairs on the

1 Johannes' diffidence about speaking up in meetings reflects a German-style deference to hierarchy. He overcame his reticence in public situations in a few years.

balcony, and in the park the first crocuses are in bloom. But today, Sunday, it's raining cats and dogs.

This is now the 4th Ultimo that I have more or less behind me. Once I send the requisitions for Krefeld and Düsseldorf tomorrow, I'll have the bulk of it done. When it's all done you'll get the subscription numbers for the last couple of months.

I'm sorry you were needlessly upset by my report about Susanne's reaction to the eventual America plans. You really shouldn't get mad at Mrs. Freyberger because of that. It's sheer chance I didn't slip up myself a long time ago and it's almost time to prepare her anyway. She reacted positively to the plan for English lessons, I think because that will present another opportunity for showing off. On 1 April she will end her gymnastics lessons so she'll have more time. I'm not worried about Susie much anyway. Her cheerful temperament always leads her to see the positive side of things more than the negative. Her current reaction to leaving friends and Oma and uncles is certainly understandable. Even for a grownup it's not always easy to comfort yourself over the loss of pleasant surroundings with the uncertain possibilities of the future. And it would be hard to explain to a child our actual reasons for leaving.

Monday afternoon

Subscriptions are down. In most places it's the disappearance of Jewish subscribers, of whom there are only a few left. Some new subscribers will be lined up by Schell, whose specialty after the church people is now the Aryanized companies.[2] It seems to me as though the financial status overall is still trending upward.

I'm keeping the Christmas present from your parents in reserve for Susie's and my summer trip.[3] I can't save much on household costs right now. Everything is expensive, especially fruit and vegetables, and it's upsetting when you write me how cheap a dozen eggs are where you are. But the chickens here have also begun to recognize that the approaching Easter holidays impose certain responsibilities on them.

Did I write you that I entered into a new payment agreement with Schindler, upon which I do not place the slightest hope? Beginning with RM 15!! on the 1st of April, then monthly payments of RM 30 beginning on the 1st of May and ending, God willing, on the 1st of August. What's important is that he starts paying at all.

I have to stop because I need to go to Duisburg and the *Île-de-France* is supposed to take this letter.

2 *Aryanized* firms were "Jewish" business concerns expropriated by the Nazis and sold to non-"Jews" at minimal prices. How Schell—whoever he was—secured subscriptions from these businesses is not explained.

3 *Summer trip* = Elfriede and Susanne's anticipated move to the United States. The Christmas present from Rudolf and Josephine was cash.

Bis bald!

Deine Friedel

THURSDAY, MARCH 7, 1939

Letter from Johannes in Philadelphia to Elfriede in Düsseldorf. Among other important matters, this letter discusses the Form 575 confirming Johannes and Rudolf's residence in the United States. Johannes sent the form to the Immigration and Naturalization Service (INS) in Washington DC, which then forwarded it to the American Consul in Stuttgart

---

Philadelphia, 3/7/39

Liebster Schatz,

Alea est jacta [the die is cast]*!* This expression, which was used twice in recent years to announce bad news in the Höber household, is going to be rehabilitated today by introducing some really good news. Jo has a job. Just a tiny little one so far as money is concerned, but a very decent one as far as content and prospects are concerned. I am Research Assistant for the City Charter Committee. I'll be doing the same thing I've been doing for the last four weeks, and I didn't even ask them to consider promoting me from volunteer to employee. I had firmly decided I wouldn't be the first one to mention that I was looking for a job. Instead, for two weeks I just did everything that was asked of me to the best of my ability. Then, a week ago last Friday, Mr. Phillips suddenly approached me on behalf of the Executive Director to ask if I would be able to give full time to the Charter Committee. He said they couldn't pay me anywhere near what my work would be worth to them; on the contrary, it would hardly be more than an expense allowance, but it would at least give me official standing if I were made an employee, and perhaps that would be useful for me later on.

Peter, can you imagine what those three sentences meant to me? You hold your tongue, you do what you're supposed to do, secretly hoping all the time that it will pay off—and after three weeks someone does indeed come and offer you exactly what you were hoping for in the most hidden corner of your heart. Someone *comes to me* and offers *me* a job! I don't have to hide from you how I reacted: I was barely able to make it out of the office and into the elevator. Then, however, I couldn't help myself, so that the elevator operator was visibly astonished by the extensive amount of business that my handkerchief had to do with my eyes. *Peterchen*, it's really only a very tiny little job, and I'll get only $65, so I could hardly even support even myself on that and any week now the whole thing could be over when we finish the bulk of our work. But it's a beginning, and it's in a field I would have chosen over all others. It's this beginning that's so important to me psychologically, that I found this kind of start after only two months and the way I found it. Because—and this is what pleases me most about the whole thing—this time there's not the slightest hint of connections or anybody's recommendation involved in the process. These people don't even have a résumé from me; they only know I had some experience in municipal administration, but otherwise they only know the research papers I produced for them, and every one of those is on a purely American subject.

When I came home from the Charter lunch last Friday after Phillips made me his offer, the letter I had begun writing you before I drove into town was still in the typewriter. But I knew that Phillips still had to get the final approval of the board of directors, so I sent off my letter to you without including the good news. Then Saturday the final confirmation came in the form of my first-ever American paycheck. Again, Peter, this is only an initial little skirmish that I've won, and this first bit of conquered ground can easily be lost again. You know how it is, you're hired and you're fired. But this first small achievement may be the beginning of a thread that will lead further. In any event, I'm meeting a lot of like-minded people and they're getting to know me.

Whether this job will continue to give me pleasure is the least of my worries right now. Since yesterday, I've been sitting here working on a new paper on labor and the city manager. I'm digging into newspaper reports about how a city manager handled a big industrial strike a couple of years ago, and I'm trying to compare the labor relations with police and firemen in cities that have city managers and those that don't, etc., etc. Then at 3:30 Phillips called up and said that by 4:30 the Chairman needed the most recent articles on the charter movement in other cities. So the staff librarian and I did a whirlwind search and found there wasn't much new with respect to New York and Chicago, and I wrote two quick memos in a half hour on the status of the charter revision process in these two cities. Thus it's been a very hectic day for me, but I'd rather have it that way than have it be quiet and peaceful. This evening I'm going with Phillips to the second of ten lectures on "Housing." He went to the first one and thought it was so good he let me know about it.

So, *Schatz*, now I've chattered on enough about myself, so let me get to your letters of the 21st and the 24th. If the last week hadn't been so exciting for me, I would probably have registered even more painfully the fact that for a whole week, for 10 days, in fact, I got no mail from you.

My time and my endurance aren't sufficient today for completing the tax stuff, but at the latest you'll get it with the next mail ship, which goes on Saturday.

Today the official confirmation arrived that the 575 has gone off to Stuttgart. Have you by any chance heard from anyone anything about analogous cases and how quickly this process functions? We have no idea whether there is anything further we can do.

Gri just whistled—7:15—to call the family to dinner, a quarter hour earlier than usual, because Walter Phillips is picking me up in his car at 7:45.

Enough. At the same time I mail this letter I'm sending you separately a copy of *American Home* magazine to give you and Susie, my sweet little Sparrow, a little foretaste. Please, please intercede with her on my behalf and help her understand why I haven't yet written to her. Even Lilly Reiff and Bill Abbott didn't get their well-earned letters until this past Sunday.

I could write every time that your letters make me happy and proud, but today I want to do so particularly.

In Liebe,

Jo

WEDNESDAY AND FRIDAY, MARCH 8 AND 10, 1939

Letter from Elfriede in Düsseldorf to Johannes in Philadelphia. This letter again contains a deliberately obscure paragraph about the "Sulden document." That term is code for a form requiring "Jews," as defined by the Nazis, to register all their property with the Finance Bureau. Non-Jews were also required to file if they had "Jewish" spouses. Rudolf filed the form with an office in Berlin in September 1938 because Josephine's parents were Jewish. See Johannes' letter to Rudolf of September 4, 1938 (Chapter 2) and his letter to Elfriede of February 14 (Chapter 6). Months after he filed the report, the Finance Bureau demanded that Rudolf comply with a levy on all Jewish property, a percentage of the holdings he reported. The complication was that Rudolf was not Jewish but had filed the report because it was required of the spouses of Jews. The "factual error" to which Elfriede is referring is the Nazis' belief that Rudolf was Jewish, and her reference to people who cannot understand percentages refers to Elfriede's belief that Rudolf's percentage of Jewish ancestors should have exempted him from the payment requirement. The second half of the paragraph deliberately obscures its meaning from officials who might open the letter. Elfriede is referring to the parentage defining who is a Jew. If one has two fully Jewish parents ("100 plus 100") then one is Jewish. But if one has one fully Jewish parent and one who is one-half or one-quarter Jewish ("100 plus 50 or 100 plus 25") then one is not Jewish ("zero"). It is not clear, by the way, that Elfriede's interpretation of the "racial" laws would be shared by German officials. The application of Nazi anti-Jewish laws to mixed couples and individuals of mixed parentage remained an area of confusion and arbitrary interpretation for years.

Düsseldorf, 8th March 1939

Lieber Schatz!

I want to write you at least briefly via the *Hansa*, which leaves tomorrow, after having packed up three pairs of underwear for you. I don't know whether I will get much writing done because I neglected the business a little yesterday and have to catch up today. Occasionally the household demands a little of me too even though I've gotten most of that work off my back. Still, when there isn't a single sock in the closet that doesn't have holes and when Helma can't be persuaded that window washing is important because it's only four weeks until Easter then I have to step in. Since I don't do so much in the house myself anymore, Helma's tyranny has naturally grown and I don't have the energy to fight it. When you feel like you're preparing to move, a lot things that might otherwise seem of greater importance become quite peripheral.

3/10

Now I've been a bad woman and haven't gotten this letter off to the *Hansa*. Only the underwear has gone off.

Your letter from the *Normandie* came today. I think it's terribly diligent of you that you already spit out another paper and I'm anxious to see what this work will lead to. Your role as "technical expert" is very appealing to me. I can imagine that it's often hard for you to hold your very charming tongue, but I think that's a smart move. I do, however, have one slight worry about all of this, namely that this might somehow, somewhere lead to a career as a public official. Heaven protect me from that! If anything was nice about the last few years [in Düsseldorf], it was the private nature of our lives, which is now dissolving, but the most positive thing was what we were able to do in these years.[4]

The pediatrician's wife fills me with serious concern. Watch out, I will revenge myself for everything as much as I possibly can. Don't rely too much on my lacking the ability to take up with someone else. When the

4 During the first five years of their marriage (1928–1933), Johannes worked in the Mannheim city administration and was an activist in the Social Democratic Party. The responsibility was intense, and he was often away from home in the evenings. The newspaper business Johannes and Elfriede began in Düsseldorf in 1934 was tedious but also less demanding of Johannes' time.

chips are down I can do it. Unexpected situations can bring out unanticipated capabilities in people. I strongly recommend that you exercise care. Nevertheless, I'm happy that you're developing your own social circle. I recently read excerpts of your last letter at the Magicians' and had great success with that. They're so appreciative of hearing about you.

I talked to a friend recently about not being invited out. When I'm invited out alone I sometimes feel so incomplete that I wouldn't mind if people didn't invite me. I always have the feeling that I don't have as much to offer by myself as the two of us together. On the other hand, when I'm alone I come across to much better advantage than together with you. For example when I'm at the Magicians' by myself I'm a good social person in every way, even when I'm not full of news. Because of that I'm terrified when I think that someday I'll have to appear alongside you in front of a new hostile world.

In the matter of your father's Sulden document, the fact is that the demand is based on a factual error. It's not so uncommon for things like that to happen. If a report is filed, the official thinks there has to be a payment as well. As I wrote you some time back, I had a very hard time making the man with whom I spoke about this on the phone understand what the circumstances were and how the thing should be handled properly. You can't overestimate the gross ignorance of people who somehow are involved with calculating percentages. As soon as there's anything having to do in any way with some part of a hundred it's all over. For all practical purposes there's either 100 or zero. And everyone knows that 100 plus 100 equals 100, but it's hard to grasp that 100 plus 50 or 100 plus 25 also equals zero.

When I read through what I've written so far I find it to be very mixed up, but I really like just typing whatever comes into my mind on a quiet evening. As I write I think about what you would say back if you were here and then it feels like a comfortable conversation.

I keep Sundays free of any work. Not because I have so much to do and feel the need to rest up, but just so Sunday has a little more to it than the monotony of the other days. I even turn the telephone work over to Helma on Sundays because I don't want to get aggravated by complaining subscribers. At any rate, the day before yesterday I raised so much hell with two carriers that I'm now looking forward to a fairly peaceful Monday morning. I get terribly angry about the collections habits of these people. I hardly have the heart to tell you that nearly RM 200 are still outstanding as of today. As far as I know, the Schindler case was transferred from the state prosecutor's office to the administrative prosecutor's office, but otherwise I haven't heard anything about it. It will undoubtedly still come up. Now here I am talking business on Sunday night, but generally I don't get as worked up about it as I did at first.

I've been following your reports about your work on behalf of the City Charter Committee with great interest and satisfaction. It's certainly odd when political objectives are supposed to be "supported" by antiquated texts on constitutional law. Or even if they aren't antiquated, it's still odd to have classical theorists re-examined for their probative value on a contemporary issue. On the other hand, this is just one of many possible approaches, and if that's what's usual there, you could say it's no worse a basis for support or affirmation than many others. The enrichment of your knowledge on the one hand and the insight into alternative ways of thinking on the other is in any event no bad thing. By the way, don't let yourself get discouraged if everything in your career efforts doesn't work out as you would like it to right away. I think it's already a great thing that you succeeded right at the beginning in getting involved with something like this, and it would be remarkable if it kept on going like this and turned itself into a job with dollars. If you don't become a great success, and become a little one instead, I don't think that's so important. Stirring things up in the big American pot will soon stir something useful to the top. Fortunately it doesn't have to be today or tomorrow. I can wait.

That's all for today. In another three days the *Queen Mary* goes, the only good ship at the moment.

Deine Friedel

FRIDAY, MARCH 10, 1939

Letter from Johannes in Philadelphia to Elfriede in Düsseldorf

---

Philadelphia, 3/10/39

Liebster Peter,

I have a bad conscience because this letter too has to go off without the tax return. You didn't realize when you pressured me that I'm now occupied all day long again and in the second place, fortunately, the deadline for filing the tax return is less serious than the deadline for paying the taxes. Since I didn't get home until 7:30 today and 6:30 yesterday and only had a twenty-minute lunch break both times, I just wasn't able to do it, but the weekend begins tomorrow afternoon and then the thing will get done.

My hearty felicitations on the return of the watch. If one knew for sure that they would come back so quickly, one would lose cherished objects more frequently just to experience the joy of their return. That little watch would have been irreplaceable in its sentimental value and I rejoice with you that it's back.

I would happily partake of some Cold Duck and chicken broth, KD and the Film Ball, but I'd really travel a long way for a glass of Cologne beer and a Cologne cheese sandwich with onions and mustard. Right now, however, I manage not to feel pangs of regret over any of these pleasant memories. That undoubtedly has something to do with the fact that other things here are equally therapeutic.

Now here I am chatting away the way you did in your letter of 2/26, but there's nothing wrong with that and I'm happy to follow your example. I am genuinely worried about all the problems you're having with the carriers. After Schindler now the others, that's really bad. And why is good old Wulff abandoning you? Oh if only Uncle [Karl] would relieve you of these troubles soon along with all of your and my other troubles!

I had a very impressive experience yesterday. I attended the public hearing for the Charter Bill before the Joint Committee of the Pennsylvania Senate and House of Representatives, which came to Philadelphia for that purpose. Such a public hearing is held for every important bill and sometimes for the more important appointments as well. I'll come back to that [in my next letter].

In Liebe,

Jo

SATURDAY, MONDAY AND TUESDAY, MARCH 11, 13, AND 14, 1939

Letter from Elfriede in Düsseldorf to Johannes in Philadelphia.

Düsseldorf, 11 March 1939

Liebster Peter,

It's Saturday morning and I really have more urgent things to do, but your letter of 2/28, with the City Manager report, which was subsequently overtaken by the letter you sent on the *Normandie*, made me feel so good that I at least want to start this quickly. Your first American opus impresses me immensely. Your English, which is so English that sometimes I don't understand it at all, amazes me (and gives me a serious inferiority complex that I will never be able to overcome).

I was comforted by the fact that your second paragraph was a quote. At first I missed the quotation marks and only recovered from my initial shock when I saw the source citation. Even with the help of a dictionary I have a hard time imagining what "passing the buck" means. From the context, however, I'll try to make sense of it. What a hard worker you are! What has happened to you that you show up for work promptly at 9 o'clock in the morning? Presumably the Höber family's active regime has swept you along with it. I can foresee that by the time I get there you'll have used up your entire inventory of good qualities for the next five years.

I'm getting to the point where I think it would be alright if Uncle Karl would let me hear something from him. But he hasn't and I swore to myself I wouldn't get impatient.

My carrier worries aren't diminishing any. The carrier I just hired didn't show up. I don't know what I'll do next. Probably advertise. There's a shortage of people everywhere, and we only get the rejects.

3/13. Monday after a quiet Sunday. On Saturday morning Betz came by and I read from your letter that I was so proud of. I'm very much convinced that you are doing things the right way. I showed off mightily with your successes, and everybody was happy to listen. On Saturday afternoon I spent an hour with Hilde, who has a lot on her back and finds it so hard to correspond with Karl. He is one of those people who's all too ready to put things off. You seem to be a gem in this regard.

Then a call came from the Finance Bureau on account of your father. He wrote them that your power of attorney was extinguished, so they wanted to know who holds the power of attorney now. I said nobody. Well, to whom should they now send the tax notice? I said directly to him. That's no good. There has to be someone with a power of attorney inside the country. Notices etc. aren't sent to foreign countries. I told him that if it's only a matter of an address they can send things here and we'll forward them. He was satisfied with that.

Saturday evening we had a drink here at home and then went for chicken soup at the train station restaurant again. Sunday afternoon a walk on the Rhine. Cold sunshine, blooming forsythia, yellow and red shimmering meadows. Elegant midday dinner at Mother's, coffee here, a really ideal and relaxing Sunday.

Günter went to the draft office here today and got [placed in the] unarmed militia, i.e., Supplementary Reserve II. At Easter he wants to go to Cambridge for a hockey game and got a military leave permission slip and was mustered in today in advance [of having to report]. I don't know whether unarmed militia means being excused from the 3-month training period. I haven't spoken to him yet.

Mrs. Freyberger just called to say she is coming over.

Tuesday morning.

This is becoming a letter in stages, which isn't really what I had in mind. It was nice and relaxed with Mrs. Freyberger. She now has several people involved in her England matter. She can get a position any time, but people have advised her to be patient in order to find something that would be more than just "something." The Magician was just here in considerable need of comforting, 1st his wife is away, 2nd, he's going to lose a couple of teeth, 3rd, his daughter and her husband are moving to Montreal in May, and that's really hitting him hard. Apparently it's a very nice, big thing with good prospects, but he recognizes that if they go it's uncertain if he'll ever see her again. On a more cheerful note, they're going to England for Easter.

Things are very sad with Hannaschs [unidentified]. He was already sick last year and now it turns out that he has a malignant tumor. He was operated on on Friday, but the malignancy is so far advanced that it's completely hopeless. It's so dreadful and upsets everyone terribly.

This letter hasn't turned out to be as nice as I hoped it would. But the *Queen Mary* is leaving in three days and maybe I can write something better before then.

Gruß und Kuss,

Deine Friedel

UNDATED FRAGMENT, MARCH 1939

Letter from Elfriede in Düsseldorf to Johannes in Philadelphia.

I'm looking forward to the issue of *American Home* you told me you're sending and I'll make it as appealing as possible for Susanne. But you absolutely must write her. She says, not without justification, that a single letter in such a long time is really very little. When she said that, she almost had tears in her eyes.

What's up with the honorable Blaschy family [Gri and Manfred]? You don't write anything about them anymore, and Gri seems to have turned her writing abilities to more worthwhile objectives. Oh Jonny, I like you much more than Manfred, indeed I really like you very much. Maybe you knew that already. I've worked hard here for three days and now I can enjoy this dark morning at the typewriter. I need a lamp because of the dark sky, which is allowing snow to fall in contravention of its obligation to provide me with a Rhineland spring. The yards and gardens are all white. Still, everybody is looking forward to warm Easter weather, including me, though I have no idea how I can make use of those days.

All the people I meet tell me to send their best wishes to you, which mostly I don't do. At any rate yesterday the Magicians, recently K.Z. [unidentified], Gerhard and Marlies, and I don't remember who all else. But the main thing is that you are in everybody's good thoughts and your absence is noticed. That should make you feel as good as it makes me feel. I find life brighter at this moment than in a long time. Mr. Heck was just here—you remember, the Magicians' handyman —and he offered to work for me [as a carrier] again. So he will start tomorrow, which means I have to go to the train station at 6 tomorrow morning [for his orientation].

Please work on the taxes, but I hope they're already on the way. 3/31 is the absolute last deadline. And don't forget that your daughter Susanne made her appearance in the world under a little waxing moon on 4/3. I just made an appointment for her first English lesson tomorrow. It costs RM 1.50 each time, but if she learns something that's not too much.

1000 Grüße und alles Liebe für meinen Tüchtigen.
[1000 greetings and all my love to my diligent one.]

Deine Friedel

TUESDAY, MARCH 14, 1939

Letter from Johannes in Philadelphia to Elfriede in Düsseldorf. This letter responds, in part, to Elfriede's "tax letter" of February 20. At the beginning of the letter, Johannes refers to "the events in Czechoslovakia." Under Hitler's threat of invasion and bombardment, the government of Czechoslovakia surrendered the territories of Moravia and Bohemia to the Germans without a shot being fired. German troops occupied the area on March 15, 1939. Johannes' casual mention of this pivotal event in world politics in the middle of a discussion of Johannes and Elfriede's tax returns epitomizes the confluence of events in the "Macrocosm" and "Microcosm" that characterized Elfriede and Johannes' life at this time. This single paragraph also highlights what the letters did not say. While Johannes could tell Elfriede he was listening to reports of the Nazi takeover of half of Czechoslovakia, the fear of Gestapo surveillance caused him to omit any comments about those events, which took the world a step closer to war.

Johannes' discussion of policy issues in Philadelphia underscores the differences in presumptions about government in Europe and America. Europeans expected a larger degree of government intervention in the economy and basic services like public utilities and infrastructure. Americans were less accustomed to government involvement in these matters, so the means of financing public projects was the subject of endless debate.

Philadelphia, 3/14/39

Liebes Peterchen,

I have been using a morning at home—albeit interrupted repeatedly by trips to the radio, which is reporting every half hour on the events in Czechoslovakia—to turn my attention to the tax return. So this will be a tax letter.

I filled out in pencil everything on the five forms that I was able to. Unfortunately there are still some blanks that you are going to have to do something about.

[*Several paragraphs of technical questions about business expense deductions are omitted here.*]

So I signed all the [blank] forms and I'm now confidently turning the rest over to you.

I was only in the office for a half day today because, first, Phillips is traveling, second, there isn't much to do and, third, I wanted to make myself a little scarce so that they don't somehow think I feel I'm obligated to stick to full office hours.

The public hearing for the Charter bill, which I mentioned on Friday, was in retrospect a phenomenon in several ways. Admission was open to the general public but the proceeding was nevertheless a model of order. I had expected that at such an event all sorts of reformers, who otherwise never find a public platform, would appear, the way we used to get free money people or land reformers or other sectarians. Instead of that, all day long amazingly good speeches were delivered to an attentive audience. The Charter Committee had prepared very well and lined up a whole team of prominent people as speakers, but the opposition made its points very well too. As a result this institution of a public hearing has made a positive impression on me. Otherwise, however, the similarity of the way policy problems are presented is surprising. In the housing lecture that I attended last Tuesday—today is the second—the talk was primarily about whether rent supplements or cheap capital should be provided for home construction, whether houses should be built with publicly employed labor or private contractors, etc. At Sweeney's the subject the last time was public utilities and turned on the question of which services should be in public hands and which not, whether one should tax them and how high the service fees should be set for the average household. And during the Charter testimony I found even in this discussion that the port of Philadelphia suffers because other ports are given an advantage by means of exemptions from rail tariffs.

That's all for today. Yesterday evening all five of us went to a really good Clark Gable film, *Idiot's Delight*, which you probably won't get to see. Tomorrow I may go out a bit with Ulli and Priscilla Brisco, Daddy's assistant. Seppchen thought I could safely go out with her alone, but Daddy and I were of the opinion that Ulli had to go along. She's a Catholic society girl from the Midwest. That's something, isn't it?

So long. On Saturday the *Île-de-France* leaves at about the same time the *Harding* arrives.

Dein Jo

THURSDAY AND FRIDAY, MARCH 16 AND 17, 1939

Letter from Elfriede in Düsseldorf to Johannes in Philadelphia, immediately following Hitler's occupation of Czechoslovakia. The second part of this letter responds to Johannes' March 7 letter in which he told Elfriede he had been hired by the Charter Committee and wrote about his steps to expedite her immigration visa.

Düsseldorf, 3/16 1939

Lieber kleiner Peter,

As usual I have to write a letter to send on the *Queen Mary* before I've gotten the one she's sure to bring me. I don't like doing that, but after the *Queen* there's a big shipping pause and I think you wouldn't like if I let her go without a letter. I'm doing better than I have in a long time. I've gotten through almost two weeks without a mood crisis and that's a lot. I'm eating well again, sleep wonderfully, and feel in good balance generally. Everybody thinks I look much better, and it seems that way to me too. Yesterday evening at the Trömels it was suggested that I have now overcome the emotional stress of separation. That does in fact now seem diminished. And right now, when upsetting things are taking place again all over the world, I really feel like half a person without you. But the feeling of greater stability is also quite helpful.

I've been having a lot of problems with the business. The newly hired carrier fell through again, because he has to go into the military. I'm placing an ad tomorrow to find a new one. Hopefully I will have at least half as much success as you did last summer. You can imagine, or rather you can't imagine, how much energy I've devoted to overcoming my telephone shyness.

Paul got a new job in Berlin. I don't know if I already wrote that the Leather Industry Economic Association approached him because their legal division was overloaded. So he sent Heidi ahead on the ski trip and went to Berlin to finalize the contract, apparently on excellent terms. The only question is when he will start. The people in Berlin want him on 1 April, but it's questionable whether his current employer will release him that soon. Finding a place to live will also present some difficulties in Berlin, but before he gets involved in that he has gone off after Heidi to the Seis Alps.

Everyone at my Mother's place is laughing about Günter's [placement in] "Supplementary Reserve 2," but it's of great business significance for them that he won't have to serve the three months' training. That will also be decided for Herbert in the next few weeks, but he doesn't have a dislocated shoulder [as Günter has]. Günter now has no military reporting obligations for the moment; he can travel overseas as he likes and so on. Now nothing stands in the way of his Cambridge trip. He will also visit our friends there. If you have some tips to give him, send them to him at Trumpington Road. He can be reached there from 6–13 April.[5]

I packed up and sent off a shirt for you so that you'll have a clean collar for Easter.

Uncle Karl is simply not to be heard from, but the four weeks I set myself as a waiting period aren't up yet. According to reports, his business practices are often somewhat messed up and a woman from here recently had to make a special trip there just to haul a matter that had disappeared back to the light of day. Next time I won't just register the letter but send it with a return receipt requested. I'm armed with an amazing amount of patience.

Friday, 17th of March 1939

Mein liebster, bester Peter,

I didn't dare to hope for the arrival of the *Queen Mary* letter, and then yours of 3/7 from the *Hamburg* shows up. What mail!!! I really don't know how to say it. Oh Peter, it's too wonderful!!! I'm overwhelmed with pride and so happy, both for you and for us. My recommendation is that

5 *Trumpington Road* = home of Johannes and Elfriede's and Günter's mutual friends, the Schlossmanns in Cambridge, England.

from now on every two months you improve your position by 65 dollars, and then we could predict approximately when it would be sufficient for me and Susie. This start! And no one can say that this was a gift from God—in my opinion you really earned this. It's very sad to be separated by several thousand miles at a time like this. I saved up the last bottle of Forster Musenhang 1931 to toast this moment. May you succeed quickly in spinning this strand into a usable cord!

I'm glad you heard from Washington that the 575 is on the way to Stuttgart, because that means I couldn't have heard anything from there yet. I did write in my cover letter that something additional would be coming and they undoubtedly waited for it, so I should be prepared to wait several more weeks without getting fidgety. Besides, I have no idea what influence Ütli has on the matter. I hope it has some, because otherwise the prospects seem pretty dark at least until the end of June.[6]

What is "housing?" I think it must have something to do with "house," but what? You have to remember that I am a poor, simple housewife, completely inexperienced in the ways of the world. How am I supposed to know all of the things you write about so knowledgably? "Explain me" we said as children, when our father was supposed to explain something to us.[6] You are known there, you can converse, and I'm a poor nobody. I already feel sorry for myself. But all of that belongs to my fate, which I am determined to meet head on. All those things that I cannot now predict I place under the rubric of "fate," and then they are in their proper place. But lady pediatricians do not fall under that rubric. Out of caution, I reserve to myself the right to decide what I want to place under that rubric—lost collar buttons and grouchy Jonnys also don't belong there. I'm disposed to bear with composure everything called fate, but some things aren't fate at all. You'll have a very hard time with me when we're finally together again. With the beginning of the 3rd stage of our life together—or should I say the 4th—I expect that you will have grown up so I won't be plagued with childish errors any more. If you want to, when you answer this you can read me the riot act.

Give my regards to Mr. Phillips. I like him a lot from your description.

Give your father an extra greeting from me. It would be quite worthwhile to begin a separate correspondence with him. His reaction to my Sicily proposal is absolutely charming. If you think it's possible that one day we'll end up in Philadelphia, you should think it over very carefully from your father's perspective. I can't guarantee my virtue with respect to your father. He is without question the most captivating father-in-law one could imagine and his mere existence can reconcile me to many of the world's hardships. I will devote myself assiduously to the task of his dye

6 *Ütli* again is code for Switzerland, referring to the fact that Johannes was born there and the hope that Elfriede might fall under the undersubscribed Swiss quota. The German quota had been exhausted until the end of the fiscal year on June 30.

7 The term *housing* denoted governmental policies designed to provide adequate residences for all citizens, particularly the poor. Housing policy was regarded as a pivotal social issue in America at the time.

packets. I'm not a good packer but will do my best so they don't change the color of the ocean.[8]

I want to tell you a nice story about Susie that I find characteristic of our times. Two days ago we were eating meatballs with caper sauce and she wondered what capers actually were. I wasn't quite sure myself, but guessed they were the buds of a foreign shrub, indeed the caper bush. It turns out that she has heard something about foreign exchange and imports, and thought that capers are not so essential for life that you should have to spend money for them—there are other things that are scarce and surely more important. Thereupon I delivered a small lecture on reciprocity in imports (note, by the way, that we were using trade economics terminology throughout) and that it's often necessary, if we want to export things, for us to take the things that other countries want to sell us. Further conversation about what things we import from foreign countries and which ones we export. She knew that quite well. These days international economics are not merely a topic of study for adults but also quite current among eight-year-olds. Then she wanted to talk about what we have in this country and what things we make ourselves. Among these was sugar, and in response to my question as to what sugar is made out of came the prompt response: out of trees. This kid has already heard or read something about sugar maples, but sugar beets were unknown to her. I predict that one day we'll be able to learn a lot from our children.

I'm reading another American book, Edmonds' *Drums Along the Mohawk*, in German. Peacock feathers and cockades, a story about the War for Independence. With this and *Arundel* you can end up getting a pretty good idea about the independence war, though it's hard to understand how these poorly trained, poorly equipped Americans with their militias were able to defeat the regular English troops. The Mohawk is a river in the vicinity of Saratoga that flows into the Hudson, but maybe you knew that already, though I have the impression that you're more familiar with the government of the United States than you are with its geography. Some day we have to drive up the Hudson to Lake Champlain and to the sources of the Susquehanna. But I'm afraid there's not much left of either the Indian romance or the Indian reality, and that in the intervening period that area has become more civilized and therefore less interesting. So let's drive south instead to Mount Vernon, which I don't know much about, and then through Florida to Key West. From there it's only a short way to Cuba. Traveling in the USA is something I can readily imagine and that I think I would like a lot. That's why I often think about what we would do on vacation, if we ever have a vacation again.

8 In a letter that was not preserved, Rudolf evidently asked Elfriede to send him packets of dye for his use in laboratory experiments.

There's nothing at all left of spring here anymore. It's horribly cold and the sun only puts in an occasional appearance. On top of that there was a thunderstorm yesterday of a kind I have seldom experienced, with hail and snow. It's good I was home because Susie woke up terrified and it was truly unbelievably loud. It wouldn't have surprised me if our house had flown away. Three-fourths of the local pages of the *Düsseldorfer Nachrichten* were full of it for two days, but Helma showed up intact the next morning.

Our wine cellar could accommodate one more evening, but I think I'll soon have to augment it. After that there's only cognac and soda. After [Dr.] Wehrmann offered apple and grape juice as a spring cure I broke off relations with him. I find that unworthy. Tradition, too, is a value one shouldn't casually toss on the dust heap. You won't be very impressed by the fact that I got a new recipe for wonderful cookies made of almonds and chocolate, but they impressed my guests.

Now it's almost 6 o'clock and since I plan to get out of here as punctually as a bureaucrat I will now bring this to a close.

Alles liebe,

Deine Friedel

FRIDAY, MARCH 17, 1939

Letter from Johannes in Philadelphia to Elfriede in Düsseldorf.

Philadelphia, 3/17/39

Liebstes Peterchen,

This afternoon I mailed a package containing a dress that Seppchen and I picked out for Susie. And enclosed you will find a supplement to my tax letter [i.e., a draft letter to the Finance Bureau] which I ask that, at your discretion, you either send off or hold back or retype on one of the blank sheets of my stationery that you have. I don't think any comment on it is necessary.

Last night I went to dinner at Walter Phillips' house, that is to say I just stayed there after I drove him first to the Sweeney seminar in Blue Boy and then drove him home, where we talked so intently over cocktails that I just never left. His wife is nice but fairly quiet. The subject of conversation last night—and always—was central Europe. You can't imagine how much people here pump me for information these days.

It was very nice in the office again today after we three young fellows had been feeling for the last few days that the work of our research department was coming to an end (that includes me and Phillips and Roger Scattergood, also a young lawyer and from a no less rich old Pennsylvania society family than Phillips). But now we're suddenly under pressure to develop very quickly a briefing memo for the Governor personally, and the three of us had a lot of fun working on it together. My topic was how much WPA and PWA money has Philadelphia gotten from the federal government and how much other cities have gotten. In Germany I think we call that financial equivalency.

Many thanks for your business letter, which I find quite heartening in view of the overall situation. I'm simultaneously a little disappointed and a little pleased at the balance sheet. Disappointed because the negative balance has not yet turned into a positive balance and pleased that apparently my absence hasn't had a very negative impact. Or do you see it differently?

Gri and Manfred have gone to Saratoga Springs for the weekend in Blue Boy, so we three grownups are here alone and Seppchen is full-time baby sitter. For this reason I have to finish this and be the substitute for the children for the nightly reading in the living room, a religiously observed ritual. Speaking of that, I will send Susie *Ferdinand the Bull* as printed matter. Commentary to follow.

Tausend Grüße,

Jo

SUNDAY, MARCH 19, 1939

Postcard from Günter Fischer and three unidentified women ("Hella," "Else," "Steffie") in Düsseldorf to Johannes in Philadelphia.

Dear Jo—in memory of a year ago—which was so nice—on my birthday—we're thinking of you today—I'm writing to you with faded lotus flowers on my head—in this tender mood we have to go to the theater now—dear Jo all good things to you—from your Düsseldorf girlfriend Hella.

Regards from another girlfriend, who also wishes you all the best. Else

[*In English*] Dear old Jo! That's still a little more lovely than last year, especially our dear old (28) girl Hella. We are so sorry not to have you among us. Next time I'll write you again from England (in a very short time). Best wishes to you. G[ünter]

[*In English*] Darling mine, this is to show you that I am in love with you as much as ever. When do you come back to your bonnie Steffie?

MONDAY, MARCH 20, 1939

Letter from Johannes in Philadelphia to Elfriede in Düsseldorf written five days after Hitler's annexation of Bohemia and Moravia. The references to the previous October relate to the Sudeten crisis, when war was avoided despite the appearance then that it was inevitable. Johannes' obscure discussion of world events once more shows the circumlocutions required by the expectation that mail might be opened by German authorities.

Philadelphia, 3/20/39

Liebster Peter,

It's always horrible to have you so far away, but for the last few days it has been unbearable, and if we hadn't all become a little smarter as a result of the events of last October, I would now begin to worry about you. But I've decided not to do that under any circumstances and to rely entirely on your wisdom and your judgment.

The reality once more is that I begin every day by turning on the radio. Some of the stations have started broadcasting reports every hour on the hour again, and several times a day there are network roundtables in which a speaker in Berlin, one in London, one in Paris and one here participate. But it's endlessly difficult to judge whether the situation is threatening to become really dramatic or to what extent the radio stations, which depend on sensationalism—in this sense they are hard to distinguish from the newspapers—are dramatizing things. Which in no way diminishes the fact that the last week has been really and truly dramatic. With all skepticism as to American methods, I still have the uneasy feeling that we are just at the beginning of cataclysmic events and not anywhere near the end. What has disconcerted me most about the events of the last week is that for the first time they appear to have burst through ideological frameworks and for that reason alone have led to unpredictable developments. This is, moreover, the point most discussed by the best news commentators here—and there is no lack of them—and all kinds of historical parallels are brought up to make the current events understandable.

In the face of such events it's not easy to turn your attention to an undertaking as peaceful as the City Charter. I have been concentrating on the problems here with such engagement that I experience this sudden distraction of my thoughts [by events in Europe] as a burden. The peculiar thing about the current situation is that, although newspapers and the radio devote a huge amount of time and space to events in Europe, American life, outside of actual government circles, remains unaffected. These events are taking place on another continent and you pay attention to them, but there is no direct impact on your own daily life. Add to that the experience the Americans had with their participation in the last war, which continues to have a strong effect. It's not just that many here still judge the motives that brought America in on the side of the Allies very skeptically. For the moment the isolationists represent popular opinion far more than the administration does.

Now from macrocosm back to microcosm. Yesterday Gri and Manfred came back from their weekend trip to Saratoga Springs in high spirits. They ran into deep snow in upper New York, while here we had warm sunshine. Seppchen had taken off from the laboratory for that time to take care of the children and I helped occasionally, for example by giving my favorite niece her bottle twice. On Saturday evening I was supposed to go out with Ulli and Priscilla Brisco, but not much came of it. First, the movie we went to—*Gunga Din*, a bad new version about the Bengal Lancers—didn't get out until 12 o'clock, second, Philadelphia tries to prove that it was once a pious city, at least externally, in that it forbids dispensing alcoholic beverages from midnight Saturday until midnight Sunday—that is called a blue law, I don't know why—and third the last train to Germantown left at 12:30 and since we didn't have Blue Boy and a young woman—namely Priscilla—ostensibly cannot drive at night from Germantown back into the city, our intended decadence came to an unforeseen early end. It will be rescheduled in the near future.

Nonetheless, I can declare with satisfaction that for the first time in a full three months I exchanged at least a few words with a being who can be described as *feminini generis*. I had this satisfaction again this afternoon when Walter Phillips attached his baby sister—sweet seventeen going on twenty—to me as helper in doing some boring statistics. Since he recently told me she asked him, "Who is this attractive man with the foreign accent and the polished manners," I took care to make the most of this teamwork, which succeeded admirably with the help of an adding machine that neither of us understood and a dividing machine which is electrically driven and therefore even more sinister.

At the moment I don't have anything more important to report, and so that's all for today.

Dein Jo

WEDNESDAY, MARCH 22, 1939

Letter from Johannes in Philadelphia to Susanne in Düsseldorf (written for her birthday on April 3).

Philadelphia, 3/22/39

Mein liebes kleines Spätzchen,

[My dear little Sparrow,]

It's a good thing that there's such a thing as birthdays and that you have to write birthday letters for them, because you are right to complain that I haven't written you for so long. But Mutti is also a little to blame for that because she got so many letters from me that there weren't any more left for you. But all that is going to be fixed today. While I don't know if you already know how to read Roman characters when I write them, and while it would take too long to write in German characters if I write as long a letter as I want to, I have decided to use the typewriter. You will certainly be able to read that.

The main thing is that I send you best wishes for your birthday. Mutti and Oma will certainly help you celebrate it properly. Will you have a children's party? Who will you invite? My old friends Tinni and Ilse? Claudia and Johannes? Of course Sonia! And Ruth, with whom you must make up quickly if you have quarreled with her. It's dumb that your birthday is on Monday. But maybe you'll just have the birthday party ahead of time, on Saturday. I hope my birthday present for you arrives on the right day. It's a picture book called *Ferdinand the Bull*, in German *Der Ochse Ferdinand*. Now that's not any ordinary picture book, because American children know Ferdinand as well as German children know Max and Moritz or Struwelpeter. I recently visited friends of Oma Seppi and Opa Rudi in Washington. That's America's capital city the way Berlin is the capital of Germany. These friends have two little girls, one is three and the other is four and both can't read yet. But when I wanted to play with them for a while, the first thing they brought me was their *Ferdinand* and then they recited the whole book from beginning to end from memory, and when I was about to turn the page each of them wanted to tell me first which words went with the picture and they were in such a hurry that all their words just tumbled out over each other. The book is so famous here that it has already been made into a movie by the same man who created Mickey Mouse. Gri and Manfred and Janka went to see the movie recently and thought it was very funny. Hopefully you too will have fun with the book and for my birthday I hope you will recite it for me as a birthday poem.

By the way, I knew about this book even before Barbara and Edith—those are the names of the two little girls in Washington—recited it to me. I saw it for the first time at the home of some German children who live near us here and who knew it just as well by heart. With the German children—and there are a lot of them here—there's a funny thing that happens. They all learn English so amazingly quickly that they sometimes can do it much more quickly than their parents, so they talk to each other in English and often even speak English with their parents. You have sometimes gotten aggravated when Mutti and I speak English with one another when you weren't supposed to understand something. I recently had the experience when two children your age turned this old trick around and spoke so quickly in English that the parents couldn't understand THEM. A fine thing! It's true that these children had already been here for about two years, but even our little sprout Janka is beginning English already. She learns in a very funny way. I think that Mutti and I told you that Oma Seppi and Opa Rudi have a black maid named Suzy. And she is Janka's English teacher. She points to an object and tells her what it's called in English and then Janka is supposed to repeat it. Janka gets mad when Suzy laughs at her if she pronounces something wrong, so now she does it the other way around and teaches Suzy German the same way. In addition to that she goes shopping with Gri every day and already knows what a lot of things are called in English. Soon she'll go to kindergarten and learn even faster. Recently she had a birthday party with English and German children together and it was very funny but it went quite well. The older German children who go to school here—we know a lot of them your age—have learned English so well that they're already the best in their classes. With children who have just arrived here, it's sometimes arranged so they start all over again in the lowest class and then are promoted every two or three months until they have caught up with their old class again.

You have probably figured out already, little Sparrow, why I am telling you so much about the children and their experiences here, namely, I have decided to stay here in America and you and Mutti should follow me as soon as possible. I hope that you will not only feel sad about leaving Düsseldorf, but will also look forward a little bit to coming here. It's not a bad exchange. The worst, of course, is that Oma Clara will stay in Düsseldorf and you must make her promise that she will come to visit us here soon. But Opa Rudi and Oma Seppi haven't seen you for so long that they recently said they don't know what you look like at all anymore, and when they saw the photograph of the picture that Brüdi painted of you—it hangs over my bed now—they hardly recognized you at first. And then Aunt Gri and Aunt Ulli and Uncle Manfred and Janka and Monika are all here and they are all very jealous of Uncle Günter and Uncle Herbert and of Franz Peter Cornelius who get to see you all the time. It's also sad, of course, to leave all of your nice friends. But just think of the fact that the same thing happened to Ursula and Klaus when their father was transferred and they found new friends a long time ago.

And then a world trip like this is a wonderful adventure, and it's wonderful not just to read about that kind of an adventure in books but actually to experience it. First there is the boat ride! For seven days or even longer you'll ride in a real floating house, and for five days you won't see anything at all except the sky and the water. You'll get all your meals in an elegant dining room, and for breakfast and lunch and supper you can pick out whatever you want to eat. When you arrive in New York you'll think at first that you are riding right into a high mountain range. Those are the skyscrapers, some of which are 70 and more stories tall, three times as high as the Wilhelm Marx building [in Düsseldorf]. There are skyscrapers like that in every big city here. I now work every day in a building that has 32 stories, and more than a thousand people work here at the same time. It's just the other way around with the house where Oma and Opa and all of us live—nobody else lives there but us and it has a garden too and a wooden porch in front of the house, which is a lot like our balcony [in Düsseldorf] except that it's on the front side, but the street we live on doesn't have a streetcar on it. And here in America there are still real live Indians and when we have a vacation, we can drive and see their wigwams. And there are many Negroes here too. So you see, Sparrow, there are all kinds of things to experience here and Mutti can certainly tell you a lot more about America when you talk to her about all this, and of course you'll do that. If you want to ask me something, just write me and I'll be sure to answer you. So you will believe me when I tell you that, I'm going to finish up by answering your last letter. We all had a lot of fun with your drawings of Schlingel, the washer woman, and the rider. Imagine, those kinds of comic stories with pictures are in the newspapers here every day, and on Sundays there's a whole extra section with lots of pictures like that and they are in color. People here call them the "funny papers" and if you go to a family's house where there are children on Sunday morning, then they will all be lying on the floor on their stomachs studying the funny papers. Maybe next time I'll send you some. What the people in these newspapers are saying is printed in a balloon that comes out of their mouths, just like in yours.

If I go on writing any more then this letter will grow and grow up to your ears. So let me give you another fat birthday kiss and you give Mutti one for me and comfort her for the fact that she isn't getting any letter from me this time because of course you are the special person today.

Alles liebe, Papi

WEDNESDAY, MARCH 22, 1939

Cable from Elfriede in Düsseldorf to Johannes in Philadelphia.

PAF2 CABLE=DUESSELDORF 3 22 1303
LC HOEBER-6701 CRESHEIM PHILA=

URGENTLY REQUEST TAX PAPERS

WEDNESDAY, MARCH 22, 1939

Cable from Johannes in Philadelphia to Elfriede in Düsseldorf.

WESTERN UNION MARCH 22 1939
TO HOEBER
PEMPELFORTERSTR. 11
DUESSELDORF (GERMANY)

SENT FOURTEENTH

THURSDAY, MARCH 23, 1939

Letter from Elfriede in Düsseldorf to Johannes in Philadelphia. Johannes was by nature somewhat lackadaisical about paying bills and meeting bureaucratic deadlines, while Elfriede believed it important to be punctual in such matters. These different approaches were a source of conflict between them throughout their marriage. This difference made it especially difficult for Elfriede to persuade Johannes that circumstances had really changed with respect to the German taxing authorities and that under the Nazis a casual approach to tax deadlines could have dangerous consequences.

Düsseldorf, 23 March 1939.

Mein lieber Peter,

I'm a poor, afflicted girl. I've rarely lived through such a mountain of aggravation and trouble as in the last week. That includes you. I was happy to get your cable, which arrived at 7 o'clock after I sent mine yesterday at 1 o'clock. It's comforting to know that if we need to we can communicate with each other in less than 24 hours. The reason for my cable was that yesterday I got a demand from the Finance Bureau saying that the tax return has to be filed by the 25th of the month or else, and I don't want to have any trouble over things like that. I was very angry because in spite of my pleading with you you still didn't do the taxes right away. As usual you wrote it off as fussiness on my part, but the process has changed significantly [since you left]. I wrote you a letter yesterday when I was angry, but when I reread it today I decided it was inappropriate and consigned it to the waste basket. Now that I know the material is on the way, I'll work things out somehow with the Finance Bureau. But the cable was necessary because no extensions at all will be granted after the 31st of the month and it would have been impossible to meet this deadline without the cable if you hadn't already sent the things off, which I had no way of knowing. It didn't occur to me that you would cable back, otherwise I would have paid for the answer from here. Well, at least it's now halfway fixed, though I can't hope that I'll get the things from you tomorrow and I may still have to telephone the Finance Bureau for another extension. I beg you to respect my wishes a little more in such matters. It's not always fussiness, and I would have been happy to avoid the demand [of the Finance Bureau] in this case. I can leave it to you to complain later on, but as long as I have to do everything here myself, I would prefer you to do what I ask. Everybody says you have the laudable characteristic of a long memory, but conditions change here every day.

This morning I was awakened by a phone call at 6 o'clock. Mr. Heck was in Rath and smashed up his bike in an accident, broken spokes and so on. With the help of the train station shipping office I succeeded in getting Schouten on the phone, who then did Heck's route after he did his own. It's a little strenuous to have to think up work reassignments all of a sudden when you've just been awakened from a bad night's sleep.

That was today, Thursday. Yesterday the Finance Bureau got me all anxious. Tuesday I brought a new carrier on and had to orient him. On Monday Mrs. Mugler was suddenly absent, so with Herbert's help I had a very unpleasant conversation with her. It turns out she collected from subscribers on part of her route and then used the money for herself. Now there's an agreement to pay it off in weekly installments and if she doesn't stick to it I'll turn it over to the prosecutor right away. It's as if my luck abandoned me completely with the departure of Wulff, who did his route for the last time on Monday. You can't be paid enough to put up with a week like this one.

I'm rather in need of comforting. The day before yesterday I went to the movies with Mother just to stop thinking about things. Last night I looked through the *American Home* [magazine] and liked it a lot. I like the way a residence is handled as a place you live and not just a piece of design. There's a nice directness about it that leads to practical solutions because it puts the status issue on the back burner. In that way, living without household help is transformed into an exercise in the pleasant virtues of modesty and practicality. I didn't find the text easy to read all the time, because there are so many words you don't find in books. I also studied the recipes with pleasure. Don't we maybe want to move to California? In the face of our weeks and weeks of miserable, wet, icy cold weather it seems very attractive. The crocus started blooming three weeks ago, but it makes you feel terrible when you see them frozen on the lawns. Every day it snows, it rains, at night it freezes, and the apartment is horribly cold. The office is a real ice box. I'll never be free of my woolen underwear and Susanne will never be free of her long stockings. That's what they call a Rhineland spring. I might as well live at the North Pole.

So now you're getting a complaint letter when last week I was in such high spirits. I can hardly remember what that was like.

Susie started taking English lessons this week and she likes them a lot, though she thinks they shouldn't continue during her vacation. She wanted to know if you knew she was taking lessons. I told her I wrote you that she was going to be doing that. She thinks it would be so nice if she could do it without your knowing and then could surprise you by understanding when you say something secret to me in English. She thinks the effect of the surprise when you fall into the trap, so to speak, would be terrific.

I hope you understand that I still have of all kinds of problems with the business and the Finance Bureau. I feel as if I've been beaten over the head with a mallet. The only thing I don't have is a cold or the grippe.

1000 Grüße von deinem geplagten Weibe Elfriede
[Love and kisses from your afflicted spouse Elfriede]

MONDAY, MARCH 27, 1939

Letter from Johannes in Philadelphia to Elfriede in Düsseldorf.

Philadelphia, 3/27/39

Liebster Peter,

Since I wrote the last letter to Susie instead of to you, it feels as though it's been forever since you heard from me and as though our whole correspondence was interrupted. Even today a really long letter won't be possible because I just got home at 6, still have to write a tax letter for Daddy and review one in English for him, write a German letter for a Charter colleague and at 8:30 I have to be in town again for another Committee. That's what you call a peaceful life in a foreign city. But things are happening and I would rather have it that way than the other way around. This afternoon I was invited to lunch with the Executive Director of the Charter Committee and the main topic was my past activities and future plans. He seems to have a sincere desire to help me. Hopefully he can. Last evening we were at the Bazett's[9] for dinner, i.e., only Pa-Mu and me along with the director of a large life insurance company and his wife. After dinner he cornered me for the rest of the evening and acted as though he was genuinely interested too. In any event we all had the impression that this meeting was prearranged by the Bazetts, who are very kind.

I recently got Ulli's guided tour of her whole hospital on Saturday, an imposing institute in which the kid holds an amazingly responsible position. By the way, she has now confirmed her decision to specialize in obstetrics after having delivered no fewer than 90 babies over the last few months.

My last few days haven't been very restful and sometimes I've been really beat at night. You have to remember that I speak almost only English from early in the morning until quite late. On Friday I had lunch with two young lawyers and Thursday evening I went to a lecture about a new institute for propaganda analysis. Before that from 10 in the morning until 5 a second public hearing for the Charter.

Now to the most immediate matters. What could possibly have prompted your tax cable on Wednesday? Hopefully only impatience and nothing else. By now I'm sure everything is in your hands, and the note in your letter of the 17th that the 31st is the absolute deadline calmed me somewhat.

There was a lot of amusement here over what is and what is not possible involving Günter's dislocated shoulder. I'm looking forward to mail from his excursion to England and equally to the fresh collars that you promised me for Easter. Á propos Easter! I almost forgot the main item: today the Stös[10] let us know that they will be here as house guests for the holiday (which, by the way, does not include Monday here).

There's nothing else to answer in your letter. It's funny that the nicest letters require the shortest answers. Oh, if only you were here!

In Liebe,

Jo

---

9 *H.C. Bazett*, professor of Physiology at the University of Pennsylvania Medical School, was instrumental in bringing Rudolf to the University after the Nazis expelled him from the University of Kiel in 1933.

10 *Stös* = Erich and Friedel Stötzner, friends who emigrated from Frankfurt to New York.

TUESDAY, MARCH 28, 1939

Letter from Elfriede in Düsseldorf to Johannes in Philadelphia.

Düsseldorf, 28 March 1939.

Lieber Peter,

Once again your two letters from the *Europa* lifted my spirits. They could use some lifting. The last week has been a nightmare and at the end there was the tax business too, which pretty well did me in. Your sending me the tax stuff in bits and pieces after you first messed it up was a bit much. Of course in spite of the availability of the *Île-de-France* your second letter came two days after the first, so [your draft letter to the Finance Bureau] turned out to be useless. I had, in fact, written [them] a letter with great difficulty on Saturday because it was the last minute for filing the return. Now I hope to God and all His saints that everything is more or less OK. In any event, I'm going to do everything myself now. The ocean is too wide and telegrams are too expensive [to consult you on everything]. It's like the way Karl [Lenzberg] is always asking questions that Hilde can't answer and she's always supposed to do things that she can't do. Still, she's pretty far along with her affairs. She has the packers there and next week Till will probably come and stay with me for a couple of days.

Now I have to face doing all the monthly invoices. It's always an effort doing things I never liked doing much even when I did them with you. But since your letters put me in a good mood, I have to write you before I do the invoices. Yesterday I sent off the second pair of pajamas and hope they meet with your approval. They are not intended to increase your attractiveness to other girls, which is unnecessary, even though they might not be ineffectual in that regard.

On Saturday we had a big crowd to celebrate Günter's birthday, for which you could at least have sent good wishes. Sixteen people from Cold Duck punch through pink champagne to chicken soup in the kitchen. It was really nice, especially after most people had left and only the Trömels, Miss Scholl, and we were left sitting in the kitchen. Mother was of the opinion that we are not very refined people since we always think it's nicest in the kitchen. I wasn't even one of the last to leave but just slipped out quietly at some point.

It's cold and nasty here. For weeks a northeast wind has been sweeping snow and cold across the lakes. Given this situation I've decided to stay here over Easter unless the weather changes substantially. I still have the heating on. [Pause] But now Hilde phoned a minute ago and suggested we should go away for a few days [at Easter] in her little Olympia with the children and her sister Ilse. It's the first Easter proposal that appeals to me.

Now I have to talk some business. More than anything else, I was upset at your expressing disappointment that the negative balance hasn't turned into a positive balance. I always knew you had illusions about the magnitude of the negative balance, specifically as to how small it was. When you left, there was still a substantial chunk of negative balance, which would be closer to disappearing were it not for the dreadful receivables outstanding from the carriers. It has also become apparent that a lot of our ads aren't being renewed, a fact reflected both in the advertising commissions and the overall sales figures. I estimate an average of RM 100 less revenue [this month]. The household doesn't cost any less than before. There are two reasons for that. It is not that we are gorging ourselves and indulging in luxuries, far from it. But the price of fruit and vegetables is extremely high at this time of year. Second, I just don't have the time to do by myself some of the things I did before. For example, I now buy cookies instead of baking them and I have your pajamas made for you rather than sewing them myself. And Susanne didn't have anything to wear—her arms were sticking out of all her sleeves. And I can't do much to reduce the overall household expenses because the big items—rent, maid, light—are high and they are constant. But in your whole life you never had a phone bill as low as RM 11.40. So while I'm being as frugal as possible, my success isn't as great as we would like it to be for reasons totally beyond my control.

I want to tell you a couple of nice stories about Susie. She recently declared herself to be so strongly opposed to marriage that I was afraid someone had prematurely explained to her what was involved. I brought up the subject again so I could intervene if necessary and set things straight. But her opinion arose from higher philosophical considerations. Yes, marrying would be very nice, because then you would always have a good friend, but if you didn't marry you would have more for yourself. And she didn't want to choose between these two possibilities, which is of course the heart of the matter. Then I asked her what kind of husband she would consider. "He has to be nice, a gentleman." Me: like Papi. "No, a little more gentlemanly." So you see where your failings are. I didn't think it would be right to withhold your daughter's opinion from you. By the way, I almost forgot to tell you about her brilliant report card. Reading and Oral Expression "outstanding" all the others "very good." She claims it's the best in the class. Well, that's fine with me. I really can't get excited over it any more than my mother could get outraged over her sons' bad grades. She will write to you about it herself once vacation starts, because she doesn't have much time now, what with a lot of school, recorder, gymnastics, and English. She was absent 27 days this winter semester but now she is as healthy as can be. Given the miserable weather I find it quite respectable that I haven't had another cold since Christmas. Any time I have to so much as wipe my nose I take quinine/vitamin C tablets and every morning I drink the undiluted juice of half a lemon. That's German folk medicine. I read *Drums Along the Mohawk* in German. I didn't know how to get the English edition and I didn't have the energy to read it in English. I'm going to get there as a complete illiterate in English, if I ever get there at all. Uncle Karl is still silent. I'm afraid I'm going to have to poke him soon.

Note: The reference in the next paragraph to Hilde paying "a great deal of money" probably refers to her payment of the Homeland Abandonment Tax and the German Discount Bank Gold Levy, two taxes on émigré property that amounted to the government's expropriation of 90 percent of the value of everything they owned. Such taxes had to be paid before clearance to leave the country would be issued.

3/30

I've gotten a little further with the invoices and accounts. And for the first time in four weeks there's a little sunshine. Yesterday afternoon I was at Hilde's. With the help of a great deal of money (actually a very great deal) she now has all the clearances and even got her passport extended by a year. So now maybe we'll go to Heidelberg for Easter. I pressed my dressmaker to finish my dress with the matching jacket. If we're going to be in that neighborhood, then it has to be chic, but it's not certain yet. I am sending you a pair of gloves as an Easter present that I hope will meet with your approval. And the history of England should be helpful to you in your historical studies.

Alles Gute
Alles liebe, Deine Friedel

FRIDAY, MARCH 31, 1939

Letter from Johannes in Philadelphia to Elfriede in Düsseldorf. In reading Johannes' discussion of Walter Phillips, remember that Johannes was 34 at the time, and Walter was 26.

Philadelphia, 3/31/39

Liebster Peter,

We seem to have figured it out so that the same ship that brings me a letter from you takes my answer back, and that's really nice and fast. I found your letter of the 23rd, which the *Normandie* brought, when I got home after picking up Pa-Mu as I often do. It wasn't here yet when we left this morning, although we always leave after the morning mail, which comes at 8. (Which means, by the way, that I get up every morning at 7:30. Me!) The regular schedule with Blue Boy has now become a routine. Since Manfred isn't working in the x-ray department anymore and is studying full time for the oral exam in April, the crew usually consists of Pa, Mu and me (Wednesday and Saturday only Pa and me). At 8:50 I drop the two of them off at the lab and then, after overcoming the chronic parking difficulties, I'm in my office at 9.

Since Monday I've been sharing an office with Walter Phillips in the Charter office on the 7th floor of a skyscraper on Broad Street. Roger Scattergood, at whose desk I now sit, has returned to his law practice, and with every passing day Walter and I are becoming more and more an inseparable team. It's a funny marriage that has developed between us, built, as is so often the case, on the polarity of our characters.

He is in many ways a kind of Peer Gynt, the child of a very wealthy prominent Presbyterian family that is very skeptical of their younger generation.[11] He is a beginner in matters of politics and government, with a very lively political interest but little conception of what one person can and cannot accomplish as a relatively small cog in a very large organization. (He's a little bit like our old friend Alwine Stolteroff [unidentified], as if to say, "But I'm Walter Phillips!"). On the other hand, he is incredibly earnest and hardworking and full of inferiority complexes about what his social position is or should be. He tries to camouflage these complexes with a self-confident manner but then gets into trouble when his abruptness and his reaching beyond the level of his competence causes him to land on his head, and then he is unhappier about it than anyone else.

Since, as you know, I'm very sociable and end up being a father confessor to a lot of people, Walter and I get along wonderfully. He allows me to give him lots of advice out of the rich store of my experience, lets me admonish him and reassure him, and in the process, without even being aware of it, he ends up being a great comfort and teacher to me. Above all, Walter is a thoroughly decent human being. Not only can he readily put himself mentally into the position of people who are far from being among the Walter Phillipses of this world, he also has a rare capacity for giving people credit for their accomplishments, a kind of personal loyalty to people, something our Peer Gynt certainly didn't have.

11 *Peer Gynt*, the title character in an Ibsen play, was the spoiled son of a well-to-do family. Walter Phillips' family was Episcopalian, not Presbyterian.

A typical example: You know that I have tried to limit my role with the Charter crowd to that of a technical expert. Yesterday, the following took place: for the first time, I was invited to attend a staff meeting that Walter always attended himself. The discussion came around to the Charter Bill now being in a slack period between its approval by the Charter Commission and full Senate consideration. It has been agreed that we should do something to liven up this lull. We (Walter and I) had discussed this point the previous day, and I suggested the idea of publishing a weekly Charter Newsletter for our speakers and others. Walter jumped at this idea, and we agreed he would present it to the Executive Director. But when the subject came up yesterday at the staff meeting, Walter called on me to present my plan to those who were there. I immediately passed the ball back to him, and expected that he would explain the plan. Whereupon Walter began a wonderful speech that began, "Dr. H. has suggested that . . . " I turned beet red, but the idea received general acclaim and today the first Newsletter was born (although I had to go over and edit the manuscript discreetly before it could go out).

All that is by the way. As you see, I have once again attached myself to a man who is my quasi-boss and have earned his trust. May heaven protect me from any disappointment! In any event, I'm learning in a few weeks things that many other people don't even get to see in years. He drags me to thousands of luncheons and meetings and speeches and lectures. Afterwards he has to explain specific American things to me that I didn't understand, and I have to explain to him the substance of some of the problems under discussion that he didn't grasp. On Sunday we have invited him and his wife to coffee; hopefully things will work out between him and the other Höbers.

To stick with the Phillips family for the moment, I have to tell you a cute story about Walter's younger sister, who also works for the Charter Committee. When we were working on the rather substantial Charter paragraphs relating to city planning, I expressed an interest in seeing a little more of the city itself, whereupon the young Phillips girl was put at my disposal with an incredibly huge car. We amused ourselves for three and a half hours in beautiful sunshine, first up on the tower of City Hall and then on the Delaware and the Schuylkill, in West Philadelphia and in the slum areas, in the Negro areas, in the Italian areas, in the Jewish areas and in the Chinese area and throughout this exceptionally ugly city.[12] Unfortunately my attention was sharply divided between the city and the first real live society girl I had ever met (and who, I had reason to believe from Walter, was not unsympathetic to me).

12 In 1939, Philadelphia had been governed by a political machine for sixty years, it had extremely poor municipal services, its air and water were badly polluted, and its streets and buildings were filthy and dilapidated. It was a far cry from the Philadelphia of today.

She told me quite unselfconsciously that she was supposed to have gotten engaged as a debutante at age 18, and now that she was 23 and still unmarried she really didn't know how to begin her life. She was particularly unfortunate in that she wasn't stupid enough to be satisfied by parties and clubs and movies, but on the other hand was restricted on all sides by iron conventions. She seemed to be quite comfortable in conversing with me until, about three hours into the conversation, in reply to some remark of hers, I mentioned that I had gotten engaged quite early. In response, she asked how long I have been engaged, and when I told her with some shock that I was married, she responded with such furious blushing that I almost laughed. I subsequently concluded that I need to have a critical conversation with Walter about the poor quality of his information service. The girl's name is Becky, a shortening of Rebecca. The next promised step in my entry into this family is a tennis match on the parents' estate on the Delaware. If things keep going like this we're going to end up in the social register. Daddy said yesterday he thought that it would be good for me to learn all about debutantes, so that I will be prepared for Susie.[13]

Good heavens! Now I'm gossiping along here about myself, when to begin with I was very concerned that you were so concerned when you wrote me. What on earth has gotten into your carriers?! First Schindler and now Mrs. Mugler! Even if I can't be of any help to you I would like to have a bit of a more detailed report. Doesn't the woman work for the RWZ [*Rheinish-Westfälische Zeitung*—a local paper] anymore? Why did she just not come to work on Monday? Her husband is working, isn't he? And why was the confrontation with her inconclusive? And how much did she embezzle? And if it was a lot, how did she still have so much money on the 19th? Did Schindler make his first April payment? I'm a little concerned about all this and would like some more details. Also about the tax matter, which hopefully is now wrapped up. What was the concrete threat that would have followed if you hadn't gotten the thing in by the 25th? And what does it mean that no more returns would be accepted after the 31st? What would have happened then? While my interest is only theoretical, still I am interested. And to answer your question in your last letter: "housing" is simply residential construction, an area in which intervention by the state and municipal governments is really just at the most elementary level, even though public intervention is more essential here than in any other country.

Stop, I don't want to get started again with American topics; otherwise the mail will have been picked up and the *Normandie* will sail without this letter.

So long my dear.

Dein Jo

---

13 Later Walter did, in fact, ask Johannes to allow himself be listed in the Social Register, an offer he declined.

CHAPTER 8

Uncle Karl Says No

TUESDAY, APRIL 4, 1939

Letter from Elfriede in Düsseldorf to Johannes in Philadelphia.

Düsseldorf, 4 April 1939

Mein liebstes Peterchen,

The work load has been running very high and shows no sign of abating. That's the way it's been for three weeks now: first troubles with the carriers and then the Ultimo, and I'm nowhere near done. The sales tax return is due on the 10th and the 7th is Good Friday. And when I'm drowning in work as I am now (I allowed myself a cigarette and this letter as a momentary break) I quickly end up in the dumps.

You can gauge how unstable I've been feeling by the fact that I was out almost every night last week, mostly at my mother's and once at von Baeyers, just because I couldn't stand my own company any more. When I found myself all alone on Saturday, it got very bad and all the obstacles we face looked insurmountable. This is already the 5th Ultimo, and it can get on your nerves to be totally in the dark as to how many more of them there will be. Don't get mad at me for pouring out all my worries. I'm sure you can imagine that I can't always be on top of things. Sunday evening the Trömels rescued me from myself and that was good. A lot of cognac and soda did the rest.

Till has been staying here since yesterday. Today the last packers are at Hilde's house and she was dreadfully upset, which is not surprising. On Friday we're supposed to go to Heidelberg with her, but I don't see how I can get everything finished by then, even though it seems to me that I've earned four days of vacation. On Sunday one of the bundles of newspapers didn't get here again—something is always wrong with the shipping system. It's terrible. There weren't these kinds of problems when you were here.

And then I wouldn't want to deprive you of the contents a bulletin that came from Frankfurt yesterday:

> Dear Dr. Höber, as your husband is not in a position to continue to conduct the business of our Agency any longer, we are prepared to

transfer our Agency contract with your husband to you, effective 1 March 1939. The same conditions will be in effect for this Agency agreement as were in place for your husband, so that the rights and obligations are the same. We must merely reserve the right to cancel the contract with one month's notice. We request that you inform us that you agree to these terms. Sincerely yours and heil Hitler! F.S.D. [*Frankfurter Sozietätsdruckerei*, the publishing company], signed by Hecht and Schreiber.

Well, I was flabbergasted and at first didn't know how I should take this, but everybody I talked to about it, Günter, Gerhard, congratulated me. Apparently I'm a capable girl. What do you think? I called Betz today because I would like my reply to be in line with his thoughts. He wasn't there but will probably call tomorrow. This wouldn't really change anything and it's understandable that they want to pin someone down who will be responsible, but somehow it goes against my grain. I much prefer doing it the way it has been up to now, with everything being done in your name and on your behalf, but I suppose I can only answer this letter in the affirmative. Once I've discussed the answer with Betz and have it written, I'll write you too. I do recognize that the work here over the last four months could have been done a lot worse.

The last couple of weeks could have given me the comfortable feeling of work well done, just as much as the time around Christmas did, but that didn't happen. The feeling of personal emptiness seemed even greater then than it does now. Men are different that way. It's very tiresome when one has a perfectly useful intellect combined with so many superfluous, subjective, female emotions. More is demanded of one's mind than one's emotions can deliver. But what else can I do? I'll just go on playing the role of the capable woman, even though I'd much rather be taken care of occasionally.

Your truly sweet letter that the *Europa* brought me, containing the conversation with the Executive Director of the Committee, really did me good. I undoubtedly have the worst low point behind me, but for some time there will still be the fear that the next day something could rain into my soup.

Now let me tell you about Susie's birthday. First thing in the morning in bed—she was sleeping in yours because Till was staying overnight in her room—we read the four Philadelphia letters together. Yours was really sweet and nicely done and I was very touched. Ferdinand arrived with the afternoon mail and everyone got to enjoy it, because in the meantime Mother and Herbert and Gerlinde with Müschelchen and the Trömels with their children had come over. We didn't have a big children's party because I couldn't manage that on the third of the month on top of everything else. Last night I didn't finish work until 11 o'clock, and I had begun at 8 o'clock and worked through without lunch. It's going that way again today, without a break, but I think I've overcome the problems again. The sun is so bright and warm that if you had the time you could sit on the balcony in the sun, but unfortunately I don't have any time. I have to go in town in a little while to get a couple of things for Easter. With a vivid imagination one could picture that it would be charming to lie on a hillside in the sun, but I shouldn't let my fantasies run wild—where would that lead?

I think of you and I think it would be much nicer to drive with you to some pleasant place.

Alles gute und liebe,

Deine Friedel

FRIDAY, APRIL 7, 1939 (Good Friday).

Letter from Johannes in Philadelphia to Elfriede in Düsseldorf. In this letter, Johannes discusses his family's financial situation, noting that, "There are really too many people for one salary ..." Rudolf received a limited stipend of $4,000 per year from the University of Pennsylvania and on this income was supporting himself and Josephine, Manfred and Gri and their two children, and Johannes—seven people in all. Because the University provided insufficient support for Rudolf's research, Josephine worked with him in the lab five days a week as an unpaid collaborator. Johannes' pay from the Charter Committee was of only slight help in supporting the household. Moreover, Rudolf's salary arrangements with the University had to be renewed annually and had not yet been approved at the time of this letter. "The book" discussed in the letter was the eighth edition of Rudolf's Textbook of Physiology [Lehrbuch der Physiologie des Menschen], *published in Switzerland in late 1938. Royalties on earlier editions had in the past provided a substantial supplement to Rudolf's income, but the returns from the new edition had not yet started coming in.*

Philadelphia, 4/7/39.

Liebster Peter,

If only I hadn't crowed so much about our good mail connections last time! The gods are now taking their revenge, and when I went to the mailbox this morning, confident that I would find a *Queen Mary* letter, none was there. But first, one might still come and, second, the *Europa* arrives tomorrow and she may have one. But since your last one arrived a week ago, this unexpected break feels like an eternity. So I decided to go into the office an hour late this morning, Good Friday, which is not a holiday here, so this letter can still go out tonight. As consolation, yesterday three packages arrived from you all at once—the two PJs and the shirt, which I put on right away this morning. Am I right that the PJs are handmade? I think they're incredibly nice, so nice that I almost think it's crazy of you to send something like that to a bachelor husband. They cry out for an audience who can appreciate them. But you don't have to worry about any improper use. To my considerable amazement, Gri recently made the same observation you often did, which I always took as self-interested, namely that I look so intellectual when I have been working so intently. I don't know whether she's right, but the cause is certainly correctly stated. I have to go back a long way to find a time when my work fulfilled me as much as it does now. For the first time I realize how wrong the newspaper business has been for us. In any event, right now there's nothing else in my life that plays any role for me other than my work. I'm often with Charter people even outside of office hours, mostly with Walter, and I have lunch every day with one or another of my colleagues so I miss other things less than I otherwise would.

But to get back to the PJs. They are so nice that it was of no importance that—for the first time with any of your packages—we had to pay 75 cents customs duty. Surprisingly also, there was 15 cents postage due on top of that because they were classified as small packages instead of commercial samples. Maybe you can write that on the package in the future. This is meant only by way of information and is in no way intended as criticism.

If the Stös weren't coming tomorrow we would barely notice that it's Easter. As I said, Good Friday isn't a holiday and neither is Easter Monday. On top of that, it's beastly cold here and yesterday there was a thunder storm that would have been worthy of April weather in the Rhineland. Pa-Mu are working insanely hard again and we are seriously plotting some way to get them away from their jobs for a while. If only money weren't so tight! There are really too many people for one salary. The book hasn't brought in anything at all yet—it couldn't have since it just came out in December—but on top of everything else the sword of Damocles of the appointment extension is hanging over Daddy's head, made more difficult this year because 65 is the normal retirement age. Well, somehow it will work out. In two weeks he's going to a physiology convention in Toronto where he is to speak on what I understand to be the good results of some new work. Three more articles are being published and in addition he has lectures, supervision of interns, exams, and ongoing experiments. Sometimes it's impossible to understand how those two manage all this work; it's becoming a little worrisome for all of us. But in the end it has always been our experience that this pace doesn't hurt them. What a difference between their generation and ours!

Prof. Rudolf Höber and Dr. Josephine Höber photographed in Rudolf's physiological laboratory at the University of Pennsylvania.

On Tuesday evening there was the weekly housing lecture. They are still just making baby steps here, even though a third of the population is very poorly housed and the slums are worse than in Oberblick or Neckarstadt.[1] The mostly young people who started this movement treat it as a crusade and seem to be having some success in getting a big program started. On Tuesday the subject was the selection of tenants and the shared facilities in the housing developments. For me, the most impressive thing again was the way a relatively young woman, the Research Director of the Philadelphia Housing Association, delivered a lecture that was exceedingly competent as well as cogent and charming. Once again it could have been you, and I've been dreaming up the most unlikely possibilities for you. Catherine Bauer recently and this time Dorothy Schoell—that was the girl's name—are absolutely like you in their combination of intellect and femininity.[2] So, hurry up!

On Thursday I had a second big tour of the city. To Becky's apparent disappointment, I had spoken to Walter about it so much that he came along. Since we were passing by, we had tea at his parents' beautiful estate on the Delaware and in the evening I went to a first class dinner and party at the home of the Executive Secretary of the Charter Committee.

1 *Oberblick* was a rundown section of Düsseldorf. *Neckarstadt* was a poor section of Mannheim.

2 Johannes' mention of Dorothy Schoell was portentous. Six years later, Dorothy Schoell became head of the Philadelphia Housing Association and hired Elfriede as Research Director, the position Schoell held at the time she made this speech.

Well Peter, it's almost 10 A.M.. That's OK, since I was in the office until 6 yesterday, but I don't want it to get any later. In addition, we have a planning meeting today about starting up Charter Clubs. I wrote you recently about my newsletter idea. That proposal fell on such fertile ground that the second issue already came out yesterday. In the next few days you'll receive a free sample of our product.

So long my dear. Tomorrow and the day after tomorrow we'll be talking about you a lot with the Stös.

Dein Jo

SATURDAY, APRIL 8, 1939

Picture postcard from Elfriede, Hilde Lenzberg, and Hilde Lenzberg's sister, Ilse, in Frankfurt to Johannes in Philadelphia. They were on a four-day Easter vacation trip to Heidelberg. The picture on the postcard is a view of the restaurant in the Frankhof Hotel, where they stayed.

Lieber Jo. Happy Easter. Are you willing to entrust Elfriede to me? We drove here in my little car and tomorrow we're going to Heidelberg. Our route goes by water [unexplained]. Cheers Jo. Till is the man of the house, do you believe it?! But still. ...

Hildchen. Friedel. Ilse Melke

SUNDAY APRIL 9, 1939 (Easter).

Picture postcard from Elfriede and Hilde Lenzberg in Heidelberg to Johannes in Philadelphia. The picture on the card shows the Neckar Bridge and castle in Heidelberg.

Lieber Peter, this is how the "war widows" pass their brief days: in the [Hotel] Europ in Heidelberg, so you can hold your nose in the air. It's still one of the better places on this continent and I have been happily meandering in the footsteps of our past.

Friedel

... Once again in the big world, completely between the past and the future. Nothing like postcards!

Hildchen

TUESDAY, WEDENESDAY AND THURSDAY, APRIL 11–13, 1939

Letter from Elfriede in Düsseldorf to Johannes in Philadelphia. Elfriede's trip to Heidelberg was paid for by Hilde Lenzberg. She and her husband Karl were permitted by the Nazis to take only a small part of their money when they left Germany. Hilde and others in her position decided to spend extravagantly in their last weeks in Germany rather than letting their money go to the state. This was the "overall situation" in which Elfriede felt she could comfortably accept Hilde's generosity on the trip. The Heidelberg visit brought up memories of Johannes and Elfriede's days there as students ten years earlier.

Düsseldorf, 11 April 1939.

Liebster Peter,

A minute ago it was still winter, and all of a sudden it's not just spring but real summer. On the balcony the thermometer reads 75 and I put the typewriter on the desk in the living room so the sun will shine on me and improve my appearance a bit.

The apricot tree in the garden next door is in bloom, the chestnuts have big leaves, and it's beautiful everywhere. Our Easter trip didn't begin until Saturday afternoon because Hilde hadn't yet finished all her business. As you might expect, she wasn't exactly in good shape. The house is empty and rented, the furniture at sea since this morning, but there's still no way for her to get to Karl, and Mussolini is in Albania.[3] All those things could push someone weaker over the edge, and all the details connected to leaving have been preying on her. Still, the [travel] days did her good, and the sunny skies of Baden, which she loves so much, will do her more good. At any rate we took off on Saturday afternoon, Hilde, Till, and her sister Ilse, who is a very decent sort. (I'm making even more typing mistakes than usual because the sun is shining in my eyes, but I don't want to turn away either.) We had coffee in that sweet little corner place in Altenkirchen. In Wiesbaden, where we wanted to stay, there were no rooms, so we drove on to Frankfurt and ate and slept well in the Frankhof. Too fancy for your modest wife. We had four single rooms, of which Hilde's and mine were joined by a passageway, providing the opportunity for charming night wanderings for chats but which could have been used for better purposes. Wonder what those might be!!

Sunday morning we had them call from Frankfurt to Heidelberg and reserve rooms for us in the Europ, and it was good we did because by

3 In the week of April 4, Italian troops attacked and quickly subdued Albania, adding to the concerns about the approach of a wider European war.

Easter trip to Frankfurt and Heidelberg, April 8–10, 1939. Hilde and her son Till; Hilde and Elfriede.

afternoon we wouldn't have gotten anything. We spent the day driving around on the truly magical Bergstrasse, ate lunch outside in Bernheim, afternoon walk in Heidelberg to the castle and the Scheffel Terrace. These are as beautiful as they ever were and the magic of the soft lines of the mountains really made an impression on me. I can walk with carefree pleasure in the footsteps of this Heidelberg past, perhaps because it's the one period of our lives that came to an end organically. There are a lot of memories here, from 37 Brückner Street and 23 Anlage Street to rehearsals in the courtyard of the castle and many others. Supper in the Europ, which was packed with people, but not one familiar face popped up.

Yesterday morning we drove all the way through the Neckar Valley to Wimpfen, climbed through the ruins and the churches, aroused considerable amusement with Hilde's inadequate driving skills, drove back via the Oden Forrest with a last detour to the Dilsberg, and finally back to the Europ for tea. Around 7 o'clock my train left, which was totally packed, but with my 2nd class ticket (also underwritten by Hilde) I got back quite well sitting in a corner seat.

Yes, I was a guest for the whole trip and in view of the overall situation I thought I could accept. It was wonderful from beginning to end, only too short. During the trip I had to comfort Hilde, a role for which you would probably be better suited than I, but I did what I could. By yesterday evening I could do it more easily than at the beginning. In the last few months she has had to summon up more intellectual and emotional strength than she actually had.

On top of everything else, there's the thing with Mac Hannasch [dying of cancer] which is so gruesome and absolutely hopeless. The Magician says we can only hope that it comes to an end soon. It's too horrible for him and his poor wife. Everyone in our circle has done everything they could and now it's coming to such a dreadful end. In the face of tragedies like this your own troubles look pretty small.

I've decided to wait out this week for an answer from Uncle Karl and then follow up. My first letter was sent on 2/15. Some people seem to have an odd sense of time.

Your letter of 3/31, which I received on Good Friday, that is on the 7th, pleased me a great deal. On Saturday morning Susanne surprised me with a huge Easter egg, bigger and prettier than any I ever saw. I was afraid she had spent at least half of the contents of her savings bank on it. She went shopping for it with Mother, and when I suggested to Mother that she shouldn't have let her spend so much money, she said Susanne thought that now Papi wasn't here she had to substitute for him and give me something so nice I couldn't have gotten anything better even from Papi. And she succeeded. I was really very touched. Mother treated me to a very elegant blouse to go with my new dress, which I got just in time on Thursday evening so I could look suitable in Hilde's company.

Hilde is no expert driver. As a wife she never got behind the wheel when Karl was here. As a result her driving has been pretty much limited to the city, and her current battered mental state didn't help things. We blamed everything on the new, unfamiliar car. We had plenty of time and it didn't bother us in the least when other cars passed us. The Easter traffic generally wasn't too bad considering the beautiful weather. It was still quite cold on Friday, and until a week ago it was so wintry that a lot of people hadn't made plans. This was also true of the landscape, and the Neckar Valley was at least as lovely as the Mosel Valley, though the little wine bars weren't open yet. The waves of these gentle mountains are well suited to smoothing out the waves of one's mood, and they did just that. I think I fulfilled my role of cheering Hilde up quite well.

4/12/39

Do you know where I'm sitting? On the balcony, which we cleaned up and furnished this morning. The sun is as warm as summertime and the night rain brought out the greenery even more and the pear trees on the trellis, which only had little buds yesterday, are in full bloom today. It's much too pretty to work.

4/13/39

Günter came back from Cambridge on Tuesday, very impressed by the country you like so well. His passion for Sweden is in danger of being obliterated by a passion for England. He now can speak only broken

Elfriede on the balcony of Johannes and Elfriede's apartment on Pempleforterstrasse 11, Düsseldorf, spring 1939.

German and instead speaks fluent English.[4] He went to Trumpington Road, where people were angry about your inadequate writing performance. Please do me the favor of letting them hear from you; it's still possible that I might want to visit them.[5]

That's enough for today.

Alles liebe, Deine Friedel

4 This is a joke; Günter was in England only a few days, and here Elfriede is making fun of his enthusiasm.

5 *Trumpington Road* was the home of the Schlossmanns, Johannes and Elfriede's friends in Cambridge. When Elfriede writes about "visiting" them, she probably means holding on to the Schlossmans as a backup escape route out of Germany.

THURSDAY, APRIL 13, 1939

Letter from Johannes in Philadelphia to Elfriede in Düsseldorf, a little over a week after Mussolini's troops occupied Albania.

Philadelphia, 4/13/39.

Liebster Peter,

It's half past 11 at night. I worked from 9 until 3:30, had a seminar from 4–6, was invited for dinner at 6:30 and just came home. I'd rather wait for the letter that the *Bremen* will undoubtedly bring me tomorrow—hopefully also one from Susie and maybe one from Günter as well—but stupidly the ship arrives in the afternoon and leaves again at night and I don't want it to leave empty.

It seems like I haven't heard from you forever, and it also seems like I haven't written forever, but neither of those things is true: I wrote last Friday and your letter of the 30th came Saturday. I'm a little worried by your last two letters, and I think it's OK for me to write you that. You've spoiled me with your letters, not only in their number but in their content, so much so that I have to adjust to it when you sometimes send me a letter that isn't as cheerful as usual. For this reason may I suggest that you only write when you are really in the mood to? I wouldn't want writing to me to become an obligation or even a chore, so that you heave some big sigh, oh God, now I have to write again and I'm dead tired, so that I'd rather go to bed or read something pleasant. I hope you know without my saying so that I wait for the mail every morning and have to take care not to let the others see my disappointment if nothing's there. Why am I a little saddened by your last letters? Because you made such a terrible fuss over the tax matters and otherwise scolded me for nearly two pages in your last letter. While I know I run the risk of being scolded again, I still have to defend myself somewhat. You got the tax forms on 2/6 and forwarded them to me on 2/20. I got them on 3/6 and returned them on 3/14 (the supplement on 3/17). There was no way I could know that the 3/31 date has now come to play such an important role. And on the subject of net or gross revenue, you didn't have to bite my head off about that comment. I know precisely how frugal a woman you are, but I worry that you may have some illusions about the possibilities from [Rudolf's bank account in] Kiel that might influence your arrangements.[6] I'm not at all surprised that the income went down by RM 100 because of advertising and cancellations. I'm only writing all this to show you that I'm not as stupid and heartless as you think and not to criticize you. So for God's sake don't be worried about this letter now. I think it's better to write things than to swallow them, and to be fair this defensive speech of mine should be followed by a hug and a kiss.

6 *Possibilities from Kiel* refers to the fact that Johannes and Elfriede's income had been supplemented from Rudolf's retirement account in Kiel, which could only be expended in Germany. Johannes felt it necessary to remind Elfriede that Nazi regulations might limit their further access to those funds.

Á propos worried—this past week was not so ideal for me for a change. It can't be denied that once in a while all kinds of nightmares suddenly come crashing down on me. This week it was the events "on the other side" (which is the funny expression everyone here uses for Europe) that were responsible for my pessimism. When I think about the fact that you haven't heard anything at all from Stuttgart, that my plans for a more permanent job have resulted in some friendly letters but nothing else so far, as well as other similar things, then the most pleasant activities are insufficient to interrupt the *circulus vitiosus.*

At the same time, I don't really have any good reason to complain. I already wrote you that one of the board members of the Charter Committee permitted me to use his name when writing to four governmental research agencies and that another of them, who is even better known nationwide, offered on his own initiative to support my applications with a personal letter. Today I got a copy of it, and I have to share the main paragraph with you:

> Since last fall I have had to rely on Dr. H. very greatly for the preparation of memoranda to deal with the myriad questions and objections that are flung at you by friend and foe in a campaign to secure for a great city a really good apparatus for local government. Dr. H. has shown himself all that one could ask not only in discovering all the important sources of information about a certain question, but in arranging the data so that others can grasp its significance. A mind that is as good at synthesis as it is at analysis is a rarity and any organization in the general field of local government that could find a way to use it on a more permanent basis than a charter campaign can offer, will be benefitting itself and the community it is serving.

Now that is really a pretty nice outcome for three months of work. If only it would lead to something!

The weekend with the Stös was really nice. They were in great form and my whole family was enthusiastic about them and vice versa. I first showed them a little of the city, Independence Hall and the wonderful Flemish exhibit in the Art Museum, then here for coffee, a walk around the neighborhood, and a cozy family evening. Sunday Swarthmore and Bryn Mawr, in the afternoon guests and in the evening a nice movie. And when they decided to stay on Monday morning I got Walter to give me the morning off and drove out to Valley Forge with them. (You don't know that place yet, and it's really pretty now with spring beginning.) In between times endless chatting. Stö's plans are unfortunately still quite nebulous. He has picked up on a lot of connections here but up to now he's had the same experience I have: lots of good will but nothing concrete.

My week was busy in other ways as well. On Tuesday I drove with Walter and his wife out to the suburb where they want to build or buy [a house] and then stayed on for a cozy dinner. We even played an hour of bridge. I think Walter had noticed my upset over the newspapers in the morning and wanted to cheer me up a bit. This evening we are invited to a formal dinner—that means tuxedo—at the Wilsons, friends of Pa-Mu. I think they're very fancy people again.

Although I didn't go out Wednesday evening, I still had a less than restful night since Janka and Moni have been sick for three days. Moni got it first, then Janka was put in with me and got me out of bed four times and then in the morning had [a fever of] 102.7. Now she is back in Moni's room and both of them are doing a lot better. Diagnosis is still unclear in spite of four doctors. All eyes are on the skin for the least sign of redness, which declines to appear.

Speaking of children, I was highly amused by Susie's marriage philosophy—"more gentlemanly" will have to be entered as a family joke into our lexicon—but also greatly pleased by her letters and her good report card. As long as she doesn't follow in the footsteps of her father, whose good grades came to a fairly abrupt end at the end of third grade, only to climb to unexpected heights at the end of secondary school. I brag about her report card every chance I get and I think her first letter in Roman characters is a lot nicer than her German letters. By the way, she should write a lot in Roman characters—she will need that here.

I have to tell you something else sad. The sleeves of my nice blue suit are already beginning to wear through. It's true that I've worn it a lot, but that's still annoying. If you by any chance saved a piece of the cloth for a patch, please send it to me. *Á propos* sending: we still have one request. We would all like to read Karl Schurz. You were finished with it, so maybe you could give it up for us.[7]

Where did you end up spending Easter?[8] I'm really looking forward to your account. And did you take the Little Sparrow with you? Let me know the details.

Schluss, Kuss,

Dein Jo

MONDAY, APRIL 17, 1939

Letter from Elfriede in Düsseldorf to Johannes in Philadelphia, enclosing a letter from the American Consul in Stuttgart turning down her visa application. Instead of summoning Elfriede for an interview, the letter (not preserved) demanded additional documents to prove that Elfriede and Susanne would have adequate financial support in the United States. Elfriede's original application had included an affidavit of support from

7 *Karl Schurz* refers to the three-volume memoirs of Karl Schurz, who emigrated to the United States from Germany in 1854 and became a Union General in the Civil War and a Senator from Missouri.

8 Johannes had not yet received Elfriede's letter of April 11–13 describing her Easter trip.

Rudolf, but the Consul questioned whether his salary was sufficient since he was already supporting seven people. The Consul apparently requested additional bank and salary information before a visa would be considered.

Düsseldorf, 17 April 1939.

Mein lieber Peter,

I can't say I was exactly pleased when I got the enclosed letter as a Sunday morning treat yesterday. I had already decided that if I didn't hear anything I would send a follow-up letter today, and then yesterday this completely unexpected mess arrived. Why, how come, is a mystery. I can't understand why something that was sufficient for you and Manfred and Gri isn't enough for Susie and me. In order to avoid any misunderstanding [when I submitted my application], I enclosed the materials from the University and the bank that you sent me. Now I have to ask you all to provide me with the requested additional certifications. Then I will forward them with the requested cover letter and then start to wait all over again. Somebody who doesn't learn patience in my position will never learn it. It's a good thing I have a gentle disposition. I'm not going to throw a tantrum, I'm not screaming, I'm not throwing vases at the wall—I'm just waiting. You can't do anything about it, and there's nothing at all that I can do to help in producing the requested information. At least I don't have to go to Stuttgart now, which would have been hard for me. I'll just wait a little longer. It makes you want to throw up (I only write that; I don't actually do it.) Mother, whom I met in town, thought I looked like I had been throwing up, but sometimes I look like that anyway and it doesn't matter because there's nobody here to look at me. It would be really, really nice if you could get the necessary papers for me in a hurry.

I really enjoy the way you write about your work, but I can't agree with your assertion that the newspaper business was the wrong track for us. You shouldn't isolate the work aspect [of your life], and if you look at it from a broad perspective it looks quite different. You evaluate the work aspect differently from where you are today, and it's certainly nice that everything is going so well for you, but I wouldn't want to erase these last few years. They provided us with skills that only the newspaper business could have taught us, and I wouldn't have wanted to miss out on them. Don't forget that.

I read parts of your last letter, which arrived on Saturday with the *Europa*, to Günter and Mother, and your compliment addressed to me on the basis of [my] intellect and femininity evoked strong misgivings about your moral conduct, but only from the two of them, not me!

I have to add something to a sentence I wrote above: if you live in historically significant times—and there is certainly no doubt on that score—I think there's a lot to be said for experiencing things from right in the center of it all and not *par distance*, and from this perspective the last few years have been really important to me. In exactly the way they occurred.

Schindler's trial was on Saturday. He was sentenced to a month. I had previously told the Criminal Police I would be agreeable to holding the case in abeyance temporarily to give Mr. Schindler the chance to remedy the matter, and on 4/1 he paid RM 15, but they still held the trial yesterday at which he was sentenced to a month in jail. He persisted in telling the court he had lost the money, which no one believed. He now has the right to file an appeal. I would have preferred to leave the case in a pending status, but I couldn't do anything about it.

If nothing unforeseen occurs I have a quieter week ahead of me, but most of the recent disruptions had causes that couldn't be foreseen. Yesterday, Sunday, was very quiet and peaceful. We had planned in the morning to go for a drive, but then it got so cold and ugly again that we withdrew within our four walls. In the last week everything has gotten all green here. Even if it's cold again, it's not so very cold, and the beautiful blooming magnolias still look wonderful even after a rainstorm.

I think the *Columbus*, which gets to Cherbourg tomorrow, will bring your account of Easter.

Alles liebe,

Deine Friedel

TUESDAY, APRIL 18, 1939

Letter from Elfriede in Düsseldorf to Johannes in Philadelphia. Tischendorf, the mover, was requesting payment to ship Rudolf and Josephine's remaining belongings from Kiel to the United States. Although Elfriede had some blank checks on Rudolf's account at the Kiel Savings and Loan, she did not know whether government restrictions limited how those funds could be used.

The letter also discusses Susanne's school situation. In 1938, the Nazis ordered the closure of all private and religious schools. In a Catholic city like Düsseldorf, this entailed merging a large number of Catholic school students into the public school system. This move was part of a program to use the schools to indoctrinate children in Nazi ideology and was one of the reasons Johannes and Elfriede decided to leave Germany. The plan was implemented in the spring of 1939.

Düsseldorf, 18 April 1939.

Liebes Peterchen,

The enclosed letter from Tischendorf, which I'm forwarding for you to handle as quickly as possible, is causing me to try to catch the *Europa*, which leaves tomorrow. Until I hear back from you I'll send Tischendorf a response to delay things. I still have a blank check here, but I don't have the slightest idea how things stand with the Savings and Loan [Rudolf's bank in Kiel], and whether it's OK just to write a check or not. I think it's better for Mrs. Tischendorf to wait before I make some kind of mistake. I never got any information from you about how the [bank] matter is proceeding, and I really have enough to do.

Today Susanne had her first classes following vacation, and starting tomorrow has to go to the Franklin School and will lose her nice Miss Anuschewski. The German school system, i.e., the unified school system, was recently instituted here Now the children will be newly assigned depending on their parents' residence. Sonja and Ruth are being transferred with Susanne to the new school, which she dreads a little. She's afraid the new teacher could be stricter and make it harder to earn good grades. Some of the teachers are coming from other schools, and it's uncertain whether the children from Susanne's former class who are remaining in the Blücher School will keep Miss Anuschewski. The day after tomorrow there's another day off for the Führer's 50th birthday. All houses are to be illuminated.

Hilde writes happy postcards from Freiburg, where she's still resting up a little. From there she goes to see her relatives almost every day and in the mornings Till has typing lessons. He'll drop out of school at the end of the current year and immediately enter an apprenticeship over there.[9]

Tonight I'm going to the movies with Mother to cheer myself up with a comedy. Otherwise I don't have any news to add to yesterday's letter. I'm enjoying the fact that the business is pretty quiet.

I've now decided just to transcribe the letter from Tischendorf so I can keep the original here to answer, which I will do tomorrow.

Dear Dr. Höber, I am herewith advising you that your father-in-law's furniture will be packed for shipping on the 18th and 19th of this month. The shipment will take place then the following week. I have

9 *Over there* = Venezuela, where Karl and Hilde Lenzberg and Hilde's son Till were moving.

received from the Foreign Exchange Office the authorization for the transfer of 2500 and request that you transmit your bank order to us. Since some of the furniture is remaining in Kiel, please advise me whether it should remain in my warehouse for the time being.

So, please transmit the bank order and let me know what's supposed to happen with the rest.

That was the business!

And this is my love!

Deine Friedel

THURSDAY, APRIL 20, 1939

Letter from Johannes in Philadelphia to Elfriede in Düsseldorf. Johannes is replying to Elfriede's letter of April 4, 1939 at the beginning of this chapter, in which Elfriede wrote about how hard the work was, about her "feeling of personal emptiness," and how "it would be worth a whole lot more to me to be taken care of occasionally." Johannes also refers obliquely to his worry that "some impediment" to Elfriede's departure might arise. Potential "impediments" included war breaking out, Germany forbidding people to leave, or the United States not allowing Elfriede and Susanne to enter the country.

Philadelphia, 4/20/39.

It was so nice, *mein Schatz*, when I came home just now and found the two postcards from you and Hilde here. The picture of Heidelberg was touching, and the cheerfulness of the postcards helped to relieve my constant worrying about you. Those worries were increased by your last letter and by Günter's letter that arrived today, which was so different from the way he usually writes. I think about you a lot and wrack my brains over whether there isn't something I could do to speed things up. My family gives me a thousand suggestions every day but I don't see any practical possibility, and I'm not inclined to do something just to make up some activity. That would only make you, me, and the others more nervous without accomplishing anything. If only there weren't this constant concern that suddenly there could be some impediment other than just having to wait!

Forgive me for worrying so much. Sometimes the worries take hold of me so strongly that I lose sight of the fact that things are going incredibly well for me here. Please, please if you think I should be doing anything differently, for God's sake write me. Sometimes I imagine that you—not just you but Mother, Günter, maybe also Herbert, in short all of you who are so dear to me—are perhaps sitting together in Düsseldorf and disapproving of something I'm doing or not doing, or I don't know what. The letter from Günter was so unusual, maybe just sad, but maybe also unfriendly. And it's so important, Peter, that when you finally get here, we don't somehow have to begin from the beginning or have to overcome some barrier between us, but rather that our letters have really contained everything meaningful.

I was struck by how unlike you your last letter was when Daddy read it aloud for everyone, even more than when I read it myself. You had every reason to be proud of the recognition as an equal that Frankfurt has accorded you. You accomplished that all by yourself and God knows not easily. You have very much earned my family's growing admiration and this confirmed it again.

I wish I could have been there when you and Susie read our letters in our big beds on the morning of her birthday. Susie's letter about her birthday was again very sweet, but I'd really like to hear from her and from you how she reacted to my very sincerely intended birthday letter. Or didn't she react at all?

The only thing of substance I have to report is that my life at the moment is going on in much the same way it has for the last few weeks. On Tuesday I was invited to dinner by the Phillips family, that is, by the parents, the occasion being the fact that Walter was to speak in a public debate about the charter in Torresdale, the suburb where the parents have their estate. He did his part badly—with a peculiar mix of hesitation and indifference—and I felt like a father who sees his son disgracing himself. In addition, I knew it all much better than he and could have presented it much better and I couldn't say a word, first because I just couldn't and second because I was sitting between his wife and Becky, sort of stuck there as a quasi-member of the family. Papa, the big man, was genial and friendly with me and only began raving about Roosevelt at dessert. I didn't say a word in response to that either, although just two days earlier someone told me that the most scandalous health conditions are rampant in his factory.

On Sunday I had two invitations at the same time, to lunch at the home of Miss Eleanor Davis, a thoroughly sexless but otherwise nice spinster in her thirties who is interested in politics and social policy—primary interest is housing questions—and who can afford to use her time in useful ways for many useful things. She introduced me to her uncle, former U.S. Commissioner for Rural Electrification under the first

Roosevelt administration, who impressed me when he recently spoke at Sweeney's seminar. And last night Ulli, Dr. Sampter [unidentified], Priscilla, and I finally carried out a long delayed plan and "went out." But it wasn't a success, other than that I enjoyed dancing again. You shouldn't go out here when you have to watch the money sooo carefully as we do. Night clubs aren't for us anyway. (I hope it's understood that every bar here that has music calls itself a "night club.")

The work doesn't let up and the pleasure I take in it doesn't either. Today I had to deliver a big paper on the differences between our charter and one now being proposed for Pittsburgh. To have to work through 300 pages of legal text word by word is a wonderful way to force oneself to become familiar with the mechanics of that kind of law. I was very proud when I had my six typed page overview on my desk ten minutes before the office closed. On top of that I was doing this work directly for Millard and Gruenberg—that's the name of our Executive Secretary.

That's all, otherwise the *Queen Mary* will get away from me. Now that I've chatted with you for an hour I feel much better. And tomorrow morning I'll get a letter from you.

In liebe,

Dein Jo

FRIDAY AND SUNDAY, APRIL 21 AND 23, 1939

Letter from Elfriede in Düsseldorf to Johannes in Philadelphia. Here, Elfriede is replying to Johannes' letter of April 13. She refers to a "holiday" the day before, which was Hitler's 50th birthday, when businesses were ordered to close and citizens were ordered to put out flags and lights. Elfriede writes about her compliance with these orders. Her failure to do so would have brought her under suspicion, as Nazi block wardens were required to note the name and address of any person who failed to fly a swastika flag on this day and report it to the Party. Dr. Antonio, with whom Elfriede consulted about the decorations, was a manager for the Frankfurter Zeitung. *Since Elfriede's apartment was also an office of the newspaper, hanging the flag was a matter of safety for the newspaper as well. From her description of how she spent the day, Johannes would have known she was doing whatever she safely could to avoid the "celebrations."*

Düsseldorf, 21 April 1939.

Mein liebstes, bestes Peterchen,

The day after a holiday means no business mail so I have time—and a letter from you. Mrs. Freyberger is coming later, so I'll start the day at 9 o'clock with a letter to you.

When I read your letter, for the first time in—how long is it? months?—I came within a hair's breadth of really crying. A sentence like "I wouldn't want writing to me to become an obligation or even a chore, etc." is something I never, never want to hear again and never, never want to read again. Of course I write letters in different moods, sometimes with more of a positive outlook, sometimes less—you do the same. But these letters, both those that I write and those that I get, have simply become my daily bread and I have to write them, even when I'm feeling completely miserable and even when I'm dead tired.

We don't have to do anything else about the taxes for now. This whole tax thing got so bad because at the same time I had to replace two carriers and deal with an embezzlement and multiple late deliveries of the papers and a dreadful amount of work for the end of the month. The taxes were just one thing too many. And there are also a lot of things going in the Big World on that really give you a headache. There are times when you just ask yourself whether all this effort will ever get you where you want to be. Sometimes I feel like I have an awful lot of weight on my shoulders, even on top of the work, and there are people out there who think I could have managed all this a whole lot worse than I have. So it's really rotten on your part when, at the end of a set of accusations or an attempt to defend your position, you finish without even trying to make up. That would do me a whole lot of good.

This damned business with Uncle Karl hasn't exactly improved my disposition, but don't worry, I'll be a good patient little girl and never complain about taxes again. And you aren't allowed to give me a hard time about money issues ever again. I have to do things here as best I can. Afterwards, if you think I did it wrong, based on the wisdom you derive from being so far away from the actual work, then I'll take it with greater equanimity, based on the superiority that my knowledge of what is actually going on gives me over those who don't know anything at all. Right now I have to cope with more things simultaneously than are usually required of average people. And don't start telling me I'm not average—I'd rather just be average and have less to worry about.

It's an indescribably beautiful spring here. In the past ten days the leaves have come out on the trees that were completely bare, and when the weather is as pleasant as it was yesterday the world looks particularly nice. Yesterday was a national holiday here. In the morning Susanne and I went to the Rhine to see the parade on the Oberkassel field. We were on this side and couldn't see much, so we walked along the Rhine Park and enjoyed the trees and flowers. It's wonderful everywhere. It even got warm enough to sit outside. In the afternoon, Günter drove Mother and us to Bauernhaus.[10] There we first had coffee and then took a long walk in the park. Maybe you remember that we once walked there on a Sunday morning in spring. It was lovely and it did me good to go for a nice long walk again. Given the beautiful weather it was amazingly quiet, though many people were undoubtedly kept away by the numerous events in the city.

In the evening I went to Trömels, but it was an evening when nothing could have kept you at home. The city has been decorated to an unimaginable degree since Wednesday and yesterday evening everything was illuminated as well. Every house, I mean <u>every</u> house, had little colored lamps that were lit at 8 o'clock. It was an indescribable show. On the window grates in the office and the kitchen I had built a little barrier for the lamps with wire, right over the flags that we hung on the window grates. It was very effective. I had discussed the number and type with Dr. Antonio a few days earlier. In addition in the city there were processions of the SS, SA, police, fire department a torchlight parade and finally a big fireworks show on the Rhine. It was impressive.

I find it less impressive that your suit is wearing through, and there are no patches left. I can't say I'm surprised—you've worn the suit almost every day for a year and a half and that's a lot. I'm sorry the situation with your suits is so impoverished and I can't do anything about it from here. Too bad I can't send you my new dress. It's so pretty and elegant that Susanne thought: since you're so elegant now you could find another man if you didn't want Papi anymore. But you still want him, don't you? Yes, I still want him, which you probably figured out.

I think your report about Janka and Moni's illness is wonderful. Four doctors and no diagnosis but six treatments is grand. How about getting a pediatrician as well? Or a mother of average common sense? Anything that can't be defined, or any fever or other symptom, is called "grippe" in German. Treatment: none. Heaven shield me from any illness in Chateau Höber!

I also find impressive—how many other things have I already found "impressive" in this letter?—the letter of recommendation from your boss or whoever he is. It makes me feel good—I think it's well-earned and I endorse it. I hope it will serve a good purpose in the future.

By the way, didn't you get the pigskin Easter gloves? Well, maybe they'll still get there. It would be too bad if they disappeared, but the German mails and the International Postal Union haven't left us in the lurch yet.

10 *Bauernhaus* was a comfortable old restaurant in Grafenberg Park on the outskirts of Düsseldorf, far from the Nazi demonstrations going on in the city.

4/23/39

Something unexpected always comes up and something always keeps me from finishing a letter I've begun. It's Sunday morning, cold wind, no thought of going out. This afternoon Günter and Mother for dinner. Last night Mother and I drank a bottle of pink champagne all by ourselves. We really are very degenerate. These endless women's gatherings are getting on my nerves, but it's a lot better than if I'm alone with myself. Right now I'm not good company for anyone. Next Sunday is part of a long weekend because 1 May falls on a Monday and Mother and I want to use that for a trip, destination still uncertain. It will probably do me good but right now I don't feel like it.

Mrs. Freyberger is planning to change her domicile to England in about six weeks.

I recently got a beautiful (not at all expensive) evening dress. When will I be able to put that to some appropriate use? It's really a sad sign when even a new dress doesn't cheer me up. In addition, after the warm days of the last couple of weeks it has been so terrible that I'm wearing my warmest knit dress again, though the chestnuts are in bloom and Düsseldorf really looks pretty in its spring radiance.

Write me soon, write me a lot, write me sweetly. I sure can use it.

Sehr in liebe, deine Friedel

TUESDAY, APRIL 25, 1939

Letter from Johannes in Philadelphia to Elfriede in Düsseldorf.

Philadelphia, 4/25/39

Liebster Peter,

I didn't write my planned letter last night because I wanted to wait for yours from the *Europa* and because I was so tired that when I lay down on the couch to rest for a few minutes after supper I didn't wake up again until 10. Now I stayed at home this morning and the letter didn't arrive. No doubt the second mail will bring it, but by then I have to be in town.

Spring broke out here also a few days ago. And how! I haven't experienced it like this since our Heidelberg days. The garden suburb of Germantown is in a great state of blooming beauty, and it's hard to believe on the daily 25-minute morning car ride, of which 20 minutes are through the blossoming Wissahickon and Schuylkill valleys, that this is supposed to be the route into the ugly city of a million people. I spent a highly unusual weekend in a manner appropriate to the environment and the weather—namely mostly in our garden. It was badly neglected by our predecessors and when I recently set out to pretty it up superficially, it became clear that nothing at all could be done superficially. So I charged into tying the ivy up on the house and getting rid of the wildest overgrowth, clearing the lawn of its weeds, mainly onion grass, and raking two years' worth of old leaves out of the hedges, etc. This unfamiliar work was great fun for me and I'm far from being finished with it. My plans even include planting flower seeds and fresh grass. Yes, the old frontier spirit is still alive in this country! Could that be shown any more vividly than when it turns Jo into a gardener?

The frontier spirit could also be seen in the part of the weekend I didn't devote to the garden. It began when Walter and I, at first accompanied by his wife, who later had to go home to take care of her baby, made a sightseeing tour of Philadelphia's residential areas. The tour was supposed to make concrete what we learned in our housing lectures, which are unfortunately coming to an end this evening. The two developments we saw, each of which encompassed three hundred residences, were very different. One, built by the city, consists of a great many single family homes or some that accommodate two families but have two separate house entrances.[11] The agency doesn't provide rent supplements but instead rent subsidies, as a result of which the rents are very low, ca. $7.50 per room. People can only rent there if their income is below a certain level—ca. $100. The architect who built these developments evidently heard or saw something about modern construction, which is to say they are done in a rectangular shape with flat roofs, but what came out is a hideous mix of romanticism and mass production, which even the playgrounds, community rooms, and green spaces don't make up for.

The second development[12] is very different. There in the middle of Philadelphia is a multistory apartment building that could be in Frankfurt, Mannheim, Berlin, or Amsterdam. It was built five years ago by a large union without rent subsidies or supplements, and as a result it is considerably more costly (about $10–15 per room, both rents by the way including heat and electric light, full electric kitchen, and built-in refrigerator). The most impressive things—apart from the truly skillful architectonic solution—are the community facilities in this building. They built a large swimming pool that children can use for 6 cents and adults for 12. The only street that cuts through the development has been placed underground and is flanked on either side by garages. The daycare

11 Johannes here describes the Hill Creek public housing project in Northeast Philadelphia built by the Philadelphia Housing Authority. The architect was an appointee of the Republican machine that then controlled the city.

12 The complex Johannes describes here is the Carl Mackley Houses built by the American Federation of Hosiery Workers in 1933–34 and still in use as private apartments. The project was designed by architect Oskar Stonorov, a Bauhaus-trained German refugee.

center is beautiful, where children can be cared for for 10 cents for the whole day. The entire flat roof of this 300-unit building is fitted out as a roof garden, broken up in just two places by large communal laundry rooms, whose views of the skyline of Philadelphia must make doing laundry a pleasure. Walter and I succeeded in getting the manager of this complex, who had given a guided tour to the 100 or so people taking the course, to come over to my car so we could talk to him for an hour or so about things he wouldn't have wanted to discuss in the larger group.

The weekend was a well-earned and much appreciated break from three very intense days in the office. Last week a new citizens' group formed to oppose the new charter published two long flyers that got me so fired up I attempted my first English propaganda piece. Walter joined in my enthusiasm and wrote the section on city finances, about which he is a specialist, and we were happy to discover that we had both written in the same style, and submitted our joint product to the organization's leaders, who not only forgave but endorsed our having gone beyond our assigned area of responsibility—we are, after all, technical advisors, not propagandists. Today 650 copies of our work are being distributed to close and not-so-close campaign workers who are being asked to comment on it and then it will probably be printed.

In addition to this substantive satisfaction I also experienced a great personal satisfaction in the office on Saturday. On the recommendation of our Executive Director I wrote the Public Administration Clearing House in Chicago, which is the central personnel source for all governmental research agencies and such organizations. They sent me their personnel form, and since I named our Executive Director as one of the three requested references, on Saturday he received an inquiry about me. I would not want to withhold from you the answer he sent—he gave me a copy of it. In the thirty-fourth year of my life it made me acquainted with characteristics that were totally unknown to me until now and so I would by no means wish to assume that they were familiar to you:

> Dr. H. came to us some months ago, and with the exception of a little time that he has given to some courses in the Graduate School at the University of Pennsylvania, has given all of his time to our work. His assignments have been primarily along the lines of research. I have been very much impressed with the careful quality of his work, the fine training and skill shown in what he has produced and his complete dependability under very trying circumstances. He is industrious, loyal, cooperative and above all extremely flexible. Working

> under high pressure, he has kept cheerful, and in a large organization of varying personalities, he has been in every way been a distinct asset not only on the technical side but for his contribution towards morale. Dr. Höber, although in this country only a few months, has acquired an excellent mastery of written and spoken English, and I am satisfied would have no language handicaps in any work in an educational institution, research agency or similar organization. His personality is pleasing. He is courteous and affable at all times, has an excellent sense of humor, is intellectually honest and has a genuinely social point of view, all of which are assets equal in importance, in my judgment, to his academic and technical equipment. I should unhesitatingly recommend Dr. H for any position for which he considers himself qualified, and shall be glad, if you so desire, to respond to specific inquiries from your office, or from anyone contemplating availing himself of his services.

Can you recognize your husband in this glowing picture??? But I don't want to repay his kindness with bad behavior and subject myself to criticism for playing hooky too long, so I have to bring this letter to a close. Actually, I still wanted to write a few lines to Lilly Reiff, from whom I just got a charming letter from Nervi. I was worried that she was annoyed with me because I hadn't written in so long.[13]

Tomorrow our house is emptying out a little. Under pressure from the family, Seppchen accepted a warm invitation from Catherine[14] to come to New York and is driving with Manfred in Blue Boy, because tomorrow he has to take the first written half of his medical exams. Heaven protect him and us from his failing! Once he has that behind him, and if he makes out reasonably well in Saratoga Springs, then hopefully he will become somewhat more stable than he is in his current period of unemployment. Daddy had originally planned to go to the physiological congress in Toronto, but gave it up in view of his terrible end-of-semester overload.

The spring and Easter letter you wrote from the balcony on the 11th, 12th, and 13th sounds really recovered and relaxed despite the sad news about Hilde and about Mac. Make it as comfortable for yourself as you can. There are still plenty of things that you can't make comfortable. A letter to Karl [Lenzberg] is very much on my mind. After Hilde's good deeds toward you there's now a double reason to write, and in addition Daddy recently decided to give him a copy of his *Textbook* as a present. He mentioned it in his letter and I think he will be pleased with that.

13 *Lilly Reiff* = Johannes' godmother, whose hospitality he enjoyed in Zürich when he first left Germany.

14 Catherine Hoeber was the widow of Paul B. Hoeber, Rudolf's second cousin, who died the previous year.

If Günter begins taking pictures this spring, he should take some of you and Susie again. It's almost fifteen years since you have had to make do with just a picture of me.

In liebe,

Jo

WEDNESDAY AND FRIDAY, APRIL 26 AND 28, 1939

Letter from Elfriede in Düsseldorf to Johannes in Philadelphia.

4/26/39

Liebes Peterchen,

Sometime this month I misplaced the ship schedule so I'm never sure when I might get mail from you. I know this letter has until the day after tomorrow, but tomorrow the invoices are supposed to arrive and then I will be fully occupied. I just packed a shirt and a couple of pairs of socks for you and will put them in the mail shortly.

4/28/39

Early morning and the mail isn't here yet. Yesterday Mrs. Freyberger was here to help me organize the invoices, but the invoices didn't arrive [from Frankfurt]. In Frankfurt they don't take account of the fact that it's very tiresome to have to work through 900 invoices in a day and a half. I want to finish them by tomorrow, Saturday afternoon, so I can have a 2½ day weekend,[15] even if the cold weather makes us stay in our well-heated apartment rather than go to a poorly heated hotel.

Mrs. Freyberger is going into the hospital in Cologne for an operation. She has an abdominal fibroid tumor that has to be removed. Her England job, which looked so promising last week, has once more been cancelled. But she's still hoping for something.

The mail was just delivered and it didn't include the invoices. And it's already the 28th! I have to call Frankfurt to be sure they're delivered tomorrow.

[Later]

I just called Frankfurt. They had a backlog and the invoices just got sent off today. How lovely, now Sunday is down the drain. And they didn't tell us that there won't be any paper on Monday [May Day] (which I assumed but didn't know for sure). "Oh yes, we'll be sending out a notice." I shall take my revenge!

15 That Monday, May 1st, was a national holiday.

It may interest you to know that the advertising revenue for April, which admittedly had five Sundays, came to RM 606.50, not counting what might still come in today. In addition, there were enough new subscriptions to balance any cancellations. I got 20 new unsolicited subscribers each in March and April. I am blooming and so is the business, and gradually I've gotten the business and the customers into my head the way you had. It's only the more difficult aspects that I don't know as well, but I'm getting there.

Hilde, who is still in Freiburg, sent me a bottle of plum brandy yesterday. (There's an old saying that he who has troubles also has liquor. But plum brandy is even better.) When I unwrapped the bottle from its careful packaging, I regretted greatly that I couldn't send you something like that. It wouldn't even have to be plum brandy or one of those other men's drinks that you normally shun (and which always remind me of mountain huts in the rain), it could also be something more delicate. But I can't do that, so instead you'll get some lightweight summer undershorts in the next few weeks.

Friday afternoon

It's nice that your letter from the *Queen Mary* got here just before I have to rush off to take this letter to the train so that the *Europa* can take it along, even if your letter is full of care and worry. Don't let your family make you crazy with suggestions. The worry about impediments other than just time is substantial (and according to the von Baeyers' opinion more from outside than from here) but avoiding such difficulties is not in our power. I trust that in the meantime you have done everything necessary to satisfy Uncle Karl's wishes. That's the only effective action we can take. If it makes you feel better, I can assure you that nobody here is critical of you, that everybody thinks that the way you're doing things is sensible and sound. I think things are going absolutely right and think it's fabulous that you can already supplement any job applications with American letters of recommendation. What I need from you is that you don't criticize me too much when I complain about the taxes and spend too much money.

Günter's letter [to you] was definitely not unfriendly, at least it wasn't meant that way. But he undoubtedly took great pains not to say things he wasn't supposed to say.[16] Besides that, the time he had was very short, between all the obligations and visits.

And now I simply must quit or the Paris train will leave without this letter. More soon. The *Queen Mary* goes on the 3rd and should take another letter.

Alles liebe Deine Friedel

16 Günter had to be reminded to omit matters from his letters that might attract the notice of German censors.

THURSDAY, APRIL 27, 1939

Letter from Johannes in Philadelphia to Elfriede in Düsseldorf. He is responding to Elfriede's letter of April 17, in which she forwarded the American Consul's letter demanding additional documentation before her visa application would be considered. Johannes tells Elfriede they sent Stuttgart the documents confirming Rudolf's income and the security of his position at the University.

Philadelphia, the 27th of April 39.

Liebstes Peterchen,

Even though this letter doesn't have to get mailed until tomorrow, I'm starting it tonight. Since your letter arrived early yesterday with the damned notice from Stuttgart, you are more than usually at the center of my thoughts and those of my whole family. What's the use of raging at this irrational and inconsistent bureaucracy? I'm trying to commit myself to this stoic principle, but I'm not succeeding very well. It's impossible to be stoic when I realize that if it weren't for the affidavit [they're now demanding], the Stuttgart letter could just as readily have contained an invitation [for an interview and medical examination]. You really are a courageous girl, and if I didn't know how little you value courageousness in yourself and how much you would prefer to give it up, I would philosophize about it a bit more. Since yesterday, we have put our engine into high gear, all the while fighting with greater or lesser success against the depression it has engendered. The product of our efforts are enclosed, namely:

a notarized statement from the Dean [of the Medical School],
a notarized statement from the bank, and
notarized duplicates of [Rudolf's] income tax returns for 37 and 38, together with the checks by which the [tax] obligations were satisfied.

In addition, Daddy is sending his Form 575 to Washington again, just in case, and yesterday I started pursuing further efforts to mobilize reinforcements too. But since I don't know if and when those efforts will succeed, and since they hopefully will not be necessary, we don't want to delay sending off the documents the Consul first requested.

What we are sending is absolutely everything that was requested and I believe in the best possible form, so you don't have to add anything else in your cover letter. I would not mention the fact that Daddy sent the 575 to Washington, otherwise they might wait for it even if otherwise they might not think about it. That way if they do ask about it you can tell them it's already on the way.

Walter Phillips and Johannes in a casual moment, possibly at the Phillips' home.

We all think it's awful that at this very moment the Tischendorf problem crops up again. We thought that at least we would have heard from the woman before she started taking such definitive steps. And the timing is particularly bad, especially because it burdens you and us even more by having to make decisions about it right now. But there's probably no way to change it.[17]

Accordingly, you will also find enclosed our orders to the Savings and Loan and to Mrs. Tischendorf. We are sending them to you and not directly to her for the simple reason that we think the bill for RM 2500 should be at least superficially reviewed and that can only be done on the basis of the prior correspondence that you have in Düsseldorf. The amount sounds an awful lot like it was pulled out of thin air. Our concern is less about what it includes than what it might not include. So if you have any reservations, or if you can determine anything from the previous correspondence, then make any changes you think are necessary with the help of the enclosed blank checks. You should burden

17 In an earlier letter (February 9), Johannes indicated he wanted to postpone selling securities from Rudolf's blocked accounts at the Kiel Savings and Loan in order to avoid drawing the attention of the authorities to Elfriede. Mrs. Tischendorf's insistence on shipping the Höbers' furniture would now require him to draw on those funds.

yourself with this only if it seems necessary and worthwhile based on the previous correspondence; otherwise just send it on as is. If you see any advantage at all in our handling the matter from here in the future, then send us the complete file with your next letter.

There's not much to tell about me since Monday. Walter has been particularly nice to me since yesterday [when I got the bad news about Uncle Karl] and when I got home last night his wife had already called to invite me for Sunday evening. It's sometimes almost comical how much we both avoid recognizing too directly how much we like each other—after all, men don't recognize such things.

If it weren't for the huge concern about Stuttgart, I think the change in Susie's school situation would have been the matter of concern for me in yesterday's mail. Why don't you think about doing something nice for her old teacher? Maybe this [change of schools] will actually ease Susie's attitude about the coming separation.[18]

That's all. I have the noble intention of getting up at 6 tomorrow morning. All stations here will be carrying the Reichstag speech[19] and I want to hear it despite the not very appealing hour. I probably won't be able to think about you doing the same thing at the same time, but I will think about you all the same.

In Liebe,

Dein Jo

---

18 *Coming separation* = Susanne and Elfriede's coming departure to the United States.

19 A few days before this date, President Roosevelt had sent Hitler a telegram demanding assurances that Germany would not invade other European countries. Hitler was scheduled to give a speech the next day (April 28) responding to the telegram. Hitler's speech coarsely insulted Roosevelt and the United States, adding to the rising fear of war.

CHAPTER 9

True Friends

MONDAY, MAY 1 1939

Letter from Elfriede in Düsseldorf to Johannes in Philadelphia.

5/1/39

Mein liebes Peterchen.

It's the first of May but the sunshine that's supposed to be here isn't, though plenty of work is. Since I worked yesterday, there's lots of mail that I have to take to the train station along with this letter because they don't collect from the mail boxes today. The invoices didn't arrive until Saturday, so *nolens volens* I had to spend Sunday working on them.[1] Now everything is finished and all the invoices have been sent out.

Then this morning Frankfurt sent a young man to bother me—he is our presumptive successor for Düsseldorf; I told him everything he wanted to know for two hours. I was very pleasant and accommodating. I think that with Betz's help it will work out for me to set my own termination date. After these two days, though, it seems to me that God didn't invent Sunday by accident but that He really had a good idea. Now I have a week of heavy work ahead of me—tomorrow Duisburg, the day after tomorrow Gladbach and Krefeld—so I'm thinking about whether I can put together some kind of little excursion for next Sunday.

I have to come back to your letter of 4/20, which I could only go into briefly last time. It worries me that sometimes I write to you when I'm not completely "up" and in a good mood, but I can't pretend to be cheerful when I'm not. Your sentence saying it might be possible that, when I get there, we might have to overcome some barriers between us gave me a real shock. I didn't think that before and I don't think it now, even if it takes another six months [for me to get there] and even if it takes longer than that. And even if, at worst, you get mixed up with someone else (with your talent for doing precisely what is least suited to the circumstances). Even when I have found a lot of things really awful to deal with, and even if I have sometimes been terribly down and depressed, it never once occurred to me that all of this could possibly disturb our relationship. In the end, we are doing all of this solely so we can live our lives together on a relatively normal basis. It is true that you

1 May Day was, of course, a national holiday throughout Europe, and mail was not collected.

sometimes find it as hard as I do to escape the feeling that the mountains we have to traverse are much too exposed to the elements and often even impassable,. But I believe as much as ever that we have taken on this challenge in basically the right way, and I don't doubt that if we manage to get across them, then on the other side of the mountains it could be quite lovely, sort of like Lake Como. By the time we get that far, however, my entire supply of patience will have been exhausted for the rest of my life. Impatience really doesn't help anything. I have also learned, by the way, that a trip to Stuttgart doesn't speed anything up. So I'll wait patiently for you to send me the certifications I need [for the Consulate]. My reminders to myself to be patient don't stop me from occasionally thinking about whether I couldn't "do" something, but I still think that off-the-cuff decisions won't make the situation easier for any of us, and could, in fact, lead to major complications.

I think sometime, somewhere I will still get to spend another weekend with Hilde. Her mixture of a cool head and a warm heart is very comforting.

How did Susie react to your birthday letter, you ask? As she should have. I thought it was the nicest, sweetest, cleverest letter that one could write to a child, and the idea of America is now very real to her. Her easygoing approach to life will make the whole thing easy if we are careful with her at the beginning. It's funny how she looks at everything from the perspective of her desire to be special. An important argument for her is, there I will know German and others won't and here I'll know English and others won't. We speak English together on Saturday nights at dinner. I'm not convinced her English lessons will be very useful, though she is making nice progress, but they are important for her self-confidence because they make her feel more prepared for a new, unfamiliar situation. By the way, you're not allowed to say anything about Susanne's English, because it's supposed to be a big surprise for you that she understands what you say when she isn't supposed to. Her faith in my discretion would be destroyed if she learned you knew about it.

I gave her a book of German legends for her birthday in a very nice edition by Severin Rüttgers put out by Insel. Now she's on a hero craze, and her prejudice against war is vanishing in the face of these real heroes who "fight with swords" because "it's cowardly to shoot if you can't see the enemy." She's in favor of an international treaty to conduct wars with swords again, or to let the leaders fight with swords. Modern technology in this arena doesn't impress her at all. I felt like Prof. Alfred Weber when I tried to make it clear to her that the progress of civilization isn't reversible. Our conversations are often very complicated anyway. She is doing fine in her new school and doesn't mind that the teacher is stricter. The teacher even told her she was eager and attentive and that was very nice, but said she may not call out the answers in class because that doesn't work with 60 children and the others wanted to and needed to come up with the answers themselves.

Mother just arrived to get me out into the fresh air. She is truly sweet with me.

Alles Liebe Deine Friedel

THURSDAY AND FRIDAY, MAY 4 AND 5, 1939

Letter from Elfriede in Düsseldorf to Johannes in Philadelphia.

5/4/39

Liebes Peterchen,

It's really awkward that your letters always arrive just after I have to send mine off [to reach the mail ship]. At the moment I'm anxious about your next letter, because it should contain your response to Uncle Karl's behavior, and then I'll be able to "do" something, even if it's only forwarding completed documents with a transmittal letter. Your letter of 4/25, which I got on 5/2, exactly a week after it was sent, was such a pleasure. I read the letter of recommendation from your executive director with the help of the dictionary so I wouldn't miss a single point and thereby discovered that the last year has effected an unimaginable transformation in your character. The word "dependability" impressed me particularly. If you continue in this fashion I will have a hard time recognizing you. Nevertheless, I was able to recognize you in a good many of the characteristics described. Of course I immediately shared this hoax with Mother and my brothers, and they appreciated it as much as I did. And that you are even becoming a gardener is great. Please send me more of your writing!

The Ultimo, which was such a terrible rush last month, went off very well this time. RM 2800 are already on the way to Frankfurt and I already have the requisition done. The total number of subscribers is down a little bit only in Krefeld due to people emigrating, otherwise stable and in Düsseldorf even up by two subscriptions. Yesterday evening I was in Krefeld. I went there by train and met Günter, who drove me from there to Gladbach. Then we picked Mother up and we all went to eat at Mulfinger's restaurant. That has now become the routine on the day I go to pick up the collections. Since it's always at least 9 o'clock when we get back we're very hungry and a good meal once a month isn't too much of a luxury.

It has been warm again since yesterday, and the chestnuts don't look so premature any more. In the next few weeks Mother is going to go for a course of treatment at Wildbad [spa]. The cold wet winter weather didn't do her arthritic knee any good, and she's afraid it could get as bad again as two years ago. We quietly insinuated the idea of Bad Wildbad into our conversations and she quickly came to a decision about it. Paul tells Mother in every second letter how happy he is. At the moment his life is divided between Berlin and Leipzig, but he hopes to be able to get an apartment in Berlin soon.

I just got a very nice letter from Hilde. She also wrote me that Max Hannasch died in the night from the 2nd to the 3rd. Even though we knew it was coming, it still affects all of us—it's so senseless and hard to take in. It just shows that it's absurd to worry a lot about the future. It always turns out to be something you didn't think of that gets you in the end. Can you imagine that there will never again be any of those great festive evenings at Freiligrathstraße? Maybe you can, since you're already in a new place, but for those of us who are still here it feels like everything is coming apart.

5/5/39

Another day. Susanne asked recently, "Will Paul have a son soon?" We couldn't answer the question for her, but the background was that she is now happily reading Scott's *Quentin Durward*, which belonged to Paul when he was a child. If Paul wasn't going to have a son, then she could write him and ask if he would give her the book, but otherwise the son would have to get it.

Susanne is always full of new expressions, sometimes funny, sometimes wise. We had a very wise conversation yesterday after her religion class. It's always hard to deal with a child with our relativistic outlook on things, but she is already too smart to be satisfied with formulaic answers. She really can drive you crazy with her questions.

Mrs. Freyberger wasn't operated on after all. So many doctors, so many diagnoses. The first one said, yes, operate, but there's no hurry. The second: you must have an operation immediately. The third: you don't need an operation for that. Next Tuesday a fourth is supposed to give his opinion. In the meantime she's coming here on Monday.

Dear *Peterchen*, this letter is sort of mixed up, but now that fast ships are going twice a week, if you don't like one letter you can comfort yourself with the thought of the next one.

In any event, I send you all my love!

Deine Friedel

FRIDAY, MAY 5, 1939

Birthday letter from Johannes in Philadelphia to Elfriede in Düsseldorf.

Philadelphia, 5/5/39.

Liebster Peter,

I couldn't possibly have thought more about you than I have yesterday and today in preparation for writing this birthday letter. Despite the fact that the Charter campaign is approaching its most intense stage, since yesterday morning Walter and I have hardly done anything, thought about anything, or spoken about anything other than for you and about you.

I had firmly intended to be able to send you a first class supplemental affidavit [of support] as a birthday present. Walter and his wife, who, I can assure you, are good for more than one affidavit,[2] offered it spontaneously as soon as they heard that Uncle Karl was nagging you for more. But despite our greatest efforts it hasn't been possible to put the whole thing together quite yet. It is Walter's desire to make it as splendid as possible. He has written a personal letter that couldn't possibly be more impressive. He got the most respected judge in Philadelphia to write a letter about his character and he is getting a second one from our Committee chairman, a very well-known lawyer. But the two banks that he and his wife use didn't work quickly enough for us to be able to send everything off today, so we have to wait for the next boat. As a result, this advance notice will have to suffice for [your birthday on] the 12th. I hope the fact that you are at the center of all my thoughts is more important to you than the concrete results these thoughts will lead to.

It's a good thing that when Pa-Mu said shortly after Christmas that we would celebrate your birthday here together I said categorically that that wasn't even a possibility, partly for pedagogic reasons and partly to avoid getting my own hopes up. If I hadn't kept telling myself that, and hopefully you told yourself that too, then the current delay would be even more infuriating than it already is. I will have to entrust to Mother's, Günter's, Herbert's, and Elisabeth's hands the task of making the day as nice for you as I would like to. Based on her stellar performance at Easter, I do not doubt that Susanne will substitute for me as well as she can. You can't imagine how much I would spoil you if I were there, but you may and should remind me of this promise every day

2 The meaning here is that Walter and Mary Phillips were sufficiently well off to guarantee the support of a number of people.

when we are together again. It's funny that of all your birthdays, the one I remember best is the one in 1924, and we weren't even together for that. My everyday thoughts just now are often hard to distinguish from those of fifteen years ago, despite the fact that I now only get mail from you twice a week instead of every day.

"Good" people would probably argue that a separated situation like the one we are living in is a wonderful testing time for a marriage and so on. I am damned sick of that kind of thinking or even talking, and find that we have no need at all of such a stress test. Besides, that represents a very American but nevertheless very monastic and hateful puritanism. On the 12th, make a toast for me to our united and not at all puritanical future together.

I have made an effort to select for you two presents suitable for that ideal American type of woman, a mixture of intellect and femininity, whom I recently described for the sole purpose of drawing the parallel to you. Hopefully you've already received the first half of this—Femininity Department. For very good reasons, the second half will follow not today but soon. The present for the Intellect Department has hopefully also already reached you in the form of a package with a Wanamakers Department Store return address. It is *Middletown*,[3] an urban sociological study written by a married couple that has practically become a classic here. If you agree, then at the next occasion you'll get the second volume, *Middletown in Transition*, which has subsequently come out. If you start reading it then we can read it together, which I would really enjoy!

Today I would rather not speak of business here nor of business at your end, neither of the macrocosmic nor the microcosmic. I am thinking of you with great love, I long for you greatly, and send you my love and kiss you in my thoughts even more warmly than usual, if that is possible.

And I wish you all the wonderful things the world has to offer.

Dein Jo

TUESDAY, MAY 9, 1939

Letter from Johannes in Philadelphia to Elfriede in Düsseldorf, responding, in part, to her letter of May 1. Johannes' letter included two additional affidavits of support (on top of Rudolf's) and other documents with which Elfriede could supplement her application for an American immigration visa. One supplemental affidavit of support came from Walter and Mary Phillips, with holdings in excess of $50,000 available

3 *Middletown: A Study in Modern American Culture*, by Robert S. Lynd and Helen Merrell Lynd examines the social structure and mores of a medium-size American city in the Midwest.

for Elfriede's support, and the other from Eugene Hoeber, a distant cousin whose branch of the Höber family immigrated to New York in the 1850s. His affidavit of support indicated he owned $230,000 in stocks and bonds, the equivalent of several million dollars today. The various documents follow this letter.

Philadelphia, 5/9/39.

My darling,

Enclosed you find the results of what we call "putting on the steamroller." I think it's pretty respectable. Eugene Hoeber is a second cousin once removed of mine, whom Pa-Mu met years ago and whom Seppchen's memory conjured up when we decided to anticipate all eventualities and feed you additional affidavits. Under pressure from the whole family, she had gone to visit Catherine[4] last week for five days, and seized the opportunity to flirt with the old gentleman on your behalf for so long that he delivered himself of this nice little affidavit—no, rather, this big fat affidavit. When it arrived no one was more astounded than we at the wonders that exist in our family.

I don't have to tell you anything else about Walter and Mary—who recently insisted that we should now be on a first name basis. Specifically, the two of them drafted the accompanying letter entirely on their own—not one word is mine—but I can't imagine how anyone could have done it better or more lovingly. It is doubly important to me because I am in a position to evaluate exactly what taking such a stance means in the circles the two of them come from.

What you are getting as enclosures are only third carbon copies of the affidavits and Walter's cover letter. The originals and an unimaginable pack of documents were sent today in two registered packages directly to Stuttgart. I don't think any Uncle in the world could ask for more and the next steps in the [visa] process should follow in short order.

Now that this complex of things is finally off my mind, I can return to my normal news coverage. It seems to me that I have badly neglected that lately. First the Charter: in the interim it has happily been approved in the Senate and now is sitting in the House of Representatives (Pennsylvania has the traditional two-chamber system). It has to be approved there by the 20th of May so on the 20th of June there can be referendum, which has to take place before the 24th of June because there are new municipal elections in the fall and people need to know whether they will take place under the old or the new Charter. It's funny how the Republican Party organization, which is now in power in

4 As described in the previous chapter, Catherine was the widow of Paul B. Hoeber, Rudolf's second cousin. Eugene was Paul Hoeber's uncle.

Philadelphia, is searching for arguments to make against the Charter, because everyone knows the only real question is whether the spoils system will be continued or not. They are stuck uncomfortably between the devil and the deep blue sea: the Charter is popular because the current city administration is more than ordinarily corrupt. If the Republicans turn the Charter down in the Legislature, they will probably lose the municipal elections in the fall and then they won't just have lost the spoils, the spoils will go to the Democrats. If they let the Charter through, they will also lose the spoils, but at least they won't go to the enemy, the possibility will remain that they might win the election, etc. etc. The nicest part of the whole thing is the way a small, focused group is able to develop the possibility of pushing through a really important reform. America in transition!

There are also some things to report on my society page. On Sunday we made a great family expedition into the country. Everyone went along, from Daddy to Monica, including Ulli and Priscilla, Daddy's assistant. She brought her car along to help with the transportation of the masses of people, and when it became apparent that she doesn't like to drive, I took over her nice three-seater and Manfred, Ulli, and Seppchen alternated as chaperone to me and the owner. Our destination was the Mennonite communities west of Philadelphia, immaculate settlements in charming hill country, on the horizon the Blue Mountains, in the area somewhere between Reading and Lancaster in case you want to track us on a map. It was a very merry although also very hot undertaking. I spent a lot of the day trying to learn many possible and impossible American songs and taking my revenge with *Alt Heidelberg* and other old favorites.

The evening before that I was invited to a big party by people I had never met before, three lawyer couples, the Director of the University of Pennsylvania School of Social Work, and two administration officials from Washington. It came about this way. To be sure he was doing things the best way possible for you, Walter wanted some expert advice. We went together to the expert, who talked to me for a long time—and then she called me the same evening and invited me to come to the party at the home of friends of theirs. It turned out not to be especially charming. Two nights earlier we had a really nice gathering at our place, Eleanor Davis, my housing expert, the Gruenbergs, and a doctor couple named Steadye. Saturday was our big Charter luncheon, planned by Walter, set up in our office and only the first of a whole series. The speaker was Charles Taft, a son of the former President, great success. On this occasion I entered the Ritz Hotel for the first time, which was only known to me from Anita Loos' books. What a

Hoeber Family excursion into the country near Philadelphia, May 7, 1939. Left to right, Rudolf, Ulli, Manfred, Gri holding Monika, Josephine holding Janka, Johannes.

Rudolf with his research assistant, Priscilla Briscoe.

letdown! Cold splendor and bad food. On the other hand, on Thursday I ate lunch at the even more elegant Bellevue-Stratford. The occasion was an invitation to Walter and me from Eleanor Davis—who has baptized us "the heavenly twins"—to have us meet Dorothy Schoell, the Research Director of the Philadelphia Housing Authority of whom I wrote so enthusiastically recently. The Friday before I was invited to a social evening, i.e., concert and dance in tux, at the Ethical Culture Society, and last but not least to Sunday supper at Walter and Mary's.

"Supper" is something that will interest your housewifely side—it differs from "dinner" in the lightness of the meal and the informality with which it is served. At the Phillipses, for example, supper was cold ham and a mixed salad put on the table in a big wooden bowl. Afterwards just strawberries. Very much to my taste and yours too. The limits on extravagant drinking are also beneficial—that is, financially beneficial. There is almost never wine. You get a cocktail before dinner, but afterwards usually nothing; a glass of beer or a whiskey is usually the most you can hope for. I have not yet experienced any of those occasions of true American drunkenness.

The highlight of my social life is yet to come—I have been invited to a formal dance at Swarthmore College. True, it is in an honorary role rather than a masculine one, but nevertheless: Bettina Meyerhof,[5] who started there after the beginning of the semester and who doesn't have a boyfriend yet and is also not very much the type for that, is now worried that she will have to sit alone all evening and asked me to protect her from this disgrace. I am excited about this enterprise. The combination of a college dance with Quaker tradition will be interesting. The event takes place two weeks from Saturday.

It's rotten that Frankfurt did you out of a long weekend by sending the invoices so late. The ad revenue for April is great. Isn't that a record? After that kind of accomplishment you don't have to worry about my ever criticizing anything again. Especially, *Schatz*, when you write me letter like the one of 1 May, which arrived today. What pleases me most is the extent to which our view of things is the same. You wrote in your letter exactly what I wrote in mine just four days later, so the bridge building problem that I suddenly imagined on the horizon when I was having a bad day is a matter we can declare closed. Instead, let's inscribe your lovely Lake-Como-over-the-mountains on our banner. We still travel best when we travel together, and that is a destination I can really look forward to.

Sehr in Liebe,

Dein Jo

5 Bettina Meyerhof was the daughter of Otto Meyerhof, winner of the 1922 Nobel Prize in medicine. He had been Rudolf's assistant at the Physiological Institute at Kiel.

Enclosure in Johannes' letter of May 9, 1939. Letter from Walter M. Phillips to United States Consul in Stuttgart.

WALTER M. PHILLIPS
9500 MARSTAN ROAD
CHESTNUT HILL, PENNSYLVANIA

May 8, 1939

Honorable Consul General
Stuttgart (Germany)

Honorable Sir,

I am informed that Mrs. Elfriede Höber, a Ph.D. of Heidelberg University, and Susanne Höber, Düsseldorf (Germany), Pempelforterstr. 11, have applied at your consulate for permanent residence. Mrs. Elfriede Höber and her daughter wish to come to Philadelphia to join their husband and father and his family who were admitted to the United States for permanent residence some time ago.

Dr. Johannes Höber, the husband, also a Ph.D. of Heidelberg, has been working for me for about three months as a research assistant. He has proved himself to be an extraordinarily bright, intellectually honest, public spirited and able person. I am so much interested in keeping him in Philadelphia that I am willing to give my personal guarantee that his wife, after being admitted to the United States, will never become a public charge.

For my own identification you may be interested in the following facts:

My family on all branches have lived in the United States since before the Revolutionary War. I am a graduate of Princeton University and also the Harvard Law School. I graduated at Princeton in the School of Public and International Affairs under Clinton D. Poole. At present I am volunteering my time to the Philadelphia City Charter Committee in the interest of good local government. After this job is done, I expect to practice law in Philadelphia.

As shown by a separate affidavit the financial responsibility of my wife and me together—we are giving a joint affidavit—should be sufficient to give the necessary guarantee required by law.

May I say again that Dr. Johannes Höber has in my opinion the makings of a fine American citizen and that to have his wife here would help him to be even more of an asset. She too, I have every reason to believe, would contribute much to America.

Quite aware of how much overworked and rushed you must be, I nevertheless ask you personally to see that the promptest possible action is taken in regard to Mrs. Elfriede Höber's and her daughter's visas and

I would appreciate a reply from you informing me exactly how things stand in their case. This is, I believe, a matter of acquiring good talent for the United States, and realizing that you too are interested in that, I presume to trouble you individually with the matter.

Very sincerely yours,

[signed] *Walter M. Phillips*

Walter M. Phillips

Enclosure in Johannes' letter of May 9, 1939. Notarized Statement of Alfred G. Scattergood, Vice President, Provident Trust Company of Philadelphia.

PROVIDENT TRUST COMPANY
OF PHILADELPHIA
SEVENTEENTH AND CHESTNUT STREETS

May 5, 1939

Provident Trust Company of Philadelphia certifies that on or about October 13, 1938, Mary Bird Phillips rented a box in its Safe Deposit Department and placed therein stocks and bonds belonging to her of marketable value in excess of $50,000., and today inspection revealed the fact that there were in the said box, still rented by said Mary Bird Phillips, stocks and bonds of marketable value in excess of $50,000.

PROVIDENT TRUST COMPANY OF PHILADELPHIA

By [signed] *Alfred G. Scattergood*
Vice President

WEDNESDAY, MAY 10, 1939

Letter from Elfriede in Düsseldorf to Johannes in Philadelphia, with an accompanying letter from Susanne. Elfriede's letter responds to Johannes' of April 27, in which he sent further documents to supplement Rudolf's affidavit of support in connection with her visa application. This was, however, before she received the additional affidavits of Walter and Mary Phillips and Eugene Hoeber.

5/10/39

Liebes Peterchen,

The *Normandie* is leaving today without a letter from me, and the fact that the *Columbus* leaves tomorrow makes me feel only slightly less guilty. The reason is that I have been enjoying life too much and for two whole days didn't look at the shipping schedule, and then all of a sudden it was too late. I thank you and all of you for the *Aquitania* letter and its weighty contents. You really have worked things out wonderfully; no one could do it better, quicker or more completely. Now everything has been sent off again with just a one-day delay, which comically resulted when I discovered, as I was putting the papers in the mail, that American paper is wider than ours and I first had to buy new envelopes big enough to hold them. By the time I got the envelopes the post office was closed, but it added only one day to the endless months this has been going on.

And now I have to confess what it was that kept me from getting a letter to the *Normandie*. Hear and be amazed: a 2½ day (!) weekend in and around Bremen, arranged by a couple of people from Paul's crowd, aided and abetted by me. The sentence in your letter before last, that I should make things as nice as possible for myself since there are so many things I can't make nice, gave me the last incentive I needed and it turned out to be a good thing. I feel fresh and reinvigorated, a little tanned by the sun, so that for the moment I feel somewhat fortified for life here again. The days away were even more refreshing than the days around Easter with Hilde, which were heavily overshadowed by the pressures on her. It's lovely everywhere right now, and Bremen-Worpswede was very convenient as the midpoint between Hannover, Hamburg, and Düsseldorf. I admire my own initiative immensely. Am I developing new and undiscovered abilities? I almost feel like I did when I was a student a long time ago. Since I still weigh only 117 pounds I look almost the same, apart from the wrinkles, and the tan even covers those up some, and I still look decent in one of those very short dresses.

I have to do something about my birthday this coming Friday. I already invited the Trömels and the Maxhis, and I'm debating whether to ask the Baeyers. If I'm lucky Hilde will be here too. I also phoned the wine store, because the last bottles from the fall 1938 order were completely gone except for one first-class bottle of *Pfälzer*. Otherwise I just offer my guests liqueur and congac, of which I always have some around, but this time that probably won't do. I'll even straighten up the house as if it had to undergo your critical inspection. Mother is leaving tomorrow for [the spa at] Wildbad. We convinced her not to wait until Saturday on account of my birthday, because finding a place to stay is easier during the week.

I forwarded the letters you sent for Tischendorf and the bank to Mrs. Tischendorf without doing anything more to them. No doubt she will make a lot of money on the deal, but I think your letter is right. She wrote something about two crates and it seems to me she will get the whole thing done on the RM 2500. There shouldn't be any additional costs. I also think it's best if I don't get into the middle of it too much at this point. Shipping the things now is probably better than doing it later.

You may remember that I once expressed the hope that we could celebrate my birthday together. Today I think it would take more than a little bit of luck for me and Susie to show up for your birthday [on August 7]. Through all my mood swings, I still basically believe there's no sense in getting upset over a few months more or less. If we knew for sure that our escape route couldn't be cut off we would both worry a lot less; patience can get us past all the other obstacles. The frequency of my use of the word "patience" in my letters is almost worth a philological treatise. In any event, my belief in fate has expanded considerably over the last six months, as has my readiness to accept whatever fate imposes. Everything we did had to be done the way it was—with Gri and Manfred going in September but you only in November. I'm not suggesting we should accept things passively, but rather that we should be prepared to manage somehow with whatever fate imposes on us and to make the best of it—not just to accept things but to turn them into something positive. Don't be surprised at the amount of wisdom your wife has amassed; if I haven't added to my stock of wisdom and reason in the last year then I never will. Unfortunately wisdom isn't enough to get rid of all of my mood swings, but on good days—and there are always some of those—I feel like I'm on my way to a sturdier mental state.

The *Bremen* arrives in Cherbourg on the 11th. Since we can't have our usual birthday celebration with just the two of us in the middle of the night, it would be nice if the International Postal Union and the German mail would deliver your letter for breakfast on [my birthday on] 12 May. If not, then I'll know that the best still lies ahead. I will feel close to you anyway. Sometimes it's hard for me to remember that 5000 km (or however many it is) separate us. So, now I have reached the limits of my wisdom again.

The underwear that I told you I'd send just went off today as well as the two remaining volumes of the Karl Schurz biography. In the second volume, don't bother reading the tedious description of the Civil War. The second volume is interesting up to the beginning of the Civil War and afterwards too. You have to write off a few things in the whole book to senescence, particularly later on, but there's still a lot in it that's quite worthwhile.

Alles Liebe Deine Friedel.

Accompanying letter from Susanne.

Lieber Papi.

I am giving Mutti a coffee warmer with an embroidered outside and the inside part. Then I am giving her a march I composed myself and a song I also composed myself. The words are: I wish you a very Happy Birthday, while the May Bugs also dance and play.

Susie

FRIDAY, MAY 12, ELFRIEDE'S BIRTHDAY, AND SUNDAY, MAY 14, 1939

Letter from Elfriede in Düsseldorf to Johannes in Philadelphia, accompanied by a letter from Susanne. As usual, Elfriede mentions "the Stuttgart people," i.e., the American Consulate. She was surprised that Johannes felt supplemental affidavits of support were necessary. She and Johannes did not know, however, that for every visa being granted by American consulates in Germany ten were being rejected. As Johannes noted in an earlier letter, the Consul had great discretion in granting and denying visas, and ultimately the supplemental affidavits from Walter and Mary Phillips and from Eugene Hoeber may have been decisive in Elfriede and Susanne getting their visas and getting out of Germany.

5/12/39

Liebstes Peterchen,

A half hour of quiet before I start making the sandwiches for this evening, because I'm having a big party. Eleven people—everyone's coming, except for you, of course. On a day like this I need to get a good grip on my slightly precarious cheerfulness.

Susie greeted me early this morning with a birthday march she composed herself and a little song to go with it, a lovely little cozy for the coffee pot that she sewed herself, and some pretty irises. She has been really cute in her impatience over the last few days. She was so full of her plans that it's sheer luck that she didn't spill it all in advance. The coffee table had lovely flowers, partly from Mother, partly from Helma, and a painted poster that Susie made saying Happy Birthday. Then the mail came, your *Normandie* letter of 5/1 as well as mail from Marianne and Mrs. Daniels. With the second mail there was a letter from Mother, who arrived at the spa in Wildbad last night. And then this afternoon your sweet, moving letter of the 5th, the one from your mother and one from Hilde. I feel very well attended to and taken care of. Susanne said, "A lot of people love you!" Mother also gave me, in addition to very pretty (and very transparent) underwear, a metalwork candle holder and a lovely glass plate for snacks or for butter on our American table. I'm looking forward to the book from you. I'll read it along with you if I possibly can.

I was very moved by your efforts and those of Mr. Phillips for a supplemental affidavit. It hadn't occurred to me that that would now be necessary, but as they say, double stitching is doubly strong, and a double bombardment may soften up even the Stuttgart people. From your letter and from Seppchen's [not preserved], I see that Stuttgart's refusal business had a greater impact on you than on me, perhaps because you are the ones who can do something about it while I can only play a more or less passive role. Hilde is coming here tomorrow, and I am looking forward to chatting with her. She is better suited to chatting than anyone else in the world.

[Sunday] 5/14/39

I seem to be a little fractured today. The Friday party was very lively, first with very comfortable conversation and then, after the Magicians and the Maxhis left, very decadent, with Günter and Marlies in a roller skating competition. I was so hung over the next day that I stayed in bed until 3 in the afternoon, because then the children's party came crashing down on me and I needed more strength for that than I had in the morning. Now I'm very much enjoying my quiet Sunday. The gardens are more beautiful and elegant than ever—chestnuts, lilacs, wisteria, hawthorn, laburnum, all in full bloom. It's really not the kind of weather when you want to be alone. If you can believe it, Erich von Baeyer submitted Susanne's portrait along with several others for a big exhibition in Cleveland, and it was accepted along with one other. But he has more or less given up painting now because he's preparing for the State [medical] examination which is coming up on 1 July.

Susanne began her most recent school assignment with the sentence, "If war breaks out we will be informed of it by means of wailing sirens." I am greatly comforted to know now that I won't miss out on it by mistake. At the end of the paragraph she wrote, "There is a shovel in the bomb cellar and also a rake. If the house falls in, the house will be raked up." Perhaps you can put her talents and knowledge of such things to better use in gardening. This afternoon I am sending her to Herbert and Elisabeth's to go for a drive with them and their friends the Leglers, but then their car is full. I miss our car greatly as a means of Sunday pleasure. As you know, Günter is no use for that kind of thing and everyone else is pretty much filled up without us. But it's so nice on our balcony today that you could almost believe you were far away from the big city. You hear the trolley clanging in the distance once in a while, but there aren't any cars in the city today.

I am glad for Mother that the weather that was so cold and rainy yesterday looks like it is going to get nice [for her stay at Bad Wildbad]. Elisabeth and Ilse Legler want to go to Ahrenshoop [on the Baltic] with the children for four weeks and then the men would join them for the last two weeks. Günter is making serious plans to go to England. And me? It seems to me that my planned summer trip is turning into a fall trip.[6] But if Mrs. Freyberger is available, I'm thinking about taking 8–10 days' vacation, though whether and where is still uncertain. The idea of lying in the sun with nothing to worry about sounds like a pleasant vacation right now. I guess I'm getting old, or maybe it's just the result of all the upset of the last few months.

And you? I gather from Seppchen's letter that you are making all kinds of plans, and that when Manfred goes to Saratoga he'll be going without his wife and children. I think it would be good if you could keep Gri from going along to Woods Hole[7] with the children. There is no question that having two little children close by would be a substantial burden on your parents' nerves and wouldn't help them if they want to rest up. While your family has used vacations in the past as the occasion for the family to get together, this year it would be good if it could be used to get the family separated from each other. While you people sometimes deny it, everybody has as much need for distance as for closeness, and in my non-expert opinion Woods Hole would be much better for your parents if they were by themselves.

How are you holding your own in this family ocean? You can picture my life here minutely from morning to night because there's almost nothing that isn't pretty much the same as when you were here; you know the atmosphere of this apartment, the people who come here and so on pretty exactly. On the other hand, I can imagine how you spend your days, but what is the atmosphere like on Cresheim Road? To what extent do individual problems become collective problems? What is it like to be a bachelor in the family fortress?

Gerlinde invited Susanne to visit Schalkenmehren over the long Pentecost weekend [at the end of May]. If it works out I'll give her to Günter to take [when he goes] but I don't know yet what I'll do. I could always go along to Schalkenmehren too, but it doesn't appeal to me very much and Günter will undoubtedly want to stay longer than just the holiday so I would be relegated to the train, which isn't much fun with the holiday crowds. But it's still two weeks away and I'll see what comes up.

6 *Summer trip* = Elfriede's planned emigration to the United States.

7 *Woods Hole*: The Woods Hole Marine Biological Laboratory on Cape Cod in Massachusetts is a major center of bioscientific research. Rudolf and Josephine spent summers there for many years, using the research facilities and enjoying a vacation at the seashore at the same time.

Mrs. Freyberger is going to be operated on after all next week. A "majority" of the four doctors who eventually got involved agreed that it was the right thing to do. What's the majority? The majority is nonsense; sense has always been present only in the minority. Dig into your literary knowledge to find the classical origin of this piece of wisdom.[8]

Alles Liebe Deine Friedel.

Accompanying letter from Susanne in Düsseldorf to Johannes in Philadelphia.

14th of May 39.

Lieber Papi,

It was very nice on Friday. I was out of bed already at 7 o'clock. I gave Helma brandy-filled chocolates and I gave Mutti a leather case for sewing things but the sewing things were already in it. Mutti liked the coffee pot warmer and the march I composed myself and she thought the song was very pretty. I wrote that I was already out of bed at 7. I now go to the Franklin school. That is too bad, because now we don't have Mrs. Anuschewski anymore but she wrote in my poetry album. On Saturday we had an after-birthday party. I got a wall vase made of a hand forged heart. I got the heart and the vase that goes with it from Helgard Helmerdig. I got a toy post office from Sonja and a bag of candies and a box of candied fruits from Uschel Diekmann. I got a book called *Homeless* by Johanna Spyri from Ruth. There are two stories in it the 1st is called "On Lake Silser" and the 2nd "How the Wiseli Was Provided For." I got this stationery I'm writing on from the Gumpenberg children. We put on a play.

Love to you and the others. Susie.
Read this to the others [in Philadelphia].

TUESDAY, MAY 16, 1939

Letter from Johannes in Philadelphia to Elfriede in Düsseldorf.

Philadelphia, 5/16/39.

Liebster Peter,

This is a gray morning. First the weather is gray after two days of such bright sunshine that I even got a little sunburned from my Sunday

8 "The majority? What is the majority? The majority is nonsense, as sense has always been present only in a minority. The State must perish, sooner or later, where the majority rules and irrationality decides." ["*Die Mehrheit? Was ist die Mehrheit? Mehrheit ist der Unsinn, Verstand ist stets bei wen'gen nur gewesen. Der Staat muß untergehen, früh oder spät, wo Mehrheit siegt und Unverstand entscheidet.*"] Friedrich Schiller, *Demetrius (I), "Der Reichstag zu Krakau."*

morning garden work. Second it's gray because there was no letter from you. And third and worst because, for the second night in a row, I had a crazy dream that I had a terrible fight with you and I woke up exhausted. My analytic capacities have totally failed me in the search for the origin of these dreams. Nor can I remember, when I am awake, why we were fighting, nor am I conscious of anything I did wrong that could have given me a guilty conscience for which I had to compensate at night by having a blowup with you. In the daytime I think of you so lovingly and at a distance of 5000 miles I am conscious only of your good side, so I don't understand at all why we should fight with each other at night. Can you think of any plausible explanation? Maybe you were thinking something bad about me yesterday or the day before for which I have to reciprocate telepathically in my dreams.

Your last two letters were as sweet as they could be, especially the last one [of 4–5 May], which you wrongly thought was all mixed up. Susanne's worries about her *Quentin Durward* inheritance are really cute, and I would have liked to have been there to hear the questions with which she was driving you crazy. Please save up some of the things she says for your letters and ask her to write me again, even though I haven't answered her last one yet. Did Günter take pictures of the two of you yet? If not he should do so soon. Is Mother in Wildbad already?

I got a post card from Hilde at the same time as your letter. Mac Hannasch's death is really one of those events that are hard to take in. For me he was one of those men I felt I could become friends with if I knew him better. I also think he was one of those people who had a very rational understanding of things and strong emotions at the same time. This event must be terrible for our circle of friends. What is still left of Düsseldorf?

And now to things here. Thirty seconds ago Gri interrupted me with the news that Moni has measles. She's had a fever since Saturday, at first very high then a lot less after getting the usual medicines, but this morning she's completely broken out in a rash. Janka undoubtedly caught it too, though right now she's quite cheerful, Moni too actually. As always she is the source of great laughter for the whole family. Her newest trick is to scrunch up her nose on command, at which no one can keep from roaring. Papa, Mama, and Grandpapa walk with her regularly, but she still only walks when she has someone's hand to hold on to.

Going back to the beginning of my letter and looking for the source of my discontentment—current, perhaps even only momentary—it probably lies in the Höber family's general in-between status these days. The Charter is coming to an end. It had a first reading in the lower house, but at the second reading was buried in a Committee from which

Photograph of Johannes taken by professional photographer Otzi Pfeiffer, Düsseldorf, 1938.

it will probably never emerge before the session is adjourned indefinitely at the end of next week. This is one of the usual ways to kill a bill that isn't favored. All of my writing so far has only gotten me letters of recommendation, and after a while you get tired of the game of referring you down the line to the next person. Experienced Americans assure me all the time that my start has been sensationally positive and that I shouldn't become impatient. What's worse is that it's already the 16th of May and Manfred still hasn't heard anything from Saratoga. When he visited there [in March] his future boss left him with the impression that he would call him at the beginning of May. The 16th isn't terrible, but since he took the written part of his exams the other day, he doesn't have any real occupation anymore. And now Gri too has finally started wandering around looking for a job and goes around from company to company with her papers and wallpaper patterns and is always received nicely everywhere and referred on to two or three other places, but that's as far as it goes. It would actually be amazing if it were otherwise, given the current job market, but these days you have to count on the amazing.[9]

9 Gri was an artist and designer basing her job search on samples of her design work.

So those are our worries. No acute ones, none that affect our spirits permanently, but still we'd rather not have them. By the way, I got a postcard recently from Erich and Annemarie saying that his portrait of Susie along with another one has been accepted for a big exhibition in Cleveland, but otherwise after July they are completely up in the air. I don't know whether that news is intended for his parents, however. I wrote them a long letter back full of fatherly pride [that Susie's portrait is going to be in this show].

Now I have to close, Peter. At 12 Mr. Paul Kern, the Personnel Director of the city of New York—age 31—is speaking at the second of our Charter luncheons.

Two more requests:

1. The copies of the Otzi pictures. I need them for job applications.[10]
2. I'd like to have a letter of recommendation from Frankfurt, as extensive as possible. I think they owe me that. Talk to Antonio about it and do it right away. I need it.

Moreover: write.

Last Friday the notarized copies of Walter and Mary's income tax returns went off to Stuttgart. We weren't able to send them off with the earlier things, but wanted to be thorough about it in any case.

In Liebe, Jo

WEDNESDAY AND FRIDAY, MAY 17 AND 19, 1939

Letter from Elfriede in Düsseldorf to Johannes in Philadelphia. This letter responds to Johannes' of May 9, in which he sent Elfriede copies of the supplemental affidavits of support from Walter and Mary Phillips and Eugene Hoeber ("Eugenius"). Elfriede was now sufficiently encouraged to go to the local police authorities (Uncle Paul) to renew her passport and get a certification that she had no criminal record. She did not know whether the Nazis would give her a hard time because Johannes had emigrated. She also could not know what problems they might raise for Susanne, who was technically 3/8 "Jewish" under the Nuremberg laws.

Düsseldorf, 17 May 1939.

Mein liebstes bestes Peterchen,

Even if I hadn't been in a good mood already, the worst hypochondriac couldn't feel bad after the riches the mail brought me today, and no

10 *Otzi* Pfeiffer was a photographer who had taken Johannes' passport picture. In 1939 it was customary in the United States to include a photograph when applying for a job.

amount of disarray in European or other politics could cause me to worry a lot after this. It's really terrific—on your part, the Phillipses, the hitherto unimagined Uncle Eugenius—well if this doesn't melt Uncle Karl's heart! I feel like he should send me a telegram summoning me for an interview right now. In view of this development I've decided to pay a visit to Uncle Paul in the next few days. I hope he's nice.

The morning began today with your Daddy's sweet letter and I had just decided anyway that I should write a letter just for him for his birthday. I won't get to that now, but you can tell him, first, that I wish him a happy birthday. You should also tell him that he is the nicest father-in-law I have and that he is by far the greatest attraction the U.S. has to offer me, that I would be happy to wear holes in the new stockings [he sent me] going for walks with him, but that I cannot guarantee that I will be able to resist showing off my now very slender legs encased in such beautiful things. After all, a poor single woman has to have something to offer if she doesn't want to spend all her time all by herself, and I don't want to do that, even here. Still, the attractions on your side of the ocean are even greater—see above.

Then Gri's letter got here. I must voice my strenuous objections to her suggestion that work is some kind of salubrious thing. If I'm feeling pretty good right now, it's only because I <u>don't</u> have much work and because I made RM 42 selling two ads. <u>That</u> kind of work appeals to me. When things go well like that you have time for other things, like baking a cake or straightening up the woolens closet and giving away 2/3 of it to other people, such as the Krefeld carrier whom I will dress in all new clothes. Or reading books (more about that later). Or chatting with Hilde. If Gri thinks, by the way, that your letters have kept me up to date on her family then she is mistaken, and I would very much appreciate it if she would tell me more about things "over there" from her own perspective. Her reputation as a good letter writer depends on it.

To Manfred I have the following to convey: I love his observation that life isn't like being on roller skates, since I never could roller skate anyway. In this sense I have been different from my otherwise exceptionally dear brother-in-law from the beginning. And since I have a thing for the classics these days, I would say with respect to the future that both the black and the brighter prospects repose in the Womb of Time,[11] though it is still questionable whether the prospects really lie there quietly or instead make their presence quite intensely felt, as unborn children sometimes do. By the way, it comforts me to know that you have an Esslinger beer in Philadelphia and I ask you all to drink to my health with it more often.[12]

11 "For him in the womb of time // The black and the lighter lots still rest, …" ["*Ihm ruhen noch im Zeitenschoße//Die schwarzen und die heitern Lose,*" …] Schiller, *Das Lied von der Glocke.*

12 Esslinger was a brand of cheap beer sold in Philadelphia.

[*Later*]
The 2nd mail brought your letter with the many enclosures and the pretty gloves. Its thickness apparently attracted the interest of the Customs people, but fortunately they spit it out right away instead of holding on to it for three days as they did [with another letter] recently. I am boundlessly impressed by Eugen the Noble Knight. How is it possible that with your well-developed sense of family feeling you never invented this most worthwhile uncle before?[13] Many thanks to Seppchen for her willingness to put aside all moral qualms and be nice to him long enough for the affidavit to pop out. Please send me a picture of him so that I can begin preparing myself to flatter him extensively at the appropriate time. I at least have a well-developed family feeling and always show old uncles only my nicest side, which doesn't necessarily mean much by most people's standards. But I will do my best.

On the subject of the Phillipses I have to switch to a more serious tone. I think it's incredibly decent and simply wonderful, first of all on the part of the Phillipses and then on your part, that you accomplished something like that in so short a time. I am alternatively moved and excited, and words literally fail me in trying to say what I want to. It is done the way true friends would and it was done so thoughtfully. I also think it says something about these people, who live in a circle in which it is not the usual thing to believe that you have to do things for your friends. It also looks like the whole thing was done in a way that makes it easy to accept. I think it is a sign of great success on your part any way you look at it.

That you sent everything straight to Stuttgart is also nice for me.

On Monday I got the *Middletown* book from Wanamaker, and I already started to read it. It demonstrates once again that our [German-English] dictionary is totally inadequate and I can barely make out the words for jobs and technical procedures, but so far I find it to be very worthwhile reading. The mixture of statistical research and analysis laid out this way leads to new ways of understanding things. The evenhanded, objective descriptions result in totally new and unexpected findings, without flashiness but with reality and depth and meaning. Reading this, I thought of a subject I could work on if I ever find my way back to social science, namely a comparative study of the nature and scale of women's work in different countries. Since the large-scale census is now under way here, in a few years there will be completely new and reliable material available about Germany. I already have the [census] forms for all four of us,[14] namely the family, occupational, and genealogical forms, completed and ready to be picked up. In addition to the *Middletown* book I'm reading a

13 *Eugen* = Eugene Hoeber, but the reference is to a folksong about Prince Eugen of Savoy.

14 "*Four of us*" = Elfriede, Johannes, Susanne, and Helma, the housekeeper/babysitter.

Kasimir Edschmid, *The Southern Empire: A Trip through the Hohenstaufen Empire in Southern Italy*. A little superficial like all Edschmids, but charming and a good way to learn something, as long as you don't use it as a historical reference work. I read that in bed at night, but I read *Middletown* at my desk.

Hilde has been here for a couple of days. She is staying with the Magicians, who are being unusually nice and sweet to her, but it's hard for her to get away and our chats are not at all suitable for the Magicians. We like being together so much, so the Magicians' well-meaning attentiveness is a little problematic. Hilde feels obligated to report to them on everything she does and she's not used to that. Nevertheless, she came here yesterday about 7 o'clock and later I walked her part of the way back. This morning she's leaving again, meeting Till in Frankfurt and will go with him to Dresden to meet with the consul of her new country. She's having some difficulties because she doesn't have an address here anymore, at least no proper one, and she can't go to where Karl is yet and they can't go to their new place until about Christmas. Their furniture is on the way already, to the horror of her relatives, who are worried about customs and storage expenses, while from here it looks like everybody should be thankful that the shipments are already on their way. She has to fight so much naiveté, both from Karl and from her relatives, so now she has to appeal to the consul for help.

A few days ago Susanne had to write words with "ch" and one of them was grouch[15]—like Papi, as she said. I realized that I almost forgot that you've always been a grouch and probably always will be. Your letters are so unusually nice that I could easily forget the darker side of your personality. At any rate, for the moment I regard you in only the brightest of lights and you will have to make a considerable effort to shake my belief that you are the nicest possible man. If it weren't for the fact that a marriage by mail is rather limited, these letters almost make it a desirable thing. So at the moment you are in my good graces. I've been in a good mood for almost two weeks without a break.

I now have a set of carriers that is better than it had been for a long time. I recently wondered if it was a lack of intelligence on my part that made it take so long until I had everything under control—but it wasn't that. There were just more difficulties than usual over the last few months. And there are still more knots to be disentangled, for example the money that I still need to get from Mrs. Mugler and Schindler that I still don't have. I'm doing everything I can to get it, but if I don't I'm not going to give myself any more gray hairs over it. To avoid any misunderstandings: I don't have any gray hairs yet. And what does it say in *The Bride of*

15 The original German word was *Meckerer*, which may also be translated as "complainer" or "whiner."

Messina, that Schiller play which no one ever read without being forced to but which is full of so many good quotations: "Do not cling to material things, which adorn your life but fleetingly."[16] My God what an expression, when you know I've always been tight with money!

In my situation I find myself forced into a certain level of hospitality, and alcohol serves rather well when battling one's worries. Yesterday Mrs. Daniels visited and brought me a bottle of liqueur, which was very necessary since Günter and Marlies had jointly emptied the one I bought the previous week. Last Saturday at 7 o'clock Günter had to go to the recruiting office for a second time, with the same result as before, but Gerhard, who had to go to the recruiting office yesterday, was placed in classification 1 and will probably have to do three months [of training] this year.

The report about your social life sounds most pleasant. I find I can't keep the Eleanors, Dorothys, and others apart anymore, and a dance in Swarthmore is almost too much for my anxious mind. But if we have to lead our lives separately for a while, then we will have to arrange our fun separately too. It's probably in the nature of things that the pleasures I arrange for myself seem a lot more harmless than those my spouse arranges for himself. Just don't forget that somewhere out there in the wide world you have a modest little wife to whom you are rather important.

Hilde wants to come for two days next week. I decided she can stay in our bedroom, a privilege accorded to no one since Paul and Heidi. I'll move to the couch in the living room.

19 May 1939

I got this far the day before yesterday when Mrs. Freyberger came, who ended up staying here until yesterday at noon. She's going into the hospital for an operation and acted as though it was nothing, but she really didn't look that way. I'm going to see if I can find a couple of grapefruit to send her so she doesn't feel quite so abandoned, because I can't possibly visit her before Saturday or Penetcost Sunday.

I decided to send Susanne to Schalkenmehren with Günter. That way it will be a longer visit for her and there will be a lot of people there who don't appeal to me and it's so close to the Ultimo that I would just as soon prepare everything in peace. It will be very quiet here—Hilde will be back in the Black Forest, Mother still [at the spa] in Wildbad, Günter in Schalkenmehren—but I'm looking forward to spending two days with books by myself.

Yesterday and the day before yesterday you were the object of great admiration when I told various people about the various affidavits.

16 Schiller, *Die Braut von Messina*, IV, 4. ["*Nicht an die Güter hänge Dein Herz, die das Leben vergänglich zieren.*"]

Everyone is very impressed, and I think sometime all that will transform itself into a job. But you shouldn't think I'm impatient when I write that. I am entirely satisfied with your results after four months

I've decided to take a couple of days' vacation in June, as I told you I hoped to. I had a tentative discussion with Mrs. Freyberger, who hopes to be able to free up a few days for me. It's actually not a good time to make too many plans, but you know that I always like to travel around a bit in my mind, even if it ultimately comes to nothing.

Now it's time for me to end this letter, otherwise the Paris train will leave without it and the Bremen as well.

1000 Grüße von Deiner Friedel.

SUNDAY, MAY 21, 1939

Letter from Elfriede in Düsseldorf to Johannes in Philadelphia.

---

21 May 39

Liebes Peterchen,

Sunday afternoon—balcony—alone—Susanne went to sail her little boat with Helma. and the weather is nice and I can enjoy my *Middletown*. Günter was here at lunch and I went for a bit of a ride with him—it's so pretty everywhere now—and since then I've been sitting here with coffee and the rest of my birthday candy. Today is Mother's Day here, and Susie felt obliged to provide a poem, flowers, and chocolates. The contents of her savings box find their way back to me every chance she gets. She learned a very cute, sweet poem in school. Then I invited her to get in my bed but that quickly turned into an unplanned riot. She wiggled more than six puppies and a dozen fleas in bed at the same time. Sometimes I'm obligated to assume your role as regards roughhousing which, as you know, is as strenuous as it is fun. I'm not always quite up to it, but I do what I can. This coming Friday she will take the express by herself (!) to Gerolstein, where Günter will pick her up and bring her back next Tuesday. She is very excited about this great undertaking. First question was whether the train has a dining car, which she would like to go to. To her regret there is none, but she is certainly your daughter, just as curious and enterprising as you are. This way she'll have almost five days of vacation, but I'm going to pass it up because I'm not up to the trip back and forth on the train. In any case the balcony is almost a substitute for summer. It's amazing how you always forget from one year to the next how beautiful springtime is. I have to remember this one particularly well because the next one will presumably look very different in a very different place.

The *Frankfurter Zeitung* has a big special section on Cologne today, which you'll probably get too. I have RM 350—worth of ads in there myself. That's probably a record for a Sunday, but I don't have any hope of beating April's record for a single month.

I had an anxious dream about you a couple of days ago. You were driving a motorcycle on a street with packed-down, rutted snow and absolutely had to pass a car, which I watched from a distance and which made me both angry and anxious. Angry because you made me anxious. This is how the hidden anxieties of my subconscious come to light, but generally I don't worry very much. Now that my business is running well and I'm less nervous about my life—even though the problems aren't completely gone—I realize for the first time how dominant this anxiety was for a long time. The big fears that torment all people don't bother me all that much, because you can't do anything about them.

Otherwise I don't have much to add since my long letter of last week, especially since I haven't heard from you since my last one.

Alles Liebe Deine Friedel.

THURSDAY, MAY 25, 1939

First air mail letter from Johannes in Philadelphia to Elfriede in Düsseldorf. Mail went by train to New York, where it was transferred to a Boeing Clipper operated by Pan American Airways. The plane refueled in Newfoundland before crossing the Atlantic and landing in Shannon, Ireland and then either Paris or Lisbon. Unfortunately the service turned out to be both expensive and unreliable.

This letter includes an extended discussion of American municipal politics, a description of life on Cresheim Road, and a surprise about Johannes' job. The letter also discusses the family's finances again. From the time he came to the University of Pennsylvania in 1934, Rudolf's $4,000 annual salary came from multiple sources. $1,000 came from the University, $1,000 came from the Emergency Committee in Aid of Displaced German Scholars (part of the Rockefeller Foundation), and $2,000 came from a Philadelphia-based foundation. Josephine worked full-time as Rudolf's collaborator at his research lab at the University of Pennsylvania, but her work was uncompensated. Rudolf's summer research at the Woods Hole Marine Biological Laboratory was supported by grants from the American Philosophical Society in Philadelphia. Rudolf's situation at the time of this letter was complicated by the death of Dr. Alfred

Stengel, Dean of the Medical School, who had brought Rudolf to Philadelphia and who had assisted in securing the grants over the years. Dr. Stengel was replaced by Dr. A. N. Richards, who was not familiar with these arrangements. As a result, Rudolf did not get approval of his salary until July 1939.[17]

Philadelphia, the 25th of May 39

Liesbster Peter,

Such is life: when I was writing a letter for the *Queen Mary* the day before yesterday I hardly knew which way was up, there was that much to do. And today I hardly know what to do with myself to justify my being in the office. So I'll start my day by writing to you.

This is going to be an historic letter, which hopefully you will get at the latest on the third day after it leaves Philadelphia. It will go by the *American Clipper*, which completed its first mail flight from New York to Lisbon in 24 hours last week. Make a note of when you get it so we can check it.

My lack of work today is due to the fact that the atmosphere around the Charter has gotten all cloudy again. Since I have time today and since it will certainly interest you, I'm going to try to sort it out for you a bit. The fact that there is a Charter fight at all stems from the fact that for decades Philadelphia has been in the hands of a party machine that is as entrenched as it is corrupt. This machine controls 21 of the 22 seats in the city council. Since this is Philadelphia it hardly needs to be mentioned that the machine is Republican. The power of this machine, like all the others, depends in part on the spoils system and in part on the election system. The council members are elected by districts. The candidates are nominated in so-called "primaries" in which all voters are eligible. You have to register either as a Democrat or a Republican and you can only vote in the primary of your party. This is how the machine gets its candidates in: The city government has about 19,000 employees, and their jobs are controlled by the machine henchmen. Since each job can control about 10 votes, that means a bloc of about 200,000 votes, and there are rarely more than 400,000 votes in either party's primary. If there is ever a danger that a group of independents might put up a good independent candidate, the machine puts up some other independent candidate and campaigns for him in order to split the independent vote so the machine candidate wins by a plurality.

This is how the Charter fight began. In the Roosevelt landslide six years ago, the Democrats took Pennsylvania for the first time in forty years,

17 Records related to Rudolf's grants are in the papers of the Emergency Committee in Aid of Displaced German Scholars at the New York Public Library and in the records of the American Philosophical Society in Philadelphia.

but just a year later failed to get a majority in the Philadelphia municipal elections. As a result, the [Democratic] Governor, in the last year of his administration, appointed a commission to draw up a new Charter for Philadelphia. The idea was that if the politicians couldn't control the city jobs then municipal reform would be possible.

Municipal frames of government, however, are established by state law here, so the Pennsylvania House and Senate are in control. By the time the Charter Commission, which was appointed by a Democrat, issued its report late last year, Pennsylvania had become Republican again, and a Republican legislature had no reason to make trouble for the Republican machine in Philadelphia. But that's what the new Charter would do. It doesn't just make civil service compulsory for all city jobs other than the political heads, it would also get rid of the primaries and the district elections and instead institute a system of proportional representation.[18] This system would be a threat to any machine. As a result, and probably primarily for this reason, the Charter got stopped in the legislature. But that's not the end of the matter, because there are municipal elections in Philadelphia in the fall. The balance of power in Philadelphia between Republicans and Democrats is 54% to 46%. In the last election the Republicans promised the cities home rule, and if now they don't give Philadelphia the Charter then they will probably lose the election to the Democrats in the fall. That's something they really don't want, because there's a presidential election in 1940 and they need the machine for that and for the machine they need the city jobs. This situation and only this situation lends great influence to the relatively small Charter group, which consists mostly of influential Republicans who are independent of the machine.

The Republicans [in the State Legislature] are now looking for a way out of this predicament, so since yesterday we now have three Charter bills instead of one: the original one with proportional representation, city manager, civil service, finance reform, etc.; a second one without proportional representation but with everything else; and a third one that just authorizes Philadelphia to adopt a new Charter via a plebiscite or to elect a Charter commission to develop a new charter. This is how the Republicans hope to turn away the animosity resulting from the fact that they promised a Charter and then rejected it.

Here you have the entire American political system in a nutshell: two parties that originally were nothing more than two big patronage parties and that to some extent still are; the pressure of historical developments moving in the direction of establishing more rational methods of governing; the resistance of many organized interest groups to the

18 In the European system of proportional representation, candidates are elected to a legislature in proportion to the votes the party receives of all votes cast in the election. Thus, if a party receives only 10 percent of the vote, it still occupies 10 percent of the seats in the legislature. This is distinguished from the American system, in which candidates for the legislature are elected based on a simple majority (or plurality) vote for each legislator in a single district.

transformation of these spoils machines, because these interest groups are far less likely to compromise than ideologically and socially amorphous groups are.

What interests me most about this Charter work is, first of all, the opportunity to study American politics, especially municipal politics, as a living organism. Secondly, I believe the defeat of the spoils system is more than necessary and desirable from every perspective, so I back the civil service idea lock, stock, and barrel. On the other hand, I am more than skeptical about proportional representation, and all attempts by Walter, by Millard, and by Gruenberg have failed to convince me that it would be a useful way to end the influence of both party machines and to bring an end to the spoils system.

Finally: what further prospects are there for the Charter and Charter work? The State Legislature meets the day after tomorrow. It meets only for a few weeks every two years. By the day after tomorrow, therefore, all proposed bills must be finished. One of the three bills will probably be adopted. In any event it won't be ours. The second, which is identical to ours except for proportional representation, would have to be submitted to a public vote in Philadelphia within 4 weeks. The third would result in either an immediate referendum on our Charter or provide for the appointment of a new Charter Commission. Hence the next week will decide what will become of our Charter Committee and thus what will become of me. If none of the three bills becomes law, then I think there is reason to hope the work will continue, though whether with me or without me is another question.

And now for something completely different. You asked in your last letter about the atmosphere on Cresheim Road. Most of the time it's as comfortable as it can be in a family where everyone likes each other, though it's sometimes burdened with irrational tensions that inevitably arise when five adults and two children and three generations and very different personalities live together for a long time in the same space. It is sometimes made more complicated than is absolutely necessary by the Höber habit of everyone worrying about what everyone else is doing, and it has recently been somewhat dampened by our all worrying about our economic future. Daddy apparently had hoped that I would find something more quickly than is now the case, and the disappointment caused when Walter innocently offered me a job prematurely[19] has given Daddy even more to deal with than me. The fact that Manfred still hasn't heard anything from Saratoga Springs isn't necessarily a reason to worry—the season is probably starting abnormally late due to the bad weather and the man wants to save the salary for the month of May—

19 The question of Walter's job offer is discussed more in a later letter.

but it's also not exactly comforting. And last but not least we are now in the weeks in which we have to wait for the extension of Daddy's grant. I believe this is a fair summary of the overall situation. Mostly we are comfortable and content with one another, sometimes more than content, which is to a large extent attributable to Monika's exceptional comic cheerfulness. And sometimes we are less so, and sometimes there is an unavoidable small blowup, but it doesn't last long and in 90 percent of the cases it's Seppchen's fault or mine or both of ours.

We're always together for breakfast, except that Manfred sleeps late once in a while. Since Daddy and Seppchen want to be in the lab at 9 and since I have to be in the office at 9, Blue Boy always leaves Cresheim Road promptly at 8:20. I should mention again how enchanting the drive into town is along the Wissahickon and Schuylkill valleys. Daddy and Seppchen have lunch in the lab. I occasionally eat alone—in which case cheaply, for 15 or 20 cents—or with Walter or Wistar and Becky, for 35 cents, or even with Walter and his wife when she comes into town to go shopping, then fancy for 40 or even 45 cents, or once in a while invited by Gruenberg or someone else, then very fancy, for example twice at the Princeton Club. Then I pick up Daddy and Seppchen from the lab at 5:30, and we drive home for a family dinner at 7:30.

After dinner we sit together in the living room until we drop into bed one after the other at 10:30. The evenings do have one problem we haven't solved, which is that some of us want to read and others of us want to talk. Seppchen can't read at night because she has clothes to mend, and it's understandable that she likes to talk when she's doing that. Gri almost always joins her in her sewing role. The appropriate solution would be reading aloud, but Daddy is so tired in the evening that he's always on the verge of dozing off. Once in a while Daddy and I prevail in enforcing silence for reading and once in a while Seppchen and Gri prevail in forcing a conversation. And Manfred avoids taking a position by withdrawing to his and Gri's room to read. This family idyll has recently been threatened by my increasingly being out. I am gradually getting to the point again where I have something going on three times a week, and oddly enough in all my activities I'm almost always exclusively with Americans. I'm too accustomed to building my own circle of friends to fit in with one put together for me by my family.

On Sunday we had a family picnic, the annual Höber trip to Valley Forge that has already become a tradition. 21 adults and children, with the exception of Tönnies a completely dark-complexioned and exclusively German company. Valley Forge is another one of the many amazing beauty spots here. We roasted hotdogs over an open fire in the fireplace there, cooked coffee, played badminton, egg races, 1, 2, 3 and other pleasant things, all of it under a clear blue sky and weather that wasn't too hot. Then in the evening Priscilla and Co. and I decided we had a terrible thirst for beer—that is, actually, the two men, because Priscilla is too dignified for beer—and since Pennsylvania prohibits alcohol on Sunday we went abroad to Weber's Hofbräu, on the other side of the Delaware in Camden and thus in New Jersey, where that which is immoral in Pennsylvania is moral. And there we danced to the swing tunes of a band dressed in Bavarian folk costumes, periodically interrupted by a floor show whose stars were five small Negro boys. More tomorrow.

Sehr in Liebe, Jo

THURSDAY AND FRIDAY, MAY 25 AND 26, 1939

Letter from Elfriede in Düsseldorf to Johannes in Philadelphia.

5/25/39

Liebstes Peterchen,

This week is going to be devoted to a visit from Hilde. She came back from Berlin on Monday and tomorrow she's going back to Freiburg. I don't see much of her during the day, since her life is fully taken up with people, friends, lawyers, etc. As a result, on two different occasions the blackbirds had started singing and it was pretty light out by the time we finally decided to go to bed. This morning before getting up she spent an hour in your bed next to mine, and we chatted cheerfully and I think that would be a nice picture for you—this visit to your bed. What do we talk about all the time? I don't know quite what, but there's no break and it's always lively. This life of excessive cigarettes and cognac and insufficient sleep isn't really good for me, so I'll recover on Pentecost.

I don't much like your question about getting a letter of recommendation from the *Frankfurter Zeitung*. That belongs in the category of sleeping dogs. I'll talk to Antonio when he's here again, but my feeling is that I'm against stirring the thing up. A lot of things are dependent on maintaining the current arrangement [with the paper]. I don't want to saw off the limb I'm sitting on.

I don't much like the stories about Manfred and Gri, and I can imagine it's worrisome and depressing for all of you. I must say, however, that it doesn't surprise me that you come to a dead end [in job hunting] once in a while. You are doing everything well and properly, and nobody's mood barometer points to "fair weather" all the time. I know that only too well myself. Hilde and I manufacture artificial "fair weather" for ourselves. She's tossing around perfume, champagne, wine, flowers, and more flowers so that our place looks like we're very wealthy. The last few evenings have even raised fears that we are falling into decadence, but I've been at the edge of the fair weather period and the forecast is for "unsettled and changeable, partly cloudy with rain showers" and so I can stand to have my spirits lifted. The bit of equilibrium I'm able to achieve once in a while is always easily endangered, and Hilde's well-justified nervousness isn't suited to stabilizing that equilibrium. With time I'm learning to follow in your footsteps and to play the role of a cheerful pillar of strength, not just for Hilde but for others as well. It probably amuses you how much I try to follow your example (though not in the area of dissoluteness). In the business—when I actually work at it — there are only a few things in which I don't succeed. At any rate, I've learned a lot from you in ten years, or if you will almost 16(!) and I like that.[20] I think that the modest capacities I was born with have expanded substantially with you, that without you I would never have arrived at the strong attitude toward life and the world around us that I sometimes feel. Even your detours with girls don't seem so terrible to me anymore (though you shouldn't take this as a license for more of them).

Sometimes I allow myself the illusion that when we're finally together again we could have a really very tidy and well-ordered life. Cool reason tells me that this is probably an illusion, but after all this disorder my craving for order has become enormous. You'll have to make a lot of effort if you want to satisfy it. Hilde recently said very nicely, "The independence we once fought for has now become a reality for us and now we don't know what to do with it."

5/26/39

Hilde just left and I'm going back to work and the serious things of life. Yesterday evening with champagne and goose liver was comfortable and fun, but now it's nice that the turmoil is over.

One more thing. I think the Kiel Savings and Loan made a mess of the stock shares. According to my information the prohibition on selling stocks only applies to Jewish accounts (whether blocked or not) but not to others. That means that no official approval of the Reich is necessary. Maybe it would be appropriate to let the Savings and Loan know that, now that there has been a ruling from Berlin.[21] This is only a suggestion. I leave it to your smarter heads to decide whether to approach them.

20 Although Johannes and Elfriede had been married for ten years, they had known each other for sixteen.

21 *Ruling from Berlin*: In February, the regime's Finance Bureau notified Rudolf that he was subject to the levy on "Jews'" property imposed after *Kristallnacht*. Rudolf's appeal, claiming he was not "Jewish," was upheld in May.

The sun has been shining here for the last week while in Wildbad Mother is in danger of drowning in the rain.

Alles Liebe Deine Friedel.

MONDAY, MAY 29, 1939

Letter from Elfriede in Düsseldorf to Johannes in Philadelphia. It includes the news (hidden in circumlocutions) that with the exhaustion of the German immigration visa quota, the American Consulate in Stuttgart had suspended the issuance of visas until a new quota year began with the fiscal year on July 1.

Pentecost Monday, 5/29/39

Mein liebes Peterchen,

On Friday as I was putting our daughter on the train [to Schalkenmehren for the long weekend] I was suddenly seized with terrible anxiety. The little kid looked so forlorn in the overcrowded train, but it all went so quickly. I was hardly off when the train started moving. At 6:30 Hendrik phoned that he and Günter had safely picked her up. Tomorrow she's coming back with Günter and on Wednesday Mother's coming back.

Recently when Susie had been at the Gumpertz', on the way back she said with a deep sigh, "Oh, I really do miss Papi very, very much." I was very moved by how attached the child is, but the following sentence, "I hate to go on the trolley or to walk, it's much nicer with the car," brought me back to reality.

My quiet Pentecost days have actually not been so quiet up to now. On Saturday afternoon Thilo and Charlo Neudeck called up to say they were here and whether I would like to go out to eat with them somewhere. I would very much, also found it much more pleasant than if I had them here for dinner. So we went to the Kurfürstendamm. Charlo, now somewhat fuller, looks younger and prettier than ever. I have seen few women whose looks were so much improved by pregnancy. A friend of Charlo's from Stuttgart was with them who is on her way to Rhodesia with her husband and child. Since she knew about a lot of worrisome matters, I asked her what she might have heard about the conditions at the place that is of interest to me. Everything there is pretty much suspended, which in my opinion has to do with the accounting year that comes to an end on 6/30. Since, however, the anxiety about the possible outbreak of events beyond anyone's control has gotten much less recently, it didn't bother me as much as it would have a couple of weeks ago. You can only do what you can do, and that will be done by all of us.

Yesterday morning I was in Cologne and visited Mrs. Freyberger [in the hospital]. She's doing quite well. It will be another 10 days before she can go home, but things are going the way they're supposed to. Then I went in town where I wanted to eat at the *Bastei* but ended up at the *Ewige Lampe*, then wandered around Cologne a little and then went home and enjoyed the chaise lounge on the balcony. Later I visited the Baeyers and in the evening went to Herbert and Elisabeth's. The last was for the sole purpose of seeing Elisabeth's gray flannel slacks (here the *dernier cri*), which she got for her trip to Ahrenshoop [on the Baltic Sea] and which have aroused my envy. Overall I was quite satisfied with the way I arranged this day, which was completely my own. It seems I'm beginning to learn to be independent and am gradually recovering the ability to stand on my own two feet. When I went into the *Ewige Lampe* by myself I even felt quite important. I'll be delighted to submit myself once again to dependence upon my husband (though not to husbandly tyranny), but it's a good thing I don't feel so helpless and depressed on holidays any more. It would have been even better by car, but I don't worry about things that can't be changed.

I'm continuing writing this letter on the chaise lounge on the balcony. In an hour, when the sun disappears behind the houses, I'll go to the station and mail this letter and some others. I'm acting as though it's summer, letting the sun shine on my belly, but instead of getting a bit of a tan and some color, which I could use, I only get freckles and some sniffles. But it really is idyllic here. A few children are playing in the garden space, and there are some skimpily clad people to be seen on the other balconies. I'm making plans to tear myself away from here for a few days this month or next.

And so I'll bring this not very significant letter to a close. Tomorrow the mail should bring me something from you, but the *Queen Mary*, which leaves from Cherbourg the day after tomorrow, should at least carry some greetings from me to you.

Alles Liebe Deine Friedel.

TUESDAY, MAY 30, 1939

Letter from Johannes in Philadelphia to Elfriede in Düsseldorf.

Philadelphia 5/30/39.

Liebstes Peterchen,

As a result of the *American Clipper* and my handwritten letter I have completely lost track of the order of our letters, and it's probably worse for you because the airmail letter undoubtedly reached you before others that were written earlier. Still, I find the *Clipper* so appealing that I'll probably use it again this Saturday, recognizing that you'll have to read my letters twice, once when they arrive and a second time in chronological order.

It's Tuesday evening, the end of 3½ days off that I got unexpectedly, not because it was Pentecost—nobody here pays any attention to that—but because Memorial Day is observed here, sort of like *Heldengedenktag* in Germany, and our boss gave us the day off and closed the office on Tuesday. Touch wood that the closing is only temporary. The Charter has indeed been killed in the state legislature and not just the one bill but all three and no one knows right now what will become of the Charter Committee. For the moment the office will open again tomorrow at the usual time.

Yesterday the Höber family went on a delightful expedition. This included Ulli, who began a two-week vacation yesterday before she takes over as Chief Resident of her hospital for two months (which means, incidentally, that she'll get \$50 a month instead of \$25). We left at 7 in two cars for New York and the World's Fair. It was tremendous. Even getting there in the sunny—later very hot—weather was a pleasure. The Pulaski Skyway going into New York is even more impressive than in the opposite direction because you have the skyscraper skyline in front of you the whole time.[22] You go under the Hudson through a new tunnel, whose access on the New Jersey side winds down the steep bank of the river across from the uptown skyscrapers. On the other side you go uptown to 125th Street on an equally new skyway along the Hudson and then diagonaotzilly across the city to the Triborough Bridge. In style the Fair is in many ways like the "*Schaffendes Volk*"[23] but it's very much bigger, and the emblem of the Trylon and Perisphere that you see in all the pictures has a tremendous architectonic impact. Like a lot of things, the overall effect is more impressive than the details of the individual elements, though some of the individual exhibits are very striking, such as, for example, the presentation of artificial lightning by General Electric. One day is only enough to get a general overview, and I would really like to come here a second time, with you.

If I go back further in the chronology, then I need to tell you about the dance at Swarthmore, which took place on Saturday. The report comes in two parts. Imagine a warm summer evening on a campus with old buildings, broad lawns, flowers, trees, and a blue sky. Add about 400 students in white tuxes and flowing light colored evening dresses, tasteful

22 *The Pulaski Skyway*, then new, is an elevated highway several miles long carrying U.S. Route 1 through New Jersey to the Holland Tunnel. At the time it was the most modern high-speed roadway in the world.

23 The "*Reichsausstellung Schaffendes Volk*" was a large international exposition built under Hermann Göring's mandate in the northern outskirts of Düsseldorf. It was open from May through October 1937.

Johannes' photograph of the New York World's Fair, May 29, 1939.

rooms in which the ball is taking place—and you have an overall impression that would remind you of the best scenes in a lovely film with a very special charm. This ball could have been enchanting—with a different companion. As expected, Bettina turned out to be as unsuited to this event as possible, and the formal dance was really so formal that out of the 200 girls I only met two, with each of whom Bettina had arranged a dance for me in advance. Even during the intermission, when we quickly drove into Media—Swarthmore is absolutely dry—to gulp down a cocktail, it still wasn't possible to get much reaction from her. And that was with me! As happy as I was to have seen something like that once, I declined when at the end of the evening Bettina invited me to a second dance next Friday. At least I was able to conceal a bit the coolness of my feelings about the whole thing.

Now to something very positive. Yesterday evening when we came back from New York there was a letter from Comstock [the doctor in Saratoga Springs] saying that Manfred should start [working for him] on 6/1, that is, the day after tomorrow. One less worry! Gri will stay here with the children for the moment and then will go to Saratoga with Janka in August when Daddy and Seppchen come back from Woods Hole. So next week Gri, Ulli, and the children will be here alone, and starting the week after next Gri and I alone with the kids.

And then something very sad. There's an article in the paper today reporting that Lederer[24] died very suddenly of a thrombosis following two operations. He was just 53. I had always hoped to be able to speak to him more extensively after those disappointing ten minutes in January. In all, we really owe him quite a lot.

24 Emil Lederer, a professor of economics, was Johannes' doctoral thesis advisor at Heidelberg. The Nazis expelled Lederer from the university in 1933. He emigrated to the United States in 1934 and co-founded the New School for Social Research in New York.

And of course I must mention your sweet letter of the 17th and 19th, which was obviously written when you had time to relax. You told me about so many amusing things that I have the feeling that you couldn't possibly have experienced any more. I'm very impressed by Susie's letter and above all by her nice Roman writing. Is that the result of the new school? At any rate, give her a big kiss from me.

In Liebe, Jo

WEDNESDAY AND THURSDAY, MAY 31 AND JUNE 1, 1939

Letter from Elfriede in Düsseldorf to Johannes in Philadelphia responding to his airmail letter of May 25.

5/31/39

Liebes Peterchen,

The 31st of a month is certainly no time for a *Frankfurter Zeitung* girl to write a letter. Stacked up in front of me are piles of invoices, subscription slips and cancellation slips, subscriber index cards, and mounds of receipts for classified ads—but while the business side of my life is showing all the signs of high tide, my private life is at a yawning ebb tide. The *Columbus* came—without mail from you. The *Queen Mary* came—without mail from you. I got your last letter a week ago today—oh it's just awful! And all I have to comfort me is a picture postcard from Hilde, "View from Feldberg in the Wiesental," leaning up in front of me on the desk. It's only slight comfort, but I have to latch onto whatever I can in my loneliness. Since I don't have much to report about my work-filled but otherwise uneventful life, I packed up your white flannel trousers and sent them off. I thought it's getting to be summer where you are and you can use them. Today I'll follow that up with a shirt and a pair of socks.

I was able to work out doing the collections in Gladbach on Saturday afternoon with the Trömels. I was especially happy about being able to ride in a fancy open DKW convertible again. Tonight I'm going to air defense again. I missed the last night of my course, and now I have to repeat it. Last evening Susie came home sunburned from Schalkenmehren, very excited about her time in the Eifel Mountains. It must have been very nice.

[*Later.*]
I had given up all hope of hearing from you before the day after tomorrow, because the next ship doesn't arrive until tomorrow, and then this afternoon the mailman brought your airmail letter. I must say the 30

cents for postage were well spent this time because that letter gives my pining heart the boost it so desperately needs. The letter, written on the 25th, cancelled in Philadelphia early on the 26th got here on the 31st, but the letter from the *Queen Mary*, which arrived in Cherbourg the day before yesterday, isn't here yet. What on earth is wrong with the post office? As to your treatise on the Charter, I'll wait for a quieter hour to study it thoroughly, first because you wrote it, second because it interests me, and third because I don't like to look stupid. Also because your continuing employment depends on it. From one of your sentences I think I have to conclude that the $65 didn't come to pass after all? Or was that about a continuing position that you were hoping for that didn't come about? Earlier you wrote about your first American check. Can you explain? I'd like to know just for my sense of our finances. Also apart from my sense of our finances.

Because my supply of suits is rather slim, I also wanted to ask you if a tailor is something very expensive where you are, for example if one had the cloth for a suit. I had a good idea for having something made, but it only makes sense if a tailor alone isn't more expensive than buying the finished suit.

I really liked your description of your family life. Now I can picture everything much more accurately, although a family argument is almost beyond the realm of anything I could imagine. I don't doubt you, but is it really true that you might occasionally cause an argument? After six months' participation in your family's life by means of letters, that possibility would never have occurred to me. As for me, I'm a poor lonely girl with literally no one with whom I could quarrel, and I haven't cried in just as long—aside from a couple of tears I had to suppress when reading one of your letters, and that's already quite a while ago.

1 June 1939

Mein liebstes Peterchen, the month is beginning well. The Post Office is showering me with everything, the *Columbus* letter, the *Queen Mary* letter—I really should start this letter all over again, that's how different everything looks to me compared to yesterday. See how much my mood depends on your letters? With all my worries I never manage to keep upbeat all the time. But the hole wasn't so deep that I couldn't scramble up out of it pretty quickly.

Many thanks for the Charter essays. I will have to postpone reading them to a quieter time.

My desk is a nightmare, but writing this letter has to come before everything else since the *Columbus* is leaving from Cherbourg tomorrow night. It may have been bad on your part that you concealed from me the snag over your employment.[25] I can imagine that it caused you some rather bitter heartache, but I really didn't deserve it that you didn't write me about it right away. It wouldn't be the first time we had to bear up under some trouble together, and there's a suitable role for me with respect to the good things too. I can imagine how awful it was for you when you got my letter reacting to your first success when by then everything had already turned into a disappointment. Life really isn't ever pretty. Not for you and not for me. But on days when I get this much mail from you it's a lot easier to endure.

But that's enough for now. Unfortunately the work has to get done too somehow.

More soon! *Alles Liebe Deine Friedel.*

---

25 *Snag over your employment*: Apparently the "first paid American job" of which Johannes wrote so movingly in March was, in fact, a misunderstanding. He worked for the Charter Committee, but he didn't get paid, so all this time he was living off of Rudolf's income. The explanation was probably in one of the letters that was not preserved.

CHAPTER 10

Uncle Karl Says Yes

SUNDAY AND TUESDAY, JUNE 4 AND 6, 1939

Letter from Elfriede in Düsseldorf to Johannes in Philadelphia, containing the news that she had been called to the office of the American Consul in Stuttgart for an interview and medical examination. This meant her written visa application, resubmitted on May 10 with additional support affidavits, had been deemed adequate and that she had passed the first hurdle in getting permission for herself and Susanne to enter the United States as permanent residents. Elfriede's relief over this achievement was dampened by her anxiety over dealing with "Uncle Paul," i.e., the German authorities. She needed to obtain a new German passport for herself and Susanne, as well as a police good conduct certificate to present the American Consulate. She knew that the Nazis' police bureaucrats were abusive to anyone seeking to leave the country.

6/4/39 Sunday

Liebes Peterchen,

I'm still enjoying the riches of the letters I got this week. Yesterday I finally had time to read the charter enclosures in peace. Your Americanization is progressing amazingly quickly.

This was a really wild week and yesterday, Saturday, put the proverbial icing on the cake. I successfully finished off the collections from the outlying areas by means of an afternoon drive with the Trömels to Gladbach. Afterwards we went for coffee to the pretty Reydt Castle, which I had never been to. You are probably familiar with it from one of your devious business side trips.

Today I went to the hospital in Cologne to see Mrs. Freyberger, who's really doing very well. She has to rest all day, but on a balcony lying on a very practical cross between a bed and a reclining wheelchair, and can move around some, but has to stay there for at least another week to recover completely. Her weight, which has gone up from 86 to 90 pounds, still has to go up some more. The last year has injured some people's nerves, and for them a bit of a rest cure is advisable and not at all a luxury. (A propos: my weight is now stable.)

Tuesday, 6 June

Alea iacta est, the die has been cast yet again! I have to go to Stuttgart on 11 July and I have been directed to advise you and others near you who are interested in this matter. The steam all of you generated has driven the engine into formidable motion, and it's now running at a positively undreamt of tempo.

Three days ago I called Betz, who is now in Frankfurt. First I broached the matter of a letter of recommendation [from the *Frankfurter Zeitung*], which he will take care of. He didn't think it's risky to ask for that, and as always I will submit myself to the wiser counsel of smart men. He then wanted to feel me out a bit about the timing of the takeover [of the news agency] and mentioned 1 October. That scared me a little because I don't know if everything can be taken care of by then, and I didn't commit myself. I don't want to abandon my place here until I see the outlines of the new one more clearly.

Now there are lots of decisions to make again and that scares me a little. Tomorrow there's Uncle Paul to deal with. I have to face that now. The date of the termination of the business is something I'll determine after [my interview in] Stuttgart, either 1 September or 1 October. That won't be too difficult, since I have enough money on hand for the final expenses.

The other concern is whether you are ready yet to have us there with you. I don't want you to be under pressure to do something quickly that would be better organized over a longer period of time. From the end of July, when I will presumably have the papers, I will have four months to use them, but the end of those four months is a mandatory cutoff. We'll have to hope that by then everything will have advanced pretty much as far as we would like.[1] *Lieber Peter*, I would have liked to spare you these concerns, but I can't help it and somehow it will work out. It really worries me a lot because I can imagine that this new reality, however positive it may be, adds to all your worries.

Still, the idea of arriving, of having you (alone) pick me up, of dropping Susanne off and then being with you for a couple of solid days, until you've gotten used to your old dragon again, is so wonderful that I don't even know how to say it. But the worries that are connected to the whole thing can't be ignored. Mother just said to me on the phone that God will make it turn out alright. *Peterchen*, you have to understand that this new development leaves me with something of a feeling of trepidation. It's not in the least because of you. What kinds of adventures and upheavals have you and I stumbled into? It would be much better if we were together. As usual, Mother is very comforting, even though she is

1 The immigration visa had to be used to enter the United States within four months of its issuance. Elfriede was concerned that Johannes would have difficulty supporting her and Susanne without a good job.

affected just as much as we are. I'll have to dig out my equanimity, which I have cultivated relatively well over the last few months, from under the rubbish heap, and be gentle with it a little bit, since no one is here to be gentle with me. I could actually use some of that.

Hilde is coming at the end of the week. I'm happy about that; she'll do me good. Her affairs are getting stretched out all over again. Now she and Karl won't be able to go to their relatives [in Venezuela] until Christmas. Till was supposed to go earlier, but more difficulties keep cropping up from the other side [of the Atlantic]. It's not very nice to have to live month after month in that kind of state of uncertainty. She and I will comfort each other with alcohol.

We've been living through an American-style heat wave here since yesterday. On the balcony the thermometer went up to 120 F in the direct sun, and even in the shade it's 86. I'm not suffering much in the heat because the apartment is nice and cool. It's wonderful on the balcony in the morning, but much too hot in the afternoon. How do American women manage with their short skirts when the weather is too hot for knee stockings?

Everybody says hello and misses you.

Deine Friedel

Enclosed is your father's tax notice. It came today!

TUESDAY, JUNE 6, 1939

Letter with a poem enclosed, from Johannes in Philadelphia to Elfriede in Düsseldorf. When he wrote this letter, Johannes had not yet received Elfriede's letter of June 4 and 6 telling him she had been summoned to the American Consulate in Stuttgart. The most recent developments in "current events," to which Johannes refers, were the Pact of Steel of May 22, 1939 formalizing the alliance between Fascist Italy and Nazi Germany, Hitler's statements on May 29 threatening Poland, and British Prime Minister Chamberlain's immediate response that England would intervene if Germany invaded Poland. Such war rhetoric would continue to escalate throughout that summer.

Philadelphia 6/6/39.

Liebstes Peterchen,

This will be the last typewritten letter for some time. In the future you'll have to make do with my handwriting, because Pa-Mu are leaving for

Woods Hole tomorrow morning and taking the typewriter with them.[2] Unfortunately they are also taking Blue Boy and I will miss that even more than the typewriter. Once Ulli goes back to work at the hospital, Gri and I will be taking care of the house and the children by ourselves. This year Pa-Mu are only going to spend June and July in Woods Hole and will spend August on vacation here in Germantown, when Gri will go to Saratoga Springs with Janka and leave Moni here with grandmother Seppchen. What becomes of me this summer depends entirely on what the Charter Committee decides. If they keep me, which should be decided in the next few days, then I'll point out to these gentlemen that I regarded the four months of volunteer time as work time and that they should give me two weeks of paid vacation. In that case I think I would head for Cape Cod. But in the first place they probably won't keep me, and in the second place they probably won't give me any paid vacation.

I've done everything I can do to increase my status as much as possible before tomorrow's meeting, which may be decisive. Just before the office closed today, I finished the draft of my memo on what could be reformed in the city government under the current Charter, i.e., even without a new one, and now it just remains to be edited tomorrow. When I was writing it and when I was consulting with two experts about it yesterday, I had the uncomfortable feeling that I had to write it as though I knew a lot more than I actually do.

This morning your letter about the Pentecost Monday you spent alone arrived, along with a postcard from Susie from Schalkenmehren. Fortunately the letter sounds a lot more contented than it might have, given the world situation, but you've always been better than your husband at keeping yourself busy when you're on your own. I only hope that what you write about the Stuttgart uncle [suspending activity until the new fiscal year begins on July 1] doesn't mean a delay of a full three months. I've heard similar rumors here, of course, but maybe that just means new applications won't be accepted but those already on file will be processed further. For reasons related to the perspective on current events, three months would seriously scare me. Apart from sometimes feeling that I've come to the end of my patience with all this waiting, Mary Phillips, with whom I had lunch today along with Walter, recognized that she hit me in a tender spot when she asked whether there was any mail from you, and then was particularly nice to me. On Monday she's taking the baby to Cape Cod, where her mother has a house. Walter will follow her in the middle of July.

With some amazement I followed you on your independent wandering through Cologne and was almost happy that you didn't get into the

2 Up to this time, Johannes had made carbon copies of all his letters. Since it wasn't possible to make carbon copies of handwritten letters, there are no copies of the letters Johannes sent Elfriede after this one, except for three letters Johannes wrote on July 3 using a typewriter in the Charter Committee office.

Bastei without me. For some reason that place is much more real to me than the *Ewige Lampe*, as a result of the nice lunch you and I had there in the spring of 1937. *Schatz*, you're going to have to learn to make phone calls as well as Hilde does. It's incredibly important here, and just try to imagine what it will be like when you have to speak English and the person on the other end of the line is being unpleasant.

Your inquisitiveness about Elisabeth's grey flannel trousers amused me greatly. "Slacks" are practically the summer fashion here. Priscilla told me just yesterday that she bought a reddish-purple pair and wondered what Daddy will say about it when she shows up in the lab in them. But grey flannel is much more distinguished, and this judgment on my part should make you feel justified in getting a pair.

I think the ad sales figures are sensational. Please let me know what kinds of ads they are. All help wanted ads? I don't have any sense of that anymore. I recently had a chance to read the Cologne supplement [in the *Frankfurte Zeitung*] at leisure and thought it was really good. In fact I read the whole of the last weekly edition with great interest. It's sometimes unnerving how quickly you get separated from things that were familiar.

Gri just whistled to come to dinner. She roasted a duck for the family farewell dinner, and since duck is better hot than cold I'm going to interrupt my writing for a while. I don't know yet whether I'll be able to write more later.

Later. *Plenus venter non studet libenter*,[3] but I can still manage a little more chatting. The duck has been consumed. It weighed 5 ½ American pounds and cost 94 cents; Gri thought that would interest you. While the duck was roasting she put the kids to bed. They were even dirtier than usual today because the sand pile in the garden was put to use for the first time. After Janka finally put all the shovels and rakes in the cellar after being asked to do so several times, she came in almost in tears and asked, "Do I have to carry all the sand into the cellar too?!"

I just read some of your last letter aloud downstairs. The things that I pick out to read always have a grateful audience here. It would be really nice if you could write separately to Woods Hole sometime; in return I'm willing to sacrifice a third of a three-page letter you might otherwise write me. Pa-Mu can't manage for two months without getting a letter from you; they are too fond of them after two months of having heard at least part of them twice a week. Reading letters aloud will play an important role when Gri and I have meals together in the future. Yesterday morning the first, very contented letter came from Manfred in Saratoga. That guy can really write letters!

3 *Plenus venter ...* = A full stomach doesn't like studying.

Now we want to have something of a family evening together. We mostly sit on the porch these days, but we won't be able to do that much longer because the mosquitos will be starting up.

A two-piece bathing suit would certainly be too much for this puritanical city, or rather too little, but certainly right for the seashore. When?????

In Liebe,

Jo

Poem enclosed in Johannes' letter of June 6, 1939 celebrating the fifteenth anniversary of Johannes and Elfriede's engagement on June 13, 1924. They got engaged in Grömitz, a resort on the Baltic Sea. Both were students at Freiburg at the time. The next semester, Elfriede attended the University of Berlin while Johannes transferred to the University of Kiel, but he rejoined Elfriede in Berlin for the spring semester. They then both transferred to the University of Heidelberg. After a five-year engagement, they married on December 22, 1928. This translation seeks to reflect the rhyme and meter of the German original.

For the 13th of June 1939.

Is it really possible that Grömitz
Was fifteen years ago today?
When I read our recent letters
It's hard for me to think that way.

It seems to me it's still, for us,
Just as it was in that earlier way,
When we sent endearments again and again
In the letters we wrote to each other each day.

My God, was I mad when you suddenly said
In the summer you'd go all alone to Berlin,
And commanded me also to go off by myself
Shutting me out, not letting me in.

My God, was I happy when you quickly discovered
That that was precisely the wrong thing my dear,
And that it was only from yourself you were hiding
And from the closeness of our Freiburg year.

[*This verse is in English in the original.*]
How young we were and how very romantic
Reaching for all the stars above
Would you believe, if it were not authentic,
That we slept in one room and didn't make love?

[*In German again.*]
Since that time long ago, at the beginning and later,
You didn't always have things so easy with me,
But we mostly did alright anyway Peter,
Moving bravely along, side by side, day by day.

Let us keep all of our romance alive, my darling
Just as strong and as young as it was way back then,
And build a good life for ourselves and our family
Past and future—together as one once again.

THURSDAY, JUNE 8, 1939

Letter from Elfriede in Düsseldorf to Johannes in Philadelphia, accompanied by a note from Susanne. Elfriede refers regretfully to her letter of June 6, in which she wrote Johannes about having been invited to Stuttgart but expressed trepidation about the next steps in the emigration process.

Düsseldorf, 8 June 1939

Liebes Peterchen,

Air mail is something really wonderful. You sit here not quite sure whether a letter could get here yet, and suddenly it flutters down on you some morning while you're still in bed. "In bed" requires some elucidation: today is Corpus Christi [a holiday], and for that reason I was in bed when the mail came, which is otherwise never the case. I wonder if you knew when you wrote this letter [*not preserved*] on the 2nd how much it would relieve my despondency of the last few days. I'm truly ashamed that I wrote you that whining letter two days ago. Instead of being happy about having overcome this major hurdle [by being called to Stuttgart], I only saw the obstacles that still have to be surmounted and I was suddenly overcome with fear. I hope you won't think I'm too wretched and bad, but also a little understandable. I will do better.

The fact that today of all days you wrote me so sweetly about life over there and what it may be like for us makes me feel very good. It's easy for things to make you afraid in this kind of in-between period, when the things you'll have to give up are so starkly in front of you (the summer is so beautiful here) and the new things are so much less tangible. I worry about the English language most of all. I imagine that you'll be there with nice, smart people and that I'll be sitting there and only understand half of it and won't be able to contribute a tenth of what's going on in my quite intelligent mind, and that's not a situation I can comfortably imagine myself being in. Maybe you told people something nice about me, but then I'll end up looking like an inadequate cow! It's not that I'm short on inferiority complexes anyway, but I often think that you and others expect a lot more of me than I can do. I can do the things I have to here reasonably well, at least I have up to this point, but I can't predict what it will be like in the future. At the outset my only ambition for over there is having you take care of me. I'm pretty much worn out in terms of being competent, and I'd just like to live comfortably with you. Please don't get mad and don't be sad either that I wrote you when I was in such terrible shape yesterday. Some people's skin is just too thin.

Hilde called yesterday—she just wanted to hear from the tone of my voice whether I wanted to have her here. She's coming on Saturday and I'm sure we'll have a nice time again.

Did I write you that Anni's husband Richard [unidentified] has been in the Sioli [psychiatric hospital] for several months? It's really sad. After people voiced every sort of opinion about the situation, it now turns out that he has lung cancer that metastasized into the brain. Ask your doctor's to explain it! It's a hopeless situation. He had gotten a little better for a while, but he's now been in the locked ward for some time. So other people have their troubles too, and then your own, which you can still do something about, don't seem so huge. You and I have always pressed on with resolution and forethought, even when there were difficulties. Somehow we'll get over the obstacles that lie ahead of us too.

It's really something when I hear back from you only ten days after I write. Actually your airmail letter didn't arrive on Monday, as you expected, but only today, Thursday, but still. I'd just like to know where the letter sat for so long between Lisbon and here. I've heard that air mail goes from Lisbon to Southampton by mail plane too, but if that's the case it should have been here much sooner. Still, it's great. When I think I might have gotten it on Monday along with the letter from Stuttgart, that would have been a lot better for my emotional state and I would have spared you the whining letter. My emotional equilibrium is so delicately and carefully stabilized, and hangs by such a thin thread, that it can't stand being unsettled even by things that otherwise help my stability, like fresh air and being outdoors and swimming. Maybe it will work out for me to make another trip north in a little while. The way you reacted to my trip to Worpswede was very nice, and a change of scenery like that does me good. I'm getting restless and something has to be done about that.

This morning I was at Ruth Fischer's [unidentified] to pick up a smart summer hat. She's expecting her baby any day and can't go out anymore. Dressed in white from head to toe I looked rather chic and almost pretty—I thought—but I need you here to really enjoy that. It's a little like Hilde recently wrote me in a poem-letter:

> The sun shone brightly in vain today,
> I felt too much alone to enjoy it at all.
> What is the sense in living this way
> If the things around you only make you feel small?

She wrote this along with many other verses on the trip from Düsseldorf to Freiburg. She sent a new bottle of plum brandy to replace the old one and today two *dirndl* aprons and fabric for a matching dress arrived. Can you wear a *dirndl* in Philadelphia? Everything we do is planned around Philadelphia and next summer. It's hardly worth it to me to make plans for things around here.

When I was at the Magicians' on Monday—I already wrote about that—they had just gotten a letter from Annemarie [in Cleveland]. From that I was able to calculate the advantage of air mail. Her letter was written one day before you wrote your first airmail letter and despite the fact that it came on the *Bremen* it arrived four days later. Her letter included a newspaper clipping in which [her husband] Erich was highlighted as a particularly noteworthy new arrival, referring to two of his paintings. The art exhibit brought him a large new commission, the portrait of a famous but unfortunately deceased man for the lobby of the hospital. So they are more or less free of money worries, even if he doesn't find something new starting right on 1 July. Annemarie's advice for me in this letter is really sort of funny. All the things we have been running ourselves ragged doing and all the plans we've been working toward all along are things she now presents as though they are brilliant new ideas she just discovered.

The day before yesterday I drove out to Neandertal[4] with Marlies and we two ladies ate outside. It was nice and cool out there after the heat, which everyone has been complaining about in the worst way. I feel quite

4 The *Neandertal* Nature Preserve, a short drive from Düsseldorf, includes a restaurant in the park. In writing of the hot weather in Düsseldorf, Elfriede was anticipating the far greater heat of a Philadelphia summer.

comfortable in the heat because I want to feel well in it in preparation for what's coming. Last night the temperature was still 77 degrees on the balcony at 11 P.M.. But at night we open the windows for cross-ventilation, and in the morning the apartment is nice and cool. Helma has to sleep downstairs because upstairs she would literally boil and she has a hard time taking the heat anyway.

The accompanying letter from Susie will make you feel guilty about your sins. You really must do something for her so she doesn't completely forget she has a Papi too.

Alles liebe, Deine Friedel

Accompanying note from Susanne written on a small slip of paper along with a tiny drawing of Susanne sticking out her tongue.

Lieber Papi.

Since you haven't written me I'm only writing you this little scrap. In my birthday letter you promised you would write me again soon. I watched and nothing and again nothing came in the mail. I know nice things, but I won't write them until you write me. Blaaat and sticking my tongue out, from Susanne.

TUESDAY, JUNE 13, 1939

The fifteenth anniversary of Johannes and Elfriede's engagement. Letter from Elfriede in Düsseldorf to Johannes in Philadelphia. She writes again that "Uncle Paul's old evilness has proven to be truly inhuman," referring to the actions of the Nazis, who increased their persecution of Jews throughout the spring of 1939, affecting many of Johannes and Elfriede's closest friends. In addition, the public schools had been transformed into centers of Nazi indoctrination, and parents were being pressured to enroll children Susanne's age in the Hitlerjugend *[Hitler Youth], an intolerable proposition for the Höbers. The understatement and circumspection of Elfriede's writing highlight her horror at what life had become under the Nazis.*

Düsseldorf, 13 June 1939, morning.

Mein liebstes Peterchen,

This is an especially good day for writing, and even though my time is very tight the *Europa* shouldn't leave without a letter from me.

Fifteen years is a long time; it actually makes up our whole adult life. Sometimes up, sometimes down, but in the end I can't imagine it being any other way. Today I'm thinking about all the positive things out of this whole time that had to be the way they were and that were so right. All the sad things we've faced are sort of like a trailing shadow that lends the proper contours to the bright side of things. Overall I can only say that it was right this way, it is right this way and presumably it will keep on being the right thing for the two of us. I think I would feel better if you were with me, today most of all.

I'm beginning to find it hard to bear things here. Yesterday, on Sunday, I fell into a deep, dark hole for the first time in these seven months and was totally overcome with despair, and it seemed to me that there would never, ever be a way to escape from all these things. Today it's better already, but not good yet. Getting the big things resolved is almost the easiest part, but all of the little junk I now have to deal with scares me. Don't be mad at me for writing this way but I want you to know that even I can't always be in good spirits, and these seven months have been a terrible test of nerves. I would like to go to bed and be sick and pull the blankets over my head so nobody can ask me for anything else. Or I'd like to close my eyes and have a carriage come and when I open my eyes I would be with you. But that's not the way it works, not in the least. Uncle Paul's old evilness has proven to be truly inhuman. I can still evade it somewhat, but in Susanne's case he's behaving in a way that's really ugly. But I'll stay on his back until I make him swallow all of that too. I'm beginning to realize that the hardest part of this year is still ahead of me and that my reserves of strength have been severely depleted.

I got a notice from the carrier in Gladbach that he's resigning as of 1 July, which was just what I needed. I hoped things had stabilized, but now he got a full-time job and you can't blame him for taking it. But everything was going so smoothly since I hired him.

Hilde has been here since Saturday and will stay until Thursday. She brings so much fuss and nervousness with her, but on the other hand she's really sweet and we have a lot to talk about. Her continued state of uncertainty, which has just been extended again, is no fun either. Sometimes it seems to us that we're supposed to ride into a tournament without armor and without weapons against an enemy in heavy armor, and you're completely helpless in defending yourself against pinpricks. No, it's not pretty in the least.

I was in Cologne again last night. Our Natalie [Freyberger] is home again and is doing well. And whom did she meet while lying on her bed of thorns? Nurse Maria, formerly Marianne Blaustein. After the latter heard that Natalie lives in Düsseldorf, she took a shot in the dark and asked whether she perhaps knew Johannes Höber? Mrs. Freyberger asked me to tell you that she is very disappointed in your taste. How could you possibly endure such a stupid person? Then Nurse Maria inquired as to whether it wouldn't be possible to arrange a meeting with me. I thought that was pretty funny. Well, *Peterchen*, you sure have had some funny affairs, and they keep on popping up all over the place. Right!??

Oh *Peterlein*, this letter isn't at all worthy of this day. And you might think this whining also isn't worthy of me either. But just dig around in your memory, and you'll realize that there are situations that just cause you to despair. By the way, don't worry about the "situation" here, but just think, as all the people around me do: she'll manage that too. Someone put it nicely to me by saying that if you can do it for seven months you can also do it for ten. But I'm very tired.

Alles Liebe Deine Friedel.

Handwritten postcript to the foregoing letter:

6/13/39
afternoon

Maybe things aren't so bad after all, when even the mail had pity on me and brought me your poem for the 13th right on time this afternoon. It makes me feel so good that it makes me want to cry, not out of sorrow but out of happiness that even from 5000 miles away there can be this kind of comfort and intimacy. Things will get better eventually. Hilde just sent me a beautiful vase of peonies with a note saying, "May he who is in America remember all the commotion as well as the 15th anniversary of your engagement." We'll drink a bottle of champagne to that sentiment tonight.

Thanks so much, *liebstes Peterchen.*

Friedel

TUESDAY, JUNE 13, 1939

Postcard from Johannes in Philadelphia to Rudolf and Josephine in Woods Hole, Massachusetts.

6/13/39

Ihr Lieben,

A letter just came from Friedel: she has been summoned to the consulate in Stuttgart on 11 July. I keep reminding myself that there can still be a thousand more delays, but this summons is the first and most important step. I just wrote her back, because now she'll probably be more impatient than at any time up to now.

In Liebe,

Euer Jo

FRIDAY, JUNE 16, 1939.

Letter from Elfriede in Düsseldorf to Johannes in Philadelphia. In this letter she refers to "Paolo," an alternate code for Uncle Paul, meaning the German authorities, from whom Elfriede had been seeking a new passport for over a month. See Elfriede's letter to Johannes of May 17, 1939. In fact, Elfriede did obtain a new joint passport for herself and Susanne on June 22, 1939, a week after this letter.

6/16/39

Liebes Peterchen,

Very quickly, because I have no time and lots of work. I just need to tell you quickly that I'm much better today than I was the day before yesterday. Hilde's gone again, and she brought a lot of uproar and nervousness. But she was very sweet, with lots of flowers and other nice things—she's been playing Santa Claus with graciousness and success. Whenever she's here we live sumptuously.

Paolo hasn't been able to resist my repeated visits—six so far—and it now looks like he's had second thoughts. We won't know until next week, however, what those second thoughts will look like. These visits take so much time, and old men are sometimes difficult. But for now I've gotten past the low point and I'm now on an upward trajectory. You will undoubtedly think it was excessive for me to write you so much whining, but that's the way I felt and I thought all my strength had completely abandoned me. I can't go into the details, but the double drama of the last few days would require a more gifted pen than mine.

To prop up my mood, I'm going away tomorrow through Monday. I feel a bit the way I often do when I've arranged something like this, that maybe I should stay here at home and not go out into the hostile world. But with my newly discovered love of North Germany I'm leaving tomorrow for Bremen. What happens after that is something I've left up to the others. If there's one thing I'm looking forward to, it's that I won't have to make any decisions for three days. If I enjoy it as much as I did the last time then it will be easier for me over the next few weeks. The weather doesn't look entirely certain; I'm hoping for a little sun and I'd love to go swimming. I think you won't begrudge me the pleasure and won't worry too much about my mental health. Mrs. Freyberger is coming this evening and will mind the office while I'm away.

Your chatty letter sent by the *Queen Mary*, which arrived after your airmail letter, made me feel good. As an obedient wife I wouldn't dream of contradicting your suggestion that I buy myself grey flannels. You'll like me in them.

I'm very anxious to hear how the Charter things proceed and I'm crossing all my fingers.

I'll be happy to write to Woods Hole. It's such a nice place and I like to think about it.

This letter is a little thin, but since I didn't leave much out of the last one I don't want you to worry about me too much. I'm as worn out as I've ever been, and tomorrow at noon I'll start resting up. When I get back there will undoubtedly be a *Columbus* letter here from you.

Alles Liebe Deine Friedel

MONDAY, JUNE 19, 1939

Letter from Elfriede to Johannes in Philadelphia. She was returning from a weekend driving trip with her brother and friends along the North Sea coast of Schleswig-Holstein.

6/19/39 On the train between Bremen and Düsseldorf

Mein liebes Peterchen,

The *Normandie* is leaving the day after tomorrow—this time I watched out and you shouldn't have to wait in vain for a letter because I was pursuing my private pleasures. That's why I'm writing somewhat shakily on the train, but I hope you'll be able to read it anyway. It was really a nice little vacation. I haven't read a paper for three days and now I'm on my way home well rested.

Do you know the town of St. Peter? I don't think so, but now I do. Wonderful beach, sun, I've got a pretty tan and was able to go swimming twice. You know how much I enjoy that. When I get out like this I realize how much I miss fresh air and sunshine and how much a car is essential to a comfortable life. When will we ever have one of our own again? Driving through the Holstein landscape in a car is charming, not to mention the moors. Getting stuck in the hidden gullies in the moors so that we couldn't get out without a shovel reminded me of our off-road driving. I'll always remember our drive up to the fortress at Bernkastel. I have a weakness for off-road cars and off-road drivers. After all, anybody can drive on the autobahn. And yesterday I encountered for the first time the nutritious and praiseworthy drink called egg grog. It consists mostly of eggs and rum, and if you have any rum or whisky there I won't hide the recipe from you—I made them explain it to me exactly. [Recipe: in a mug, beat an egg yolk with a tablespoon of sugar, then pour on 1/3 cup rum and 1/3 cup boiling water. Stir vigorously.] I could imagine you could make yourself popular with it over there, though not when it's 95 in the shade.

There was something else nice about the trip. We went through some of the places you and I went through in 1927. Do you know Friedrichstadt on the Eider, which looks as though you were in Flanders? Supposedly it was originally a Dutch settlement. Do you know the huge flat gravestones in the cemetery in Lunden? It isn't exactly a cemetery, but around the church, which is slightly elevated, is a large lawn on which these huge slabs lie, the gravestones of the farmer families of Dittmar. It was amazing how much this trip reminded me of the trip along the New England coast two years ago, though I'm not quite sure why that is. Maybe it's the low houses with the high fences around them, or maybe it's just that the green is so intense here even after six weeks without rain and got even more intense after a thunderstorm on Saturday. I just don't know, but that's what always happens to me on every trip in the country—it reminds me of one of our trips together. Your ears must have been burning. What am I going to talk about if it's not about you? You're my most fertile and worthwhile subject of conversation.

Here I am on the train writing you a cheerful travel account, far from the problems of our times. It's precisely that distance from the problems of our times that makes this trip feel so good, that just for once I'm away from the maelstrom of concerns and traveling with people who understand the whole situation here but who are sufficiently removed from it themselves that they don't have to talk about it all the time. That's what makes Hilde's visits such a strain, that we always end up talking incessantly about "it," so that in addition to your own problems you also have to live through those of the other person as well.

We're about to get to the Teutoburgerwald Tunnel, which means the industrial area is approaching literally at the speed of an express train. Vacationing in bits and pieces is OK, but I still need a real vacation. I'm looking forward to the sea voyage for that, if the fall storms don't mess it up and turn what should be a restful time into a long trial.

Now I have used up the third piece of paper. Your letter should be waiting for me at home, which I am looking forward to. But I still have to get this letter into the mailbox today.

Alles Liebe Deine Friedel.

Elfriede and Susanne's joint passport issued by the German government on June 22, 1939.

MONDAY, JULY 3, 1939

Letter from Johannes in Philadelphia to Elfriede in Düsseldorf. He wrote this letter and the next one on a Charter Committee typewriter, so he was able to make carbon copies. Johannes is responding to a letter from Elfriede (not preserved) that she wrote just after she got her new German passport. In that letter she apparently again expressed her anxiety about leaving Germany and moving to America. This was still a week before Elfriede was to appear at the American consulate in Stuttgart.

The vehemence of Johannes' letter demonstrates the depth of his concern, engendered both by his fear that war was imminent and by proposals in the U.S. Congress to cut off all immigration.

On the latter point, the Wagner-Rogers Bill was introduced by liberal Senator Robert F. Wagner of New York and Representative Edith Nourse Rogers of Massachusetts after Kristallnacht. *The Bill would have increased the German immigration quota—previously 27,000 annually—by 20,000 German children under 14. In Senate Committee hearings, the bill was opposed by veterans' groups, Southerners, isolationists, and outspoken anti-Semites. At hearings in June 1939, the Senate Committee amended the bill so the 20,000 children's visas would be provided by reducing the number of adult visas by the same number. Finding this amendment intolerable, Senator Wagner withdrew the bill. The Reynolds-Starnes Bill, introduced by Senator Robert R. Reynolds of South Carolina and Representative Joe Starnes of Alabama, would have cut all immigration visas by 90 percent. While neither of these bills was adopted and the pre-existing immigration quotas were unaffected, the hostility expressed in the Congressional debate raised great concern among those seeking to rescue refugees fleeing the Nazis.*[5]

The letter also discusses the plans Johannes and Elfriede still had to ship their belongings to America.

Phila 7/3/39

Liebster Peter,

By the time you get this letter, your initial anger about my cable on Friday will probably have subsided somewhat. I know you hate cables, and you shouldn't think I've forgotten that or that I've been infected by my family's cable mania. But since the Clipper isn't flying until Wednesday this week I had no other choice when your letter got here on Friday.

I'm still distraught today about your letter. I understood your first reaction to the summons from Uncle Karl only too well: all of a sudden it dawned on you that what you had been hoping for for months was suddenly facing you concretely with all its problems. I hope I've been able to make it clear to you how well I understood those reactions, although—why hide it?—I was somewhat saddened that your reactions were so vehement and so exclusively negative, because my reaction was exclusively one of joy. I also recognized your comments about September, October, and all sorts of other target dates as a kind of self-suggestion against getting your hopes up prematurely when so many preconditions are still unsettled. But your last letter is really inexplicable to me. Now that you're in the clear with Uncle Paul—and I marvel at the fact that you

5 For more information on the Wagner-Rogers bill and Congressional debates on admitting refugees see Richard Breitman and Alan M. Kraut, *American Refugee Policy and European Jewry, 1933–1945* (Bloomington: Indiana University Press, 1987), 232; Barbara McDonald Stewart, *United States Government Policy on Refugees from Nazism, 1933–1940* (New York: Garland Publishing, Inc., 1982), 495–545; David S. Wyman, *Paper Walls: America and the Refugee Crisis, 1938–1941* (Amherst: University of Massachusetts Press, 1968), 67–98.

got there so quickly—there's no longer any reason not to set the termination date as quickly as possible.[6]

There are a thousand reasons in favor of that. As soon as possible, you, Susie, and I need to get out of the unsettled status we've been living in for almost a year. You yourself wrote again and again that that status was unsatisfactory and thought it should be ended as quickly as possible. You really must begin to catch up with me here as soon as possible. The more I get ahead of you in language, acclimation, familiarization, and making friends, the harder it will be for you to get to the same place in all those things. So much for the subjective side of things. Now to the objective things. I don't need to tell you that things are rapidly heading in the direction of a repeat of the same situation that Gri and Manfred encountered.[7] You know as much about all of that as I do. What you may not know is that very dark clouds are beginning to appear on the horizon over here as well. On Friday, the Senate Committee on Immigration considered about 70 proposals and came up with a bill that would suspend all [immigration] quotas for a full five years. It's not certain that this bill will become law, but there are people who think it's entirely possible. This is not an attempt to panic you—I wish it were nothing more than that—and I don't know when such a law would take effect, but the mere fact that it got this far can't be taken seriously enough.

And now the counterarguments. You can't seriously mean that you have some long-term obligation to the managers at the *Frankfurter Zeitung*. They never wanted to give us anything on a long-term basis, and now it's up to them to make the best of their own timing problems. Has some recent act of generosity on their part caused you to forget how the overall situation with them was, is, and still should be evaluated?? Or do you mean something else by "phasing out?" Everything has been so carefully thought out, so psychically prepared over all these long years and months that now the mechanics just need to be allowed to roll out. I beseech you, *Peter*, now to find the determination to see that the question of the end date, in weeks and days, is the only important thing and that everything else is secondary.

Don't let your courage and energy drop off so dramatically all of a sudden. You'll only make it harder for yourself that way. Don't forget that you'll need plenty of fighting spirit in the future too. You can't use it all up by spreading out over months what you could accomplish in a few weeks. That would use up a lot more energy, not less. The next few years won't be any picnic for the three of us, but our reserves together will be a lot greater than the sum of the reserves each of us has separately.

6 "*In the clear with Uncle Paul . . .*" refers to the speed with which Elfriede obtained a new German passport and a police certificate of good conduct for the U.S. Consul.

7 "*The situation . . . that Gri and Manfred encountered*" refers to the postponement of Manfred and Gri's departure the previous September because of the Sudeten crisis. Here Johannes anticipated the increasing likelihood that war would prevent Elfriede's departure.

Maybe I don't have to tell you any of this. Maybe you just wrote the October end date the same way I try to tell people who ask me when you'll be here, "Christmas," so as to talk myself into not counting the days in my sleep and when I'm awake. Even with the greatest pessimism there's no need to assume that October will necessarily be the earliest possible end date.

I don't know how much advice I should give you on the concrete questions. Sometimes I think you can make much better judgments there on the spot, sometimes I think you would like to know my opinion on one thing or another instead of having to decide everything yourself. The questions relating to [shipping our] furniture have been going through my head during the last few days as we've been unpacking the second Tischendorf shipment.[8] My opinion: [ship] all of the bedroom and dining room, including both of the book cases from Kiel, the couch if it was reupholstered, the steel chairs, the Eschenbach cabinet and kitchen table, some of the bookcases depending on the number of books that will be going (I favor taking as many as possible) and finally the sewing machine and maybe a desk. Whether all that travels with you or after you is secondary and depends only on whether you can get it done by the time you would otherwise be traveling. Since things have been straightened out with the Kiel Savings and Loan I strongly recommend using Tischendorf again.

And now I can't wait for your answer to this letter. If you had all of your letters from the last year in front of you the way I do, you would be amazed to see the way what you have written since the 4th of June [the day you were summoned to Stuttgart] doesn't fit at all with everything else you've written all year long. Think about the last time we met in Basel, think about what it will be like when I'm on the pier waving to you when you arrive, think about the fact that there's a big house and a garden in Germantown waiting for you and lots of nice, kind people whom I've prepared in advance to meet you, and all the other things will become much easier because they are only the means to an end.

Sehr in Liebe

Dein Jo

MONDAY, JULY 3, 1939

Letter from Johannes in Philadelphia to Rudolf and Josephine in Woods Hole, Massachusetts. Part of the letter concerns Rudolf and Josephine's furniture, which arrived a few days earlier.

8 The shipment of Rudolf and Josephine's furniture from Kiel, which had been the subject of so much aggravation with both the German banking and foreign exchange authorities and the Tischendorf shipping company, had finally arrived at the house on Cresheim Road.

Phila, 7/3/39

Ihr Lieben,

It is Monday between Sunday and a Tuesday holiday and I'm in in a dead quiet office occupied only by three men and a secretary. Gruenberg left for vacation on Saturday, when I was off because I'm on duty today. He didn't say anything before he left about what will happen after 8 July, so I optimistically assume [my job] will continue as it has up to now.

Gri and I divided our weekend between furniture and the children. Gri had arranged for a young man to come Saturday afternoon and with his help we hauled boxes that we unpacked and then repacked with things we couldn't place—mostly books—down to the cellar and hauled up things that inadvertently ended up down there [when the shipment first arrived] on Thursday. Now there's a light at the end of the tunnel, and the house looks even better than before. Your den looks excellent with the two desks, the cabinet, three bookcases, and the red leather sofa. The glass-fronted cabinet has been moved from your den down into the dining room. Filled with our nicest china, it has become a really beautiful decorative piece. I think the porch almost the nicest thing, where the table that used to be in my room is surrounded by the wicker chairs and in the back yard is all the nice white furniture. Both of these sets together cry out for a garden party. How about having one for 40 people to celebrate Elfriede's arrival?

On Friday we went to the theater—"Prelude to Swing"—at the Walnut Theater, a history of Negro music presented in music and dance by a troupe from the WPA Federal Theater, which has subsequently been killed by Congress. A really charming evening.

I'm spending a lot of time these days with Walter Phillips and Eleanor Davis in connection with a new project we are cooking up: a "good municipal government" movie, made under the direction of the Charter Committee, to be used in part in the election campaign in the fall and in part later for educating parent-teacher groups, clubs, organizations, schools, etc. Saturday Eleanor and I looked at samples of similar films at a movie company and worked on the strategy for a meeting with people who are important for financing the project. In short, we are working on figuring out new assignments for the Charter Committee.

Ulli is terribly busy. She's on duty two weekends in a row because she's chief resident now.

Rudolf, Ursula (in driver's seat), and Josephine at the Nobska Point Lighthouse near the Marine Biological Laboratory, Woods Hole, Massachusetts. In the summers, when classes were not in session at the University of Pennsylvania, Rudolf and Josephine conducted physiological research at Woods Hole.

There has been almost no mail for you, and what little there has been we take care of. I pay any bills right away. On Saturday a registered letter came from Hannah Winkler. She is supposed to submit her application [for an American visa] and asked for a new affidavit of support. We sent a letter holding things off a bit. I think you could give her the affidavit, but only after Elfriede and Susie actually have their visas. In my opinion this caution is necessary because Hannah is also within Stuttgart's jurisdiction.[9]

On Friday the good news arrived from Elfriede that she and Susie had gotten new passports valid for one year. Elfriede apparently was at first very concerned about whether she would get it. Thank God that has been gotten through. With that they at least have the ability to go to Zürich if it becomes absolutely necessary.[10]

We were happy to get both of your letters written on Sunday morning, but we are not, repeat not, in agreement with the way you are still driving yourselves so hard. Can't you do things just a little slower, as so many others do? Shouldn't you maybe have a real vacation at some point between Woods Hole and Cresheim Road? We worry that after the last year you really need some thorough relaxation time and don't think you'll get that by being here in August. If you insist on being here, then I think it would be nice if we three grownups take care of the house and the baby together and when I come home in the evenings I would alternately take Pa or Mu out for an excursion for an hour or two and

9 Hannah Winkler was a second cousin of Johannes living in Offenbach, Germany. With the crush of Germans seeking American visas, and with Rudolf's ability to give affidavits of support overextended, Johannes wanted to wait until after Elfriede's interview with the American Consul in Stuttgart on July 11 before bringing this new matter to the American authorities. Rudolf did eventually provide an affidavit of support, and Hannah got to the United States before the war.

10 Johannes and Elfriede's backup plan was that if Elfriede did not get her American visa before war broke out, she would go to Switzerland and try to complete the visa application process there.

sometimes we could treat ourselves to a babysitter and all go off together.

So long,

Jo

P.S. I almost forgot to tell you that Gri came back quite pleased from her job interview on Saturday. She'll get the final word on Wednesday. The poor thing worked for three days well into the night to prepare.

CHAPTER 11

Getting Out, Part II

Elfriede wrote to Johannes on June 4, 1939 that she had been summoned to the American Consulate in Stuttgart on Tuesday, July 11. This meant the paperwork Elfriede and Johannes submitted was sufficient to support Elfriede's visa application. The step that remained was for Elfriede and Susanne to be interviewed at the Consulate and examined to ensure both were healthy. Earlier letters indicate that Susanne had some kind of heart ailment and had hepatitis the previous December. She also came down with a cold a week before the examination. There was, therefore, some reason to worry about this last step. Waiting for the appointment was an anxious time.

WEDNESDAY, JULY 5, 1939

Letter from Elfriede written on the train between Düsseldorf and Krefeld to Rudolf and Josephine in Woods Hole, Massachusetts.

7/5/39

Ihr Lieben,

I have to make use of this train trip if I'm going to fit a letter to you in with everything else. I'm on my way to Krefeld, and if I get to Gladbach this evening then I will have made five different trips like this in five days.

Thanks for your letter, which arrived today and brought back nice memories of dear old Woods Hole. That place is so pretty and pleasant and it's not right for you to abuse it by working. The work you do there (even if it's a lot more meaningful and productive than the work most people do) is really an inappropriate use of your time there. Unfortunately I have my doubts that you'll ever learn the wisdom of the old saying that you can overdo things.

On Sunday I'm heading for Frankfurt and Stuttgart. I have to be there very early on Tuesday and would have had to travel on Monday anyway, so we thought it would be nicer to go already on Sunday and spend Monday driving around Swabia between Heidelberg and Stuttgart, which we love so much and which isn't like anyplace else in the world. At the moment I'm being visited by Hilde Lenzberg, who is leaving for South America on 7/29. I will meet up with her and her son (and her car) on Sunday [July 9] afternoon in Frankfurt, and then we'll spend the next two days wandering around the area. In the meantime our nice and truly irreplaceable Mrs. Freyberger will substitute for me here [in Düsseldorf]. Without people like her it would be impossible to imagine the last few months. I'll go back on Wednesday the 12th. I'm not worried about anything going wrong there, and I hope that the cold Susanne came down with this morning is nothing more than a cold.

[Later.]
Now I'm on my way back from Krefeld, and I'm replacing lunch with a stalwart demeanor and a glass of lemonade. It's so hot that eating is just as uncalled-for as working. I'm quite anxious to see how things will go from here on in. I am tired of this in-between status and have a great need for a normal and stable environment. Somehow it seems to me that our life has been provisional for the last ten years, and that's quite enough. Let's just hope that higher powers don't decide to spit in our soup. In such circumstances, Susanne always says, "If I were the Empress of the World . . . ." Unfortunately we're not!

Be well and best wishes from

Eurer Friedel

The trip from Düsseldorf to Stuttgart was over 400 kilometers, so it required an overnight stay, and Elfriede made it a leisurely trip. On Sunday, July 9, she and Susanne took the train to Frankfurt, where Hilde Lenzberg picked them up and drove them to Maulbronn. They stayed overnight in Maulbronn, where Hilde's father was a schoolmaster, and spent Monday touring the countryside around Maulbronn. Early Tuesday morning, Hilde drove Elfriede and Susanne into Stuttgart, about an hour away, and to the American Consulate there.

Decades later, Susanne was still able to recall the physical examination vividly and understood its significance, even as a nine-year-old. She and Elfriede were led into a large, noisy hall filled with women and children waiting to be examined by the doctors there. She was upset at being told she had to undress in public, in front of all the people in the room. There were a few screens, but they afforded little privacy. Elfriede comforted her and told her to be brave and helped Susanne understand this was something she had to do. Elfriede was good at giving her courage. Susanne undressed (top only, she said) and was examined by a doctor who spoke English. Very near where she and Elfriede waited and were examined, another mother and daughter suddenly burst into loud and bitter weeping because they were told they did not pass the examination and would not get visas. Though just a young girl, Susanne understood that this was a terrible thing to happen. Though they did not know it then, for most the denial of a visa was a death sentence.

TUESDAY, JULY 11, 1939

Entries in the single German passport issued to Elfriede and valid for both her and Susanne. The entries, made with a rubber stamp and the blanks filled in in ink, were the anxiously sought permits that would allow Elfriede and Susanne to escape from Germany to America.

~~Nonquota~~ Immigration Visa
Quota No. **608**
Dated JUL 11 1939
Issued to *K.S. Elfriede F. Hoeber*
(Name)
[signed] *Boies C. Hart Jr.*
Boies C. Hart, Jr.
American Vice Consul at Stuttgart, Germany
IMMIGRANT IDENTIFICATION CARD
No. *1083233* Issued

~~Nonquota~~ Immigration Visa
Quota No. **609**
Dated JUL 11 1939
Issued to *Susanne K. J. Hoeber*
(Name)
[signed] *Boies C. Hart Jr.*
Boies C. Hart, Jr.
American Vice Consul at Stuttgart, Germany
IMMIGRANT IDENTIFICATION CARD
No. *1083234* Issued

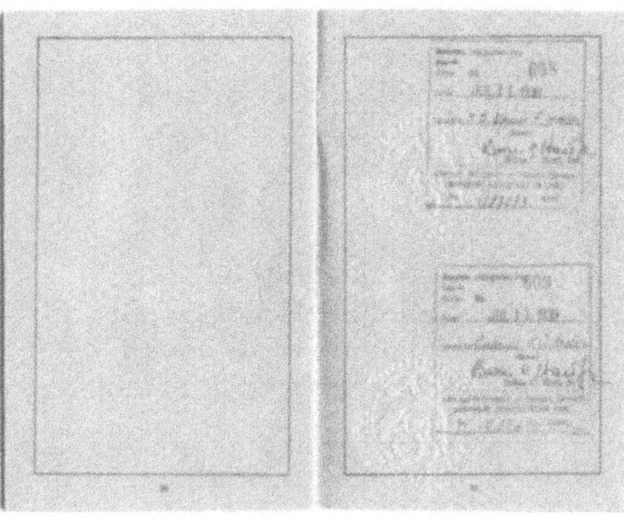

Page from Elfriede and Susanne's joint passport showing the immigration visa stamps for each of them, July 12, 1939.

TUESDAY, JULY 11, 1939

Postcard from Johannes in Philadelphia to Rudolf and Josephine in Woods Hole, Massachusetts.

7/11/39

Ihr Lieben,

Gri just called me in the office and read the following telegram from Stuttgart: "Got it. We're happy." Despite the fact that my desk is still overloaded with mail that has to go out before 5, I must dash this postcard off quickly so that you can be happy along with us as quickly as possible.

Thank God that we've gotten this far. Now they will get over the rest of the hurdles quicker and more easily.

Euer glücklich und dankbarer Jo
[Your happy and thankful Jo]

After receiving her American visa, Elfriede began serious preparations for her departure from Germany. These preparations included purchasing passage for herself and Susanne, transferring the newspaper business to the successor selected by Dr. Betz, and packing up the household belongings for shipment. While all these preparations were underway, Elfriede arranged for Susanne to stay for several weeks at her family's farm in the village of Küingdorf in Westphalia.

SUNDAY, AUGUST 6, 1939

Letter from Susanne at the Fischer family farm in Küingdorf in Westphalia to Johannes in Philadelphia. The farm belonged to August Fischer and Alwine Fischer, unmarried siblings of Elfriede's father. Other relatives lived there occasionally as well, and Susanne often visited over summer vacations. The Fischer farm's main product was pork, and the adjacent fields of grain produced feed for the animals. Behind the main farm land was a well-tended forest on a hill, whose cool shade and icy springs were a favorite in summertime. The large eighteenth-century farmhouse included a barn for some thirty pigs and their feed, work horses, farm equipment, the family's living quarters, a small Bierstube *patronized by the local farmers, and a tiny grocery store and post office. At age nine, Susanne occasionally served beer to patrons in the* Bierstube.

This letter included a little paper folder of pressed flowers.

8/6/1939

Lieber Papi.

Since today is Sunday and Annemarie and Tea Schulte are going to the movies I didn't know what I should do. So I borrowed paper from Mieken and I'm writing to you. But now I have to stop already because I'm going up the mountain with Aunt Berta to see if the oats are ripe yet. We'll probably harvest them on Tuesday. Our little pussycats are sweet (but not housebroken) and have fleas too, unfortunately. The creek that runs through the farm overran the meadow even though it [normally] is only as wide as our house door in Düsseldorf.

[Later.] It was very nice in the forest just now. I climbed up on Uncle August's high seat [on the wagon]. Then we rode on the bike for a while and it was all uphill but then it was downhill. Hey, the radio's hissing, must be storm interference. Oh, now it's working again and it's pretty, but then the storm interference doesn't stop and it's awful. Uncle August has the *Bierstube* full of cheerful people again, haha. Hey, if you built a café or a hotel up on the mountain in the clearing with the nice view, then you would have a whole hotel or café full of cheerful people, because what you see there is so beautiful. Since I can't figure out from here when the ships go, I'm afraid that you'll get this letter at the same time you get the card that I wrote about 3 days ago. I sometimes work in the *Bierstube* and pour beer for the customers. Since I've been here, Uncle August shot a buck. The pressed flowers I'm sending are pea flowers and bean flowers. Well, I don't know what else to write so I'll close this letter.

Viele 1000000000 O O O O O und Grüße von Susa

P.S. Write soon. Aunt Alwine, Uncle August, Annemarie, Aunt Berta, and Lottchen send their greetings.

WEDNESDAY, AUGUST 9, 1939

Letter from Elfriede to the Düsseldorf branch of the Foreign Exchange Control Office.

*In deciding how to handle their permanent relocation to the United States, Elfriede and Johannes had to take into account the provisions of the taxes placed on emigrants. These included the "Reich Abandonment Tax" and the "German Gold Discount Bank Levy." Under the latter law, all property transferred out of Germany was subject to a 90 percent tax. The exception was that emigrants were permitted to take, free of taxes, personal belongings that were essential for establishing a modest existence [*Bescheidende Existenz*] in the foreign country. To ensure that taxable property had not been converted into luxury goods to evade the Discount Bank Levy, departing emigrants were required to file a detailed inventory of items to be shipped and the value of any items purchased after 1933. The level of detail in the attached inventory of Johannes and Elfriede's possessions—down to the number of dust rags they had—was required by German regulations. Beginning in May 1938, personal belongings to be shipped abroad had to be packed in the presence of customs officials.*

Düsseldorf, 9th August

Pempelforterstr. 11.

To:
Foreign Exchange Control Office
D ü s s e l d o r f

For your information I wish to make the following remarks in connection with the attached application for permission to move personal effects to the USA.

We married on 12/22/1928 and acquired our set of household furnishings in the course of the year 1929. Since 1929 we have always occupied an apartment of 4 rooms and a kitchen.

The acquisition of replacement pieces was necessary only in small quantities for household linens. Our stock of clothing has been largely replaced since 1933 in the natural course of things.

We have not acquired anything specifically for our emigration. Our furnishings and our linens are adequate. We are not taking all of our furnishings with us. We have no financial assets and have always lived on the income from our work, from which we have accumulated a small amount of savings. The acquisition of clothing in the last year has been at the same level of necessity as in prior years.

[*signed*] Höber

Enclosure transmitted with the letter above:

Inventory of Personal Effects

Means of shipment: Shipping crate

Dr. Johannes Höber, Düsseldorf Pempelforterstr. 11

Dining Room
1 Buffet
1 Table with table cloth
6 Chairs
1 Sideboard
1 Cupboard
1 Tea wagon
1 Standing lamp
1 Wool rug
1 Net curtain with valance

Living Room
1 Couch
1 Small table
4 Armchairs
1 Desk
9 Sofa pillows
6 Bookcases
2 Standing lamps
1 Wool rug
1 Small velour rug
1 Pen holder
1 Postal scale
1 Letter basket
Writing utensils
1 Stool
2 Waste baskets

Bedroom
2 Beds (complete)
1 Couch
2 Night tables
2 Cupboards
1 Dressing table
1 Chest of drawers
2 Bedside rugs
2 Straw mats
2 Stools
2 Night table lamps
1 Net curtain with valance
1 Quilt
1 Pillow
1 Wool blanket
1 Duvet

Kitchen
1 Cupboard
1 Table

2 Chairs
1 Laundry basket
1 Trash can
Clothesline and clothespins
Cooking utensils
1 Ironing board
1 Sleeve board
3 Trays
1 Toaster
1 Iron

Dishes

1 Set dining dishes for 12 people
1 Set coffee dishes for 12 people
1 Set tea dishes for 12 people
1 Nickel silver tray
1 Soup tureen
1 Watering can
1 Wooden tray
1 Brass tray
1 Copper bowl
3 Straw baskets
1 Teapot
1 Tea container
5 Pottery jugs
1 Honey jar
1 Cookie jar
12 Flower vases
5 Flower pots
3 Candle holders
2 Wall sconces
2 Cigarette boxes
1 Thermos bottle
1 Sugar bowl
12 Wine glasses
12 Champagne glasses
12 Beer glasses
12 Punch glasses
12 Liqueur glasses
14 Demitasse cups
18 Water glasses
20 Glass plates
6 Shell plates
2 Fruit bowls
8 Glass bowls
12 Miniature glass plates
12 Ashtrays
2 Sardine boxes
7 Coasters
6 Tile hotplates
1 Chinese porcelain bowl, chipped

Flatware

12 Lg. spoons
12 Med. spoons
12 Teaspoons
12 Egg spoons
1 Ladle
3 Serving spoons
1 Cake server
1 Salad set
12 Lg. knives (silver)
12 Sm. knives
9 Fruit knives
1 Sugar spoon
1 Nutcracker
1 Pusher
1 Poultry shears
8 Bottle corks
1 Tea strainer
1 Bowl

Silverware

1 Breadbasket
1 Cookie dish
2 Ashtrays
1 Sm. Bowl
1 Egg cup w/ spoon
1 Napkin ring

Linens

20 Bedsheets
3 Bedspreads
14 Duvet covers
12 Pillowcases
1 Bath towel

18 Hand towels
18 Turkish towels
6 Kitchen towels
6 Glass towels
6 Washcloths
6 Dustcloths
6 Soap cloths
10 Table cloths
24 Napkins
8 Coffee table covers
30 Coffee napkins
Misc. doilies + sm. table covers

Miscellaneous
1 Sewing Machine
1 Lounge chair
1 Garden umbrella

4 Lamps
2 Mirrors
2 Pairs skis
2 Pairs ski boots
2 Pairs climbing boots
2 Pairs brogues
2 Sking outfits
1 Climbing trousers
1 Rucksack
1 Picnic basket with contents
1 Carton curtain remnants
1 Carton w/ misc. mending materials
Misc. children's games
1 Box w/ left over wool
1 Satchel

Linen acquired after 1933 (to replace used objects)

½ Doz. hand towels	7.20	1934
1 Doz. kitchen towels	9.60	1935
2 Coffee table covers (one handmade)	8.—	1936
12 Coffee napkins handmade	6.—	1936

Books etc.
Ca. 800 books on economics, art history, and aesthetics
Ca. 100 children's books
Ca. 40 art portfolios
Ca. 25 art prints
1 Sm. engraving (Heidelberg)
1 Sm. engraving (Mannheim)
1 Sm. engraving (Freiburg)
1 Drawing (London)
1 Plaster relief
1 Sm. plaster figure

Atlantic travel began to be difficult already in August 1939, before the war began. Elfriede got preliminary authority to leave Germany on August 22, but the next scheduled liner, the German ship *Hansa* of the Hamburg America Line, was cancelled.

Friday, September 1, 1939: Many years later, Susanne still remembered sitting in the quiet living room at the Küingdorf farm on the first day of September. She was reading, away from the bustle of the work of the farm, listening to the radio while she read. Her reading was interrupted by the report on the radio that German troops had crossed the Polish border. Even as a nine-year-old she understood that this was an exceedingly important happening, Susanne ran to tell Uncle August and Aunt Alwine the news. She knew that something was occurring that would have an impact on her and everyone in her family.

Two days later, on September 3, in response to Hitler's invasion of Poland, England and France declared war on Germany.

In the first week of September, Elfriede arranged with the Jonen Moving and Storage firm in Düsseldorf to come to the apartment on Pempelforterstrasse and pack all the household furnishings listed on the inventory above. Her original plan was to ship these goods to Philadelphia, but the start of the war made that impossible. As a result, Elfriede contracted with Jonen to crate the things, place them in their warehouse, and ship them to Philadelphia "as soon as there was an opportunity to do so." She paid them RM 2200, more than half a year's income, in advance for packing, storage, and eventual shipment.

TUESDAY, SEPTEMBER 5, 1939

Letter from Johannes in Philadelphia to Elfriede in Düsseldorf

---

Philadelphia, 9/5/39.

Liebes Friedelkind,

As soon as your letters of the 24th and 28th of August arrived today, I went to the local office of the Holland-America Line here and booked passage for you and Susie on the *Nieuw Amsterdam*, which leaves from Rotterdam on the 15th of September. We don't know yet whether there's enough room for you on that ship. If there is, you will be notified of that fact either directly from Rotterdam or from this line's agents either in Düsseldorf or Cologne. If you're not able to reach the ship or if it should already be sold out, you have to try to rebook on to the *Statendam* that leaves 11 days later. The passage is 3rd Class, but third class on these boats should be decent and we can't possibly afford Tourist Class.

I don't have to tell you that we will be following you in our thoughts every step of the way. There are a lot of other things that I don't have to tell you either.

In liebe, Jo

Johannes was fortunate in purchasing the tickets on September 5, because the next day the Holland-America Line issued an announcement that

"Effective as of Sept. 6, 1939, all trans-Atlantic fares ... are subject to a surcharge of 40 per cent because of increased operating costs resulting from the present European conflict."

By the time the Holland-America Line cabled its Cologne affiliate of Johannes' purchase of the tickets, passage was no longer available on the *Nieuw Amsterdam*, so on September 11 the Cologne shipping agent notified Elfriede that she and Susanne had been booked for passage on the *Veendam* leaving from Antwerp on September 23.

The *Veendam* turned out not to be a fortunate choice. As noted above, as soon as war was declared, ocean travel became extremely dangerous as the German Navy began attacking British naval vessels. The first major naval battle took place on September 17, twelve days after Johannes bought the *Veendam* tickets, and the *Veendam* was involved. On that day, the British aircraft carrier *HMS Courageous* was on submarine patrol in the Atlantic west of Ireland. It was struck by torpedoes from the German submarine U-29 and sank. 518 British sailors were killed, but over 700 survivors were picked up by the *Veendam* and by British warships. In the meantime, however, Elfriede continued to finalize her departure.

THURSDAY, SEPTEMBER 14, 1939

Exit permit entered in Elfriede and Susanne's German passport by the police authorities in Düsseldorf.

No. *1926* Fee *8,—*

ENDORSEMENT

For *Dr. Elfriede Höber and one child*

(Name of Holder)

For a one-time departure from and return to the Reich territory by means of every officially recognized German border crossing.

This endorsement may be used for border crossing until and including *1 October 1939*.

Düsseldorf, *14 Sep. 1939*

POLICE SUPERINTENDENT

By authorization:

Freuntag

(Signature)

[SEAL]

WEDNESDAY, SEPTEMBER 20, 1939

Letter from Elfriede in Düsseldorf to the Business Management Office of the Frankfurter Zeitung, *just two days before she left Germany. In this letter, Elfriede communicated the final settlement of her accounts for the business.*

Düsseldorf, 20 September 1939

Pempelforterstr 11

TO:

Business Manager
Frankfurter Societäts-Druckerei
Frankfurt/Main

Gentlemen:

In accordance with my conversation with Dr. Betz this morning, I am transmitting to you herewith my final business accounting. It concludes with a balance in your favor of RM 173.26, for which I enclose a postal money order made out to you.

Allow me to add the following details:

For the authority for my deduction of the account receivable for Espenlaub, please refer to my letter to the Advertising Department dated 9/12/39 and for the account receivable for Grosse to my letter dated today to the Business Office.

For my employment by the *Frankfurter Zeitung*, which was full time from 9/1/39 until 9/15 and thereafter in a consultant capacity, I have deducted RM 190 pursuant to my agreement with Dr. Betz.

Thank you for the letter of recommendation for my husband, which I received today. At the end of six years of employment with the *Frankfurter Zeitung* I feel I must say that my husband and I both look back on these years as a time of agreeable and productive work.

Sincerely yours,

Elfriede Fischer Hoeber

A small smudged stamp mark in Elfriede and Susanne's German passport indicates they exited Germany Friday, September 22, 1939 and entered Belgium at the border crossing at Aachen, the last German city Elfriede and Susanne saw on their way out of the country. Five years and one month later, Aachen would be the first Germany city American troops would see as they entered the country on October 21, 1944.

The train took Elfriede and Susanne to Antwerp.

They had gotten out of Germany, but they were still not safe. When they arrived in Antwerp, Elfriede and Susanne were booked for passage on the *Veendam* leaving the next day. But it didn't leave. The fear of attack at sea had disrupted all ocean travel and shipping schedules, and the prospect of taking a ship across the Atlantic in wartime was terrifying. So they waited.

Living in Antwerp in the meantime was problematic. German emigration laws allowed Elfriede to take only RM 20 in cash (less than $10) out of Germany, so she and Susanne had to rely on money wired from America for living expenses while they were waiting for a ship. Susanne remembered many years later that when they first arrived, money seemed quite plentiful, but as their departure got delayed again and again the money got tight. Rudolf and Johannes wired Elfriede money from the United States via the Holland America Line office in Rotterdam, which then transmitted the money to the Antwerp office, where Elfriede picked it up. Money was also tight for the Höber family in Philadelphia, however, so Elfriede and Susanne had to live sparingly.

At first they stayed in a nice hotel, and Elfriede was in good spirits. In those early days, they enjoyed visiting Antwerp's museums and exploring the city. Later, despite Belgium's neutrality, the museums put their pictures in storage and closed because of the danger of war. When Elfriede and Susanne couldn't visit museums anymore, life became boring and tedious. As the days and weeks wore on, their small reserve of funds dwindled. Susanne passed the time somewhat by reading—she particularly treasured a book Oma Clara gave her about a young girl traveling in America—but she couldn't read all the time. The wait dragged on.

Every morning Elfriede and Susanne went to the shipping office to find out if they could get tickets for passage on any ship. Susanne remembers the atmosphere as wild and chaotic, both inside the office and outside, where there was a kind of service window facing the street. They held tickets on the *Veendam*, but its departure was postponed again and again, and it was only on October 13 that its departure date was fixed—this time for October 28.

Elfriede and Susanne moved several times during the weeks they were in Antwerp, with the hotels getting worse and smaller each time they moved. A particularly bad room was infested with mice that kept Susanne awake at night.

Once they became "poor" (Susanne's word), they ate only at cheap restaurants. She remembered a facility resembling a cafeteria in the basement of something like a 5-and-10-cent store. One evening, Elfriede and Susanne misunderstood the wording on the menu—their knowledge of Flemish was limited—and mistakenly ordered boiled eel with some kind of green vegetable. Neither Elfriede nor Susanne could stomach it, and not having the money to order a second meal, they went hungry that night.

As indicated in the following letter—the last in the series—Elfriede was finally able on October 15 to exchange her *Veendam* ticket for a cabin on the *Westernland*, scheduled to leave on October 23.

In later life, Elfriede remembered the weeks in Antwerp as full of dread and boredom—and fear that they would never get out. She swore that she would never go back to Antwerp. And although she later traveled to more than sixty countries and even returned to Germany several times, she never returned to Antwerp.

MONDAY, OCTOBER 16, 1939

Letter from Elfriede in Antwerp to Johannes in Philadelphia (postmarked October 17). One point covered is Elfriede's handling of a remittance from Johannes for living expenses in Antwerp. Johannes deposited money with the Holland America Line office in Philadelphia for Elfriede and Susanne, since they could take only RM *20 out of Germany. Holland America's European office was in Rotterdam, and the Rotterdam office sent the $22.50 to Elfriede in Antwerp. As the result of a bookkeeping error, the Rotterdam office sent Elfriede the money a second time, and Elfriede returned that payment. Elfriede believed her honesty disposed the company to give her preference when selling tickets on the* Westernland. *This preference was of incalculable importance.*

Antwerp, 16 October 1939

Lieber Peter,

On Saturday [October 14] it was said that you could still get 1st class places on the *Statendam* leaving Rotterdam on the 22nd. After I thought about it, and even telephoned Mother [in Düsseldorf] on Saturday night, I decided to do that and to cable you again today for $100 if it turned out to be true. But this morning (really early this time, at 9 A.M.) when I went my usual way [to the shipping office], there was a phone call from Rotterdam that the *Westernland*, which actually was supposed to leave 8 days after the *Veendam*, had been released from that route and that she would sail on the 23, that is, a week from today. In the course of the morning they announced that the release of the *Veendam* in the next few days was sufficiently certain that the line confirmed the 28th as the departure date. Now I happened to have heard the previous week that additional places were going to be sold for the *Westernland*, so I went to the office at 2 P.M. when it opened again and was completely empty, and I managed to work it out so that we now have two places on the *Westernland*.

Many people wanted the same thing, of course, but I had had the opportunity to make myself popular when the $22.50 that you sent me and that I got paid out on our first day here was paid out a second time. That is to say, it was transmitted twice from Rotterdam [but I didn't take it and told them it was a mistake]. Today I got a letter from Rotterdam in which the line thanked me for my thoughtfulness. I had already told the man this morning that he should make a reservation for me on the *Westernland*, but none of the many others who were trying for the same thing have gotten it up to now. I am now very pleased, 1st finally to see the end of this idiotic waiting time, 2nd to get out of here five days before the *Veendam*. How did I manage that? The *Westernland* is a single-class ship, so I didn't have to pay a surcharge. I'm not clear whether the line might have cheated me out of a couple of dollars, but such a miniscule amount doesn't really make a difference. I didn't say or ask anything [about the price] and I'm happy with my ticket, which says it's for the *Westernland*, Cabin B-53. Unfortunately it's an inside cabin, but by then it was all the same to me. When the *Westernland* arrives [from Rotterdam] and is actually here at the pier, I will cable you again so I don't end up standing alone with my ten suitcases at the pier in New York. I'm going to be careful with the remaining money, and I hope I can even bring some of it back to you. For your information, of the money you deposited for me I received $22.50 in cash in addition to the 182 dollars and some cents that were charged for the ticket. I paid $117 in RM [*Reichmarks*] in Cologne. If you deposited more than that, see to it that you get it back. It is indeed a pile of money that this has already cost all of you, but I didn't start this war.

How have things been with you all these weeks? At this point I've heard almost nothing about you for two months, but now it seems like we'll actually get out of here and get to you. I hope we don't run into any disaster other than seasickness on the way, because as Paul aptly noted, you can take Vasano for seasickness but for torpedoes you can only take a lifeboat. To tell the truth, I'm not really very worried about the torpedoes. When cautious people at home asked me whether I wanted to risk the transatlantic trip at this time, I just answered that it was pretty much the same whether a bomb fell on my head in Düsseldorf or a torpedo hit some other part of my body on the ocean. On the other hand, a bomb shelter is warmer than the ocean in October.

The charms of Antwerp do not improve with time. Either the weather is clear, and then it's cold, or it's warm, in which case it rains. And it's not pretty when you have to put on wet shoes again because you don't have any others to change into. My cold isn't entirely gone yet, but it's not bad. Instead of that I now have a backache today, with which I can't walk, stand, sit or lie down. It's not pretty. I'll be happy if I never return to Antwerp again, even if the museums are open. It's really nice that a tragic event like this departure has been turned into a complete farce by this stupid waiting. You can't just keep on saying goodbye for weeks—so Mother gets a postcard every day (she always sends a card in return) and otherwise I write almost nothing other than the weekly letter to you.

In the meantime, the birthday time[1] has arrived at your end. I had forgotten about it because I've been living horribly detached from time and place, in an ugly unreality. Herbert wrote me a postcard before his birthday—which was evidently celebrated with the whole family following the old tradition—and said that only we, the salt of the Düsseldorf earth, were missing. What is the source of the expression, "You are the salt of the earth?" I'm really falling apart here. I do nothing, read nothing other than newspapers and that isn't always much fun.

If heaven and assorted Führers don't spit in our soup again, we'll be with you in a couple of weeks.

Alles liebe Deine Friedel

Although this letter indicates the *Westernland* was scheduled to leave Antwerp on October 23, it was again delayed and did not leave until October 28. But the Atlantic voyage was mercifully safe and uneventful.

On Sunday, November 5, 1939, Elfriede and Susanne arrived in New York and were greeted by Johannes, who came to the pier alone. Like millions of refugees before them, and like millions since, the Höbers were finally safe in America.

1 *Birthday time*: most of Johannes' family's birthdays fell in October.

Visiting the Phillipses was one of the first priorities for Johannes and Elfriede after Elfriede and Susanne arrived in America. Mary Phillips took this picture of Walter, Mary's brother Frank, Susanne, Johannes and Elfriede at the Phillips' farm in Bucks County, just outside of Philadelphia.

EPILOGUE

A Family in America

Johannes and Elfriede and Susanne were reunited in New York City on November 5, 1939. They were safe and could begin a new life. But it would not be easy.

Elfriede found it difficult to settle into the communal Höber house on Cresheim Road. She liked Rudolf and got on well with Gri and Manfred, but Elfriede and Josephine were both strong-willed, intelligent women whose very different personal styles were bound to clash. Within a few months Johannes and Elfriede moved into a tiny apartment of their own on Wayne Avenue, not far from Creshiem Road. Susanne was enrolled in the local public school and made the transition with surprising ease. The school started by placing her in first grade and moving her up every couple of months as her English caught up with each grade level. Within a few months she was in the fourth grade, where she belonged. Elfriede was pleased when the teacher told her Susanne's only problem was that she was rather too talkative—in English.

Johannes' fortunes with his work remained bumpy for years. The Charter Committee's role became superfluous when the State Legislature adjourned without taking action on the city charter. Johannes held on as a staff member until November 1939, when the Committee closed its doors. By that time he had succeeded in publishing an article analyzing the failed Philadelphia charter fight in the *National Municipal Review*, a respected professional journal with a nationwide audience.

When the Charter Committee shut down, Stephen Sweeney took Johannes on at the Fels Institute for Local and State Government at the University of Pennsylvania. He worked there for a year and then secured the position of public affairs director for the Philadelphia Housing Authority, the first of several jobs with social service agencies that enabled Johannes to support the family—modestly—through the 1940s. During a six-month period of unemployment in 1942, Walter and Mary Phillips lent Johannes and Elfriede enough money to live on. Johannes repaid the loan with a $1,000 prize he won in a newspaper contest for the best essay on "a great American" (Johannes chose President Franklin D. Roosevelt).

In 1941, Johannes and Elfriede had their second child, Thomas Rudolf, and in 1942 a third, Francis Walter (for Walter Phillips). Susanne grew into a brilliant student like her mother. In 1947 she was valedictorian at Cheltenham High School before going off to Sarah Lawrence College on a full scholarship.

Reprinted from the NATIONAL MUNICIPAL REVIEW, Vol. XXVIII, No. 9, September, 1939

Philadelphia Carries On

By JOHANNES U. HOEBER

Philadelphia City Charter Committee

Committee organized to campaign for adoption of new charter continues its efforts despite failure of legislature to enact bills; question to dominate this fall's elections of mayor and council.

WITH the adjournment of the 1939 Pennsylvania legislature *sine die* the curtain fell on another battle for municipal reform in America's third largest city, Philadelphia.

On May 2nd the State Senate passed by a vote of thirty-eight to eight the city manager-proportional representation bill sponsored jointly by Senators Woodward (Republican) and Shapiro (Democrat). Governor James, who had promised home rule for Philadelphia during his election campaign last autumn, announced early in May that he would sign the bill if passed by the House of Representatives. At that time hopes ran high that Philadelphia would achieve its long desired modern form of city government. If the legislature had passed the measure the people of Philadelphia would have been called upon to approve or reject it at a special election which, under the provisions of the bill, would have been held four weeks after its enactment.

A survey conducted in March by the *Philadelphia Evening Bulletin*, under the supervision of Dr. George H. Gallup and the American Institute of Public Opinion, showed that 72 per cent of all citizens questioned expressed an opinion on the new charter and that 76 per cent of that number would approve the proposal. But the charter never reached this final stage. After its passage through the Senate, the bill was sent to the House of Representatives. The House referred it to its Committee on Cities of the First Class which in turn appointed a subcommittee to give it "thorough and intensive study." And there it remained until the legislature finally adjourned on May 30th.

Philadelphia's fight for a new form of city government has a long history. Since 1919 the city has been operated under a mayor-council charter. This charter was hailed at the time of its enactment as a big step forward because it abolished the old-fashioned two-chambered council and reduced the city's legislative body from 145 to 22 members. It has nevertheless not worked very well. The main defects were two: (1) it could not correct the division of authority between city and county, co-extensive in Philadelphia, which had been abolished by an act of consolidation in 1854 but restored by judicial interpretation of the Pennsylvania constitution of 1874; and (2) it did not eliminate the division of authority between mayor and council, the inherent weakness of all mayor-council charters.

In November 1922, article XV, section 1, of the Pennsylvania constitution was amended to read: "Cities, or cities of any particular class, may be given the right and power to frame and adopt their own

1

Johannes U. Hoeber, "Philadelphia Carries On," National Municipal Review, *September 1939. Johannes wrote and published this article in this nationwide professional journal less than nine months after he arrived in the United States.*

Johannes continued his political activities through the 1940s. After the failure of the 1939 Charter campaign, Johannes and Walter joined a cadre of young Roosevelt-inspired liberals intent on bringing modern governance to the city. World War II, however, interrupted any serious possibility of major reform.

America entered the war on December 8, 1941. Although at age thirty-seven he was too old to join the Army, Johannes desperately wanted to assist in the war effort against the Nazis. On the day after Pearl Harbor he wrote to the local civilian defense authorities asking to be named a civil defense warden. On nearly the same day, however, the U.S. Congress passed legislation declaring him and countless other anti-Nazi refugees "enemy aliens," and his offer of service was rejected. In 1944, Johannes became an American citizen, in the minimum time legally required. Elfriede followed him in gaining citizenship a few months later.

The one area of the war effort in which Johannes was able to participate was in a pro-American propaganda effort aimed at Germans living in the United States. Before the war, Philadelphia had a German-language radio station, WTEL, with 100,000 listeners, which would regularly broadcast pro-Nazi messages. After the United States entered the war, the government seized the station and turned it over to a group of pro-American German refugees. Johannes and Elfriede each went on the air to tell the radio audience about their experiences under the Nazis and about how much more secure they felt in the United States.

The building at Pempelforterstrasse 11, where Johannes and Elfriede and Susanne lived, as it appeared after the Allied bombing of Düsseldorf in 1943.

Second floor windows at Pempelforterstrasse 11 where the Höbers' apartment was located.

Just before she left Germany, Elfriede put all of her and Johannes' belongings in storage with the Jonen Moving and Storage Company and paid for shipment to the United States when that became possible. As a result of the war, no such possibility arose, and Johannes and Elfriede never saw any of their things again. Every item on the detailed inventory was destroyed in an Allied bombing attack on Düsseldorf in June 1943.

C. J. JONEN Wwe. DÜSSELDORF

Internationale Spedition / Spediteur der Reichsbahn

Gegründet 1837

Bahnstellen: Düsseldorf-Derendorf / Fernsprech-Sammel-Nr. 20341

Reichsbank Giro-Konto Nr. 36/755 Postscheckkonto: Köln Nr. 1351 Drahtwort: Spedition Jonen

Frau Dr.
Elfriede Höber

Düsseldorf, Industriehaus, Wehrhahn 94
den 2.9.43

Abtlg. Ausl. Ref. Wi./He.

Betrifft

Bescheinigung!

Wir bescheinigen hiermit Frau Dr. Elfriede Höber, geb. Fischer, früher wohnhaft Düsseldorf, Pempelforterstr. 11, daß ihre bei uns lagernden Möbel, Einrichtungsgegenstände und Bücher etc. bei dem letzten Terrorangriff in der Nacht zum 12.Juni 1943 vernichtet wurden.

C.J. Jonen Wwe.

Notice from C. J. Jonen International Moving Company, Düsseldorf, notifying Elfriede that "your furniture, furnishings books, etc. stored with us were destroyed during the last terror attack during the night of June 12, 1943."

In the first post-war election in 1947, Johannes became a pivotal organizer for Philadelphia's reformers. He was the co-founder of the Philadelphia chapter of the Americans for Democratic Action (ADA), which developed into a national force for progressive public policies and civil rights for several decades.

At the end of the war, the Allied occupying forces in Germany appointed Hermann Heimerich as governor of the Rheinland. As Social Democratic (SPD) *Oberbürgermeister* of Mannheim before the Nazis, Heimerich had been Johannes' mentor and friend. Johannes briefly entertained the idea of returning to Germany and assuming a role in the postwar government—but only briefly. In any event, Elfriede was unalterably opposed to returning to the country from which she had been driven.

In the course of his reform work in Philadelphia, Johannes met William L. Batt, a Democratic Party activist with ties to the national organization. In 1948, Batt was asked to form a team to write speeches for President Harry S. Truman, who was facing a blistering reelection campaign. Batt invited Johannes to join this small team, and he spent the summer—in a brutally hot and non-air-conditioned Washington, DC—researching and writing confidential campaign material for the president.

And so it was that on September 30, 1948, the President of the United States delivered a plain but smart message to a cheering crowd in a sweltering auditorium in Louisville, Kentucky. His message came down to this: "The issue in this election, as I have said time and again, is the people against special privilege. Is the government of the United States going to be run in the interest of the people as a whole, or in the interest of a small group of privileged big businessmen?" The crowd roared its approval of Truman's defense of the common man. Only two or three people in the hall that night knew that the President's speech was written by a German refugee who had lived in the country less than ten years.[1]

While Johannes was spending his days managing small social welfare agencies and his nights pursuing reform politics, Elfriede also returned to work. In 1945, she obtained a position with the Philadelphia Housing Association. It was headed by Dorothy Schoell Montgomery (mentioned in Johannes' letters) and lobbied for government programs to provide homes for people with limited incomes. Elfriede's title was "Research Director," and her work included gathering facts about the kinds of housing available in Philadelphia and the kinds of people who were without adequate shelter. She kept the job for the next eighteen years. While her job allowed her to promote progressive public policies, the savings from her salary made it possible for all three children to go to college.

Not many years after their arrival in the United States, Johannes and Elfriede were anxious to explore America beyond Philadelphia, but their small salaries left little extra for travel. The solution was camping, sleeping, and cooking outdoors, so the only extra daily expense was gasoline for the car. The family took road trips every summer for twelve years so that by the time Frank, the youngest, was fifteen, the family had visited all forty-eight continental states, most of Canada, much of Mexico, and a majority of the national parks. Johannes and Elfriede, immigrants that they were, showed their children far more of their adopted country than most native-born Americans.

Johannes' work in municipal politics came to a head in 1951, when the state legislature finally allowed the city's voters to adopt the kind of char-

1 Johannes' role is documented in Philip White, *Whistle Stop: How 31,000 Miles of Train Travel, 352 Speeches and a Little Midwest Gumption saved the Presidency of Harry S Truman* (Lebanon, NH: University Press of New England, 2014).

ter he had worked for 1938. The new charter opened the door for the election of a reform administration under successive mayors Joseph S. Clark (later a U.S. senator) and Richardson Dilworth. Johannes became Deputy Commissioner of Welfare, where he was able to help build a system of care for the city's poor.

After twelve years, the reform period in Philadelphia was succeeded by a new wave of incompetent and largely corrupt administrations. Disheartened by this reversal, Johannes accepted a position in the administration of President John F. Kennedy in 1963. For several years he managed a massive stimulus initiative providing hundreds of millions of dollars to the states for job-creation projects. When that program came to an end, Lyndon Johnson was president and named Johannes to a new position in the State Department. It was 1967, and the United States was in the thick of the Vietnam War. While America was making war in the Southeast Asian countryside, it also took upon itself the job of ameliorating the suffering of those injured or displaced by the war. Johannes was appointed to head the Vietnam desk of the Agency for International Development and led the relief effort there. He travelled to Saigon and the back country repeatedly and for five years directed the program that provided hospitals, food, clothing, and shelter to hundreds of thousands of victims of the war. As a refugee himself, there was satisfaction in being able to provide assistance to refugees of another war in another part of the world.

Elfriede also found a place in the Kennedy Administration. She started with the federal Housing and Home Finance Agency, where her projects included rehabilitating dilapidated tenements in Harlem, building houses for Apaches in Arizona, and providing insulated homes in remote Eskimo villages in Alaska. Her favorite official trip involved a 400-mile flight in a single engine plane from Anchorage to the Yu'pik village of Bethel on the Bering Sea. Her plane landed on the frozen river adjacent to the new houses her agency had built in the tiny town, where she was hailed as the most important visitor in living memory.

Later, Elfriede moved to the U.S. Commission on Civil Rights, where she promoted the law prohibiting discrimination in the sale and rental of homes. After Congress adopted the Fair Housing Act in 1968, Elfriede moved to the Department of Housing and Urban Development, where she implemented enforcement of the new law around the country.

Johannes and Elfriede retired from government service in 1972. In 1977, at the age of seventy-two, Johannes suffered a sudden massive heart attack and died instantly.

Photographic portrait inscribed to Johannes by President Harry S. Truman, 1949.

During the time he was heading the refugee program in Vietnam, Johannes met frequently with members of the U.S. Congress on matters of funding and policy. He developed a good relationship with Senator Edward M. "Ted" Kennedy, a senior member of the Senate Foreign Relations Committee. Sen. Kennedy was an increasingly forceful opponent of the American war policy, and Johannes often provided him with off-the-record information that Kennedy used in the debates over bringing the war to a conclusion.

Two days after Johannes died, Senator Kennedy rose on the floor of the United States Senate and spoke:

> Mr. President, I was deeply saddened this week to learn of the death of Johannes Hoeber, a distinguished civil servant and humanitarian, who capped a long life of service in behalf of his fellow man as director of U.S. programs for refugees in Vietnam.

> Dr. Hoeber was himself a refugee—a refugee from Hitler's Germany. In 1933 he was arrested and imprisoned by the Nazis for several weeks, and subsequently spent five years working with the anti-Nazi underground until 1938, when he was faced with questioning by the Gestapo. Dr. Hoeber fled to the United States where he began a long career in social service programs to help people in need both here at home and abroad.
>
> From 1951 until 1962, Dr. Hoeber served as Philadelphia's deputy commissioner of welfare. In 1962, Dr. Hoeber became Assistant Administrator of the Area Redevelopment Administration of the Commerce Department.
>
> However, a few years later Dr. Hoeber joined the Agency for International Development—AID—to direct its programs for refugees and social welfare activities in Vietnam.
>
> It was in this capacity, Mr. President, that I came to know of Dr. Hoeber's dedicated service. As chairman of the Subcommittee on Refugees I came to know of his constant effort to upgrade AID's programs for refugees and millions of other victims of that tragic war. He often fought against the insensitivities of his own superiors in AID, who were more interested in commodity import programs to help Saigon's ailing economy than in efforts to help Saigon's orphans or the maimed or the crippled.
>
> Dr. Hoeber never lost sight of the urgent humanitarian needs in war-torn Vietnam, nor of America's great humanitarian responsibility to help meet those needs. His humanitarian service during the Vietnam conflict, like that of so many others both here in Washington and in the field, often went unnoticed and unseen. But they are the unsung heroes of America's effort to meet its humanitarian obligations to millions of innocent men, women, and children caught up in one of the most tragic wars the United States has ever been involved in.
>
> To his wife, Elfriede, and his three children, I want to offer my deepest sympathy for their loss, and to recognize the dedicated humanitarian service of their husband and father.

Johannes' sudden death was, of course, a shock for Elfriede. She stayed on alone in their house in Washington for a while. A year later, however, her son Frank and his wife Ditta bought a large old house in the center of Philadelphia that included a large apartment. Elfriede moved in and stayed for twenty-two years. When she was in her nineties she moved to a retirement home in Oakland, California, near her other son, Tom. She died on June 30, 1999.

And what of all the others named in the letters?

United States Congressional Record, *Senate, June 28, 1977: Remarks of Senator Edward M. Kennedy of Massachusetts on the Death of Johannes U. Hoeber.*

Congressional Record

United States of America

PROCEEDINGS AND DEBATES OF THE 95th CONGRESS, FIRST SESSION

Vol. 123 WASHINGTON, TUESDAY, JUNE 28, 1977 No. 112

S 10983

Senate

JOHANNES HOEBER

Mr. KENNEDY. Mr. President, I was deeply saddened this week to learn of the death of Johannes Hoeber, a distinguished civil servant and humanitarian, who capped a long life of service in behalf of his fellowman as director of U.S. programs for refugees in Vietnam.

Dr. Hoeber was himself a refugee—a refugee from Hitler's Germany. In 1933 he was arrested and imprisoned by the Nazis for several weeks, and subsequently spent 5 years working with the anti-Nazi underground until 1938, when he was faced with questioning by the Gestapo. Dr. Hoeber fled to the United States where he began a long career in social service programs to help people in need both here at home and abroad.

From 1951 until 1962, Dr. Hoeber served as Philadelphia's deputy commissioner of welfare. In 1962 Dr. Hoeber became Assistant Administrator of the Area Redevelopment Administration of the Commerce Department.

However, a few years later Dr. Hoeber joined the Agency for International Development—AID—to direct its programs for refugees and social welfare activities in Vietnam.

It was in this capacity, Mr. President, that I came to know of Dr. Hoeber's dedicated service. As chairman of the Subcommittee on Refugees I came to know of his constant effort to upgrade AID's programs for refugees and millions of other victims of that tragic war. He often fought against the insensitivities of his own superiors in AID, who were more interested in commodity import programs to help Saigon's ailing economy, than in efforts to help Saigon's orphans or the maimed or crippled.

Dr. Hoeber never lost sight of the urgent humanitarian needs in war-torn Vietnam, nor of America's great humanitarian responsibility to help meet those needs. His humanitarian service during the Vietnam conflict, like that of so many others both here in Washington and in the field, often went unnoticed and unseen. But they are the unsung heros of America's effort to meet its humanitarian obligations to millions of innocent men, women and children caught up in one of the most tragic wars the United States has ever been involved.

To his wife, Elfriede, and his three children, I want to offer my deepest sympathy for their loss, and to recognize the dedicated humanitarian service of their husband and father.

Mr. President, I ask unanimous consent that an article from today's Washington Post be printed in the Record.

There being no objection, the article was ordered to be printed in the Record, as follows:

JOHANNES U. HOEBER DIES, FOUNDING MEMBER OF ADA

(By Charles Hoepard)

Johannes U. Hoeber, 73, one of the founding members of the Americans for Democratic Action, died of a heart attack at his home here Sunday.

Born in Zurich, Switzerland, Mr. Hoeber was raised and educated in Germany receiving his Ph. D. in economics from the University of Heidelberg in 1929. He also studied at the London School of Economics.

Mr. Hoeber was arrested and imprisoned by the Nazis for several weeks in 1933 and spent the next five years working with the anti-Nazi underground in Germany.

In 1938, faced with questioning by the Gestapo, Mr. Hoeber fled to the United States, where he settled in Philadelphia. There he worked for several charitable agencies as an administrator.

He was also active in the reform campaign and in the administration of Philadelphia Mayor Joseph Clark, who later served in the U.S. Senate. From 1951 to 1962 Mr. Hoeber served as Philadelphia's deputy commissioner of welfare.

In 1962 Mr. Hoeber became assistant administrator of the Area Redevelopment Administration of the Commerce Department and five years later he became chief of the Refugee and Social Welfare staff, Vietnam bureau, of the Agency for International Development.

In 1972 Mr. Hoeber retired from the AID and received the agency's meritorious honor award. He worked for the next three years as a consultant to the Council of International Programs for Youth Leaders and Social Workers.

Looking back on his life, Mr. Hoeber recently wrote that he was most proud of "my participation in the fight for freedom and democracy in Germany . . . my success in becoming a useful and respected citizen of the United States, and the professional careers of my daughter and two sons."

Mr. Hoeber is survived by his wife, Elfriede Fischer Hoeber, of the home in Southwest; his three children, Susanne Hoeber Rudolph, a professor at The University of Chicago, Thomas R., a magazine editor who lives in Sacramento, Calif., and [illegible] who works for the National Labor Relations Board in Philadelphia; two sisters, Dr. Ursula Hoeber of Philadelphia and Gabriele [illegible] of Temple, Tex.; and eight grandchildren.

Rudolf and Josephine continued their scientific research at the University of Pennsylvania as long as they could. Three years after Johannes' arrival in the United States, in December 1941, Josephine died suddenly at the age of sixty-five of a heart attack. Rudolf was devastated but kept at his work at the university for a few more years. In 1947, the last edition of *Physikalische Chemie der Zelle und der Gewebe* was published in English under the title *Physical Chemistry of Cells and Tissues*. Not long after that, Rudolf developed Alzheimer's disease and rapidly declined. Ursula, with a large medical practice, lived with him in his home and cared for him until his death in September 1953.

Elfriede's mother and brothers and their families lived through the war in Germany, but tragedy struck them at the end. Clara Fischer stayed in Düsseldorf until an allied bombing raid destroyed her home in 1943, when she moved to safety in the Alps. Günter, Herbert, and Paul were drafted into the German Army. Günter and Herbert survived, but Herbert's wife, Elisabeth, and a young son died during the Russian advance at the end of the war. The second son, young Peter, survived.[2] Elfriede's brother Paul was captured by the Russians in Königsberg and was never heard from again.

Everyone in Europe suffered great privation for years following the war. Although Johannes and Elfriede were still struggling financially, they scraped together enough to send care packages every month to Clara and the other Fischers. In 1949, Clara moved to the United States and lived with Johannes and Elfriede for several years before returning to Germany.

In 1963, Johannes and Elfriede returned to Germany for the first time since the war to see her mother. Having done so, Elfriede insisted on leaving the country as soon as possible. She told her son, "Every time I got on an elevator or talked to a waiter I wondered what he did under the Nazis and wanted to get away from him." She nevertheless returned to Germany twice more before Clara died in 1968. On her eightieth birthday in 1984, Elfriede invited all of her American children and grandchildren to be her guests for several days at the Fischer family farm in Küingdorf.

Walter and Mary Phillips remained Johannes and Elfriede's close friends for the rest of their lives. They were the first Americans that Johannes introduced Elfriede to after her arrival in November 1939. Walter remained a leading activist for political progressivism in Philadelphia and served in the reform administration elected in 1951. He later ran for mayor (unsuccessfully) in 1963.

Manfred got a position as a staff physician at a Veterans Administration hospital in a small town in upstate New York in the mid-1940s. He stayed with the VA for many years, and he and Gri and their children eventually moved to Texas.

The fate of Mrs. Freyberger, Johannes and Elfriede's faithful office assistant, was extraordinary. She had planned as a last resort to flee to Shanghai, for which no visa was required, but she never made it there. Like countless others who were unable to get out of Germany, Mrs. Freyberger was swept up by the Nazis and imprisoned in the Theresienstadt concentration camp. She survived the camp and after the war emigrated to America. In May 1960, at the time of the Jerusalem trial of Adolf Eichmann, she wrote Johannes the following in a letter from New York:

> Eichmann's arrest has aroused all sorts of memories. He was the most feared visitor to Theresienstadt. Every time there was an announcement of his visit it set off a panic; his presence meant there would be transports to Auschwitz. He took those who were selected to Auschwitz himself. One of them even took place in Theresienstadt

2 See Peter C Fischer, *I Thought I Would Forget: Memories of a Childhood in the Twentieth Century* (Norderstedt, Germany, 2011).

> for the spouses of mixed marriages. He found me, too, to be appropriate for removal to Auschwitz.
>
> It was in October 1944 that the last transport ever went from Theresienstadt to Auschwitz. All through October there were transports of 2,500 people each to Auschwitz every second day. In this desolate confusion someone dispatched me from the main office to the telephone center, which had just been completely cleaned out by Eichmann. While I was using the nearest steps to the telephone center, Eichmann was coming down the main stairway to clean out the main office. They forgot about me in the telephone center. Everyone who was in the main office was gassed in Auschwitz, so that I alone was left over as the result of "oversight."

The fate of Rudolf's sister, Helene Höber (Tante Helene in the letters), is unknown. Rudolf and Josephine probably maintained communications with her as long as possible, but mail service between the United States and Europe was suspended after Pearl Harbor. Johannes never mentioned her to his children in his lifetime. It must be assumed that as a mentally handicapped person, and arguably a part Jew as well, she perished at the hands of the Nazis.

All three of Johannes and Elfriede's children made careers related to politics and government, as their parents had. Susanne and her husband, Lloyd Rudolph, became professors of political science at the University of Chicago. Thomas received his master's degree in political science from California State University and spent his working life writing about California politics and serving as a university administrator. Francis (Frank) graduated from Columbia University and spent forty-five years as a government executive, partly with the National Labor Relations Board and partly with the New Jersey court system.

ACKNOWLEDGMENTS

My parents and grandparents were in the habit of saving everything written. Their papers have been arranged and catalogued in a Hoeber Family Archive, from which the letters in this book have been drawn. The illustrations are also drawn from this Family Archive.

Deciphering, editing, and translating the letters of Johannes and Elfriede Hoeber has occupied me for more than twenty-five years. I am indebted to a number of individuals who helped me on the way.

My good friend Achim Bonte, historian and Deputy Director of the State and University Library of Saxony in Dresden, first made me conscious of the importance of my parents' story. It was he who suggested to me that these letters merited publishing. I am grateful for his friendship and advice over the years.

Several individuals were particularly helpful with the transcription and translation of the letters. Britta Fischer developed the knack for deciphering Elfriede's eccentric handwriting and laboriously transcribed many pages for me. She also was able to identify many of the friends who made up the landscape of Johannes and Elfriede's life in Düsseldorf. Mark McGuigan helped me unravel the meaning of numerous complex passages, particularly related to issues of public administration. Linda Hansen-Gerheuser read the draft of several early chapters and suggested useful strategies to make the English translation read more smoothly and naturally.

My sister, Susanne Hoeber Rudolph—"Susie" in the letters—helped fill in gaps in the story through her recollection of numerous incidents at a distance of seventy years.

I am indebted to those who read one or more drafts of the manuscript and provided suggestions for many of the explanatory points contained in the commentary and footnotes. Readers included Jane F. Castner, Christopher DeRosa, Sally Foreman Griffith, Patrick J. Hennessy, Thomas R. Hoeber, and Sam Stern. David W. Maxey not only read the full manuscript and provided extensive useful suggestions, but he also suggested to me the American Philosophical Society as a publisher.

Everything I have ever written has been made better by the incisive critique of Ditta Baron Hoeber. She has read many drafts of this book and provided invaluable editorial insights both as to language and content.

She was convinced of the value of this project from its beginning, and her support kept me going whenever I had doubts. For these and countless other reasons I owe her an endless debt of gratitude.

Francis W. Hoeber
Philadelphia
Spring 2015